THE KEY
STUDENT STUDY GUIDE

English Language Arts 9

THE KEY student study guide is designed to help students achieve success in school. The content in each study guide is 100% curriculum aligned and serves as an excellent source of material for review and practice. To create this book, teachers, curriculum specialists, and assessment experts have worked closely to develop the instructional pieces that explain each of the key concepts for the course. The practice questions and sample tests have detailed solutions that show problem-solving methods, highlight concepts that are likely to be tested, and point out potential sources of errors. **THE KEY** is a complete guide to be used by students throughout the school year for reviewing and understanding course content, and to prepare for assessments.

Rao, Gautam, 1961 –
THE KEY – English Language Arts 9 (2nd Edition) Alberta

1. English – Juvenile Literature. I. Title

Published by
Castle Rock Research Corp.
2410 Manulife Place
10180 – 101 Street
Edmonton, AB T5J 3S4

9 10 11 M 14 13 12

Publisher
Gautam Rao

Contributors
Toni d'Apice
Ute-Brigitta Blunck
Brigitta Goerress
Linda Mitchell
Lois Westerlund

Dedicated to the memory of Dr. V. S. Rao

THE KEY—ENGLISH LANGUAGE ARTS 9

THE KEY consists of the following sections:

KEY Tips for Being Successful at School gives examples of study and review strategies. It includes information about learning styles, study schedules, and note taking for test preparation.

Class Focus includes a unit on each area of the curriculum. Units are divided into sections, each focusing on one of the specific expectations, or main ideas, that students must learn about in that unit. Examples, definitions, and visuals help to explain each main idea. Practice questions on the main ideas are also included. At the end of each unit is a test on the important ideas covered. The practice questions and unit tests help students identify areas they know and those they need to study more. They can also be used as preparation for tests and quizzes. Each unit is prefaced by a **Table of Correlations**, which correlates questions in the unit to the specific curriculum expectations. Answers and solutions are found at the end of each unit.

KEY Strategies for Success on Tests helps students get ready for tests. It shows students different types of questions they might see, word clues to look for when reading them, and hints for answering them.

Practice Tests includes one to three tests based on the entire course. They are very similar to the format and level of difficulty that students may encounter on final tests. In some regions, these tests may be reprinted versions of official tests, or reflect the same difficulty levels and formats as official versions. This gives students the chance to practice using real-world examples. Answers and complete solutions are provided at the end of the section.

For the complete curriculum document (including specific expectations along with examples and sample problems), visit www.education.alberta.ca/teachers/core.aspx.

THE KEY *Study Guides* are available for many courses. Check www.castlerockresearch.com for a complete listing of books available for your area.

For information about any of our resources or services, please call Castle Rock Research at 780.448.9619 or visit our website at http://www.castlerockresearch.com.

At Castle Rock Research, we strive to produce an error-free resource. If you should find an error, please contact us so that future editions can be corrected.

TABLE OF CONTENTS

KEY Tips for being Successful at School

KEY TIPS FOR BEING SUCCESSFUL AT SCHOOL

KEY FACTORS CONTRIBUTING TO SCHOOL SUCCESS

In addition to learning the content of your courses, there are some other things that you can do to help you do your best at school. You can try some of the following strategies:

- **Keep a positive attitude**: Always reflect on what you can already do and what you already know.

- **Be prepared to learn**: Have the necessary pencils, pens, notebooks, and other required materials for participating in class ready.

- **Complete all of your assignments**: Do your best to finish all of your assignments. Even if you know the material well, practice will reinforce your knowledge. If an assignment or question is difficult for you, work through it as far as you can so that your teacher can see exactly where you are having difficulty.

- **Set small goals for yourself when you are learning new material**: For example, when learning the parts of speech, do not try to learn everything in one night. Work on only one part or section each study session. When you have memorized one particular part of speech and understand it, move on to another one. Continue this process until you have memorized and learned all the parts of speech.

- **Review your classroom work regularly at home**: Review to make sure you understand the material you learned in class.

- **Ask your teacher for help**: Your teacher will help you if you do not understand something or if you are having a difficult time completing your assignments.

- **Get plenty of rest and exercise**: Concentrating in class is hard work. It is important to be well-rested and have time to relax and socialize with your friends. This helps you keep a positive attitude about your schoolwork.

- **Eat healthy meals**: A balanced diet keeps you healthy and gives you the energy you need for studying at school and at home.

HOW TO FIND YOUR LEARNING STYLE

Every student learns differently. The manner in which you learn best is called your learning style. By knowing your learning style, you can increase your success at school. Most students use a combination of learning styles. Do you know what type of learner you are? Read the following descriptions. Which of these common learning styles do you use most often?

- Linguistic Learner: You may learn best by saying, hearing, and seeing words. You are probably really good at memorizing things such as dates, places, names, and facts. You may need to write down the steps in a process, a formula, or the actions that lead up to a significant event, and then say them out loud.

- Spatial Learner: You may learn best by looking at and working with pictures. You are probably really good at puzzles, imagining things, and reading maps and charts. You may need to use strategies like mind mapping and webbing to organize your information and study notes.

- Kinesthetic Learner: You may learn best by touching, moving, and figuring things out using manipulatives. You are probably really good at physical activities and learning through movement. You may need to draw your finger over a diagram to remember it, tap out the steps needed to solve a problem, or feel yourself writing or typing a formula.

SCHEDULING STUDY TIME

You should review your class notes regularly to ensure that you have a clear understanding of all the new material you learned. Reviewing your lessons on a regular basis helps you to learn and remember ideas and concepts. It also reduces the quantity of material that you need to study prior to a test. Establishing a study schedule will help you to make the best use of your time.

- Regardless of the type of study schedule you use, you may want to consider the following suggestions to maximize your study time and effort:

- Organize your work so that you begin with the most challenging material first.

- Divide the subject's content into small, manageable chunks.

- Alternate regularly between your different subjects and types of study activities in order to maintain your interest and motivation.

- Make a daily list with headings like "Must Do," "Should Do," and "Could Do."

- Begin each study session by quickly reviewing what you studied the day before.

- Maintain your usual routine of eating, sleeping, and exercising to help you concentrate better for extended periods of time.

CREATING STUDY NOTES

MIND-MAPPING OR WEBBING

Use the key words, ideas, or concepts from your class notes to create a mind map or web, which is a diagram or visual representation of the given information. A mind map or web is sometimes referred to as a knowledge map. Use the following steps to create a mind map or web:

1. Write the key word, concept, theory, or formula in the centre of your page.

2. Write down related facts, ideas, events, and information, and link them to the central concept with lines.

3. Use coloured markers, underlining, or symbols to emphasize things such as relationships, timelines, and important information.

The following mind map is an example of one that could help you develop an essay:

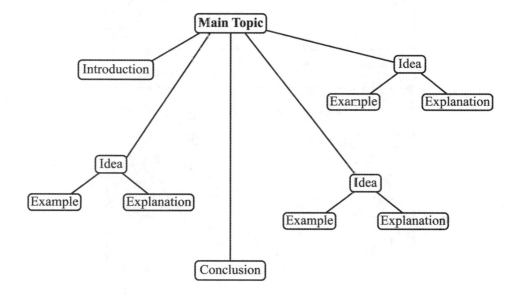

INDEX CARDS

To use index cards while studying, follow these steps:

1. Write a key word or question on one side of an index card.

2. On the reverse side, write the definition of the word, answer to the question, or any other important information that you want to remember.

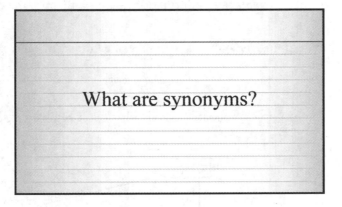

SYMBOLS AND STICKY NOTES—IDENTIFYING IMPORTANT INFORMATION

Use symbols to mark your class notes. For example, an exclamation mark (!) might be used to point out something that must be learned well because it is a very important idea. A question mark (?) may highlight something you are not certain about, and a diamond (◊) or asterisk (*) could highlight interesting information that you want to remember. Sticky notes are useful in the following situations:

• Use sticky notes when you are not allowed to put marks in books.

• Use sticky notes to mark a page in a book that contains an important diagram, formula, explanation, or other information.

• Use sticky notes to mark important facts in research books.

MEMORIZATION TECHNIQUES

The following techniques can help you when you need to memorize something:

- **Association** relates new learning to something you already know. For example, to remember the spelling difference between dessert and desert, recall that the word *sand* has only one *s*. So, because there is sand in a desert, the word *desert* has only one *s*.

- **Mnemonic** devices are sentences that you create to remember a list or group of items. For example, the first letter of each word in the phrase "**E**very **G**ood **B**oy **D**eserves **F**udge" helps you to remember the names of the lines on the treble-clef staff (E, G, B, D, and F) in music.

- **Acronyms** are words that are formed from the first letters or parts of the words in a group. For example, RADAR is actually an acronym for Radio Detecting and Ranging, and MASH is an acronym for Mobile Army Surgical Hospital. HOMES helps you to remember the names of the five Great Lakes (Huron, Ontario, Michigan, Erie, and Superior).

- **Visualizing** requires you to use your mind's eye to "see" a chart, list, map, diagram, or sentence as it is in your textbook or notes, on the chalkboard or computer screen, or in a display.

- **Initialisms** are abbreviations that are formed from the first letters or parts of the words in a group. Unlike acronyms, an initialism cannot be pronounced as a word itself. For example, BEDMAS is an initialism for the order of operations in math (Brackets, Exponents, Divide, Multiply, Add, Subtract).

KEY STRATEGIES FOR REVIEWING

Reviewing textbook material, class notes, and handouts should be an ongoing activity. Spending time reviewing becomes more critical when you are preparing for a test. You may find some of the following review strategies useful when studying during your scheduled study time:

- Before reading a selection, preview it by noting the headings, charts, graphs, and chapter questions.

- Before reviewing a unit, note the headings, charts, graphs, and chapter questions.

- Highlight key concepts, vocabulary, definitions, and formulas.

- Skim the paragraph, and note the key words, phrases, and information.

- Carefully read over each step in a procedure.

- Draw a picture or diagram to help make the concept clearer.

KEY STRATEGIES FOR SUCCESS: A CHECKLIST

Reviewing is a huge part of doing well at school and preparing for tests. Here is a checklist for you to keep track of how many suggested strategies for success you are using. Read each question, and put a check mark (✓) in the correct column. Look at the questions where you have checked the "No" column. Think about how you might try using some of these strategies to help you do your best at school.

KEY Strategies for Success	Yes	No
Do you attend school regularly?		
Do you know your personal learning style—how you learn best?		
Do you spend 15 to 30 minutes a day reviewing your notes?		
Do you study in a quiet place at home?		
Do you clearly mark the most important ideas in your study notes?		
Do you use sticky notes to mark texts and research books?		
Do you practise answering multiple-choice and written-response questions?		
Do you ask your teacher for help when you need it?		
Are you maintaining a healthy diet and sleep routine?		
Are you participating in regular physical activity?		

Comprehend and Respond to Texts

COMPREHEND AND RESPOND TO TEXTS

Table of Correlations				
Specific Expectation	**Practice Questions**	**Unit Test**	**PAT 2000**	**PAT 2001**
By the end of this course, students will:				
Students will listen, speak, read, write, view and represent to comprehend and respond personally and critically to oral, print and other media texts.				
2.1.1.2 use previous reading experiences, personal experiences and prior knowledge as a basis for reflecting on and interpreting ideas encountered in texts	8, 15, 16, 56, 61, 72	17, 15	35, 36	21
2.1.2.1 identify explicit and implicit ideas and information in texts; listen and respond to various interpretations of the same text	4, 5, 14, 40, 48, 50, 52, 60, 62, 65, 68, 73	1, 14, 16, 19	1, 10, 11, 12, 15, 17, 18, 21, 28, 30, 34	1, 5, 8, 9, 11, 16, 17, 28
2.1.2.2 select appropriate reading rate and strategies for comprehending texts less closely connected to prior knowledge and personal experiences	12, 22, 64			
2.1.2.3 preview complex texts as to their intent, content and structure, and use this information to set a purpose and select strategies for reading		27		
2.1.3.1 use knowledge of visual and textual cues and structural features when skimming and scanning various print and other media texts to locate relevant information effectively and efficiently	20, 23, 24, 25, 63, 69	20, 24	13	19, 20
2.1.3.2 analyze and discuss how the structural features of informational materials, such as textbooks, bibliographies, databases, catalogues, web sites, commercials and newscasts, enhance the effectiveness and efficiency of communication		11		
2.1.4.1 apply and explain effective procedures for identifying and comprehending words in context; adjust procedures according to the purpose for reading and the complexity of the texts	1, 3, 18, 21, 26, 27, 28, 41, 55, 57, 70	2, 13, 21, 26	9, 14, 20, 23, 25, 27, 40, 47	6, 13, 26
2.1.5.1 use reference materials, including a writer's handbook, to verify correct usage, address uncertainties and solve problems that arise	26			
2.2.1.1 experience oral, print and other media texts from a variety of cultural traditions and genres, such as essays, broadcast advertisements, novels, poetry, documentaries, films, electronic magazines and realistic fiction		10, 18		
2.2.1.2 identify and discuss how timeless themes are developed in a variety of oral, print, and other media texts			39	
2.2.2.1 analyze how the choices and motives of characters portrayed in oral, print and other media texts provide insight into those of self and others	2	7	4, 16, 45, 54	2, 3, 22, 23
2.2.2.2 identify and discuss theme and point of view in oral, print and other media texts	33, 43, 67, 74, 75	28	7, 26	14

2.2.2.3	discuss and explain various interpretations of the same oral, print or other media text	54			
2.2.2.4	relate the themes, emotions and experiences portrayed in oral, print and other media texts to issues of personal interest or significance			37	
2.2.3.1	discuss how techniques, such as irony, symbolism perspective and proportion communicate meaning and enhance effect in oral, print and other media texts	46, 51	5, 22	3, 5, 24, 33, 43, 51	15
2.2.3.2	discuss character development in terms of consistency of behaviour and plausibility of change	7, 9, 29, 30, 32, 35, 45, 66	3, 6, 23, 25	2, 8, 55	7
2.2.3.3	describe how theme, dominant impression and mood are developed and sustained through choices in language use and the interrelationship of plot, setting and character	13, 37, 42, 49, 58, 71	4, 12	31, 32, 48, 50	25
2.2.3.4	identify features that define particular oral, print, and other media texts; discuss differences in style and their effects on content and audience impression			38, 49	12
2.3.1.1	explain the relationship between purposes and characteristics of various forms and genres of oral, print and other media texts	11, 16, 38, 39	27		
2.3.2.2	evaluate the effectiveness of oral, print and other media texts, considering the believability of plot and setting the credibility of characters, and the development and resolution of conflict	6, 10, 34, 36	8, 29	6, 22, 52	24, 29
2.3.4.1	analyze creative uses of language and visuals in popular culture, such as advertisements, electronic magazines and the Internet; recognize how imagery and figurative language, such as metaphor, create a dominant impression, mood and tone	17, 31, 44, 47, 53, 59	9	29, 41, 42, 44, 46, 53	4, 10, 18, 27

COMPREHEND AND RESPOND TO TEXTS

USE STRATEGIES AND CUES

Some texts are difficult to read. The following section of your *KEY* outlines strategies you can use and indicates cues already in a text that can help you to understand texts that are easy and texts that are more difficult.

2.1.1.1 discuss how interpretations of the same text might vary, according to the prior knowledge and experiences of various readers

INTERPRETING TEXTS

Each individual interprets his or her world differently. The interpretation each classmate in your class has of a text will reflect the diversity of perception. You may think something in a novel is more important than the person sitting next to you. Each person reads a text with a different point of view. The following examples show how students can interpret the same story in different ways.

Ben Mikaelsen's novel *Touching Spirit Bear* revolves around a 15-year-old boy who has severely assaulted and injured another teenager. As a result, the boy is placed in a Circle Justice program that requires him to survive on a small island using his own skills and ingenuity for several months. A significant aspect of the boy's background is the fact that his parents are separated and that his father has been physically abusive as a disciplinarian. Because of his past, the main character is a very angry young man. Different students will read this story very differently.

For example, a student who has faced charges under the Young Offenders Act may relate to the protagonist and understand what it feels like to be so young and already have been in trouble with the law. Or students whose parents are divorced may relate to the protagonist's emotional turmoil in dealing with difficult family issues. Students who have never been in serious trouble may be able to find sympathy for the protagonist and think differently about young offenders after reading the book. Other students may not find compassion for the protagonist at all.

As you can see, interpretation has a lot to do with personal experience. That is why reading is so important. If you have not had experience with some aspect of life, reading about people who have led lives different from yours can help you understand how others see the world. You cannot live a life other than your own, but you can read about lives that you may not have imagined were possible. Literature teaches you to understand and accept different points of view.

2.1.1.2 use previous reading experiences, personal experiences, and prior knowledge as a basis for reflecting on and interpreting ideas encountered in texts

USING PRIOR KNOWLEDGE IN INTERPRETATION

Using prior knowledge means to build on your background knowledge in order to understand something. Background knowledge consists of information you already know and past experiences. When you read, you will better understand what the author is saying if you use background knowledge. Readers who actively think about the text and use their background knowledge during reading will understand more of what they read than readers who do not make these associations.

Try to make connections between what you already know and what you are reading. Ask yourself the following questions as you read:

- Does this text remind me of anything?

- What do I already know about the topic of this text?

- Does this text remind me of anything else I have read?

- Is there something in this text that is like something I already know?

The following passage describes two events during Christopher Columbus's voyage to the New World. Some of the references may be unfamiliar to you, but your knowledge and understanding of context should help you understand the passage.

Example

Journal Entry

Rodrigo spotted land today from the crow's-nest on the *Pinta*. Martin, captain of the *Pinta*, fired a cannon to alert us on the *Santa Maria*. We have finally reached Asia! The memory of the hardships we suffered to get here is somewhat lessened by the excitement of discovering a new land for King Ferdinand and Queen Isabella. Still, it is difficult to forget the smell of unwashed bodies, the lice and fleas, the scurvy, and the chronic hunger.

Later Entry

We have met the natives, who call themselves the Taino. I am very interested to learn the source of the gold that they have used to make the ornaments they hang from their noses. Through a somewhat ineffectual sign language, the chief has told me that the island with the gold is west and north from here. They call this island Colba. We will explore, rest, restock, and sail on. It seems we did not find Asia after all.

Before reading, you likely already knew that Columbus did not reach Asia. You also may have already known that Columbus sailed for Spain, so you can infer that King Ferdinand and Queen Isabella sent Columbus searching for new lands for Spain. The chronic hunger and scurvy mentioned in the journal entry should lead you to assume that the voyage was difficult and lacking in food in general, and foods rich in Vitamin C in particular, which causes scurvy. If you already know a bit about the first voyage of Columbus, then you may assume that the island of Colba is now known as Cuba. By making assumptions, as you may know using what you already know and by using the context of the story, you can understand the passage well.

2.1.2.1 identify explicit and implicit ideas and information in texts; listen and respond to various interpretations of the same text

Explicit and Implicit Ideas

Explicit ideas are clear statements that are directly stated in the text. An explicit idea states the meaning. For example, the statement "The temperature yesterday dropped to –27°C" is explicit.

Implicit ideas, which are also known as inferences, are suggested, implied, or inferred.

An implicit idea is not directly stated. In texts, conclusions and predictions are usually implicit ideas, and themes are often implicitly referred to rather than directly stated.

Practise making inferences by asking the following questions as you read:

- Why did I think that would happen?

- What do I think the text is about?

- How do I think the character feels?

- How did I know that?

- What is the author actually saying?

- What is the author leading me to believe?

Read the following article about the invention of the microwave oven. Make inferences that can be supported by explicit ideas in the text.

FORTUNATE ACCIDENTS CAN LEAD TO THE BEST INVENTIONS

Some inventions are the consequence of an idea followed by trial and error (like Edison and the light bulb) or of a flash of inspiration. Other inventions are born through fortunate accidents.

Some of the greatest inventions in history have been made because of fortunate accidents. Take the microwave oven, for example. Percy Spencer, the inventor of the microwave, was motivated to join the Navy in the area of wireless telegraphy (radar) because as a child in 1912, he had been deeply inspired by the valor of the Titanic's wireless operator. When his Navy service ended, Spencer got a job with Raytheon Company as an engineer. Raytheon specialized in defence contracts and commercial electronics.

Spencer's job at Raytheon involved working with magnetrons that generated microwave radio signals, which are essential for radar. Spencer was looking at ways to increase the production of magnetron tubes because of WWII. One of his tubes had a hole in it, and he wondered what effect this might have. He had a chocolate bar in his pocket while he was running experiments with the leaking device. Lo and behold, the chocolate bar melted. He then brought in a bag of popcorn, which popped all over the lab. He also tried the experiment with an egg, which exploded because it was still in its shell. Spencer came to realize that the microwave could be used to cook food.

Raytheon sold the first commercial microwave in 1947. It weighed 750 pounds and was nearly six feet tall. Obviously, this was not a microwave for a personal home. It was used in restaurants, rail cars, and on large ships. It was not until 1955 that the first domestic microwave was for sale, and it was still too big for the average kitchen. Plus, it cost $1300—nearly as much as an automobile in those days. In 1967, Japan manufactured a smaller magnetron and hence a smaller microwave. It sold for $495 and the world's love affair with the microwave began in earnest. Now, it would not be a stretch to say that more than 99% of the homes in North America have a mircowave in the kitchen.

The following statements are some explicit ideas from the text:

- Percy Spencer invented the microwave oven.

- Spencer got a job as an engineer.

- The first commercial microwave weighted 750 pounds.

- The first domestic microwave cost $495.

The following explicit statements lead to the inference that while popular ideas or discoveries often begin by accident, they can then spread over a large area:

- "It was used in restaurants, rail cars, and on large ships."

- "… more than 99% of the homes in North America have a microwave in the kitchen."

Inferences allow different readers to arrive at various conclusions and interpretations of the same text. The following two interpretations of this text are both logical and valid, even though they are different:

- If both the cost and the size of microwaves had not become significantly smaller, microwaves might not enjoy the great popularity and use that they have today.

- It is important to take care when cooking food in the microwave, as some foods need special preparations in order to be cooked safely in the microwave.

Were your inferences close to these? Actively make inferences as you read a text, and afterwards you will find that you probably understand more about the text than you think.

2.1.2.2 select appropriate reading rate and strategies for comprehending texts less closely connected to prior knowledge and personal experiences

SELECTING A READING RATE

Before you begin to read, you should select a reading rate. Your reading rate will vary according to the form of the text, the level of difficulty of the text, and whether you are previewing, skimming, scanning, rereading, rechecking a fact, or reading for enjoyment. For example, if you are skimming a text for information, you will read more quickly than if you are researching a particular topic.

DETERMINING IMPORTANCE

Before you begin to read, you should determine the importance of what you are reading. By identifying what is most important, you can set aside the less important ideas and pieces of information while you concentrate on the more important ideas.

Following are some techniques that are helpful for determining importance:

- Before reading, think about what you know about the topic and what you would like to learn.
- While reading, look for clues in the format of the text that might indicate importance—pay attention to the first and last lines of a paragraph, the title, any headings or subheadings, captions, or framed text.
- Pay particular attention to pictures, illustrations, charts, and diagrams.
- As you read, intend to remember.
- After reading, think about the most important information you learned from the text.

READING STRATEGIES

Reading strategies will help you to better understand every kind of text. Every time you read something, choose a strategy that works best for you and for the kind of text you are reading. When using a reading strategy, monitor your progress and level of understanding by asking yourself the following questions:

- Do I need to slow down?
- Should I reread that part to make sure I understand it?
- Should I check that word in a dictionary to be sure I understand the meaning as it is being used?
- Can I get some more information on this topic by using an encyclopedia, the Internet, or other resource from the library?
- Do I need to modify some of my reading questions now that I have read that new piece of information?

Reading comprehension strategies are tools that are used by good readers to make sure that they understand what they read. The strategies you use will depend on the type of text that you read and your purpose for reading.

Coding Text

Coding text is a simple strategy that helps you to become more involved in your reading, make decisions as you read, and clarify your understanding. Your reading rate is slowed down by this strategy, which focuses on understanding the text on a deeper, more personal level. The strategy consists of a marking system that records your reactions to what you are reading and prompts you to monitor your comprehension. Following are some symbols that can be used. These symbols are only examples—use whatever symbols that are useful and meaningful to you.

Example

- **R** this reminds me of something
- **V** creates a visual picture
- ***** this is important
- **++** main idea
- **E** evokes an emotion
- **?** do not understand
- **SD** supporting details

Monitoring for Meaning

This strategy involves checking your understanding of the material that you are reading. Continually ask yourself whether the text makes sense:

- Do I understand what I just read?
- What just happened?
- How do these ideas and details relate to each other?

Monitor your broader understanding of the text by considering:

- Who the characters are
- When it takes place
- What is the conflict
- Where it takes place
- Why the author wrote the text

Synthesizing

Synthesizing allows you to sort through the information in the text to make it make sense. Synthesizing is putting elements together to form a whole. Following are some questions that you can ask when you are synthesizing:

- What was the author's purpose in writing the text?

- What was the main idea of the text?

- What clues helped me to determine the main idea?

- How do different parts of the text connect with one another?

- Has my thinking changed after reading the text?

- Can I think of a new title for the text?

ADDITIONAL COMPREHENSION STRATEGIES

There are a variety of figure-it-out strategies that you can use when you do not understand something you are reading:

- Reread a page or section if you do not understand. Sometimes, a second reading is necessary.

- Skip ahead if you do not understand what you have just read. There may be information further on that will help you to understand that section.

- Use context clues to make sense of unfamiliar words. Familiar words can help you to determine the meaning of a new word.

- Use information from pictures to help make sense of what you have read.

- Ask for help. Ask a teacher, parent, classmate, or sibling for help when you have tried your own strategies but still do not understand something.

Strategic Reading

Asking questions while you read will help you to become an active, thoughtful, reflective, and skilled reader. Following are some questions to ask before, during, and after reading.

Before Reading

- What is my purpose for reading?

- What will I do with the information I read?

- What do I already know about the topic?

- What do I think I will learn?

- What are my predictions?

- What reading strategies should I use with this text?

- How is the text organized?

- What questions do I have before reading this text?

During Reading

- Am I meeting the purpose I set for this reading?

- Am I making sense of what I am reading?

- Do I understand what I am reading?

- Do I have a clear visual image in my mind?

- Is what I am reading what I expected?

- Are some parts different or similar to my predictions?

After Reading

- Do I need to reread any difficult parts?

- Did I learn what I wanted to learn?

- What new information did I learn and how does it fit into my background knowledge?

- What else do I still need to know about the topic?

- What are my thoughts about what I have read?

- Do I agree or disagree? Why?

- Do I like what I have read? Why or why not?

Thoughtful Reading

A thoughtful reading involves the following strategies:

- Activating background knowledge by making connections between new and known information

- Questioning the text to clarify and deepen understanding

- Drawing inferences using background knowledge and clues from the text

- Determining importance in order to distinguish details from the main ideas

- Monitoring comprehension to ensure meaning is being constructed

- Rereading to employ fix-up strategies to repair any confusion

- Using sensory imagery to deepen and enhance comprehension

- Synthesizing to create new thinking

2.1.2.3 preview complex texts as to their intent, content, and structure, and use this information to set a
purpose and select strategies for reading

PREVIEWING

When you first approach a complex text, preview the structure before you begin to read. Try to get an idea of what the author will say and how it will be said so that you know what to expect. Use this information to establish your purpose for reading. Once your purpose is established, you can better decide which strategy you should use.

When you preview a text, begin by taking a quick look over the reading selection. Are there headings or titles? Are there graphs or charts? Are there any pictures? Are there photo captions? If there are any of these, make a note in your mind to pay close attention to them when you read the text.

Your thoughts may run like this: *"Hmm, this looks interesting. The pictures sure catch my eye. I can see that there is one main section of text and then three other paragraphs with titles. There are also lots of little bits added beside the illustrations. I wonder if these have extra information or if they are just going to summarize the main text. It looks like there are some goofy cartoons as well."*

Examine the structural features of the text, such as the table of contents, section, chapters, illustrations, charts, diagrams, glossary, and index. Plan how you can use these features to:

- Find specific information

- Navigate around the text

- Answer questions and understand assignments

- Understand key concepts

ESTABLISHING A PURPOSE FOR READING

One of the most important steps to take before reading is to find your purpose. The purpose for reading a text can help you decide how to read it. Are you reading to research information for an essay, to answer questions for an assignment, or to locate the phone number, hours of operation, and address of a new clothing store? How you go about reading for any of these different tasks will change with your purpose.

When you have a purpose for reading, you can keep a closer eye on your progress. You know when to stop and reread. Sometimes, you need to revisit your purpose; at other times, your purpose changes.

PREDICTING AND QUESTIONING

While you read, predict what will happen and question what does happen. Using your background knowledge and clues from the text, you can make predictions as you read. You should be able to support your predictions with facts from the text.

To practise making predictions, try the following suggestions before you read:

- Ask yourself what you think will happen.

- Try to guess what the text is about based on its title.

- Turn information headings into questions (e.g., "Cats purr" becomes "Why do cats purr?").

As you are reading, stop and make predictions about what might happen next. After you read, ask yourself if your predictions about the text were correct, how they were similar, and how they differed.

Once you have determined your purpose for reading, you can select the strategy most appropriate to your purpose.

2.1.3.1 use knowledge of visual and textual cues and structural features when skimming and scanning various print and other media to locate relevant information effectively and efficiently

USING TEXTUAL CUES TO LOCATE INFORMATION

Two ways of using textual cues to locate information are scanning and skimming. Both scanning and skimming involve selective reading to locate specific impressions or information.

Scanning involves looking for specific words related to the information you are seeking. Scanning is not reading; it is searching. For example, you may be asked to read a passage and then answer the following question.

The author explains that the smallest bone in the body is found in the

    A. ear

    B. foot

    C. skull

    D. hand

You could scan the passage for the word *smallest* to check your answer to the question. This technique is also very useful for scrolling through books or the Internet for research. You can automatically scan on the Internet using the shortcut command "Ctrl+F" to find a specific word or phrase once you are at a website. You cannot use this method when you are reading printed text, so you will have to use your own scanning skills. Following are some situations in which scanning would be effective:

• Looking over a test to assess the number and types of questions.

• Looking over a story to assess the length, level of difficulty, introduction, and ending.

• Looking over a table of contents of a new text.

• Looking over newspaper headlines to see where certain section or articles are located.

Some textbooks have subheadings, notes under diagrams and pictures, or notes in the margins. These notes and subheadings often help to give readers a better understanding of the text by summarizing the information. When reading an expository text, it is useful to be able to summarize the author's message as you read.

Skimming involves quickly looking over all the parts of a text. You skim a text when you look at pictures, headings, and bold text, but do not read the whole piece. This is a useful strategy for before and after reading a text in detail. It is especially helpful in reading newspaper articles, textbooks, and web pages. Skimming just part of a story or report to find information that you need will save time.

Skimming is extremely useful for searching the Internet. Skimming through your search results helps you to choose which sites to view. Once you get to a site, skimming can help you to decide if the site will be helpful or not. Observant skimming skills can save you a lot of time.

Skimming a chapter of your textbook before you read it will help you to grasp more of the content and comprehend the organizational parts of the chapter. The following strategies can help you skim a chapter in a textbook:

• Before reading a chapter, preview it by noting headlines, charts, graphs, and chapter questions.

• Read the complete introduction to identify key information that is addressed in the chapter.

- Read the first sentence of each paragraph for the main idea.

- Skim each paragraph, noting key words, phrases, and information.

- Read the last sentence of each paragraph.

- Read the complete conclusion to summarize each chapter's contents.

After skimming through the chapter, it is helpful to go back and:

- Turn each heading and sub-heading in the chapter into a question before you begin your reading.

- Answer the questions you created.

- Read over any questions that are at the end of the chapter, and see how many you can answer.

2.1.3.2 analyze and discuss how the structural features of informational materials, such as textbooks, bibliographies, databases, catalogues, web sites, commercials, and newscasts, enhance the effectiveness and efficiency of communication

THE STRUCTURE OF INFORMATION

Informational materials are generally organized to be user friendly. That means that readers should be able to:

- Navigate through the information

- Locate needed information

- Find links to related information or more detailed information

- Verify information, such as facts and statistics

The structural features of information refer to how that information is organized and presented. Structural features include the title, layout, chapters, lists, and links of the information you are reading. Structural features should be effective and efficient. Just as telephone directories and dictionaries are organized for ease of use, most other information materials are also organized. Textbooks, bibliographies, catalogues, databases, websites, and commercials all have structural features. Which structural features are effective and efficient for you as a user? The following section explains different structural features of media you encounter daily.

STRUCTURAL FEATURES OF BOOKS

Informative books are organized with features that help you to find information quickly. These features can also help you recall or find information that you have already read. Following are some features with which you should be familiar.

Title Page

A title page tells you the topic of the book and its author or editor.

Table of Contents

The table of contents is found at the front of a book, usually following the title page. It lists the book's chapters or divisions in order from first to last. The starting page number of each chapter is also given. You can skim a table of contents from top to bottom to find out where a particular chapter begins and its length.

Preface or Foreword

A preface or foreword is an introduction that tells you what you can expect to be in the book. It can also mention the main idea of the book or the purpose of writing it.

Visual Layout

The visual layout of a book refers to how the book is put together and whether it contains pictures or diagrams.

Appendix

The appendix is a section found at the back of some information books. Appendices contain additional information that further discusses the material, such as notes, charts, maps, or diagrams.

Index

An index is an alphabetical list of the important topics in an information book. It tells you which pages have information on each topic.

Glossary

A glossary is often found at the back of a non-fiction book. It lists and explains the meanings of some words in the book that may be unfamiliar. When you read a book with a glossary, you can quickly check the meaning of words as they are used in context.

Example

---

air pump a device for pumping air into or out of a vessel, a room, etc.

decompression a gradual lowering of pressure on a person who has been on an underwater dive

diving bell an open-bottomed box or bell, supplied with air, in which a person can be lowered into deep water

SCUBA **S**elf **C**ontained **U**nderwater **B**reathing **A**pparatus

submarine a vessel able to operate under the water

Chapter Organizers

Often, chapters in textbooks are organized logically to help you locate Information. The following example contains elements that may appear in a chapter of a science book:

Example

- Topic-related picture on the first page
- List of chapter subtopics on the first page
- A mini story related to the topic on the first page
- Objectives and key terms at the beginning of each subtopic
- Special inserts
- Hands-on activities
- Student activities under headings, such as
  - Checking Concepts
  - Thinking Critically
  - Interpreting Visuals
  - Building Science Skills
  - Designing an Experiment
- Lab Activities
- Chapter summaries under headings, such as
  - Key Term Challenges
  - Content Challenges
  - Concept Challenges

Chapter organizers change depending on the content of a book. Chapter organizers also help you navigate around and through a chapter. This is especially useful if you want to read only certain kinds of material from each chapter as you study for an exam.

STRUCTURAL FEATURES OF BIBLIOGRAPHIES

Bibliographies are organized alphabetically and in a specific format that makes it easy to recognize the source of the information, such as a book, encyclopedia, Internet article, or magazine article.

Bibliographic listings are always in one location, which makes it easier for researchers to find other resources on the same topic, refer back to the resource for additional information, or recheck facts. Each listing includes all the information required for a quotation, citation, or footnote, and can be used as a quick reference.

Example

Bibliography

"Arctic Lemmings." <u>The American Encyclopedia</u>. 3rd ed. 2007.

Chartrand, Emily. <u>Myths About Lemmings</u>. New York: Avenue Publishers, 2001.

Doherty, Paul, John Phillips, and David Rollester. <u>Lemmings in the Wild</u>.
    Chicago: U of Chicago P, 2002.

Gallager, Stuart. <u>Lemmings in the Arctic</u>. Special report prepared at the request of
    the Alaskan Department of Conservation. August 15, 1998.

"Lemmings Unlimited," 2001 photo gallery,
    http://www.lemmingsunlimited.org/2001.html

Bibliographies are formatted to clearly show the sources an author has used for his or her writing.

Structural Features of Databases

A database is a collection of related information, usually found on a spreadsheet or in a chart. Information that is organized into a database is useful in research, particularly for scientific topics.
If you were preparing a report on global warming, for example, you might want to refer to a database of average seasonal temperatures at different world locations over a period of several hundred years. Databases are just one of many tools that you can use to locate information.

Whether the database is a chart, spreadsheet, directory, list, or set of maps, the structural features that make it appeal to users include:

- Briefly stated information that is easy to navigate

- Information that is alphabetically or chronologically organized

- Volumes of related information organized at one location

Since many people begin with the Internet when they are researching a topic, it is helpful to be aware of the most popular search sites. While the Internet has many sites from which you can gather more information about your subject, it may not be as accurate. Anyone can create a website, so even though the information may be more current than encyclopedias and textbooks, it may not always be right. Always check your facts against other sources, or find reliable websites such as online newspapers or university journals.

STRUCTURAL FEATURES OF ADVERTISEMENTS

Advertising is all around you. Each time you pay attention to an ad in a magazine, on TV, or on your computer, you evaluate that ad as a text. As you are probably aware, advertising designers use deliberate strategies with wording, photography, lighting, music, sound effects, and even ad placement to entice buyers. Certain ads are undeniably effective at persuading, influencing, or convincing potential customers.

Some structural features that can make ads more visually effective include:

• Font style

• Font size

• Ad size

• Visual layout

• Focal point

2.1.4.1 apply and explain effective procedures for identifying and comprehending words in context; adjust procedures according to the purpose for reading and the complexity of the texts

USING CONTEXT CLUES TO COMPREHEND WORDS

Usually when you read a text, you do not have to rely on a dictionary or thesaurus to understand most of the words. These tools should be a last resort. You can generally understand a text if you watch for context clues. Context clues come from the familiar words around the unfamiliar words.

When you are reading a text, you can often clarify the meaning of an unfamiliar word in one of the following ways.

• Find the definition in the text. Sometimes, the word will be bolded with the definition provided at the bottom of the page.

• An example of the word may be given in the text. Often, the example is introduced by the phrases "for example" or "for instance".

• Look for a restatement of the word or phrase. Often, this restatement follows "or" or "which is". A term may also be restated as an appositive without a cueing word or phrase.

Example

  • Softball, a form of baseball played with a larger and softer ball, is becoming more popular.

  • India braces each year for the monsoons, seasonal winds from the Indian Ocean that bring heavy rains.

• Look for contrasts. If you notice pairs of contrasts, try to predict the meaning of the unfamiliar word from the other word in the pair

Example

  • The sauerkraut was not bland, but sour and acidic ("bland" must be *neutral*).

  • How could an experience be both gratifying and frustrating at the same time? ("gratifying" must be similar to *rewarding*).

  • Anson stared at the bubbling mixture. Would it be toxic or harmless? ("toxic" must mean *harmful* or *poisonous*).

• Comparisons made by words such as "like," "similar to," or "as if" give clues to meaning.

ADJUSTING APPROACH ACCORDING TO PURPOSE AND TEXT COMPLEXITY

Two situations where you may benefit from adjusting your approach are when you encounter jargon and subject-specific terminology.

Jargon

Jargon refers to a specialized set of words and phrases commonly understood by a group, such as members of a profession, hobby, or field of study. For example, imagine going to the dentist. If, after examining your teeth and X-rays, the dentist tells you that you have a "cary on your 1-3," you would not know what she is talking about. She is using jargon that is specific to dentists, and she would have to explain to you that she has found a cavity in one of your teeth.

Jargon is common among different professions and can be confusing to someone who does not belong to the special group for whom the jargon has meaning.

Online Language

Most students are computer literate and can navigate through and communicate using the Internet with ease. Online language has become an integral part of online communication. Usually online language abbreviates normal words to make typing as quick and easy as possible. You should never use online language or abbreviations in your writing assignments. Using online language for anything other than online communication with friends looks messy and unprofessional. Even if you are communicating online, if you are writing to anyone other than a friend, make sure you do not use online language.

Subject-Specific Terminology

Subject-specific terminology refers to the terms that are central to an area or unit of study. These terms are generally introduced at the beginning of a new unit or chapter. For instance, before beginning a poetry unit, an English teacher will first review common poetry terms, such as sonnet, lyric, ballad, onomatopoeia, alliteration, etc. Some terminology has an entirely different meaning from one subject to another. Following are a few examples of common math and science terms:

Word/Term	Math Meaning	Science Meaning
Base	Side or face of a polygon from which an altitude rises	Chemical compound that acts with an acid to form a salt
Formula	Equation that shows a general relationship	Chemical or physical equation
Power	Notation of a number with a base and an exponent, such as a^n where a is called the base and n is called the exponent	Rate at which energy is used
Transformation	Any mapping of a figure resulting in a change in position, shape, size, or appearance	The process of metamorphosis, as in caterpillar to butterfly

Subject-specific words that are important are often bolded and defined at the beginning of the chapter, bottom of the page, or back of the textbook.

When new words appear in content areas, you will better understand and remember information, ideas, and concepts by adopting the new words into your vocabulary. Ensure that you know the spelling and meanings of the word, and try to use the word, when appropriate, in conversation and writing.

Subject-specific terminology is important for understanding concepts. Before plunging into a new text, learn any terms that will help you to better understand the information. If the term is not defined in the text, use the glossary. List the terms and their definitions in your notes for quick reference.

Since most subject-specific terminology is not language that you use every day, learn it as you need it. Refresh your memory occasionally, and terminology will be relatively easier to review later on if necessary.

2.1.5.1 use reference materials, including a writer's handbook, to verify correct usage, address uncertainties, and solve problems that arise

USING REFERENCES

By Grade 9, you are probably a regular user of both online and print resources. You probably refer to dictionaries to verify correct meanings and spellings of words, thesauruses to find synonyms, and encyclopedias to locate information. Another reference resource that will help you to edit your own writing is a writer's handbook. This reference will help you to ensure that your language is grammatically correct.

Computer functions such as the spelling and grammar check do help to fix some problems, but it is best if you reread and edit your writing and also have someone else check it. Often, a computer grammar check makes errors so it is important that you know correct grammar. The following references are useful for checking any problems that you find in your writing:

- The Canadian Writer's Handbook

- The Chicago Manual of Style

- The McGraw-Hill Handbook of English Grammar and Usage

- Modern Language Association Handbook

- Simon & Schuster Handbook for Writers

- Thompson Nelson-Harbrace Handbook for Canadians

RESPOND TO TEXTS

2.2.1.1 experience oral, print, and other media texts from a variety of culture traditions and genres, such as essays, broadcast advertisements, novels, poetry, documentaries, films, electronic magazines and realistic fiction

FORM AND GENRE

Genre refers to any classification of texts by form, style, or subject matter.

FORM

The form of a text is made up of the structural elements chosen by the author.

Examples of Form	Characteristics
Letter	• Generally begins with an inside address and date • Uses conventional greeting and closings, such as *Dear* and *Sincerely*
Memorandum	• Addressed to a limited group, such as the employees of a company • Limited to essential information
Short story	• Consists of 20 000 words or less • Usually few characters and only one main character • One plot
Novella	• Consists of 20 000 to 50 000 words • Shorter version of a novel
Novel	• Consists of over 50 000 words, but often 90 000 to 100 000 or more • May contain many characters and multiple plots within the main story
Screenplay	• Contains mainly dialogue and directions for the action • Special rules for margins and font size give a standard length of approximately one page to one minute of screen time

GENRE

All genres contain certain characteristic elements.

• Westerns usually include a gunfight.

• Science fiction often includes imaginary scientific developments, such as interstellar spaceships.

• Romances are always complicated with misunderstandings and difficulties.

Forms and genres are combined in various ways. For example, an epistolary novel, which is told through letters, is a combination of two forms. Novels can be written in any genre, and all genres can be combined. A science fiction story might also be a romance, and a historical novel might also be a detective story.

The following chart contains examples of forms and genres. Note how the genres relate to the forms.

	Examples of Forms		Examples of Genres
Fiction	Poetry	Metrical Free verse Sonnet	Epic Ballad Lyric
	Prose	Play Musical Motion picture Shakespearean Modern	Tragedy Comedy
		Novel Novella Short story	Historical Detective Fantasy Science fiction Realistic
Non-fiction		History	Political Social Military
		Biography Autobiography Memoir	
		Documentary film	
		Essay	Expository Persuasive Research
		Letter	Personal Business Letter to the editor
		Diary	
		References	Encyclopedia Dictionary Thesaurus Atlas
		Textbook Manual	

The author's purpose and the audience for whom the author writes determine the form. Some forms of writing, such as non-fiction, give specific, accurate, and real-life details. Other forms may use more vivid and intense language, such as poetry, and others rely heavily on dialogue, such as plays.

The following table describes different types of literature and their sub-categories.

Genre	Description
Fiction	Author's imagination
• Short story	• 3 000–4 000 words—can be read in one sitting
• Mystery	• Contains a puzzle or a riddle that needs to be solved
• Historical Fiction	• Fictitious characters participating in real events that are accurately reported
• Fantasy	• Imaginative fiction with strange, fanciful creatures and settings
• Science Fiction	• Often a futuristic story with alien characters
• Murder Mystery	• A murder occurs that needs to be solved
• Realistic Fiction	• Stories that appear to be very real or true to life
Non-Fiction	Based on facts or reality
• Biography	• The life story of a specific person, written by someone else
• Autobiography	• A biography of a person told or written by himself
• General non-fiction	• Any writing about true situations rather than about imaginary events or characters
• Plays	• Written to be acted out, based on dialogue

POETRY

Poetry has special characteristics, as do plays, short stories, and essays. Poetry is distinguished from other forms of writing by the use of figurative language, its form, and its rhyme and rhythm.

Some of the very first stories ever told were in verse. Long before books existed, people chanted about the great events they had witnessed and their brave deeds. Over time, these chants were written down and are now called epic or narrative poems.

Following are descriptions of different types of poetry.

Epic poems are long narrative poems, usually about a historical event.

Ballads are narrative poems that tell a love story, historical event, or tale of heroism. Ballads are usually written in four-line stanzas, sometimes with a repeating chorus called a refrain. Ballads were originally sung rather than written down. As a result, some older ballads seem to be missing parts of their stories.

INAUGURATION DAY

The respected man stood on the podium, humble
The whole world watching, would he stumble?
He delivered that day with such eloquent words
To inspire and explain and to push us forwards.

The ears of the world listened to his ideal
To the best of our natures his words did appeal.
We need not, he told us, accept our decline
No need to seal our greatness into a shrine

Goodbye, we will say, to past recrimination
Time now to build ourselves a better foundation.
"Worn-out dogma" is a thing of the past
Our greatness, people, it will surely last.

Embrace, Americans and citizens of the world,
An idea of humanity once more unfurled.
We all have a hand in our common fate
And we shun all you who would desecrate.

Here is your destiny, absorb the vision
It is, after all, your decision.

As you read the poem "Inauguration Day," you can hear in your head how this poem could be sung, as ballads often are. You can also gain the sense of historical importance that the author feels about this inaurgration day.

Narrative poems tell stories.

MARATHON

The distance was cruel and the pace was fast
The sun shone brightly but the air was cool
The runner wondered if she could last
A medal of completion would be her jewel.

The route was a slice of limestone, a man-made path
That bent to the will of the river.
Twenty-four down, you do the math
Just keep going, follow the path, it will deliver.

You to the finish line, there it is, in sight
Is there gas in the tank for a little kick?
She calls on her will, using all of her might
She has grown taller on her own measuring stick.

The narrative poem "Marathon" tells the story of a runner during a marathon, and the thoughts, feelings, and actions that are a part of the marathon story.

Lyric poems express a poet's emotions or feelings. Lyric poems can be any length. Some lyric poems are pages long, while others, like the following example, are only a few lines in length.

> I fail to see the beauty
> in all this white stuff.
> The land is frozen, inert, contracted,
> holding its breath until spring.

This is an example of a short lyric poem that succinctly describes the author's throughts and feelings regarding a cold and snowy winter season.

Free verse poems are poems with no rhythmical pattern or rhyme scheme. They are still poems because they express emotions and contain poetic devices and symbolism.

BRUSH

This face, at the end of the counter
it pleases me.
Hello, I say, my name is
And yours?
Will there be love
from a chance encounter?

BEFORE SUMMER

I was Spring
And full of greenness
Young and rooted
To all things Black and White.

Pliant and imperfect
But content nonetheless
Unaware of Genesis
And all the shades of grey.

Looming over
Rising up
To shake hands with the origin of my understanding
A shining Apple.

Its rare beauty had me spellbound
vaulting high, rising rising I reach for it
It is in my grasp now
Subtle shades show once shrouded detail.

Complex the variation
Exciting the new vision
Frightening and confusing
The arrival of Summer.

The poems "Brush" and "Before Summer" have no rhythmical patterns or rhyme schemes, yet they are good examples of free verse poems that express emotions and symbolism through words and images.

Elegies are poems that are written as reflections on death. They are poems of mourning.

> And how shall I be remembered
> Now I am laid in simple pine?
> Who will be bothered?
> Will my grave become a shrine
> To the memory of me?
>
> I hope that my caring nature
> Did help prepare you all,
> Propel you all, strongly into the future.
> Stumble you may, but please don't fall
> To the memory of me.

This elegy is written from the perspective of the person who died, wondering how he or she will be remembered, and reminding those left behind that they should go "strongly into the future," and not "fall to the memory of me."

Odes are lyric poems that express lofty or enthusiastic emotion. Traditional odes often follow the structural pattern of historical poems from Greek and Latin.

Sonnets are 14-line poems that follow a set rhyme scheme and a logical structure. Some sonnets are written in an octave, which consists of 8 lines, followed by a sestet, which consists of 6 lines. Others are written in 12 lines ending with a couplet.

ESSAYS

Essays are multi-paragraph compositions in which a writer develops a subject with supporting ideas and detail. A minimum of three paragraphs is required in order to develop an introduction with a thesis, a body paragraph that supports this thesis, and a conclusion. The same principles of organizing a clear paragraph can be used to organize a clear essay.

There are several genres of essays:

- **Descriptive essays**, which describe something in detail, such as an object, place, person, procedure, or emotional experience

- **Narrative essays**, which tell a story. These essays usually relate a personal experience or replay a person's involvement in an event

- **Expository essays**, which show or explain a procedure, event, or topic

- **Reflective essays**, which consider a topic in a thoughtful or reflective manner. These essays usually consider various aspects of a topic

- **Persuasive essays**, which are opinion essays that seek to win readers over to a particular viewpoint on a topic or issue

Essays are organized into an introduction, a body, and a conclusion. The most common essay is the five-paragraph essay. The Hamburger Plan, shown below, illustrates a basic structure of the essay.

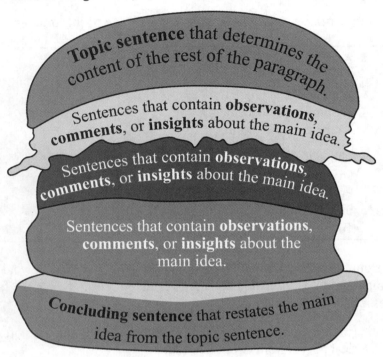

Topic sentence that determines the content of the rest of the paragraph.

Sentences that contain **observations**, **comments**, or **insights** about the main idea.

Sentences that contain **observations**, **comments**, or **insights** about the main idea.

Sentences that contain **observations**, **comments**, or **insights** about the main idea.

Concluding sentence that restates the main idea from the topic sentence.

As you read different texts, you will encounter the traditions and beliefs of other cultures. These encounters will inform you about people outside of your own cultural environment, and they enrich your understanding of others.

CULTURAL TEXTS

Many stories from different cultures are actually very similar. For example, many cultures have creation stories, flood stories, and stories that explain how the four seasons came to exist. You have probably read or heard the famous story of the "Tortoise and the Hare," which teaches the lesson that slow and steady wins the race. In this story, the tortoise wins out over a bragging hare. Though you would think that a hare could easily beat a tortoise in a race, the tortoise wins because the hare keeps getting distracted, while the tortoise wisely keeps working at his task.

Similar characters are also found among many cultures. One such character is called the trickster. The trickster character tends to be naughty and enjoys creating mischief. He is very clever and may be greedy and somewhat selfish. Most of all, he loves to outwit people who think they are smarter than he is by using special powers.

Following are some genres of cultural texts.

Myths are stories of gods. Myths help to explain events and natural occurrences, such as lightning. Most of the myths known today come from either Greek or Roman times. What is viewed as mythology today was an actual religion for the Greeks and Romans, who had many stories relating the interactions between gods and humans. For example, the story of Demeter and Persephone is a Greek myth that explains the origins of the four seasons.

Legends are stories that pass on the history and culture of a people. Legends were passed on orally by older members of a group. They were at one time regarded as true but are so fantastical that today they are seen almost as myths. For example, the legend of Achilles tells the heroic deeds of Achilles in the Trojan War. It is unlikely that Achilles existed, but the Trojan War was a real event in history.

Folktales and **fairy tales** are stories that usually teach a lesson or a moral. For example, in "Little Red Riding Hood," the lesson is to listen to your parents and to not wander into dangerous areas. Often, the stories contain magical elements, and the characters are animals that act like humans, such as in "The Three Little Pigs."

RABBIT THE TRICKSTER

A long time ago, in the days when men and animals were more similar, Otter was very highly regarded by the other animals but seldom seen. One day, the animals were debating about who had the finest coat. There was great variation among the coats, making it a difficult decision. Some had long fur, while others had short. Some had coats of one colour while some had varied colours. The animals decided to hold a council to decide who did indeed have the finest coat. Many had heard that Otter had the finest coat, but he rarely ventured down the creek to visit with the other animals. Rabbit was a very vain creature, always thinking and scheming, and he wanted to be acknowledged as having the finest coat. Immediately, he spoke up and volunteered to fetch Otter and guide him back to the council.

Rabbit travelled up creek until he found Otter and told him about the council. Rabbit had no trouble recognizing him because of his beautiful coat of soft dark-brown fur. Otter agreed to travel with him and they set out. At the end of the first day, Rabbit made a comfortable camp by cutting bushes for beds. The next day they set out again, and Rabbit gathered wood and bark that he carried on his back along the way. Otter asked what it was for, and Rabbit told him it was so they could be comfortable when they camped this night.

Once the sun began to set, the two travellers started making camp. Rabbit carved a piece of wood into the shape of a paddle. Otter asked what this was for, and Rabbit told him that he had good dreams when he slept with a paddle under his head. After that, Rabbit started clearing a path to the nearby river. Again, Otter asked what Rabbit was doing.

"This is the place where it has been known to rain fire. I want to make sure that we have a clear path to the water, just in case."

Then Rabbit hung his coat on a tree branch and advised Otter he should do the same, telling him, "You don't want to get burn marks on your lovely coat."

The two settled down to sleep, but only Otter was sleeping in earnest. Rabbit called out to Otter a couple of times to make sure he was sleeping deeply. Then Rabbit took the paddle, scooped up embers from their campfire, and tossed them into the air shouting, "It's raining fire! To the river. To the river."

Otter ran to the river and has lived there ever since.

Rabbit left his coat behind and wore Otter's much more attractive coat back to the council. The other animals recognized him from a distance because of his distinct coat and shouted, "Welcome! Make a place for Otter."

Otter seemed very bashful and kept his head down with a paw hiding his face, not making eye contact with the other animals. Bear, who was not easily fooled, pulled the paw away from Otter's face so they could have a good look, and there was Rabbit with his split nose. Bear was angry and took a big swipe at Rabbit with his large claws. Rabbit was very fast but Bear managed to pull Rabbit's tail off, and that is why rabbits ever since have had such short tails.

2.2.1.2 identify and discuss how timeless themes are developed in a variety of oral, print and other media texts

THEME

The theme of any work is its subject—what the work is about. The theme can be divided into two parts: the subject itself, and what is said about the subject. In a skillfully constructed narrative, everything contributes to the theme. The following chart shows how all of the elements of the narrative contribute to the theme.

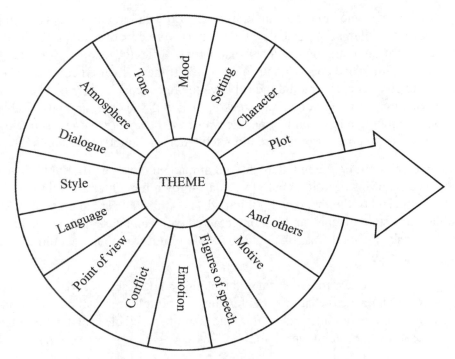

While the moral of a story and its theme are connected, they are not the same. A moral is a conclusion drawn from the events in a story. It is a statement about the best way to behave. The author may sometimes state the moral of the story, but it is more common for the moral to be left for readers to discover.

Some common themes in literature, past and present, include:

• Survival

• Man versus nature

• Triumph over adversity

• The "American Dream"

• Courage and bravery

• Freedom

• Religion

• Family

• Friendship

• Loyalty

UNIVERSAL THEMES

Timeless themes, also known as universal, common, or recurring themes, are incorporated into a variety of oral, print, and other media texts. For instance, themes important to adolescents, such as the need to belong and the need to be seen as unique, are woven into a popular novel written by S.E. Hinton at the age of 16. The novel was later adapted into a screenplay for a Hollywood movie by the same title— *The Outsiders.*

Universal themes are based on the conditions that most people experience at some time in life as members of the human race. Life and death, war and peace, questions of human suffering, goals and dreams, questions of identity, and the quest for truth are all universal themes. Universal themes in literature can easily be recognized and can be compared in two or more texts.

Theme: War

WAR	THE LAND
It was difficult to believe that this ugly, burned out pile of rubble was once his home. There, mixed into indistinguishable pieces of debris, was a recognizable piece of the porch railing. The porch had encircled his entire house and provided different, but beautiful views of the land that had been his and his family's for several generations. Presumably, the land was still his, but much of the beauty had been destroyed when the attack came. His parents had died in this house, fortunately before they had a chance to see all of it destroyed, when the neighbouring province decided to embark on a mission of expansion fueled by greed.	Throw at me what you will, Your worst, or your best, This place is mine, mine, mine. All you do is increase my zest For defiance.
Of course, they had not stood idly by and let their neighbours take what was theirs. A war had been fought, and as with all wars, the cost had been high. But the stakes had been high too—freedom, property ownership, saftey, peace. He had lost nearly everyone that he was close to in the conflict, and he had seen a few of his friends behave like animals. No, worse than animals. The human heart, he decided, is a dark and dangerous thing, and it is impossible to really know what is in another's heart, or in your own, for that matter. He was certain that if he had asked Matt before The War whether he would even consider torturing another man, his answer would have been no. Matt was the resident idealist and was always on a rant about politicians, their stretching of rules, and their creative application of law. Throwing back a pint at the local bar they would egg him on, and accuse him of being soft. But, take some things away from the idealist, brutally take some things away, and then see the colour of his character.	The lines on the map Are man-made, arbitrary. God gave us this land, Our rights to it, elementary To our well-being. What's this you say? Your God gave it to you! But whose God is right? Your words fill me with rue, Let us go to war. To make our decision, This absolutely, will solve our division?

The following table compares the two texts:

War	The Land
• Images of the ugliness and destruction of war	• Images of the reasons behind actions of war
• Claims of fighting for what is his	• Claims of fighting for what is his
• War making men do what is wrong	• War making men do what is right
• War as a symbol of destruction and anger	• War as a symbol of ownership and what is right

2.2.1.3 consider historical context when developing own points of view or interpretations of oral, print and other media texts

LITERATURE AND HISTORY

Some authors deliberately weave themes and issues from their own historical period into their work. Consider Charles Dickens' *Oliver Twist*, for example, which was written in 1838 in part to draw attention to problems that existed in English society at that time. *Oliver Twist* is considered a social novel because it:

• Exposed social problems related to industrialization

• Described the conditions accurately

• Sparked outrage in readers

• Publicized the need for social and political reform in England

Some of the themes addressed in Dickens' novel are discussed below.

Effects of Industrialization on Society

Fagin and his gang of boys represent the outcasts of society who were victims of circumstance in Victorian society. England went from being a country of gently rolling, green pastures to a land of factory-choked cities,where people of all ages laboured long hours for pennies a day. Most of the profits filled the pockets of the wealthy factory owners.

The Plight of Children in Victorian Society

Many children were orphaned, abandoned, or neglected. Orphans were placed in workhouse orphanages, similar to the one inhabited by Oliver. Because the class structure was so rigid, if you were born poor, you stayed poor. As an orphan, Oliver would never be accepted into a higher class, but after he was adopted, he could enjoy a much better quality of life, with all the perks that accompanied a middle-class lifestyle.

Conditions of the Working Poor

Dickens was angered and outraged by the Poor Laws of 1834. The legislation required the poor to earn their keep by labouring in government-run workhouses. These workhouses were literally sweatshops. Small children worked long hours for very little besides meager amounts of food and a place to sleep.

Crowded sections of London were rank with slums, garbage, violence, and criminal activity. Dickens describes the sights, smells, and sounds that were a part of everyday life in Victorian England. Images of poverty are captured in his description of Fagin's den, with its "Walls and ceilings ... black with age and dirt" reaching through streets that were "very narrow and muddy [with] air impregnated with filthy odors [and] dark and brown stains."

Corruption was the norm in such a setting. It is no wonder an orphan like Nancy turned to the hardened life of the streets at an early age and that child criminals freely roamed the streets picking pockets and committing other petty offences. They were easily recruited by cunning adults like Fagin to become part of a vicious London underworld ruled by risk and violence.

Rigid Structure of the English Class System

As the middle classes expanded under industrialization, they began to exploit the lower classes. This exploitation was personified in Oliver Twist with characters such as Mrs. Mann, Mr. Bumble, and Mrs. Sowerberry. Within the lower class itself, a "survival of the fittest" mentality caused betrayals and exploitation such as those experienced by Oliver and Nancy. It is interesting that Oliver's "salvation" comes from the upper class in the person of Mr. Brownlow. Dickens was looking to the powerbrokers, the lawmakers, and the wealthy of the upper class to bring about reforms that would improve conditions for members of the lower class. Nancy, on the other hand, both betrayed and saved Oliver. Dickens seems to be portraying the strong pull of evil forces on members of the lower class, which prevented even the good-hearted, like Nancy, from being an effective catalyst for reform.

In summary, Dickens drew attention to glaring social issues of his day, such as the workhouse conditions, issues of child labor, and criminal activity among children resulting from poverty and neglect. By advocating better conditions for these groups, he became an ambassador for change in Victorian England.

Historical literature can make history come to life with unique characters and a realistic setting. What is actually happening during an author's lifetime often directly influences the content, plots, settings, characters, and themes in the author's writing. In historical fiction, particularly, the historical context must be respected and accurately described for the writing to be authentic or realistic.

2.2.1.4 compare and contrast own life situation with themes of oral print and other media texts

THEMES AND LIFE SITUATIONS

Some themes create a strong reaction in readers or viewers because of a sense of kinship or familiarity to personal experiences.

Consider, for example, a play called *The 15th Candle*. This play, which is set in the early 1900s, is about a girl who shows promise as an artist. Her father intends to remove her from school when she turns 14 to work in a local factory. The main theme revolves around parental control and the right of a parent to influence important personal decisions in the lives of their children. In spite of the historical context of the play, when views on education and child labour were different from today, many students identify quite passionately with the personal issues raised by the theme.

Examining letters to the editor in a newspaper provides an opportunity to explore several viewpoints on a single issue. Following is an example of such a letter. This letter objects to what the writer views as an unnecessary degree of high-sticking violation in the game of hockey, which can result in serious injuries to players. After you read the original letter to the editor, read the two examples of responses to that letter. You should see three distinctly different ways that three individuals, each with a high level of interest in the game, view the issue put forward by the first writer. The theme is violence in the organized sport of community hockey.

FATHER CALLS HOCKEY A GAME OF BUTCHERY

Toronto (CP)—Norman Neeld, whose son Greg suffered a severe eye injury from a hockey stick last week while playing defence with Toronto Marlboros, says "hockey is a game of skill but butchery has taken over."

Two of his four sons have been hurt by high sticks, he said in an interview Monday, and he feels something ought to be done to prevent such incidents.

Neeld, an Air Canada pilot who lives in Vancouver, said "skilled players are subjected to fouls, many of them dangerous high-sticking offences, by the less skilled players."

"My four sons all have been excellent skaters from time they started to play hockey and they've all gone through the same thing of fouls against them. This, basically, is where the game falls apart."

Greg Neeld, 18, was hit in the eye by a stick during an Ontario Hockey Association Major Junior A game last Friday between the Marlboros and Kitchener Rangers.

Doctors at Toronto General Hospital say it will be a week before they know whether he will lose the sight in his left eye.

"We have to wait until the swelling in the eye disappears," Neeld said. He added that the doctors are not overly optimistic and do not want to give his son false hope.

Another son, 13-year-old John, was hit on the head by an opposing player in a Vancouver peewee game last year.

—Canada Press

Letters to the Editor

I wish to respond to yesterday's editorial expressing the opinion of a parent, Mr. Norman Neeld. I am a 14 year old junior player from Guelph, Ontario, and read the editorial in our local paper. Although I feel sympathy for Mr. Neeld and his injured sons, there is another perspective to consider. Without a doubt, hockey is a rough sport. It is a challenge for referees to call everything they see. Caught in the speed, excitement, and intense emotion of the game, athletes sometimes make impulsive choices that cause unnecessary injuries. I would still choose the organized risk of hockey over the random risk of hanging out with friends outside the arena. One of my friends was injured in a stabbing incident outside our arena. He was not a player. He was a fan, who happened to say the wrong thing to a fan from the town we were playing. I have the utmost respect for referees who are doing their best to keep a physical and emotional game reasonably clean and sportsmanlike.

Lyndon Glassman
Guelph A Rep Team

I read Mr. Neeld's assessment of hockey as a "game of butchery" with interest. I am a parent, too. With three sons in hockey. I am involved in the organization, as well, as co-ordinator of an Aboriginal League in our area. We play regularly with other leagues at the various age levels. My goal is to combine skill development with sportsmanlike behavior on the ice. While infractions do occur, especially with "less-skilled players," as noted by Mr. Neeld, we are constantly addressing the skill/behavior combination, not only in our coaching clinics, but in our practices and games. When a preventable injury occurs, we review the incident, email all coaches and referees in the organization, and direct the coaches to re-focus on the skill or behavior that could have prevented the injury. This philosophy has resulted in significant injury reductions in our league. We are united here in our view that high-sticking is dangerous and unnecessary, and are doing our best to eliminate the infractions at the grassroots level.

Aaron Lightfeather
High Prairie Aboriginal Hockey Association

2.2.1.5 express the themes of oral, print or other media texts in different forms or genres

EXPRESSING THEMES

You may be asked to express a theme in a different form or genre.

Sometimes the theme of a story is not so easy to locate. You may feel you understand a text, but that it is difficult to define the theme in words. Sometimes it can be easier to define the theme of a text by first expressing the theme in a different medium or genre.

REPRESENTING AND READING

Representing the theme of a text using a different medium or genre can force you to imagine concrete, visual ways of presenting some of the more abstract aspects of reading, such as theme, mood, character qualities, and symbolism. A poster, for example, could be used to express the dominant theme in a novel using nothing but pictures cut from magazines. A collage of clip art from the computer could visually express the theme of a novel, story, or poem. Title pages can also present themes.

In "The Gift of the Magi" by O. Henry, a young woman makes a difficult personal choice in order to provide a special Christmas gift for her husband. The theme is explicitly stated near the end of the story: "Of all who give and receive gifts, such as they are wisest."

If asked to express the story's theme in a different form or genre, you might choose to create a poem. In a poem, the theme of sacrifice for love would probably be expressed more indirectly. For instance, a poet could express the theme through suggestion and figurative language.

> Jim and Della
> Captives of Time
> Each bearing priceless gifts of love to the other;
> Two matchless treasure chests
> Brimming with teardrop diamonds, promise emeralds, and hope rubies;
> Promises
> Passions
> Parables
> Captured in one shining moment of truth.

2.2.1.6 consider peers' interpretations of oral, print, and other media texts, referring to the texts for supporting or contradicting evidence

CONSIDERING PEER INTERPRETATIONS

Group discussions are good times to express your views and consider the views of your peers. Perhaps they noticed something you missed, or they missed something you noticed. Whenever you are in doubt about an interpretation, go back through the text. Verify your views with supporting evidence. It is perfectly acceptable to change your mind about a character, theme, or statement of bias. The following examples demonstrate the value of considering peer interpretations to enhance your own understanding of texts.

Example

Two students have just read a short poem and looked at a one-page magazine ad. The teacher presents them with an empty Venn diagram and asks them to fill in points of similarity and contrast between the two genres or forms. Initially, the students had trouble naming shared characteristics because they had thought of a poem and an ad as being dramatically different. One student said that since imagery is word pictures, it would seem that pictures in an ad might have the same effect. The peer agreed, after checking the picture of a young man surfing in their ad. Further discussion led to agreement about the remaining shared characteristics that they placed on their Venn diagram.

Poem
- Word images suggest "mind pictures"
- Purpose is to create a mood, present a theme, etc.

Shared
- Imagery
- Appeal to senses
- May contain fragments rather than sentences
- Punctuation clarifies meaning

Advertisement
- Visual images provided to suggest results or product attributes
- Bolded words contain key ideas
- Purpose of text is persuasion

2.2.2.1 analyze how the choices and motives of characters portrayed in oral, print and other media texts provide insight into those of self and others

CHARACTER CHOICES AND MOTIVES

Before thinking about analyzing character choices and using insights from literature and media texts to better understand real people, let us review some important notions about character.

Character

In this context, *character* refers to qualities such as courage, honesty, generosity, intelligence, and their opposites. Character also refers to fundamental ideas and beliefs held by the person, which are revealed through:

- A character's actions or inactions

- Dialogue between two or more characters

- Thoughts revealed through interior speech or through other thought-revealing techniques, such as stream-of-consciousness narration

- The author's narration

One limitation of a film is the difficulty of revealing a character's thoughts in a way other than action. Voice-over narration, which is similar to first-person narration, is one method that filmmakers use to get past this limitation.

Personality

In this context, *personality* refers to features such as the attitudes, social skills, and emotional responses that constitute a character's enduring mode of behaviour. Personality is revealed the same way as character, but it is easier to show in film.

Motivation

Motive, which refers to the reasons for actions, is essential to character development and plot. Well-developed characters have believable, multiple, and conflicting motives. Motives take time to develop. Movie characters often have simple motivations because of the time constraints of the film.

Appearance

Some authors do not describe their characters' appearance at all, or only provide a brief description of their appearance.

UNDERSTANDING CHARACTER

All humans have common thoughts, emotions, and motives. Through an active and sympathetic imagination, humans can understand other people who are genuinely different.

- as we think about other people (real people and imagined characters) our own experiences and motives make them understandable

- as we observe other people (real people and imagined characters) and see something of ourselves in them

Skillful storytellers can make feelings and motives clear so that readers can understand the world and themselves in new ways.

Characterization

There are two different methods for characterization: direct and indirect characterization.

Direct characterization is expressed by:

- What one character says or thinks about another character

- The author's statements about a character

Indirect characterization is inferred from:

- What a characters says

- What a character thinks about him or her self, others, and the world

- A character's actions

- The reactions of other characters to that character

Analyzing Interactions Between Characters

As you read, you need to analyze the interactions between the main and subordinate characters and explain how these different interactions develop or affect the plot. The following types of interactions might occur between characters:

- Internal and external conflicts

- Motivations

- Relationships

- Influences

Following the introductory passage from "The Shop Door" are some conclusions that can be drawn about the main character (Rose) and the subordinate character (the stranger).

THE SHOP DOOR

The little bell that hung over the shop's door jingled merrily, making Rose look up from the task at hand. She bolted up and shot straight to the door, fully ushering in the after-hours visitor. Rose turned several locks. The "Closed" sign had been showing for some time already.

"The Master is expecting you," Rose whispered. There was no real need for silence, but the visitor's imposing and shadowed presence, combined with the lateness of the hour, had stolen Rose's voice.

Rose clasped her hands together to still their nervous trembling. "Wait here. I will go get him."

The stranger remained well back in the shadows at the front right side of the shop, where whatever camouflage the dim lighting failed to provide, a brimmed hat pulled low over his eyes. Rose parted the curtains that went to the back of the store.

She was gone only a moment. Lowered voices were heard. When she came back through the curtain, her eyes were not on the man but on what was in her hands. She held it reverently, and the bend of her head suggested awe and humility. What was it she was carrying so reverently? A book? Still with eyes only for the book, Rose crossed the room to where the visitor waited.

Rose forced herself to extend the book towards the waiting man. His eyes were on her, measuring her reaction. She still had not even looked at him. He reached out to receive the book and was amused to feel a small measure of resistance as he lifted it from her hands. She stared at her empty hands for a moment. Finally, fortified by the privilege of having held such an object in her own two hands, she raised her eyes to look at the stranger's face. He braced himself for her reaction. She surprised him by only briefly narrowing her eyes when she saw the disfiguring scars on the left side of his face.

Rose unlocked the door and started to open it.

"I hope I don't have to tell you to be careful. That which you carry is more important and valuable than either one of us."

He nodded, still comforted by her reaction, and slipped out the door deep into the shadows of the night.

Internal and external conflict—The conflict in the story is primarily internal. Both Rose and the stranger struggle with their own inner conflicts: Rose with her humility and the importance of her job, and the stranger with his shyness regarding his scars.

Motivations—As the two characters interact in this part of the story, it becomes evident that they have different motivations for what they do and say. Rose is shy and humble, the servant to her master, yet very aware of the importance of the book and its safety. The stranger is imposing yet shy and seems more concerned about Rose's reaction to his scars than to the task at hand.

Relationships—Rose and the stranger are strangers to each other; however, even from their first meeting and words, there is a sense of respect and curiosity between them. The reader should sense the deep connection that the book creates between the two characters and the importance of this book to both their relationship and a great cause.

Influences—According to the beginning of the story the following interactions influence the two characters:

- Rose's servitude to her master and the stranger

- The stranger's shyness about his appearance

- The importance of the book

These four aspects of character interaction contribute significantly to the plot. The reader learns of the separate internal conflicts and gets a glimpse that these conflicts are intertwined. This helps the reader begin to understand the motivations that cause each character to act and how these motivations may interact with each other. A relationship may be forming between Rose and the stranger, which may continue developing throughout the plot. The setting and character influences again offer a glimpse into this complicated and intertwined character relationship that leaves the reader wanting more.

GENERALIZING ABOUT INSIGHTS

When you read, observe how literary characters from the past, the present, and the future face conflicts and challenges in many different situations. Human nature remains very similar throughout history, so you will read about greedy characters, curious characters, fearful characters, and courageous characters from all literary periods. The same personality traits you might read about in books likely exist in people you know in the real world. Literature provides repeated opportunities to think about these characters and to compare and contrast their motivations and reactions as they confront similar situations and conflicts in different historical eras.

Analyzing characters from literature and other media texts provides you with valuable insights about yourself and other people. Most of the insights that you will gain from thinking about characters can fit into one of the following categories:

- **Encouragement**—we share familiar emotions, dreams, and disappointments on our journey through life. It helps to realize that characters we read about or see in movies have weathered similar or far worse and survived.

- **Warning**—some villains or failures serve as warnings or alert you to pitfalls that can be avoided in real life.

- **Inspiration**—characters who rise above challenging circumstances, such as poverty or ignorance, are a source of hope and inspiration for real people.

- **Comic relief**—laughter is healthy and contributes to well-being. Humorous characters act as a light reminder not to take life too seriously.

- **Empathy**—in Canada, we are removed from war-torn environments, so we can develop an attitude of empathy or understanding for disadvantaged people by reading about and analyzing characters from hostile environments.

- **Moral attitudes and values**—ideas about right and wrong, tolerance and justice, and searching for truth and the good in others are often conveyed through characters who requires us to examine and explore our own set of values.

- **Broadened perspectives**—characters beyond our limited sphere of experience of friends, family, and travels expand our horizons and our understanding of the world. Ideally, these characters help us to look outside ourselves at the world, its needs, its possibilities, and where we can fit in or make a contribution. A broadened perspective helps people to be less self-centered and self-absorbed.

2.2.2.2 identify and discuss theme and point of view in oral, print and other media texts

POINT OF VIEW

The perspective from which a story is told is called the author's point of view. There are three main points of view.

First person limited point of view results when the author decides to have one of the characters in the story tell the story. The pronouns "I," "me," "my," "mine," "we," and "us" are used. When first-person point of view is used, the reader usually knows only what the person who is telling the story thinks and feels.

Example

- "I was scared when I climbed the tree because I thought I might fall."

Third person limited point of view results when the author uses a narrator to describe the story objectively. The narrator has only a limited knowledge of the other characters.

Example

- "She appeared to be surprised when she heard John enter the house."

Third person omniscient point of view results when the author uses an all-knowing narrator to describe the events of the story. The pronouns "he," "she," "his," "her," "they," and "their" are used. Third person omniscient point of view allows readers to gain more information about all the characters and their thoughts.

Example

- "When Jack answered the phone, he knew instantly that it was going to be bad news."

SUBJECTIVE AND OBJECTIVE VIEWPOINTS

Viewpoints can be either subjective or objective, depending on the author's intentions.

Subjective point of view can be directly affected by a personal or emotional bias. A story that has a narrator with a subjective point of view will state opinions about the characters and their actions.

Objective point of view reports the facts of a situation without emotional overtones or bias. A newspaper reporter, for example, should report the news objectively, without inserting his or her own opinion.

A story that has a narrator with an objective point of view will try and relate the characters and actions to the reader as realistically as possible and will not offer personal commentary in narration.

2.2.2.3 discuss and explain various interpretations of the same oral, print or other media text

INTERPRETATIONS

Your new encounters are subjected to your unique viewpoint. This bias results from personal experiences and prior knowledge, and your own perspective and opinions.

Read the following excerpt from Edgar Allan Poe's "The Tell-Tale Heart." Compare the objective and subjective interpretations that follow.

Example

---

from THE TELL-TALE HEART

It is impossible to say how first the idea entered my brain; <u>but once conceived, it haunted me day and night.</u> Object there was none. Passion there was none. I loved the old man. He had never wronged me. He had never given me insult. For his gold I had no desire. I think it was his eye! Yes, it was this! <u>One of his eyes resembled that of a vulture</u>—a pale blue eye, with a film over it. Whenever it fell upon me, my blood ran cold; and so by degrees—very gradually—I made up my mind to take the life of the old man, and thus rid myself of the eye forever.

Now this is the point. You fancy me mad. Madmen know nothing. But you should have seen *me*. You should have seen how <u>wisely I proceeded—with what caution—with what foresight—with what dissimulation</u> I went to work! I was never kinder to the old man than during the whole week before I killed him.

—*by* Edgar Allan Poe

Example

Objective Interpretation

This excerpt of "The Tell-Tale Heart" describes how the narrator came to hate the old man that he wants to kill. It is from first person point of view and uses vivid language. The author uses short and long sentences and uses a variety of punctuation.

Subjective Interpretation

The plot of "The Tell-Tale Heart" seems implausible and far-fetched. I thought the author tried too hard to make the language complicated and it makes the reader feel detached from the story. Maybe that is the point, but if that is the author's style then I do not want to read more of his work.

The objective interpretation of the story included unbiased observations about techniques the author used. The subjective interpretation offered one reader's opinion about the story. Remember to check if your teacher wants an objective or a subjective interpretation of an assignment before you begin writing.

INTERPRETATION OF MEDIA TEXT

Media text refers to texts, information, and messages that are deliberately packaged for large or public audiences. Newspapers, magazines, all forms of advertising, artwork, and photographs are examples of media text. Messages hidden in the visual images of advertising are not only subtle but are also open to interpretation.

Now, read the poem, "The Blind Men and the Elephant," which summarizes text interpretation. This poem shows in just a few stanzas why making an assumption too quickly about anything is a mistake.

THE BLIND MEN AND THE ELEPHANT

It was six men of Hindostan,
  To learning much inclined,
Who went to see the elephant,
  (Though all of them were blind):
That each by observation
Might satisfy his mind.

The *first* approached the Elephant,
  And happening to fall
Against his broad and sturdy side,
  At once began to bawl:
"Bless me, it seems the Elephant
  Is very like a wall."

The *second*, feeling of his tusk,
  Cried, "Ho! What have we here
So very round and smooth and sharp?
  To me 'tis mighty clear
This wonder of an Elephant
  Is very like a spear."

The *third* approached the animal,
  And happening to take
The squirming trunk within his hands,
  Then boldly up and spake:
"I see," quoth he, "the Elephant
  Is very like a snake."

The *fourth* stretched out his eager hand
  And felt about the knee,
"What most this mighty beast is like
  Is mighty plain," quoth he;
"'Tis clear enough the Elephant
  Is very like a tree."

The *fifth* who chanced to touch the ear
  Said, "Even the blindest man
Can tell what this resembles most;
  Deny the fact who can,
This marvel of an Elephant
  Is very like a fan."

The *sixth* no sooner had begun
  About the beast to grope,
Than, seizing on the swinging tail
  That fell within his scope,
"I see," cried he, "the Elephant
  Is very like a rope."

And so these men of Hindostan
  Disputed loud and long,
Each in his own opinion
Exceeding stiff and strong,
Though each was partly in the right
  And all were in the wrong.

—*by* John Godfrey Saxe

The poem shows how looking at only one part of an issue allows you to form a very mistaken opinion on a subject. People often choose to only look at one part of an issue. The best way to avoid making biased opinions is to try and find as many viewpoints and as much information as possible about any given issue. Analyzing all sides of text or of an issue will help you form rational, balanced opinions.

2.2.3.1 discuss how techniques, such as irony, symbolism, perspective and proportion communicate meaning and enhance effect in oral, print and other media texts

ARTISTIC AND LITERARY TECHNIQUES

Techniques such as symbolism, irony, perspective, and proportion are used to communicate meaning and enhance effect in oral, print, and other media. The most significant contribution of these techniques is that they help readers to both understand and remember.

Symbolism is created when an author uses an object, a situation, or an action to suggest another meaning. A tiger, for example, might symbolize strength or fierceness, or a lamb may be used to suggest peace and gentleness.

Symbolism can be complicated or simple. There is a certain amount of creativity in trying to figure out if something is a symbol or not. After reading through a story, try and think of the images and ideas that stood out to you. This can be a good start to discovering symbols in a text.

The following list provides a number of symbols that are commonly found in literature. Knowledge of these universal symbols can help you find more meaning in what you read.

Common Symbols in Literature
- Water—fertility, life-giving, rebirth, purification, redemption
- Stagnant or polluted water—corruption, evil
- Fire—destruction, purification, passion, death
- Earth—baseness, fertility
- Air/wind—spirits, freedom, inspiration
- Sun—wisdom, vision, power, life-giving, regeneration
- Sunrise—birth, rebirth, joy, hope
- Sunset—death
- Mountains—obstacles, achievement, aspirations, awe, glory
- Storms—death, evil, inner turmoil
- Roads, ships, trains, railroads—journeys, changes
- Fork in the road/crossroads—choices, decisions
- Doors/gates/arches—escape, opportunities, utopias, fantasy worlds, freedom
- Bridges—transitions, crossing over
- Walls/fences/hedges—barriers, dividing lines, prisons
- Windows—freedom, longing, imprisonment
- Mirrors—illusion, unreality, passage to other worlds
- Birds/sky—freedom

- Circle—wholeness, unity
- Gardens—Eden, paradise, innocence, fertility
- Desert—spiritual aridity, death, hopelessness, sterility
- Lamb—innocence, Christ
- Sheep—conformity
- Black—evil, death, despair
- White—innocence, good, redemption
- Red—war, anger, blood, vengeance, love, passion
- Green—growth, renewal, life, nature, envy
- Yellow—sun, happiness, cowardice, betrayal

Symbolism plays a key role in other forms of media text, particularly films and advertising.

Because advertising consists primarily of images, the images must carry the symbolism. Many of the images communicate "symbolic codes" in such aspects as facial expressions, gestures, clothing, and setting.

Irony occurs when the reader or the audience knows information that the characters do not know or when there is an unexpected twist related to an earlier fact or idea.

Consider Shakespeare's *Romeo and Juliet*, for example. When Romeo discovers Juliet lying motionless, he assumes that she is dead and acts upon this assumption, which creates irony because the audience knows that Juliet has swallowed a sleeping potion and is only unconscious.

An example of dramatic irony can be seen in the ending of "The Most Dangerous Game."

> Rainsford did not smile. "I am still a beast at bay," he said, in a low, hoarse voice. "Get ready, General Zaroff."
>
> The general made one of his deepest bows. "I see," he said. "Splendid! One of us is to furnish a repast for the hounds. The other will sleep in this very excellent bed. On guard, Rainsford …
>
> He had never slept in a better bed, Rainsford decided.

The irony occurs in the role reversal that occurs at the end of the story. Rainsford is not really "a beast at bay," as he says. Knowing that his life truly depends on the outcome of this final encounter, Raindford takes over a predator, forcing his pursuer, Zaroff, to become the prey. The "winner" of the deadly contest initiated by Zaroff is identified in the closing sentence of the story. Ironically, Zaroff becomes the loser in the game he had set up as a win-win situation for himself.

2.2.3.2 discuss character development in terms of consistency of behavior and plausibility of change

CHARACTER DEVELOPMENT: CONSISTENCY AND PLAUSIBILITY

Literature is about real or fictional people and the conflicts they have to overcome. Characters are important because they are the action doers. They set goals for themselves that they try to reach. Characters in fiction must be realistic; they might be good or bad, happy or sad, humble or arrogant. If a character in a story is well developed, their strengths, weaknesses, motivations, conflicts, points of view and relationships are disclosed. They act like real people act in the real world.

Guy de Maupassant's "The Diamond Necklace" shows the humanness of characters as they face the conflicts that occur in the story.

The conflicts begin when Matilda Loisel borrows a necklace from a wealthy friend to wear to a party. Matilda loses the necklace. She and her husband spend the next ten years working to pay off the expensive replacement necklace. In the end, they discover that their descent into poverty has been a waste because the original necklace borrowed from the friend was actually an inexpensive fake.

Matilda Loisel and her husband are major characters. Matilda is considered the protagonist, and the author has unfolded the story from her point of view. Mme. Forestier is a minor character; she has a fairly insignificant part in the plot.

There are two main aspects of character: personality and appearance. Look at what the author has told us about Matilda Loisel.

Example

Matilda Loisel (before the loss of the necklace)	
Personality	**Physical Appearance**
Unhappy Vain Selfish Dissatisfied Materialistic Flirtatious	Pretty

This following excerpt from early in the story reveals the two major characters.

Example

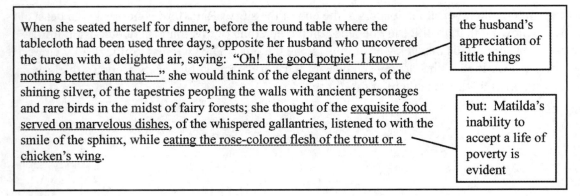

When she seated herself for dinner, before the round table where the tablecloth had been used three days, opposite her husband who uncovered the tureen with a delighted air, saying: "Oh! the good potpie! I know nothing better than that—" she would think of the elegant dinners, of the shining silver, of the tapestries peopling the walls with ancient personages and rare birds in the midst of fairy forests; she thought of the exquisite food served on marvelous dishes, of the whispered gallantries, listened to with the smile of the sphinx, while eating the rose-colored flesh of the trout or a chicken's wing.

the husband's appreciation of little things

but: Matilda's inability to accept a life of poverty is evident

After the missing necklace is replaced by an identical but much more expensive one, Matilda begins to exhibit character changes. In a less dramatic way, so does her husband.

Example

> Mrs. Loisel now knew the horrible life of necessity. She did her part, however, completely, heroically. It was necessary to pay this frightful debt. She would pay it. They sent away the maid; they changed their lodgings; they rented some rooms under a mansard roof. She learned the heavy cares of a household, the odious work of a kitchen. She washed the dishes, using her rosy nails upon the greasy pots and the bottoms of the stewpans. She washed the soiled linen, the chemises and dishcloths, which she hung on the line to dry; she took down the refuse to the street each morning and brought up the water, stopping at each landing to breathe. And, clothed like a woman of the people, she went to the grocer's, the butcher's, and the fruiterer's, with her basket on her arm, shopping, haggling, defending to the last sou her miserable money.

How a life of poverty affected and changed Matilda, and what she had to do, and how she accomplished these tasks.

> The husband worked evenings, putting the books of some merchants in order, and nights he often did copying at five sous a page.

In contrast: a very short sentence that tells how the husband was affected. Also the fact that his name is not given shows that the story is about Matilda and the effects of the loss of necklace.

The following chart summarizes the changes in Matilda Loisel.

Example

Matilda Loisel (after the loss of the necklace)					
Personality			**Physical Appearance**		
Loud Voiced	Hardworking	Thrifty	Old	Common	Stringy hair
Uncomplaining	Strong	Hard	Untidy clothes	Red hands	
Crude	Sad	Unselfish			

A comparison of the two charts shows how the loss of the necklace affected Matilda and changed the pretty but spoilt, discontented woman into a common, hardworking, and strong woman.

While Matilda's character changed, she did still wonder what life could have been like if her circumstances had been different.

Example

> How would it have been if she had not lost that necklace? Who knows? How singular is life, and how full of changes!

Are the changes in Matilda Loisel's character plausible to readers? In the story, Guy de Maupassant explores a reality about human nature that we have all experienced, to a greater or lesser degree. The depth of Matilda's obsession with appearances is hinted in a quote very early in the story:

Example

> She had a rich friend, a schoolmate at the convent, whom she did not like to visit, she suffered so much when she returned. And she wept for whole days from chagrin, from regret, from despair, and disappointment.

What was it that motivated the Loisels to work so hard for 10 years? It could be said that it was to repay the loan, but the real motivation was that the Loisels were dishonest. Matilda was dishonest about the necklace primarily because she was ashamed of her poverty and envious of her friend's success.

Plausible changes generally happen to realistic characters. Realistic characters are revealed through their actions, manner of speaking, thoughts, and description. Characters from everyday life, dealing with real issues are plausible to readers. This is why many authors develop characters with whom readers can easily identify. Some characters become very real to their readers because their creators developed them consistently so they, like real people, have familiar, predictable personalities.

2.2.3.3 describe how theme, dominant impression, and mood are developed and sustained through choices in language use and the interrelationship of plot, setting and character

TEXT DEVELOPMENT

Dominant impression is the tone generated by the author. It is the author's apparent attitude toward characters, settings, and conflicts. Tone can be thoughtful, chatty, formal, tragic, silly, or a combination of attitudes. The author's tone produces a certain mood, which readers can sense as they read. Dominant impressions like theme and mood are developed and sustained through language and the interrelationships of plot, setting, and character.

In the following passage, the narrator's frustration and anger are expressed through the use of repetition, choice of diction, and punctuation.

Example

> Garbage! Garbage! Garbage! Why is there so much garbage in the world? Do they think it will just go away if we stick it in landfills? Every year they take truckloads of garbage to new and bigger landfills! There is no end to it!

Mood is usually created through tone and descriptions of settings and characters. Just as in real life, the mood of a story can be angry, sad, frightening, suspenseful, enthusiastic, or scary.

In the following passage from "The Storm", the author creates a mood of eeriness, suspense, and loneliness. Readers wonder what is going to happen and can feel the suspense and fury. It is the author's style of writing—short simple sentences and diction, and phrases such as "voices in the wind, screaming", "furious gale", and "pushed it down like a playground bully", that create the mood the readers experience.

Example

> The storm advances with chaos and purpose combined. There is a noise to the wind like a vast machine. Are there voices in the wind, screaming? Or, is it just a trick of the furious gale as it struts among the buildings and signs and trees? A large tree rips free of its moorings and topples over. One hundred years of growing undone in one capricious moment. The rain, having fallen for hours, loosened the tree's roots, and its co-conspirator, the wind, pushed it down like a playground bully.

When you read a poem, the poet's language often includes imagery, which contributes to the overall mood of the text. The use of imagery can stir an emotional response or connection in readers. This influences the mood and the personal meaning of a poem for readers.

Example

> **RAIN**
>
> Friend or foe
> this time?
>
> Will you be like a mother's
> gentle caress, soothing,
> easing, quenching?
>
> Or will you be the brute
> wearing torrential boots, washing
> away, knocking down,
> deluge?

The following excerpt is from Gilbert Highet's short story, "Another Solution." In the story, the main character thinks he has survived the capsizing of his small boat in the Mediterranean. Vivid descriptions of the watery setting as the plot draws to a sudden and unexpected conclusion and the character faces his inevitable fate, creates a mood of horror for readers. The theme that human beings are no match for the forces of nature is also suggested.

> A piece of seaweed touched his foot, and he pushed it away. It drifted back, and he kicked it off. When it returned and glided along his knee, he lowered one arm to catch it. Perhaps it was not seaweed, perhaps it was poor Concha's handkerchief.
>
> As he felt about in the water, something gripped his knee. Instantly, the same grip was on his hand. He could not move. He glared down into the dark water, where beside his own body he saw nothing. But it was necessary to see the gray shape with the long arms, the great octopus which clung to the rock and now grasped both his wrists and threw another tentacle round his waist and drew him down. He had not thought of that.

The language chosen by the author is straightforward and matter-of-fact. This creates a dominant impression of near scientific and impersonal detachment. The author's tone heightens the surprise, despair, and utter terror of the swimmer's final moments.

2.2.3.4 identify features that define particular oral, print, and other media texts; discuss differences in style and their effects on content and audience impression

TEXT FEATURES

All texts have certain defining features. These features serve to:

- Set texts apart from other similar texts

- Make texts user friendly

- Make texts appealing to readers

Following are some examples of text features that serve to distinguish texts:

- Fonts, font sizes, and bolding

- Visuals, such as diagrams, maps, graphs, illustrations, photographs, and cartoons

- Organizational features, such as table of contents and chapter headings

- Reference features, such as index, glossary, bibliography of linked references, and appendix

These features affect the overall impression or style of a text. If a text contains numerous visuals, for instance, it is usually perceived by readers as easier to understand, especially when the reader reads about something that is clarified or explained in more detail by an illustration.

UNDERSTAND FORMS, ELEMENTS, AND TECHNIQUES

2.3.1.1 explain the relationships between purposes and characteristics of various forms and genres of oral, print, and other media texts

CHARACTERISTICS OF TEXTS

AUTHOR'S PURPOSE

Every author writes for a specific reason or purpose. When you know the author's purpose, it is easier to understand the meaning. There are five main purposes for writing that you should be able to recognize when you read.

To inform: An author whose purpose is to inform wants the reader to understand the facts of a situation.

> The incident occurred on Saturday evening across from the community centre. No injuries were reported, but several citizens were rattled by the commotion.

To explain: An author whose purpose is to explain wants to give the reader the *why* or *how* of a situation So that they understand the situation.

> An arctic flow of chilled air can cause icy precipitation and blizzard conditions even as late as March.

To entertain: An author whose purpose is to entertain tries to amuse the readers, make them laugh, or help them escape the real world for a while. The purpose of most fiction is to entertain or amuse the reader.

> **SUMMER DREAMIN'**
>
> The sudden blizzard made me slip
> It also made me slide;
> I looked up at my calendar
> To see March tucked inside;
> I shook my fist at heaven…
> Can't tell you how it hurt
> To sadly turn away from them,
> My shorts and muscle shirt!

To influence: An author whose purpose is to influence tries to make readers feel strongly about something.

> I am confident that serious accidents could be prevented if snow removal were to increase. The inconvenience of the equipment must be accepted to reduce the hazards of winter driving.

To convince: An author whose purpose is to convince tries to change readers' minds about something. The author wants readers to see things from his or her point of view.

> Following a sudden blizzard with unexpectedly heavy snowfall, the swift and efficient clearing of all major and secondary roadways is essential, for three reasons. First of all, the traffic hazard created by large snow-moving equipment is not to be compared with the greater safety hazard of leaving snow on the roads.

Sometimes, an author may write for more than one purpose. Consider, for example, a funny and entertaining story that also teaches a lesson or a moral.

You can usually determine or explain a logical or inferred relationship between the author's purpose and form. For example, if your purpose as a writer were to complain about a faulty product you had received by mail, the most logical form would be to write a business letter or email to the company. When author Charles Dickens wanted to influence middle class English people to improve the appalling conditions for the poor, his choice of form was the serial novel, which was printed in weekly installments in local newspapers.

2.3.1.2 evaluate the effectiveness of different types of media texts for presenting ideas and information

EFFECTIVENESS OF DIFFERENT MEDIA TEXTS

The various means of presenting ideas and information are referred to as forms and genres. Every form of text is effective for a type of communication. Following are a few examples of news media forms.

Summary Newscast

A summary newscast is a brief recap of the daily news. It is effective for people who may not have time on certain days to read a full newspaper, but who still want to be aware of what is happening locally and in the world.

Morning Newspaper

The morning newspaper is an effective form for people who read the news with their breakfast or as they commute by bus or subway to work.

Editorials and Letters to the Editor

Editorials and letters to the editor are effective forms for addressing different aspects and points of view on current issues. This also allows a newspaper to fulfill one of its valuable roles as a forum for discussion.

Examine how one subject can be treated completely differently in different kinds of texts. In the poem "The Dare" and in the article "Seeking New Experiences," the writers treat the subject of teenage risk-taking very differently.

THE DARE

Go on, I dare you
Come on down!

Was it me they called?
Pretend you haven't heard,
a voice commanded in my mind.
Walk past, walk fast
and don't look down,
don't look behind.

Come on, it's easy!

The banks were steep,
the water low
and flanked with oozing brown.
Easy? Walk fast
but don't look down.
Walk straight, walk on,
even risk their jeers
and run…

Never go near those dykes,
my mother said.
No need to tell me.
I'd seen stones sucked in
and covered without trace,
gulls slide to bobbing safety,
grasses drown as water rose.
No need to tell me
to avoid the place.

She ca-a-a-n't, she ca-a-a-n't!
Cowardly, cowardly custard!

> *There's no such word as 'can't,'*
> my father said.
> I slowed my pace.
> The voices stopped,
> waited as I wavered, grasping breath.
> My mother's wrath? My father's scorn?
> A watery death?
>
> I hesitated then turned back,
> forced myself to see the mud below.
> After all, it was a dare…
> There was no choice;
> I had to go

"The Dare" is a poem written in the first person. The narrator hears the voices of those who dared her to walk along the dykes. In her head, she also hears the voices of her mother and father. Throughout the poem, the reader knows how the narrator feels because of her self-talk ("Walk past, walk fast / and don't look down,/don't look behind"), her fears ("The banks were steep, / the water low"), and her realization that she cannot turn away from the dare.

SEEKING NEW EXPERIENCES

Why do teenagers take dangerous risks more often than people in other age groups? "A normal part of adolescence is seeking new experiences and trying on new roles," says Dr. Beatrix A. Hamburg, a child psychiatrist at New York City's Mount Sinai Hospital. As you move toward adulthood, Dr. Hamburg notes, risk-taking helps you feel more independent.

Unfortunately, Dr. Hamburg adds, many young people haven't yet developed the sense of judgment they need to tell an acceptable risk from a dangerous one.

Poor judgment isn't the only reason why teens take dangerous risks, says Randy Cornelius, a developmental psychologist at Vassar College in New York. Many teenagers, he says, feel that they simply cannot be hurt by actions such as drinking and driving. "Most adults have been to enough funerals and visited enough hospitals to know that human life is a fragile thing," Cornelius says. "Teenagers who haven't had this exposure sometimes think of themselves as invulnerable or superhuman."

"That's true," admits Eric Fischer, a 16-year-old from Salt Lake City, Utah. Eric's brother Matt was paralyzed from the waist down in a skiing accident. "Before Matt got hurt, I used to be a real radical skier—pushing myself as fast as I could and jumping without looking out for what might be below. Now that I know I could get totalled, I ski carefully and try to stay in control."

Unlike "The Dare," "Seeking New Experiences" is a third-person exposition explaining why teenagers take more dangerous risks than people in other age groups. The author refers to the findings of a child psychiatrist and a developmental psychologist in order to back up the deductions that many teenagers feel themselves to be invulnerable. This thought is supported by relevant detail in the form of the testimony from an accident victim's brother.

Both pieces of writing deal with risk-taking, but they are presented very differently. If you were researching the topic of teenage risk-taking, the article could be an effective resource for some key information on your topic. On the other hand, the poem might provide you with an effective way to introduce your topic to a reader or listening audience. Part of evaluating the effectiveness of a text is determining which form is most suitable for the situation.

2.3.2.1 compare the development of character, plot, and theme in two oral, print, or other media texts

COMPARING DEVELOPMENT OF CHARACTER, PLOT, AND THEME

Comparing allows you to think about similarities and differences between:

• Two different stories on a similar theme

• The same story presented in two different ways (print and film, for example)

• Two variations of a story, such as the original and an adaptation

Comparing is easier if you organize your information systematically. Consider the following two characters:

	Oliver Twist	**Harry Potter**
Similarities	• Orphan • Family problems—desertion, abusive adults • Dreamer—dreamed of the big city, London	• Orphan • Family problems—abusive uncle, aunts, cousins • Dreamer—dreamed of power over his situation, revenge
Differences	• Physical survival challenges • Manipulated by people such as Jack Hawkins (Fagin) • Was seen as vulnerable, an "underdog"	• Emotional survival problems • Learned to use his "gifts" to have power over enemies • Was seen as a leader, a champion of "underdogs"

Charles Dickens' *Oliver Twist* and J. K. Rowling's *Harry Potter* share a similar universal theme of good versus evil. If you select one of the Harry Potter novels, you could make a comparison chart of the characters, the plot, and the theme.

2.3.2.2 evaluate the effectiveness of oral, print and other media texts, considering the believability of plot and setting, the credibility of characters, and the development and resolution of conflict

BELIEVABILITY IN TEXTS

As you evaluate the different types of text you read, your critical thinking skills will enable you to use the text effectively and confidently, for a variety of purposes. While you read, ask yourself the following questions:

- Why is the story believable?

- Why is the plot so convincing?

- How has the author created a realistic setting?

- Why is the main character so credible?

- Is the conflict authentic and genuine?

- Is the story plausible?

On the surface, these are simple, direct questions. However, answering them by providing supporting evidence from the text can become fairly complex.

Anything that makes a story realistic, authentic, or believable to readers is called verisimilitude, which means similar to the truth. There are several elements involved in creating realistic stories:

- A **realistic plot** is created with readers can imagine the events actually taking place

- A **realistic setting** is created when the author includes descriptions that give readers a visual image

- **Realistic characters** are created through description, dialogue, actions, and thoughts. These characters are often subject to the hardships with which readers are familiar

- **Realistic subject matter** is created by issues that are either current or historical

- **Realistic life situations** are created when plausible issues arise and are resolved in ways that are not always positive

For a story to be realistic, it must contain believable conflicts. Stories are about the conflicts that characters encounter. Conflicts can be either internal or external.

Internal Conflict	External Conflict
Person against self	Person against person
	Person against society
	Person against nature

By the end of the story, the conflict is usually resolved in some way for the main character. Sometimes, a major conflict is not resolved and you are left with an unsettled feeling. This can make the resolution more plausible than one where the outcome is directly stated.

Evaluating Believability

Believability is evaluated through comparisons with real life. When you read consider whether the relationships in the text are similar to relationships that you have or have observed. If there are moral dilemmas in the text, are they reflections of real life dilemmas? Is the setting realistic?

2.3.2.4 identify ways that a change in narrator might affect the overall meaning of oral, print, and other media texts

NARRATION

Most texts you read are written from one of the following points of view:

- **First-person**—the narrator tells the story from a subjective perspective using the pronouns "I" and "me."

- **Third person limited**—the story is written objectively about someone else using the pronouns "he," "she," and "they."

- **Third person omniscient**—the narrator knows everything about the characters including their thoughts.

Consider the following excerpt from Edgar Allen Poe's "The Tell-Tale Heart."

> True!—Nervous—very, very dreadfully nervous I had been and am; but why will you say that I am mad? The disease has sharpened my sense—not destroyed—not dulled them. Above all was the sense of hearing acute. I heard all things in the heaven and in the earth. I heard many things in hell. How, then, am I mad? Hearken! And observe how healthily—how calmly I can tell you the whole story.
>
> It is impossible to say how first the idea entered my brain; but once conceived, it haunted me day and night. Object there was none. Passion there was none. I loved the old man. He has never wronged me. He had never given me insult. For his gold I had no desire. I think it was his eye! Yes, it was this! One of his eyes resembled that of a vulture—a pale blue eye, with a film over it. Whenever it fell upon me, my blood ran cold; and so by degrees—very gradually—I made up my mind to take the life of the old man, and thus rid myself of the eye forever.

The narrator's point of view is first person. It is the persona of a strangely obsessed, probably insane housemate of an elderly man who has been murdered as he slept. This viewpoint **affects**:

- **Character claims**, which heighten the sense of a madman possessed by an evil idea. The first-person protestations of sanity strengthen the perception that the main character is criminally insane.

- **Tone**, which conveys the writer's attitude toward the story or characters. The punctuation in the introduction implies the tone of an insane person. This is further exemplified in the next paragraph when the narrator exclaims that he decided to take the old man's life because he didn't like his eye.

- **Plot**, which is affected by the narrator's perspective. Since the story is centred on the narrator, it is his perspective that establishes the plot.

- **Credibility**, which the story changes as a result of the obsession and insanity that is conveyed through the persona of the narrator. The stealth, cunning, suspense, and guilty outcome of the plot become believable because the narrator's sanity is questioned.

In a theatrical adaptation of this story, the "madman" speeches, which are not changed from the original, are spoken in an insane asylum, where the murderer is relating his tale to a medical professional. The first person viewpoint of the mad character was counterbalanced by the sane viewpoint of the psychiatrist. Were the psychiatrist to also gain a perspective, it may read as:

Although this is our third interview since his admission last Thursday, the patient continues to be extremely agitated in my presence, pacing rapidly back and forth before me as he speaks, gesturing wildly to make points, and stopping frequently to wag his forefinger in my face, as though to command my full and rapt attention. In his dissociative state, he accepts no responsibility whatsoever in the incident which brought him here. On the contrary, he continues to blame his unfortunate victim, the gentleman with the pale blue eye.

My report shall remain inconclusive, at this point, until I can have him observed by my department colleagues, Drs. Leonard and Christiansen. Meanwhile, I do not feel threatened or in danger. This patient is disturbed, but is not of a violent nature.

You can see by this example that a different narrator viewpoint can affect the overall meaning by altering the tone or by adding a further dimension to character portrayal. As shown, a different narrative viewpoint can change the tone of the story and add dimension to a character.

2.3.2.5 summarize the content of media texts and suggest alternative treatments

ALTERNATE TREATMENTS OF MEDIA TEXTS

What happens to an animated television commercial when it is adapted to a magazine ad? Which scene from the movie's trailer would you use as the backdrop for a theatre poster? Would the short story you just finished reading make a good play? Adapting any work into a different medium can help you to understand the content of the original work. The new form can still communicate the same message or messages—sometimes with more impact than the original.

Example

DEEP FREEZE INCREASES RISK TO HOMELESS
FEARS GROW FOR UNSHELTERED

Edmonton – While most of us struggle with getting the car to start and risking a fender-bender on the way to work, the homeless of our city struggle with survival in the frigid temperatures that have gripped the region this past week.

Ellen McCall, spokesperson for city shelter co-ordination, reports that 800 beds prepared for weather emergencies are being filled nightly.

While no one is being turned away from shelter facilities, it is feared that some people needing shelter may not be finding it for a variety of reasons, including voluntary choices to spend the night in makeshift temporary shelters outside.

Bus drivers and police have been cautioned to be on the alert for anyone needing assistance or shelter. Commuters and other citizens are asked to report possible shelter-related emergencies to the shelter hotline at 780-SHELTER (743-5837). All calls will be treated as urgent.

So far, there have been no reported deaths due to freezing. However, each period of severe cold in the past has generated at least one fatality in the city. It is hoped that 2008 will remain fatality-free.

—by E. Meyer

BALLAD OF A COLD MAN

The winds they chill me to the bone,
A man who calls Edmonton home,
My cardboard walls are way too thin
I wish I could go home again.

Chorus
Home again, yes home again,
I wish I could go home again,
To Mother's stew without the pain,
I wish I could go home again.

The streets they mock me with their ice,
The cops assume I act with vice,
My cardboard walls no shelter give,
Must move if I expect to live.

Chorus, etc.

How did I reach this point so low?
How did my dreams descend below?
The ice outside, that's not so bad,
It's ice within, that makes me sad.

And so if winter's got you down,
And risky drivers make you frown,
Just pause while at that traffic light,
And say a prayer for someone's plight.

I too was once a man like you,
The drive to work my trial too,
But life can change and paths can turn,
So don't complain, be still, and learn.

Most news stories are objective, whereas most poems are subjective and emotional. Adapting the news article into a poem allowed the student to understand the emotional consequences of information that was originally presented as objective and unbiased. By adapting information into a new medium or genre, new understanding and perspective can be attained.

2.3.3.1 analyze creative uses of language and visuals in popular culture, such as advertisements, electronic magazines and the Internet; recognize how imagery and figurative language, such as metaphor, create a dominant impression, mood and tone

CREATIVE LANGUAGE AND VISUALS

Language can be manipulated creatively, using both figurative language and imagery. Figurative language inspires emotional reactions, creates mental pictures, and stimulates the senses. Figurative language and visuals can evoke a powerful and memorable response. Figurative language is not only used in poetry, but also in advertising, music videos, and online.

When you interpret the meaning of a piece of writing, keep in mind that many different kinds of authors—not just poets—use words and phrases figuratively. This means that words and phrases are used to convey meanings other than their literal or dictionary interpretations. The following literary devices are examples of the variety of figurative language that authors use:

• **Simile** is a comparison of two unlike things using the words *like* or *as*.

  • The kite flew like a bird.

  • She was as quiet as a mouse.

• **Metaphor** is a comparison of two or more things or ideas without using the words *like* or *as*. A metaphor can occur within a sentence, a paragraph, or throughout an entire piece of writing.

  • The stars were diamonds in the sky.

- **Personification** is the attribution of human characteristics to an inanimate object.

  - The north wind wailed like a lost child.

- **Hyperbole** is an extreme and deliberate exaggeration.

  - I ate a mountain of pancakes for breakfast.

- **Alliteration** is the repeated use of the first letter or sound in two or more words set closely together.

  - The frightened fox fought fiercely.

- **Onomatopoeia** is the use of a word that imitates the sound that it describes.

  - Lightning crackled overhead.

Read the following paragraph, paying close attention to the underlined phrases.

Example

> Out in the bay, treacherous currents sizzle and leap among the underlying rocks with the relentless (1) purpose of a hungry dragon. Which unsuspecting ship will be (2) on the menu today? (3) Like a spoiled child, the (4) waves demand their favourite meal, the creaking timbers of a vessel too weak to escape the (5) cruel, crunching (6) jaws of the (7) ravenously hungry sea.

The figurative and metaphorical uses of the underlined words in the paragraph are explained below.

1. "purpose of a hungry dragon" is a metaphor that compares the sea with a dragon

2. "on the menu" is a metaphor that compares the sea with a restaurant

3. "Like a spoiled child" is a simile that compares the sea with a child in the middle of a temper tantrum

4. "waves demand their favourite meal" is a metaphor that compares the waves with customers ordering food at a restaurant

5. "cruel, crunching" is alliteration—the repetition of the beginning consonant sound of a word

6. "jaws" is a metaphor that compares the frightening waves with the jaws of a monster dragon

7. "ravenously hungry sea" is personification, giving the human characteristic of hunger to the inanimate sea

The next time you read a newspaper or a magazine article, watch for symbolism and imagery. Writers deliberately use literary devices to create emotional connections between readers and the text. Following are a few examples of literary devices from a variety of informational texts:

- *Oak Island Money Pit*—title as metaphor. It is rumoured that there is a treasure hidden deep in a pit on this island. This "money pit" has also swallowed the money of treasure seekers.

- "The inventor had a flash of inspiration"—metaphorical use of the word "flash."

- *Meals on Wheels*—title as metaphor.

FIGURATIVE LANGUAGE IN VISUALS

Visual images can project a dominant impression or mood that can be interpreted as a visual metaphor for something else.

Example

The signs throughout the cartoon could be interpreted as visual metaphors for the annoying rules and regulations of daily life.

CREATING ORIGINAL TEXT

2.4.1.1 generalize from own experience to create oral, print, and other media texts on a theme

GETTING STARTED

How do you discover good topics for writing projects? The first two places to look are:

- Your own experiences
- Areas that interest you

How should you express your ideas? Often, your teacher will assign a format, such as a story, essay, or poem. When you choose for yourself, try to be unique. The format you choose should be the one that best represents your writing. For example, you could create a:

- PowerPoint presentation
- Collection of poetry
- Digital photo essay
- Short story

Following is an example of a student's proposal for a multimedia presentation. Notice the different media: video, picture, audio interview, music, and spoken word all being used to convey an idea.

Example

Multimedia Presentation Proposal

Theme Chosen: My Dream of Peace

Personal Interest in Theme: Older brother recently returned from serving with Canadian Forces in Afghanistan

Format Chosen: Multimedia Presentation

Order of Presentation:

1. Introduction (1 minute)

2. Three minute taped interview with older brother about mission and his impressions of war

3. PowerPoint computer presentation
   - Photos of brother
   - Photos sent home from Afghanistan
   - Clip from "Saving Private Ryan" (1 minute)
   - Clips from different conflicts around the world from the past ten or fifteen years, including Iraq, Darfur, and Afghanistan (1 minute) with music playing in the background
   - Slides showing kids playing in a prairie playground, kids playing in an Afghanistan village, my brother waving at the camera

4. Conclusion (1 minute)

This student's presentation offers many different media to keep the class interested. Some people respond better to visuals, while others respond better to audio stimulus. This student has made sure that the audience will remain attentive throughout the presentation. Think about how you can use different media for your next presentation.

2.4.2.1 create oral, print, and other media texts on common literary themes

ELABORATING ON THE EXPRESSION OF IDEAS

Common literary themes are a good source of ideas for writing. Sometimes, teachers will choose the theme, and sometimes you will be asked to elaborate on the theme from a specific text. Try to plan a unique approach to expressing your ideas, such as:

- A computer presentation

- An interview

- A collage

- A play

The following example shows a student's plan for elaborating on a literary theme from a specific poem.

Text Proposal

Theme Chosen: Facing Difficult Challenges in Life

Literary Expression of Theme: Poem "Mother to Son," by Langston Hughes

Format Chosen:

- Seven-paragraph oral response assisted by five classmates

- Hamster on a treadmill object lesson

Order of Presentation:

1. Read poem "Mother to Son" by Langston Hughes

2. Introductory paragraph explaining significance of poem and references to challenges of life

3. Paragraph 1 read by classmate Mary Beth Hale as Helen Keller—"How I lived such a memorable life in spite of my double handicap"

4. Paragraph 2 read by classmate Ronnie Chiu as Winston Churchill—"How I overcame dyslexia to lead my country through the Second World War"

5. Paragraph 3 read by classmate Charles Hahn as Terry Fox—"How I used cancer as a stepping stone to a dream"

6. Paragraph 4 read by classmate Morgan Zukowski as Mother Theresa—"How I put aside my doubts to serve humanity"

7. Paragraph 5 read by classmate Abdul Majhad as Stephen Hawking—"How I used science to escape my physical limitations"

8. Showing my hamster running on his treadmill to demonstrate the principle of perseverance

9. Concluding paragraph

This student has involved many classmates in his or her presentation and has brought in an example—a hamster—to convey the main idea of the presentation. A lot of creativity and expression has gone into the presentation, and the student has taken some time to organize the presentation. No matter what methods you use to present ideas, creativity and organization will make your ideas interesting and unique.

2.4.3.1 create oral, print and other media texts that interrelate plot, setting, and character, and reveal the significance of the action

STRUCTURING TEXTS

It is enjoyable to create your own stories in any genre. Do you ever feel that your story is not working out like it is supposed to? Here are a few reminders about storytelling that may help you:

• Keep plot, setting, and characters interrelated

• Make the action significant to plot and character development

• Take time to plan or chart your story

INTERRELATING PLOT, SETTING, AND CHARACTERS

There are always reasons that characters in stories perform certain actions. Sometimes, an author does not tell you directly why a character does something. Sometimes an author will give you enough information that you can guess why a character does something. The more that you are told about the characters in a story, the more real they seem and the more interesting they are. Just like real people, characters act as they do for several reasons. In order to build a good character, an author considers the character's traits and motivations.

Traits are aspects about characters that make them unique. Traits include interests and whether they are mean or kind. Emotional and psychological traits combine to form the personality of a character. In "Snow White and the Seven Dwarfs," for example, it is Snow White's nature to be trusting, so she is not suspicious of the evil Queen. If Snow White were less trusting, she would not be tricked as often as she is by the Queen.

Motivations are what make characters do things to get what they want. For example, they may want other characters to care about them, or they may want power, money, knowledge, fame, revenge, or love. A character's motivation is the reward that he or she seeks. For example, the Queen in "Snow White and the Seven Dwarfs" selfishly wants to be the fairest in the land. Since Snow White is more beautiful than the Queen, the Queen is motivated to get rid of Snow White. The situation and the setting of a story also determine why characters act the way they do.

Other aspects of short stories, such as setting, situation, and plot contribute to characterization and are connected to how the author builds characters.

Setting is where and when a story takes place. Is the story set in a medieval castle or a high-rise building in the 20th century? Like real people, the time and place in which characters live affects how they act and how they look. Snow White, for instance, would not wear jeans, a T-shirt, and runners, nor would she sling an electric guitar over her shoulder as she walked through the woods with the huntsman.

Situation is what is going on between characters at the beginning of a story. Usually, the situation quickly leads to a problem or a conflict. Snow White's stepmother, the Queen, is very jealous of Snow White at the beginning of the story. She is also very evil by nature, while Snow White is very innocent. This situation is what leads to the Queen taking advantage of Snow White in order to get what she wants.

Characters, setting, and situation carry and give life to the plot of the story.

Plot refers to the action that happens in a story. How and why things happen are parts of plot. Plot changes according to the conflicts or problems faced by the characters.

A plot **diagram outlines** the elements of plot:

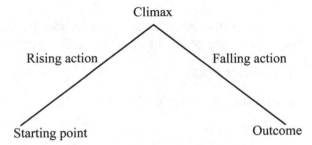

Either plot headings or a plot diagram can be used to outline the events of a short story.

THE IMPORTANCE OF PLANNING

Planning ahead helps you to stay focused on the plot of your story. Planning makes you think about the characters' actions and how they affect the plot. Your characters' actions should be significant and important to the plot. Your characters and their actions should fit the setting. You can use a graphic planner to plan your story. A graphic planner will help you to see how the story will evolve and develop.

The following plot diagram can help you organize your story.

| Story Title _____ |
| Author _____ |
| Setting _____ |
| Time _____ |
| Place _____ |
| Characters

_____   _____

_____   _____ |
| Problem

_____ |
| Plot Summary
1. _____
2. _____
3. _____ |
| Conclusion

_____ |

There are a number of ways to develop your story. Following are some examples of how to develop your story in a unique way:

- Use flashback or a variety of settings so your story does not follow a linear timeframe

- Have the two main characters communicate by postcards, emails, or letters to solve a problem

- Incorporate news items, or reports to make your story realistic

- Create a video with the help of your friends acting out your story while you read the narration

2.4.4.1 create oral, print, and other media texts that include main and minor characters, and show how the main character develops and changes as a result of the action and events

ORIGINAL CHARACTERS

You can use your knowledge of characters in literature to write convincingly about your own characters and how they develop or change as the result of events in your story.

Everything that an author does to bring characters to life is called characterization. Different characters have different purposes in moving a story forward and making it interesting. The more important a character is, the more the author describes and develops that character. You may have already learned names for some of the different types of characters. It is important to know the following functions or purposes of characters.

Character Type	Description of Function
Protagonist	• the main character and usually the most well-developed • usually the "good guy" or hero, but not always
Antagonist	• the character against whom the protagonist struggles • can be a villain, but not always
Major Character	• helps move the plot forward in some way • the author usually gives a lot of information about major characters • both the protagonist and antagonist are major characters
Minor Character	• has a minor role • minor characters affect an event in the plot, but they do not move the whole plot forward • the author will not develop these characters much

Characters are either static (unchanging) or dynamic (changing). Your main characters should be dynamic—that is, forced to change or able to change as they encounter conflict in the plot. Most good stories involve protagonists learning something about themselves or the world that changes their outlooks.

Similar to reality, things happen to characters in stories that make them change. When the ugly duckling looked into the water and saw how beautiful he was and heard the children exclaim at his beauty, he no longer felt sad, ashamed, and unwanted, and a great happiness rose in him.

The following tips can help you create more memorable dynamic characters:

- Before you begin, think about characters in stories you have read. How did they change?

- Why? Use these as models.

- Add events to your plot that force your characters to change.

- Revise your conflicts to force your characters to change.

- Get peer feedback to add events and make character actions more explicit.

- Ask your peers to explain how your characters change. If they are vague, ask them to contribute some possible ideas that would motivate your character to change.

- Consider ways to clarify your ending, such as

  - Revealing more inner thoughts of the main character
  - Adding or inserting new scenes
  - Providing more detail about the outcome of the story

If you work on your characters, you will see them grow from flat and uninteresting static characters into dynamic and more realistic characters.

PRACTICE QUESTIONS—COMPREHEND AND RESPOND TO TEXTS

Use the following passage to answer questions 1 to 11.

A WINTER'S WALK

It was an unusually mild winter, with so little snow that Anne and Diana could go to school nearly every day by way of the Birch Path. On Anne's birthday they were tripping lightly down it, keeping eyes and ears alert amid all their chatter, for Miss Stacy had told them that they must soon write a composition on "A Winter's Walk in the Woods," and it
5 behooved them to be observant.

"Just think, Diana, I'm thirteen years old today," remarked Anne in an awed voice.

"I can scarcely realize that I'm in my teens. When I woke this morning it seemed to me that everything must be different. You've been thirteen for a month, so I suppose it doesn't seem such a novelty to you as it does to me. It makes life seem so much more
10 interesting. In two more years I'll be really grown up. It's a great comfort to think that I'll be able to use big words then without being laughed at."

"Ruby Gillis says she means to have a beau as soon as she's fifteen," said Diana.

"Ruby Gillis thinks of nothing but beaus," said Anne disdainfully. "She's actually delighted when any one writes her name up in a take-notice for all she pretends to
15 be so mad.

But I'm afraid that is an uncharitable speech. Mrs. Allan says we should never make uncharitable speeches; but they do slip out so often before you think, don't they? I simply can't talk about Josie Pye without making an uncharitable speech, so I never mention her at all. You may have noticed that. I'm trying to be as much like Mrs. Allan
20 as I possibly can, for I think she's perfect. Mr. Allan thinks so too. Mrs. Lynde says he just worships the ground she treads on and she doesn't really think it right for a minister to set his affections so much on a mortal being. But then, Diana, even ministers are human and have their besetting sins just like everybody else. I had such an interesting talk with Mrs. Allan about besetting sins last Sunday afternoon. There are just a few
25 things it's proper to talk about on Sundays and that is one of them. My besetting sin is imagining too much and forgetting my duties. I'm striving very hard to overcome it and now that I'm really thirteen perhaps I'll get on better."

"In four more years we'll be able to put our hair up," said Diana. "Alice Bell is only sixteen and she is wearing hers up, but I think that's ridiculous. I shall wait until I'm
30 seventeen."

"If I had Alice Bell's crooked nose," said Anne decidedly, "I wouldn't—but there! I won't say what I was going to because it was extremely uncharitable. Besides, I was comparing it with my own nose and that's vanity. I'm afraid I think too much about my nose ever since I heard that compliment about it long ago. It really is a great
35 comfort to me. Oh, Diana, look, there's a rabbit. That's something to remember for our woods composition. I really think the woods are just as lovely in winter as in summer. They're so white and still, as if they were asleep and dreaming pretty dreams."

"I won't mind writing that composition when its time comes," sighed Diana. "I can manage to write about the woods, but the one we're to hand in Monday is terrible.
40 The idea of Miss Stacy telling us to write a story out of our own heads!"

"Why, it's as easy as a wink," said Anne.

"It's easy for you because you have an imagination," retorted Diana, "but what would you do if you had been born without one? I suppose you have your composition all done?"

45 Anne nodded, trying hard not to look virtuously complacent and failing miserably.

"I wrote it last Monday evening. It's called 'The Jealous Rival; or, In Death Not Divided.' I read it to Marilla and she said it was stuff and nonsense. Then I read it to Matthew and he said it was fine. That is the kind of critic I like. It's a sad, sweet story. I just cried like a child while I was writing it. It's about two beautiful maidens called
50 Cordelia Montmorency and Geraldine Seymour who lived in the same village and were devotedly attached to each other. Cordelia was a regal brunette with a coronet of midnight hair and dusky flashing eyes. Geraldine was a queenly blonde with hair like spun gold and velvety purple eyes."

"I never saw anybody with purple eyes," said Diana dubiously.

55 "Neither did I. I just imagined them. I wanted something out of the common. Geraldine had an alabaster brow, too. I've found out what an alabaster brow is. That is one of the advantages of being thirteen. You know so much more than you did when you were only twelve."

—*by* L.M. Montgomery

1. When she is fifteen, Ruby Gillis wants to have
   A. a boyfriend
   B. adult vocabulary
   C. an interesting life
   D. her name in the paper

2. Mrs. Allen can be **best** described as
   A. the minister's wife
   B. the girls' teacher
   C. Diana's mother
   D. Anne's mother

3. Anne most likely thinks that a "besetting sin" (lines 24–28) is
   A. a minor indiscretion
   B. being disobedient
   C. being forgetful
   D. a major fault

4. On their walk to school, Anne and Diana spend **most** of the time
   A. planning their composition
   B. observing their surroundings
   C. criticizing their school mates
   D. discovering what it means to be thirteen

5. The title of this passage refers to
   A. the girls' daily walk to school
   B. the need to be observant of nature
   C. how the girls fill their time each day
   D. Miss Stacy's composition assignment

6. The reason for Anne's excitement at being thirteen is that she
   A. is entering her teens
   B. will be grown up in two years
   C. will be able to wear her hair up
   D. knows more than she did before

7. Besides having a vivid imagination, Anne can **best** be described as being
   A. thoughtless and irresponsible
   B. self-centered and uncaring
   C. observant and talkative
   D. vain and mean-spirited

8. The genre of Anne's composition "The Jealous Rival; or, In Death Not Divided," is **most likely**
   A. romantic fiction
   B. historical adventure
   C. descriptive narrative
   D. information observation

9. The relationship between the two girls is shown **mainly** through

A. comparisons

B. description

C. friendship

D. dialogue

10. The idea that Anne has a vivid imagination is **most clearly** shown in the phrase

A. "'My besetting sin is imagining too much'" (lines 25–26)

B. "'as if they were asleep and dreaming pretty dreams'" (line 37)

C. "'I just cried like a child while I was writing it'" (line 49)

D. "'Geraldine had an alabaster brow, too'" (lines 55–56)

11. The writer's purpose in writing this passage is **most likely** to

A. show differences between Anne and Diana

B. illustrate Anne's perception of the world

C. amuse readers with teenagers' gossip

D. illustrate the closeness of two friends

Use the following passage to answer questions 12 to 18.

LETTER

When I was eight years old, my father, a union organizer in the forties and fifties, was blacklisted, accused of communist activities. It meant no work—with a vengeance. My mother, then in her forties, had twin boys that spring—premature, and in premedicare times you can imagine the devastating costs for their care. I was hungry that year, hungry
5   when I got up, hungry when I went to school, hungry when I went to sleep. In November I was asked to leave school because I only had boys' clothes to wear—hand-me-downs from a neighbour. I could come back, they said, when I dressed like a young lady.

The week before Christmas, the power and gas were disconnected. We ate soup made from carrots, potatoes, cabbage and grain meant to feed chickens, cooked on our wood
10   garbage burner. Even as an eight-year-old, I knew the kind of hunger we had was nothing compared to people in India and Africa. I don't think we could have died in our middle-class Vancouver suburb. But I do know that the pain of hunger is intensified and brutal when you live in the midst of plenty. As Christmas preparations increased, I felt more and more isolated, excluded, set apart. I felt a deep, abiding hunger for more than
15   food. Christmas Eve day came, grey and full of the bleak sleety rain of a west-coast winter. Two women, strangers, struggled up our driveway, loaded down with bags. They left before my mother answered the door. The porch was full of groceries—milk, butter, bread, cheese and Christmas oranges. We never knew who they were, and after that day, pride being what it was, we never spoke of them again. But I'm forty-five years old, and
20   I remember them well.

Since then I've crafted a life of joy and independence, if not of financial security. Several years ago, living in Victoria, my son and I were walking up the street, once more in west-coast sleet and rain. It was just before Christmas and we were, as usual, counting our pennies to see if we'd have enough for all our festive treats, juggling these against the
25 necessities. A young man stepped in front of me, very pale and carrying an old sleeping bag, and asked for spare change—not unusual in downtown Victoria. No, I said, and walked on. Something hit me like a physical blow about a block later. I left my son and walked back to find the young man. I gave him some of our Christmas luxury money—folded into a small square and tucked into his hand. It wasn't much, only ten dollars, but
30 as I turned away, I saw the look of hopelessness turn into amazement and then joy. Well, said the rational part of my mind, Judith, you are a fool, you know he's just going up the street to the King's Hotel and spend it on drink or drugs. You've taken what belongs to your family and spent it on a frivolous romantic impulse. As I was lecturing myself on gullibility and sensible charity, I noticed the young man with the sleeping bag walking
35 quickly up the opposite side of the street, heading straight for the King's. Well, let this be a lesson, said the rational Judith. To really rub it in, I decided to follow him. Just before the King's, he turned into a corner grocery store. I watched through the window, through the poinsettias and the stand-up Santas. I watched him buy milk, butter, bread, cheese and Christmas oranges.

40 Now, I have no idea how that young man arrived on the street in Victoria, nor will I ever have any real grasp of the events that had led my family to a dark and hungry December. But I do know that charity cannot be treated as an RRSP. There is no best-investment way to give, no way to insure value for our dollar. Like the Magi, these three, the two older women struggling up the driveway and the young man with the sleeping bag, gave
45 me, and continue to give me, wonderful gifts—the reminder that love and charity come most truly and abundantly from an open and unjudgemental heart.

—*by* Judith MacKenzie

12. According to the information in the passage, the narrator grew up in
   A. India
   B. Africa
   C. Victoria
   D. Vancouver

13. In the first two paragraphs, the writer recounts events in the narrator's eight-year-old life. Which of the following elements of the narrative is **most clearly** in these paragraphs?
   A. Setting
   B. Theme
   C. Mood
   D. Plot

14. The narrator's eight-year-old desperation intensified because of

   A. her father's loss of his job

   B. the premature birth of her twin brothers

   C. the embarrassment of wearing boys' clothes to school

   D. feeling hungry amidst the abundance of Christmas

15. The "physical blow" (line 27) that hit the narrator and caused her to seek out the young man she had initially refused to help was **most likely**

   A. charity

   B. value

   C. guilt

   D. joy

16. The passage was **most likely** written with the purpose of

   A. entertaining

   B. persuading

   C. describing

   D. informing

17. The phrase "Like the Magi, these three" (line 43) contains an example of

   A. hyperbole

   B. metaphor

   C. simile

   D. irony

18. The writer indicates that genuine charity comes from a giver who is

   A. impulsive

   B. impartial

   C. wealthy

   D. stable

Use the following passage to answer questions 19 to 26.

THE BONE DETECTIVES
MORE FORENSIC DETECTIVES ... AND THE CLUES THEY COLLECT
PART V

Computer Specialists

Not all criminals commit crimes with knives and guns. Some log on to trouble using computers. An estimated one trillion dollars is transferred electronically over computers each week, increasing the potential for crime. To stop computer crimes, the FBI has put
5   together a Computer Analysis and Response Team (CART). The team investigates cases involving bank theft, drug dealing, mail fraud, and gambling. In many of these cases, computers are used not only to steal money but also to store illegal business records, which can later be used as evidence. Murderers sometimes even keep computer-based diaries of their crimes. In 1993 CART successfully retrieved plans and maps connected
10   with an attempted murder and cracked one of the largest insurance fraud cases in the United States.

Forensic Pathologists

When police locate a dead body, pathologists examine it, inside and out. They determine the cause and manner of death. Did the victim commit suicide? Did someone else
15   kill him or her? Could it have been an accident? To find out, forensic pathologists investigate the scene where a person died to determine what the victim was doing and his or her health status before death. Next they comb for clues on the victim's clothes, body, and internal organs. The internal exam is called an autopsy. Hairs, threads, and fingernail scrapings are sent to the crime lab for analysis, while blood and urine samples
20   are tested by toxicologists for the presence of alcohol and drugs. Sometimes pathologists determine that victims did not die where they were found, but were moved after death. This, and other information forensic pathologists collect, is valuable to police and can help lead to a killer.

Document Examiners

25   Whether it's a forged signature on a check or a ransom note written by a kidnapper, document examiners analyze and compare handwriting to determine the author's identity. They also use microscopes to examine hand printing, typewriting, rubber stamps, photocopies, embossed seals, charred documents, and more. When a suspect pen is available, examiners can chemically analyze and compare its ink to that used in
30   a questioned document. Watermarks, translucent impressions that can be seen when paper is held up to light, also provide clues to the true age of a document and the manufacturer. One famous case cracked by document examiners involved a will said to be written by millionaire Howard Hughes. Analysis of the document, which was laced with misspellings and factual errors, revealed the handwriting to be nothing more than a
35   good imitation.

Forensic Toxicologists/Chemists

Sometimes criminals poison their victims. Other times victims poison themselves with overdoses of drugs such as cocaine. To determine whether drugs and alcohol are involved in a crime, forensic toxicologists analyze a victim's blood, urine, and stomach
40   contents. Traces of some drugs also can be found in a victim's hair and bones. Along with studying specimens, these forensic experts assist in arson investigations, where they identify substances used to accelerate fires. They also analyze explosives used in bombings by terrorists and establish the presence of drugs on items such as clothing, cars, and boats.

45   To identify drugs and explosives at a crime scene, the FBI has developed portable drug detectors called Ionscans. In one case, the equipment helped locate cocaine hidden in railroad ties. In another, it was used to find drugs concealed in dog cages.

Hair and Fiber Examiners

Strands of hair and pieces of fiber can be important clues in a crime-scene investigation.
50   When found, they can help identify the scene of a crime, place suspects at the scene, pinpoint the weapon or the instrument of the crime, or identify hit-and-run vehicles. Although an examination of hair cannot absolutely identify a suspect or victim, it can indicate whether the hair could belong to a particular person. Microscopic analysis of hair can also reveal clues to a person's race, tell which part of the body it came from,
55   and disclose whether it was bleached or burned. Stray fibers help solve crimes, too, by providing circumstantial evidence. Wayne Williams, a serial killer in Atlanta, Georgia, was arrested and eventually convicted after police matched unusual yellow-green carpet fibers found on victims to those in his bedroom.

Firearm Examiners

60   When guns and bullets are recovered from the scene of a crime, firearms experts take action. They microscopically examine and compare bullets, cartridge cases, and other ammunition components to see if they have been fired from a particular weapon. These forensic examiners also can tell whether a firearm has been discharged and determine the distance at which it was shot by analyzing gunpowder stains on the victim's clothing and
65   the weapon.

To make comparisons more efficient, the FBI recently introduced an automated firearms evidence imaging system called DRUGFIRE. This system stores firearms evidence information and images in a computer database so that police can readily collect, share, and link the evidence to solve crimes. In Baltimore, two murders and another serious
70   shooting were linked by DRUGFIRE over several weeks. Police eventually identified a suspect and recovered the firearm used in all three incidents.

—*by* Donna M. Jackson

19. As it is used in the text, the term "forensic" **most accurately** means

A. medical

B. internal

C. drug-related

D. crime-related

20. Which of the following statements about Ionscans is **most accurate**?

   A. They detect drugs transported in train cars.

   B. They were developed by the Federal Bank Reserve.

   C. They are used to analyze explosives in laboratories.

   D. They can recognize drugs and explosives on site.

21. The phrase "circumstantial evidence" (line 56) refers to evidence that

   A. leads to an obvious and clear conclusion

   B. is discerned through complete supposition

   C. is not important to a case

   D. establishes a conclusion indirectly by inference

22. A hit-and-run vehicle would **most likely** be identified by

   A. CART

   B. an Ionscan

   C. fiber analysis

   D. the study of a victim's bone

23. According to the text, firearm experts do **not** study the

   A. path of a bullet

   B. empty cartridges

   C. markings on a bullet

   D. gunpowder stains on victims

24. The introduction of DRUGFIRE allows for

   A. firearms to be used in a variety of crimes

   B. drug traffickers to be caught more easily

   C. weapons evidence to be linked and stored

   D. gunpowder stains to be examined more thoroughly

25. An increase in the incidence of technological crimes can be attributed to

   A. the introduction of CART by the FBI

   B. an increase in computer programs for databases

   C. a crack-down on fraud cases in the United States

   D. the huge amounts of monetary funds that are transferred electronically

26. The word that **best** expresses the meaning of "laced" as it is used in the phrase "laced with misspellings" (lines 33–34) is

A. threaded

B. covered

C. flavored

D. mixed

Use the following passage to answer questions 27 to 40.

THE UNSINKABLE MRS. BROWN

"There was a cyclone the day you was born," Shamus Tobin tells his daughter. "Ya musta swallered the tail a' that twister." This dialogue was a figment of a writer's imagination composed long after the events took place. But those who knew the real Margaret Tobin Brown might well have believed that she had a cyclone inside her.

5   Born July 18, 1867, Maggie Tobin grew up in Hannibal, Missouri, the sleepy hamlet on the Mississippi River where Sam Clemens (also known as Mark Twain) had romped a generation before. Like Sam, the tall, auburn-haired daughter of Irish immigrants was ambitious. When her older brother left Hannibal for Leadville, Colorado, Maggie followed. She got a job as a clerk in a department store, where she met James Joseph
10   Brown. "J. J." was thirteen years her senior and not wealthy—attributes that left Maggie unimpressed. He was persistent, though, and she married him.

The couple moved into a log cabin in Stumptown, where J. J. operated a gold mine. When the silver market collapsed in 1893 and the price of gold skyrocketed, J. J. made a fortune!

The Browns moved to the city, and Maggie set her sights on Denver society. Society,
15   however, wanted no part of an uneducated ex-clerk from Stumptown. Undaunted and determined to improve herself, Maggie went East to study languages and literature at New York's Carnegie Institute; she then began to travel abroad. Greater challenges lay ahead, but Maggie was ready.

Returning from a stay in Europe in 1912, Maggie booked passage on the *R.M.S. Titanic.*
20   On the night of April 14, she was in her stateroom reading when, in her own words, a "crash … threw me to the floor." The ship had hit an iceberg!

While other women scrambled aboard lifeboats, someone had to drop the unconcerned Maggie into a lowering craft. The one male aboard that lifeboat told the women it was futile to row away from the sinking ship as it "would take everything for miles around
25   down with suction." Ignoring his warnings, the forty-four-year-old Maggie grabbed the oars, ordered a second woman to do the same, and rowed to safety.

On board the rescue ship *Carpathia*, Maggie helped to organize the proceedings and used her knowledge of foreign languages to comfort the immigrant survivors. Maggie and other wealthy passengers also raised almost $10,000 to help the needy.

30   Later, when reporters asked how she had survived, she replied, "Typical Brown luck. We're unsinkable." After the tragedy Maggie was not only accepted into Denver society but became a national hero. After her death she inspired the Broadway musical and Hollywood film *The Unsinkable Molly Brown.*

27. In this context, the **best** meaning for the word "undaunted" is

    A. heroic

    B. energetic

    C. unshakable

    D. unwavering

28. The word "futile" (line 24) means

    A. foolish

    B. unwise

    C. useless

    D. exhausting

29. The sentence "Ya musta swallered the tail a' that twister" (lines 1–2) is an example of

    A. slang

    B. jargon

    C. dialect

    D. colloquialism

30. The main purpose of the introductory paragraph is to establish

    A. the Missouri setting

    B. the impending conflict

    C. Molly Brown's character

    D. cyclone patterns and shapes

31. An example of personification is found in the quotation

    A. "the sleepy hamlet on the Mississippi River" (lines 5–6)

    B. "the silver market collapsed" (line 13)

    C. "the price of gold sky-rocketed" (line 13)

    D. "would take everything for miles around down with suction" (lines 24–25)

32. According to the passage, both Samuel Clemens and Maggie Tobin

    A. were friends

    B. were ambitious

    C. had auburn hair

    D. had immigrant parents

33. The phrase "Maggie set her sights on Denver society" (line 14) implies that Maggie

    A. wished she could move to Denver to live

    B. was glad her husband had become so rich

    C. wanted to mingle with the rich and famous

    D. hoped to buy a house in Denver with a view

34. Maggie Brown decided to study languages in New York and travel to Europe in order to

    A. face the challenges that were ahead of her

    B. become more worldly and knowledgeable

    C. spend the money that her husband had acquired

    D. communicate with people she met on her travels

35. Maggie Brown survived the sinking of the *Titanic* **mainly** because of her

    A. fear

    B. strength

    C. knowledge

    D. determination

36. Maggie Brown's leadership qualities are **best** demonstrated when she

    A. grabs the oars and rows the lifeboat to safety

    B. raises $10,000 with other wealthy passengers

    C. is reading in her stateroom as the *Titanic* hits the iceberg

    D. helps with the organization of passengers on the *Carpathia*

37. Which of the following quotations best describes Maggie Brown's character?

    A. "she had a cyclone inside her" (line 4)

    B. "the tall, auburn-haired daughter" (line 7)

    C. "Undaunted and determined" (lines 15–16)

    D. "'Typical Brown luck. We're unsinkable.'" (line 30–31)

38. The **main** purpose of this passage is to

    A. inform

    B. instruct

    C. describe

    D. persuade

39. The writer presents his ideas **mainly** by

A. providing dates

B. using descriptions

C. making comparisons

D. providing brief details

40. The **main** purpose of this passage is to show Maggie Brown's

A. ambition and courage

B. determination and spirit

C. ability to overcome obstacles

D. survival during the sinking of the *Titanic*

Read the following passage to answer questions 41 to 49.

COOKS BROOK

At the pool where we used to swim
in Cooks Brook
not everyone had guts enough
to dive from the top ledge

5   not that it would have been
a difficult dive
except for the shelf of rock
that lay two feet below the surface
and reached quarter of the way out
10   into the width of the pool

one by one the brave few of us
would climb the cliff to the ledge
and stand poised
ready to plunge headfirst
15   into the dark water below
and always there was that moment
of terror
when you'd doubt that you could
clear the shelf
20   knowing full well
it would be better to die
skull smashed open in the water
than it would be to climb
backwards down to the beach

25   so always there was that moment
      when you prayed for wings
      then sailed arms outspread into the buoyant air
      what you feel is something
      impossible to describe
30   as the water parts like a wound
      to engulf you
      then closes just as quickly
      in a white scar where you entered

      and you are surprised always
35   to find yourself alive
      following the streaks of sunlight
      that lead you gasping to the surface
      where you make your way
      leisurely to shore
40   as though there had been nothing to it
      as though it was every day of the week
      you daringly defied the demons
      who lived so terribly
      in the haunted hours of your sleep

—by Al Pittman

41. In the line "and stand poised," (line 13) the word "poised" means

   A. excited

   B. fearfully

   C. balanced

   D. gracefully

42. Which of the following **best** describes how the speaker was feeling before the dive?

   A. "one by one the brave few of us" (line 11)

   B. "you'd doubt that you could / clear the shelf" (lines 18–19)

   C. "it would be better to die" (line 21)

   D. "there was that moment / when you prayed for wings" (lines 25–26)

43. The speaker says that "it would be better to die / skull smashed open in the water / than it would be to climb / backwards down to the beach" (lines 21–24) because the speaker

   A. likes to be challenged into doing dangerous acts

   B. would rather die than be humiliated for backing out

   C. always accepts a dare and does not want to back down

   D. is worried about getting into trouble for doing foolish things

44. An example of alliteration is found in the phrase
   A. "into the dark water below" (line 15)
   B. "sailed arms outspread" (line 27)
   C. "gasping to the surface" (line 37)
   D. "daringly defied the demons" (line 42)

45. From before the dive to the point coming out of the water, the speaker's emotions change from
   A. fear to indifference
   B. nervousness to dismay
   C. agitation to excitement
   D. frustration to composure

46. The speaker's **main** conflict with the environment is with
   A. "the shelf of rock" (line 7)
   B. "the cliff to the ledge" (line 12)
   C. "into the dark water below" (line 15)
   D. "the buoyant air" (line 27)

47. The lines "following the streaks of sunlight / that lead you gasping to the surface" (lines 36–37) are an example of
   A. tone
   B. setting
   C. contrast
   D. imagery

48. The **main** idea of this poem is that
   A. diving is a brave sport
   B. fears are more often than not unfounded
   C. people should never back down from a challenge
   D. people may experience many types of conflict when faced with a challenge

49. The characteristic of the brook that is focused on **most** in this poem is its
   A. depth
   B. width
   C. coldness
   D. swiftness

Use the following passage to answer questions 50 to 59.

SPACE SHUTTLE 51L

Whenever something terrible happens, finger-pointing, accusations, conspiracy theories, and charges usually follow. On January 28, 1986, President Ronald Reagan was going to make his State of the Union address. Like all presidents, he wanted to speak of great things. Had all gone well, he could have spoken about the first teacher being launched

5 into space to conduct lessons to thousands of classrooms from Earth orbit. In another view, NASA had been promoting its concept of routine space travel. Already, there had been three delays in launching the Space Shuttle 51L *Challenger*. NASA was condemned by the news media for its inability to reach space on time. In still another view, the teacher member of the crew was to conduct the live lessons from space on the

10 fourth day of the mission. Another delay would cause the lessons to be presented on a Sunday, when schools were closed. Which of these or other theories is correct is hard to know. Most likely, it was a combination of many things that made NASA push ahead with the launch.

Conditions for the launch of the Space Shuttle Challenger were not good. Launchpad

15 thermometers read 36 degrees Fahrenheit (2 degrees Celsius), 15 degrees lower than the coldest day a shuttle had flown before. The low temperatures concerned engineers, who were experts in solid-booster rockets. The boosters are made in tube-shaped segments that are stacked one on top of another. A tongue from the bottom edge of the segment above slips into a groove on the upper edge of the segment below. Rubber O-rings seal

20 the joints to prevent pressure from escaping when the boosters are ignited. On some previous launches, inspections of the recovered boosters revealed that the seals had come close to failing. Lower temperatures, the engineers reasoned, would make the rings stiffer and less likely to do their jobs. Their warnings to NASA went unheeded, and NASA seemed to rush to launch the mission.

25 At 11:38 A.M., Francis Scobee, Judy Resnick, Ron McNair, Michael Smith, Ellison Onizuka, Gregory Jarvis, and teacher Christa McAuliffe lifted off on a terribly short ride. Seventy-three seconds into the flight and 48,000 feet (14,630 meters) above the Atlantic Ocean, the external tank of the *Challenger* exploded in a massive fireball. The two solid-rocket boosters split off, and zigzagged away trailing smoke.

30 In the many investigations that later surveyed the wreckage and the videotapes of the launch, a sequence of probable events was pieced together. At the moment of liftoff, the launchpad was coated with ice, and icicles clung to many of the pad's structures. The overnight low temperatures, combined with outgassing of the supercold liquid hydrogen and oxygen fuel in the external tank, chilled the vehicle and pad to below

35 freezing. The rubber O-rings in the solid-rocket boosters were stiff with cold.

Upon liftoff, a tongue of flame, like a blowtorch, shot out from the lower joint on the right solid-rocket booster. The seal had failed. Flames ate through the insulation on the hydrogen end of the external tank and through the support post that held the booster to the tank. When the tank melted through, the booster started wobbling because it was

40 still attached to the upper end of the tank. The nose of the booster slammed a hole in the upper liquid oxygen tank. The liquid oxygen streamed out and met the liquid hydrogen. Some 400,000 gallons (1,514,165 liters) of fuel detonated. The crew of the *Challenger* probably never knew what happened. The cabin they were riding in remained intact. It continued to climb to 65,000 feet (19,810 meters) before tumbling into the ocean two

45 minutes and forty-five seconds after the blast. Doctors have suggested the crew would

have been unconscious for their last minutes of life. However, three of four emergency oxygen canisters were manually activated after the explosion. It is possible the crew was awake through the entire fall. They died on impact with the ocean.

50 Many investigations followed in the wake of the Challenger disaster. There was much finger-pointing. Thousands of questions were asked. Congress demanded that NASA fix its problems. Careers were ruined. Most important was the devastation that struck the families of the lost crew.

Two years passed before NASA flew another Space Shuttle. Many improvements were made in the vehicles, including increasing the number of O-rings to three in each
55 booster joint and placing electric heater bands around the joints to keep the rings warm for launch. One question has still not been answered about the Challenger disaster. Did NASA learn its lesson this time? It will be many years before the question can be answered.

Fire!

60 In 1998 the United States and fifteen other nations of the world started orbital construction of the International Space Station. As big as two football fields side by side, the ISS, as it is called, will provide world-class scientific laboratory facilities in space. To get ready for the station construction, the United States and Russia began a series of joint flights into space. Cosmonauts flew on the Space Shuttle, and astronauts flew on the
65 *Mir* space station.

The *Mir* station was launched into space in 1986. It was a series of interconnected cylinders, solar panels, and docking ports. Cosmonauts lived and worked on the station for long periods, exceeding a year in space in some cases. A string of U.S. astronauts visited *Mir*. Although the station was functional, the astronauts noted that it was wearing
70 out and much of their time in orbit was spent maintaining and repairing systems. During Jerry Linenger's stay, conditions got progressively worse.

Linenger arrived at *Mir* on board the Space Shuttle *Atlantis*. Three astronauts had already done a tour of duty on the station. Astronaut John Blaha was waiting on board *Mir* to greet Linenger. After showing Linenger the *Mir* "ropes," Blaha returned to Earth
75 on board the Atlantis. Linenger remained on *Mir* for four months until he was replaced by Michael C. Foale.

Although *Mir* was designed for permanent crews of three, periodically the number increased when visitors and replacement crews arrived. It was just after dinner, during a period of overlapping crews, that one of the cosmonauts was performing a routine
80 activity. Sasha Lazutkin drifted down a tunnel to replace a canister that provides oxygen to the station. The canister was filled with a slurry of chemicals that give off oxygen when activated. With six people on board, extra oxygen had to be provided for breathing. Replacing the canister, called a "candle," was a job that was done three times a day.

At first, the canister started working properly, but then Lazutkin was startled by a small
85 orange flame and sparks coming from the unit. In no time the flames grew, and *Mir* emergency alarms began blaring. The situation was critical. The flames shot out like a small volcano. They spread 12 inches (30 centimeters) across and extended out about 3 feet (1 meter), with sparks coming out the end. Even worse, globs of molten metal were forming. Unless brought under control, the flames could melt through *Mir*'s
90 aluminum walls and release its entire air supply. The crew would be dead in seconds.

Dense black smoke was filling the station, and the crew rushed to put on oxygen masks. Some of the masks malfunctioned, and others had to be used. It took several fire extinguishers before the fire was put out. The crew barely survived. For the next several days, the crew wore masks as they cleaned the soot from inside the station.

95 In microgravity anything not cleaned up would be deposited inside their lungs.

50. Space Shuttle 51L *Challenger* faced a launch that can **best** be described as

   A. exciting

   B. precarious

   C. scrupulous

   D. predestined

51. In regards to the *Challenger* tragedy, the fact that on previous launches the rubber O-rings had come close to failing is considered

   A. resolution

   B. complication

   C. foreshadowing

   D. antecedent action

52. Many of the conclusions presented by the investigations into the *Challenger* tragedy can be **best** described as

   A. presumed

   B. conclusive

   C. exhaustive

   D. accountable

53. The phrase "a tongue of flame, like a blowtorch," as it appears in the line "Upon liftoff, a tongue of flame, like a blowtorch, shot out from the lower joint on the right solid-rocket booster," (lines 36–37) contains an example of

   A. simile

   B. metaphor

   C. hyperbole

   D. personification

54. The fact that NASA did not seem to pay attention to the recommendations made by their own scientists and engineers and instead went ahead with the Challenger launch suggests behavior that can be **best** described as

   A. calculated

   B. negligent

   C. scientific

   D. precise

55. The word "terribly," as it is used in the phrase "lifted off on a terribly short ride" (line 26) means

    A. seriously

    B. extremely

    C. desperately

    D. thoroughly

56. To maintain a constant supply of oxygen for the astronauts aboard *Mir*, the inhabitants were required to change the canister "candles" by hand three times each day. This maintenance can **best** be described as a

    A. daily task

    B. tedious task

    C. manual task

    D. automatic task

57. The word "slurry," as it is used in the sentence "The canister was filled with a slurry of chemicals that give off oxygen when activated," (lines 81 to 82) means

    A. mess

    B. brand

    C. vessel

    D. concoction

58. The description "The flames shot out like a small volcano" (line 86 to 87) creates a sense of

    A. height

    B. disaster

    C. immediacy

    D. anxiousness

59. The phrase "The flames shot out like a small volcano" (lines 86 to 87) contains an example of

    A. simile

    B. metaphor

    C. personification

    D. imitative harmony

Use the following passage to answer questions 60 to 66.

THE BRONTË SISTERS
from IN CONTEXT BACKGROUNDER

If Charlotte, Emily, and Anne Brontë had been brought up in separate homes, they might never have found the confidence or encouragement to write their remarkable books. If their father had not had a vast and passionate love for learning and attended university— the first in his family to do so—his daughters might never have found their greatest joy

5   and achievement in literature. If their mother and two older sisters had not died when they were very young … if their only brother had not been wrapped in a tight cocoon of despondency … if their home had not been isolated in a harsh and lonely corner of England—if all of these things had not been true, the Brontë sisters might never have written the novels and poems that have fascinated the world for over a century.

10   The Brontë sisters wrote the first of their books in the autumn of 1845, when they found themselves at home together after a period of separation. Charlotte stumbled across some of Emily's poetry and recognized its "peculiar music—wild, melancholy, and elevating," and she had the idea that the three of them should put together a volume of their poems. The collection was published—at the sisters' expense—and sold only two copies. But the

15   "mere effort to success had given a wonderful zest to existence," and the sisters decided that each of them should write a novel.

Using masculine pen names to avoid unfair criticism or flattery, Charlotte (Currer Bell) wrote *The Professor*, Emily (Ellis Bell) wrote *Wuthering Heights* and Anne (Acton Bell) wrote *Agnes Grey*. *Wuthering Heights* and *Agnes Grey* were both published (at the authors'

20   expense) but *The Professor* was universally rejected. Ironically, Charlotte's second book, *Jane Eyre*, found a publisher so eager to see it in print that it was off the presses before either of her sisters' first books.

Only Charlotte's *Jane Eyre* was at all well received. Emily's *Wuthering Heights* was even thought to be an earlier, lesser work by Charlotte. But neither Emily's apparent failure nor

25   Anne's minor success with her second novel, *The Tenant of Wildfell Hall*, interfered with their determination to write better and more popular books.

Unfortunately, none of the three sisters lived long enough to realize their potential. Two of them died of tuberculosis—Emily at 30 and Anne at 29—within a few months of each other. Their brother, Branwell, whose failed dreams of being a writer had greatly

30   influenced his sisters in their work, died soon after at the age of 31.

Charlotte Brontë survived her sisters by five years. In that time of grief and loneliness, Charlotte felt "a sacred duty to wipe the dust off their gravestones" and to keep the memory of her sisters alive.

In the years since their deaths there has been growing admiration for all three Brontë

35   sisters—their seven novels and hundreds of poems have given as much pleasure to the world's readers as they gave to their three remarkable authors.

—*by* Clayton Graves

60. How many children were in the Brontë family?

    A. Three

    B. Four

    C. Five

    D. Six

61. In the phrase "Using masculine pen names to avoid unfair criticism or flattery," (line 17) the word "pen name" means

    A. a disguise

    B. an artifice

    C. a pseudonym

    D. a misrepresentation

62. The idea that a book of poetry should be written by the three sisters was proposed by

    A. their father

    B. Branwell

    C. Charlotte

    D. Emily

63. Where did the Brontë sisters live when they were writing their novels?

    A. France

    B. England

    C. Belgium

    D. Scotland

64. The Brontë novel that was **most** successful at the time of its release was

    A. *Jane Eyre*

    B. *Agnes Grey*

    C. *Wuthering Heights*

    D. *The Tenant of Wildfell Hall*

65. The Brontë sibling who experienced literary defeat was

    A. Anne

    B. Emily

    C. Branwell

    D. Charlotte

66. The **most evident** character trait that is shared by all three sisters is their

A. egotism

B eagerness

C. compassion

D. perseverance

Use the following passage to answer questions 67 to 75.

JUST FOR TODAY

Just for today I will hold my head high,
and forget my problems.
I can smile and make everyone else's day better,
even if behind that smile I cry.

5 Just for today I will walk away from a fight,
though I may feel hurt inside.
I will ignore what is said,
and continue on peacefully.

Just for today I will set an example,
10 when I feel the need to hurt.
I will laugh and walk away,
people will admire me more.

Just for today I will say only positive things,
I will treat others the way I would want to be treated,
15 instead of the way they treat me.
I will be confident that life is like a mirror,
if you smile at it, it smiles back,
and what goes around comes around,
so one day that smile will return to me.

20 Just for today I will stand tall,
I will not look at the ground,
but instead share happiness with others.
I will not compromise my morals,
instead I will offer opinions,
25 and accept reactions without question.

Just for today I will accept life's ups and downs,
and know that they only make me stronger in the end.
I will understand that doing what is right and knowing what is
      right are separate issues,
30 but with strength I can bring them together to make the world
      a better place.

Just for today I can.

—*by* Mollie Moir

67. The line "behind that smile I cry" (line 4) refers to the speaker's

    A. mood swings

    B. teenage drama

    C. hidden emotions

    D. changing feelings

68. By walking "away from a fight," (line 5) the speaker hopes to gain

    A. peace

    B. support

    C. happiness

    D. acceptance

69. The **main** reason the speaker wants to "set an example" (line 9) by walking away from a fight is so that

    A. she can avoid conflict

    B. others will admire her

    C. no one ends up with hurt feelings

    D. she can maintain a positive attitude

70. As it is used in the line "I will not compromise my morals," (line 23) the word *compromise* means to

    A. expose

    B. bring to terms

    C. reach an agreement

    D. make a dishonourable concession

71. The mood of this poem is one of

    A. anger

    B. excitement

    C. melancholy

    D. self-awareness

72. The last line of the poem "Just for today I can" presents the conclusion that

    A. accepting shows denial

    B. accepting means growing

    C. she is only working for one day

    D. she understands what she is doing

73. When the speaker says, "I will understand that doing what is right and knowing what is / right are separate issues," (lines 28–29) she means that

    A. knowing what is right is not always easy

    B. knowing what to do does not mean it will get done

    C. thinking long and hard about what is right before taking action is important

    D. taking action is easier than spending time worrying about what action to take

74. The speaker is **best** described as

    A. kind and composed

    B. confident and accepting

    C. reserved and thoughtful

    D. assertive and uncompromising

75. The point of view from which this poem is written is

    A. first person

    B. second person

    C. third person limited

    D. third person omniscient

ANSWERS AND SOLUTIONS—PRACTICE QUESTIONS

1. A	16. B	31. A	46. A	61. C
2. A	17. C	32. B	47. D	62. C
3. A	18. B	33. C	48. D	63. B
4. C	19. D	34. B	49. A	64. A
5. D	20. D	35. D	50. B	65. C
6. D	21. D	36. A	51. C	66. D
7. C	22. C	37. C	52. A	67. C
8. A	23. A	38. A	53. A	68. A
9. D	24. C	39. D	54. B	69. B
10. D	25. D	40. B	55. B	70. D
11. B	26. D	41. C	56. C	71. D
12. D	27. D	42. B	57. D	72. A
13. C	28. C	43. B	58. D	73. B
14. D	29. C	44. D	59. A	74. B
15. C	30. C	45. A	60. D	75. A

1. A

Diana says that Ruby Gillis "means to have a beau as soon as she is fifteen" (line 12). A "beau" is a boyfriend.

2. A

When Anne says that she thinks Mrs. Allen is perfect and that Mr. Allen feels the same, she adds that Mrs. Lynde does not think that a minister should have so much affection for another human being (lines 20 to 22). This statement informs readers that Mr. Allen is the minister and, therefore, that Mrs. Allen is his wife.

3. A

Anne confesses to Diana that her "besetting sin is imagining too much and forgetting my duties" (lines 25–26). This "sin" is really a minor indiscretion because it is neither deliberate nor willful.

4. C

Anne and Diana are both being unpleasant about the other girls with whom they go to school. They are uncharitable about Ruby Gillis, they have nothing nice to say about Josie Pye, and they think Alice Bell looks ridiculous. They want to observe their surroundings and think about their compositions, but they are too busy gossiping to be seriously doing so.

5. D

Miss Stacy assigned the girls a composition entitled "A Winter's Walk in the Woods." The writer has shortened the title to "A Winter's Walk" to show how the girls' daily walk to school ties in with the essay they are required to write. It is possible that the girls pay little attention to their environment as they walk to school (as is shown in this excerpt) and the teacher wants them to become more observant.

6. D

Anne summarizes her excitement at being thirteen when she says, "That is one of the advantages of being thirteen. You know so much more than you did when you were only twelve" (lines 56–57). Anne knows that she is entering her teens, but this is not the specific reason for her excitement. It is Diana who talks about being grown up in two years and being able to wear her hair up.

7. C

Anne notices all sorts of things about other people, such as Mr. Allen's fondness for Mrs. Allen and Alice's crooked nose. She is also extremely talkative, speaking at least twice as much as Diana during their walk to school.

8. A

From the description that Anne gives to Diana of her completed composition, it appears to be very much in the genre of romantic fiction. Anne has exaggerated the looks of her two heroines by giving one of them "a coronet of midnight hair and dusky flashing eyes" (lines 51 to 52) and the other "hair like spun gold and velvety purple eyes" with "an alabaster brow" (line 56). This exaggeration of physical features is typical in romances.

9. D

During the entire walk to school, Anne and Diana converse. They talk about assignments, Mrs. Allen, and their schoolmates.

10. D

Alabaster is a compact, fine-textured white and transparent material that is often carved into vases and ornaments. Anne's imagination is evident when, at barely thirteen, she can think up and describe her heroine as having an alabaster brow (forehead).

11. B

The passage consists mainly of Anne expressing her wonder at being a teenager, her views on various people in her life, and her exuberant imagination.

12. D

It is stated in the passage that she grew up in a "middle-class Vancouver suburb." (line 12)

13. C

The narrator's description of early hardships to establish mood or a feeling of desperation.

14. D

The narrator notes her hunger was experienced in a middle-class Vancouver suburb; seeing much around her made her feel worse.

15. C

In all likelihood the narrator felt guilty and perhaps recalled how the two women had given to her family when she was eight, and she realized how much her family had needed and appreciated the help.

16. B

By sharing her own experiences with charity, the writer wishes to convince the reader that true charity and love come from giving without judgment.

17. C

A simile compares two things using the words *like* or *as*.

18. B

The narrator states "love and charity come most truly and abundantly from an open and unjudgemental heart" (line 45 to 46); thus, one gives without judging.

19. D

Forensic experts use scientific knowledge and procedures to investigate crimes. Sometimes they use their knowledge of medicine, internal biology, or chemistry and drugs. However, their work is related to solving a crime.

20. D

Ionscans are most accurately described as detecting drugs and explosives at the crime scene.

21. D

Circumstantial evidence is evidence that leads to the inference of a judgment indirectly. A series of probabilities may become circumstantial evidence if some aspects of a crime are debated.

22. C

The writer states that strands of hair and pieces of fiber can help identify hit-and-run vehicles (line 49). CART is an acronym for an investigation team. Ionscans are portable drug and explosives detectors. The study of victim's bone does not provide information about specific aspects of the objects that caused injury.

23. A

Although the writer states that forensic examiners can determine the distance at which a weapon was fired, it does not discuss the path of the bullet. The study of the markings on a bullet, gunpowder stains, and empty cartridges is mentioned (lines 60–62) in the text.

24. C

The FBI introduced DRUGFIRE as a means of storing firearms information and images in a computer database. This allows for the collection, sharing, and linking of evidence in crime investigation.

25. D

Criminals are tempted by the huge amounts of money that are transferred electronically and criminal activity has increased.

26. D

There were errors and misspellings mixed with other material in the document. In this phrase, the word "laced" means mixed.

27. D

Maggie Brown was unwavering in her determination to better herself and get an education; there was nothing that was going to come between her and her ambition to be accepted in Denver society. Even though all the alternatives are synonyms for undaunted (according to Roget's Thesaurus of English Words and Phrases), in this context, "unwavering" is the best alternative.

28. C

The word "futile" means useless, purposeless, pointless, unpractical, or unworkable. The man told the women in the life boat that there was no point in rowing away from a sinking ship because, when it eventually sank, it would pull everything in the surrounding water into its eddy.

29. C

Dialect refers to speech that is spoken by a particular group of people living in a particular place. In this dialogue, Shamus Tobin is speaking with the dialect of an Irishman. The fact that the Tobins live in Missouri would not have influenced his Irish accent. Slang and colloquialism refers to words that are used in casual or everyday speech, while jargon is the use of specialized words or terms used in certain situations or occupations.

30. C

The introductory paragraph is used to introduce the reader to Maggie Brown's character. A cyclone did not really occur the day the Maggie Brown was born, nor did her father compare her to a cyclone, but Maggie Brown had such energy and determination that she acted like a cyclone when she was bent upon getting her own way.

31. A

Personification is when the writer describes an animal, an object or thing, or an idea as if it were a person. In this passage, the writer has described the village or hamlet of Hannibal as "sleepy" as if it were a tired person. The silver market collapsing and the price of gold sky-rocketing are not described as persons.

32. B

The author writes, "Like Sam, the tall, auburn-haired daughter of Irish immigrants was ambitious." The author does not tell us whether or not Sam Clemens had auburn hair, if he had immigrant parents. Sam Clemens and Maggie Brown could not have been friends since Clemens had been born a generation before Maggie Brown.

33. C

When Maggie set her sights on Denver society, she was endeavouring to become a member of the Denver social class that partied and attended functions that only the rich would have been able to afford. When Maggie Brown and her husband became rich, she thought that she would have been accepted into this prestigious group. Because she lacked formal education, she was not accepted into Denver society at this time.

34. B

Maggie Brown was not accepted into Denver society because she was uneducated. She desperately wanted to be accepted, so she set out to do all that was required of her in order to be considered a member of the exclusive rich society of Denver. She knew she had to have more education and, with traveling, she would become knowledgeable about the world and other cultures and customs. She had enough money in order to do this. Her experiences in Europe assisted her to face the challenges that were ahead of her and her study of languages enabled her to communicate with foreigners.

35. D

Maggie Brown was not going to sit back, give in and do nothing about trying to move the lifeboat out of the area that would be caught in the *Titanic*'s eddy. She ignored the man's arguments and deliberately took the oars, told another woman to do the same, and was able to row the lifeboat away from the *Titanic*. Maggie Brown's actions did not show she was afraid or show her knowledge. She would have had to be fairly strong in order to row a lifeboat full of people; however, this is not likely the main reason for her survival.

36. A

When Maggie Brown grabbed the oars and, with another woman, rowed the lifeboat to safety, she was showing strong leadership qualities. She did not need to be told what to do but just took control of the situation.

37. C

Throughout the passage, the writer gives examples of Maggie Brown's determined and fearless approach to life: leaving Hannibal, improving herself when she was not accepted into Denver society, taking the oars and rowing the lifeboat to safety, helping with the survivors of the tragedy, helping to raise money. There seems no task that faced Maggie Brown that she was unable to tackle. The passage does not give many examples of the wild and destructive behaviors that would be associated with a cyclone.

38. A

This is an informative passage about Maggie Brown and her indomitable spirit. The writer does describe some of the events that occurred in Maggie Brown's life, but these descriptions are presented as examples of how Maggie Brown overcame adversity.

39. D

The writer has provided many details to enhance the facts that are given in this passage about Maggie Brown. He briefly tells of her childhood home and its connection to Samuel Clemens, how Maggie Brown and her husband became rich, how Maggie Brown attempted to improve herself, and the sinking of the *Titanic* and the impact it had on Maggie Brown. There are a few comparisons: Maggie followed her brother to Leadville, and Maggie's determination to survive in the lifeboat. Actual dates in Maggie Brown's life are given, but these are not ways by which the writer has presented the ideas.

40. B

Maggie Brown's ambition and courage are addressed in the passage, as well as how she survived the sinking of the *Titanic*, and her ability to overcome difficulties; however, the main purpose is to show Maggie Brown's determination and spirit.

41. C

To be poised is to be balanced or composed. Therefore, the "brave few of us" who stood poised would have stood well-balanced, with composure.

42. B

Before the dive, the speaker is concerned about clearing the shelf that juts out two feet under the water. The speaker knows that death is assured if the shelf is not cleared.

43. B

The reader does not know whether the speaker always accepts dares, likes being challenged into doing dangerous things, or is particularly worried about getting into trouble. However, the speaker does feel that death would be preferred to the preferable humiliation of not performing the dive.

44. D

Alliteration is the repeated use of an initial sound in two or more words in close proximity. The sound device contributes to the melody of the writing. The phrase "daringly defied the demons" uses the repetition of the d sound.

45. A

The speaker is quite fearful and nervous before the dive, "there was that moment/of terror/when you'd doubt that you could"; but once the dive is over, a feeling of indifference, nonchalance, and composure takes over ("make your way/leisurely to shore/as though there had been nothing to it)". The speaker forgets the fear and matter-of-factly swims back to the others.

46. A

While there are various types of conflict portrayed in "Cooks Brook": human versus human, human versus self, and human versus the environment. However, the shelf of rock under the water is the main natural conflict in this poem.

47. D

Imagery is a technique poets and writers use to describe things figuratively or in a way that appeals to the senses. In this phrase, the reader can imagine the sunlight filtering down through the water and the swimmer using its rays to reach the surface.

48. D

The main idea of this poem is that a person may experience many types of conflict, all of which must be overcome when faced with difficult challenges. Sometimes it would be wise for people to back away from a difficult challenge, especially is there is danger to life.

49. A

The major environmental opponent in this poem is the "shelf of rock/that lay two feet below the surface / and reached quarter of the way out / into the width of the pool." It is the depth of the brook where the shelf lies and beyond that is mainly focused on in this poem. The poet does not discuss the temperature or swiftness of the brook. The width is mentioned to point out where the brook is too shallow and how much of it (three quarters) is deep enough for the divers.

50. B

While a shuttle launch is always dangerous, the weather conditions under which this particular launch occurred were more extreme than during any previous launch, making the *Challenger* launch especially precarious.

51. C

The previously malfunctioning O-rings foreshadowed their later failure. Had this signal been understood, then perhaps the *Challenger* tragedy would have been avoided.

52. A

The conclusions presented were at best probable, as there were many variables considered and the *Challenger* was largely destroyed because of the explosion of the fuel and the subsequent impact with the ocean.

53. A

A simile compares two things using the word *like* or *as*. In this case, the small lick of flame from the seal is compared to a blowtorch: hot and dangerous.

54. B

NASA's behavior regarding the launch could be viewed as negligent, if in fact they failed to heed the advice given by the scientists and engineers.

55. B

In the given context, the word "terribly" is synonymous with *extremely*.

56. C

The astronauts had to perform a routine replacement of the canisters by hand three times a day, making this a *manual* task.

57. D

The "slurry" of chemicals in the canister was a concoction of chemicals designed to produce oxygen under the proper conditions.

58. D

A fire aboard the space station would have been a serious one, and the fact that flames were shooting like a small volcano would have made everyone on board very anxious.

59. A

A simile is a figure of speech that compares two things using the word *like* or *as*. In this case, the flames of the fire are likened to the eruption of a volcano.

60. D

Two older sisters, an only brother, and the three famous sisters—Charlotte, Emily, and Anne—equals six children.

61. C

The word pen name is synonymous with the word pseudonym.

62. C

Charlotte proposed that the three sisters should put together a volume of their poetry.

63. B

The Brontë sisters were living in "a harsh and lonely corner of England." (lines 7–8)

64. A

Charlotte Brontë's *Jane Eyre* was the only of the sisters' books to be "at all well received." (line 23)

65. C

While Branwell had greatly influenced his sisters, his own attempts to be a writer were not successful.

66. D

Despite some failures and a lack of publishers, the Brontë sisters continued to write; they persevered at writing because it was something each of them felt passionate about.

67. C

According to the speaker, "Just for today I will hold my head high,/and forget my problems. / I can smile and make everyone else's day better, / even if behind that smile I cry." In other words, the speaker is keeping her real emotions hidden by presenting a brave front.

68. A

The speaker states that by avoiding fights and conflicts, she will be able to "continue on peacefully" (line 8).

69. B

The speaker states that she will set an example by walking away from a confrontation; that way, "people will admire me more" (line 12).

70. D

As it used in this line, the word "compromise" means to make a dishonourable or shameful concession.

71. D

Mood is a feeling inferred by a writer or poet and felt by the reader or listener. In this poem, the feeling or attitude that is expressed is one of self-awareness.

72. A

The poet is concluding that "Just for today I can," as a means of acknowledging that accepting is growing. She now realizes she must accept life's ups and downs because they will make her stronger.

73. B

The statement "I will understand that doing what is right and knowing what is right are separate issues" means that simply knowing what is right in a given situation is not the same as actually doing what is right. People often know what is right and yet do not do the right thing.

74. B

The speaker is best described as confident and accepting. Statements such as "I will be confident" (line 16) and "I will stand tall," (line 20) illustrate her self-assurance, and lines like "I will offer opinions, / and accept reactions without question" (lines 24–25) demonstrate that she is accepting and tolerant.

75. A

This poem is written using the first person point of view. First person narration allows the reader to see what the main character is thinking and also allows that character to be further developed through his or her own style of storytelling.

UNIT TEST—COMPREHEND AND RESPOND TO TEXTS

Read the following passage to answer questions 1 to 6.

OLIVER TWIST—AT THE POLICE STATION

The offence had been committed within the district, and indeed in the immediate neighbourhood of, a very notorious metropolitan police office. The crowd had only the satisfaction of accompanying Oliver through two or three streets, and down a place called Mutton Hill, when he was led beneath a low archway, and up a dirty court, into this
5   dispensary of summary justice, by the backway. It was a small paved yard into which they turned; and here they encountered a stout man with a bunch of whiskers on his face, and a bunch of keys in his hand.

"What's the matter now?" said the man carelessly.

"A young fogle-hunter," replied the man who had Oliver in charge.

10   "Are you the party that's been robbed, sir?" inquired the man with the keys.

"Yes, I am," replied the old gentleman; "but I am not sure that this boy actually took the handkerchief. I—I would rather not press the case."

"Must go before the magistrate now, sir," replied the man. "His worship will be disengaged in half a minute. Now, young gallows!"

15   This was an invitation for Oliver to enter through a door which he unlocked as he spoke, and which led into a stone cell. Here he was searched; and nothing being found upon him, locked up.

This cell was in shape and size something like an area cellar, only not so light. It was most intolerably dirty; for it was Monday morning; and it had been tenanted by six
20   drunken people, who had been locked up, elsewhere, since Saturday night. But this is little. In our station-houses, men and women are every night confined on the most trivial *charges*—the word is worth noting—in dungeons, compared with which, those in Newgate, occupied by the most atrocious felons, tried, found guilty, and under sentence of death, are palaces. Let any one who doubts this, compare the two.

25   The old gentleman looked almost as rueful as Oliver when the key grated in the lock. He turned with a sigh to the book, which had been the innocent cause of all this disturbance.

"There is something in that boy's face," said the old gentleman to himself as he walked slowly away, tapping his chin with the cover of the book, in a thoughtful manner; "something that touches and interests me. *Can* he be innocent? He looked like.—By the
30   bye," exclaimed the old gentleman, halting very abruptly, and staring up into the sky, "Bless my soul! Where have I seen something like that look before?"

After musing for some minutes, the old gentleman walked, with the same meditative face, into a back ante-room opening from the yard; and there, retiring into a corner, called up before his mind's eye a vast amphitheatre of faces over which a dusky curtain
35   had hung for many years "No," said the old gentleman, shaking his head; "it must be imagination."

—*by* Charles Dickens

1. The offence that Oliver was accused of was
   A. theft
   B. assault
   C. breaking and entering
   D. evading a police officer

2. Oliver's "invitation" (line 15) to enter the cell was actually more of a
   A. push
   B. request
   C. summons
   D. command

3. The fact that nothing was found on Oliver when he was searched means that he **probably**
   A. was innocent
   B. hid the stolen object
   C. was working with a gang
   D. threw the handkerchief away

4. The plot of this passage is **mainly** developed through
   A. dialogue
   B. description
   C. comparison
   D. characterization

5. The phrase "a vast amphitheatre of faces over which a dusky curtain had hung for many years," (lines 34–35) symbolically refers to
   A. unhappy memories of the past that the old gentleman no longer thinks about
   B. the old gentleman's long ago days as a theatre performer
   C. the old gentleman's own court trial many years ago
   D. people the old gentleman knew in the past

6. According to the information in the passage, the old gentleman is **best** described as someone who is
   A. losing his memory
   B. kind and sympathetic
   C. imaginative and patient
   D. eager to return to his book

Read the following passage to answer questions 7 to 12.

THE DELAY

An old bull terrier, a young Labrador retriever, and a tough little Siamese cat: this remarkable trio couldn't have known that their journey to rejoin the family they loved would become a harrowing trek through 400 km of northern wilderness.

Hunger was now the ruling instinct in the Labrador and it drove him out to forage in the early dawn. He was desperate enough to try some deer droppings, but spat them out immediately in disgust. While he was drinking from a marsh pool still covered with lily pads, he saw a frog staring at him with goggle eyes from a small stone; measuring the
5   distance carefully, he sprang and caught it in the air as it leaped to safety. It disappeared down his throat in one crunch and he looked around happily for more. But an hour's patient search rewarded him with only two, so he returned to his companions. They had apparently eaten, for there were feathers and fur scattered around and both were licking their lips. But something warned him not to urge his old companion on. The terrier was
10 still utterly exhausted, and in addition had lost a lot of blood from the gashes suffered at the cub's claws the day before. These were stiff and black with blood, and had a tendency to open and bleed slightly with any movement, so all that day he lay peacefully in the warm autumn sunshine on the grass, sleeping, eating what the cat provided, and wagging his tail whenever one of the others came near.

15 The young dog spent most of the day still occupied with his ceaseless foraging for food. By evening he was desperate, but his luck turned when a rabbit, already changing to its white winter coat, suddenly started up from the long grass and swerved across his path. Head down, tail flying, the young dog gave chase. Swerving and turning in pursuit, but always the rabbit was just out of reach of his hungry jaws. At last, he put all his strength
20 into one violent lunge and felt the warm, pulsating prize in his mouth. The generations fell away, and the years of training never to sink teeth into feathers or fur; for a moment the Labrador looked almost wolf-like as he tore at the warm flesh and bolted it down in ravenous gulps.

They slept in the same place that night and most of the following day, and the weather
25 mercifully continued warm and sunny. By the third day the old dog seemed almost recovered and the wounds were closed. He had spent most of the day ambling around and sleeping, so that by now he seemed almost frisky and quite eager to walk a little.

So, late in the afternoon, they left the place which had been their home for three days and trotted slowly along the track together again. By the time the moon rose they had come
30 to the edge of a small lake which the track skirted.

A moose was standing in the water among the lily pads on the far shore, his great antlered head and humped neck silhouetted clearly against the pale moon. He took no notice of the strange animals across the water but thrust his head again and again under the surface, raising it high in the air after each immersion, and arching his neck. Two or
35 three water hens swam out from the reeds, a little crested grebe popped up like a jack-in-the-box in the water beside them, and the spreading ripples of their wake caught the light of the moon. As the three sat, ears pricked, they watched the moose squelch slowly out of the muddy water, shake himself, and turn cantering up the bank out of sight.

The young dog turned his head suddenly, his nose twitching, for his keen scent
40 had caught a distant whiff of wood smoke, and of something else—something
unidentifiable.... Seconds later, the old dog caught the scent too, and started to his feet,
snuffing and questioning with his nose. His thin whippy tail began to sweep to and fro
and a bright gleam appeared in the slanted black-currant eyes. Somewhere, not too far
away, were human beings — his world. He could not mistake their message — or refuse
45 their invitation: they were undoubtedly cooking something. He trotted off determinedly
in the direction of the tantalizing smell. The young dog followed somewhat reluctantly,
and for once the cat passed them both; a little moon-mad perhaps, for he lay in wait to
dart and strike, then streaked back into the shadows, only to reappear a second later in an
elaborate stalk of their tails. Both dogs ignored him.

50 The scent on the evening breeze was a fragrant compound of roasting rice, wild-duck
stew, and wood smoke. When the animals looked down from a hill, tantalized and
hungry, they saw six or seven fires in the clearing below, their flames lighting up a
semicircle of tents and conical birch bark shelters against a dark background of trees;
flickering over the canoes drawn up on the edge of a wild rice marsh and dying redly in
55 the black waters beyond; and throwing into ruddy relief the high, flat planes of brown
Ojibwa faces gathered around the centres of warmth and brightness.

The men were a colourful lot in jeans and bright plaid shirts, but the women were dressed
in sombre colours. Two young boys, the only children there, were going from fire to fire
shaking grain in shallow pans and stirring it with paddles as it parched. One man in long
60 soft moccasins stood in a shallow pit trampling husks, half his weight supported on a
log frame. Some of the band lay back from the fires, smoking and watching idly, talking
softly among themselves, while others still ate, ladling the fragrant contents of a black
iron pot onto tin plates. Every now and then one of them would throw a bone back over
a shoulder into the bush, and the watching animals gazed hungrily after it. A woman
65 stood at the edge of the clearing pouring grain from one bark platter to another, and the
loose chaff drifted off on the slight wind like smoke.

The old dog saw nothing of this, but his ears and nose supplied all he needed to know; he
could contain himself no longer and picked his way carefully down the hillside, for his
shoulder still pained him. Halfway down he sneezed violently in an eddy of chaff. One
70 of the boys by the fire looked up at the sound, his hand closing on a stone, but the woman
nearby spoke.

—*by* Shelia Burnford

7. During the day, the young dog left the other two animals resting because he was

A. bored

B. hungry

C. restless

D. playful

8. The conflict in this story is between animals and
   A. nature
   B. society
   C. humans
   D. themselves

9. Which of the following quotations contains a simile?
   A. "staring at him with goggle eyes"
   B. "stiff and black with blood"
   C. "as he tore at the warm flesh"
   D. "popped up like a jack-in-the-box"

10. This excerpt is taken from which of the following types of writing?
    A. a fable
    B. a legend
    C. an adventure
    D. a historical account

11. The introduction is written in italics in order to
    A. show that it is not part of the original story
    B. introduce the reader to the three animals
    C. explain how difficult the animals' journey was
    D. help the reader understand what the story is about

12. This excerpt **most** conveys a sense of
    A. hope
    B. failure
    C. despair
    D. happiness

Use the following passage to answer questions 13 to 19.

WANTED: MARS ... DEAD OR ALIVE?

When *Mariner 4* flew past Mars in 1965, scientists on earth got the first-ever close-up view of the Red Planet. What they saw came as a surprise … and, as a disappointment. The Mars that *Mariner*'s television cameras revealed was a blasted, cratered desert, with an atmosphere so thin that it was barely more than a vacuum. The planet was
5   bitterly cold and dry, and had no trace of life. It was so cold that at the polar caps, Mars' atmosphere had begun to freeze into dry ice. There was no sign of life, not even microscopic plants, and no water. MARS WAS DEAD!

The news was shocking, for up until *Mariner*, scientists had thought that Mars was a planet a lot like Earth, only somewhat colder. The Red Planet has always fascinated
10 astronomers. It is certainly the most earthlike of all the planets in the solar system—far more hospitable than the furnace of Venus or the hydrogen clouds of the gas-giant planets such as Jupiter and Saturn. But the *Mariner* spacecraft found that Mars was not so much like earth after all.

As revealed by *Mariner* and its later cousins, Mars is a planet of stunning superlatives.
15 Its great volcano, *Olympus Mons*, reaches up almost 25 kilometers above sea level (or, above the level where sea level would be, if Mars had a sea). That's like three Mount Everests stacked on top of each other! *Valles Marineris*, the Grand Canyon of Mars, is so huge that Earth's Grand Canyon could fit into it sideways. If it were placed on Earth, the Valles Marineris would stretch from New York to Los Angeles. Even the sky of the Red
20 Planet is different—a pinkish yellow instead of a bright blue.

For all these marvels, it's even more disappointing that Mars doesn't have any life. Or does it?

New Evidence for Life

The robotic spacecraft that followed *Mariner* to Mars—the *Vikings*, *Pathfinder*, and
25 *Global Surveyor*—gave us a somewhat modified view of the planet. Mars is inhospitable now … but was it always cold and dry? Photographs from orbit show many places on the planet that look like dry riverbeds. How could Mars have dry riverbeds, unless it once had rivers? Scientists think that long ago, Mars had liquid water, like the earth.

They also speculate that billions of years in the past, when Mars was young, it had a
30 much thicker atmosphere. Due to the *greenhouse effect*, the thicker atmosphere made Mars much warmer than it is now. The higher temperature allowed liquid water to be present. But long ago Mars lost most of its atmosphere—nobody knows for sure how— and became cold and dry.

But could life still be there? On Earth, living things are very tenacious. From the polar
35 snows to the darkest depths of the ocean, life has learned to survive no matter how extreme the environment. So, if life started on Mars when it was warm and wet, maybe as Mars slowly grew cooler and drier, life adapted to survive.

It would have had some serious adapting to do, though, since we know that the surface of Mars today is extremely harsh. Besides no water and a very thin atmosphere with no
40 oxygen in it, the planet's surface is flooded with ultraviolet light. (Think about it: On Earth, we use ultraviolet light to sterilize surgical instruments.)

But perhaps life on Mars is hidden deep underground. Maybe the planet has underground *hydrothermal* springs. Perhaps the water of Mars is very salty. Since salt water freezes at a lower temperature than fresh water, it could still be liquid even at Mars'
45 temperatures. Recently, scientists Ken Edgett and Michael Malin of Malin Space Systems in San Diego, CA, found places on Mars where, according to their analysis, water had burst loose from underground *aquifers* and flowed across the planet's surface in geologically recent time. In some places, Mars does have underground water!

If there is underground water on Mars, it is possible that there are bacteria, living in these
50 springs. Such life would be very primitive, perhaps like the extremophile bacteria that live in underground springs on Earth.

If we do find life on Mars, even simple bacteria, we will know that life is not unique to the earth, but exists on two planets—and maybe is common across the galaxy. That would be an amazing discovery!

55 **Olympus Mons**—The largest volcano on Mars. It was named after Mount Olympus, the legendary home of the Greek gods. ("Mons" means "mountain" in Latin.)

Valles Marineris—A 3,200-kilometer-long canyon on Mars. It was named after the Mariner space craft that first took pictures of it. ("Valles" means "valley" in Latin.)

Greenhouse effect—When gases in the atmosphere of a planet hold in the solar heat,
60 causing the planet's temperature to rise

Hydrothermal—Water warmed by the geothermal heat of the planet

Aquifer—An underground layer saturated with water

—*by* Geoffrey A. Landis

13. The word "tenacious" means
   A. persistent in maintaining something valued
   B. knowledgeable about how to survive
   C. strong and determined
   D. able to adapt

14. In 1965, scientists were both surprised and disappointed at their first close-up view of Mars because they
   A. had expected to find signs of life on Mars
   B. had thought that Mars was a lot like Earth
   C. discovered larger mountains than on Earth
   D. noticed that Mars' sky was not a bright blue

15. The statement "On earth, we use ultraviolet light to sterilize surgical equipment" suggests that ultraviolet light is

    A. very safe

    B. powerful

    C. cleansing

    D. very bright

16. According to the article, the **main** reason why there is no liquid water on Mars today is that

    A. Mars is dead

    B. Mars is too cold

    C. the riverbeds have dried up

    D. there was a greenhouse effect

17. The title "Wanted: Mars…Dead or Alive"? **most likely** suggests that

    A. astronauts want to know whether Mars is alive or dead

    B. scientists want to know if life ever existed on Mars

    C. nobody knows whether Mars has life on it or not

    D. the writer wants to go to Mars

18. This passage would **most likely** have been written for

    A. future astronauts

    B. a science textbook

    C. a science magazine

    D. a science fiction novel

19. The main idea of this passage is that

    A. Mars is not really like Earth

    B. Mars is a beautifully stunning planet

    C. the Mariner 4 found no signs of life on Mars

    D. at one time, there may have been life on Mars

Read the following passage to answer questions 20 to 24.

THE OUTLAW WHO WOULDN'T GIVE UP
PART 4

Laugh in the dark fun house, 1976. A television crew is filming an episode for the *Six Million Dollar Man* inside a fun house in Long Beach, California. When they set up the cameras in a dark corner, the director doesn't like the looks of the dummy dangling from the ceiling. It is sprayed with glow-in-the-dark paint and doesn't fit the scene.

5 A technician reaches up to remove the dummy. Plunk! The arm falls off. Everyone is shocked to see that this arm has a real bone. The dummy is a mummy, and no one knows who it is or how it got there. They call a medical examiner, and another mummy mystery begins.

As usual the mummy has clues. A look at the bones and tissues reveals a man about 10 thirty years old with unhealthy lungs, probably from pneumonia. But he died from a gunshot wound in his chest. A copper bullet jacket still in the body turns out to be .32 caliber made between the 1830s and World War I.

Those are interesting clues but only the beginning. The examiner looks into the mummy's mouth. Inside is a 1924 penny and a ticket stub from "Louis Sonney's 15 Museum of Crime, So. Main St., L.A." A check of driver's license records turns up Dan Sonney, who says that his father bought the mummy (they thought it was a dummy too) in the 1920s from an unknown source. Louis had a traveling road show called "The March of Crime" and charged people twenty-five cents to see the "outlaw who would never be captured live." When Louis died in 1949, the road show was put into storage 20 until 1971. Then these items were bought by Spoony Singh, owner of the Hollywood Wax Museum.

Spoony thought the mummy was made from papier-mâché and sent it off to Mount Rushmore to be part of a haunted house. It was returned as "not being lifelike enough." Eventually the body lost its identity and ended up dangling at the fun house in 25 front of the TV crew.

It takes only a few days to get this much information, but questions still remain. Who was this man? The police want to identify the body. They keep looking and find an old partner of Louis Sonney's who remembers buying the mummy from a retired coroner in Tulsa, Oklahoma. The partner thinks the mummy had been a robber.

30 Then people in Oklahoma get involved in this mummy mystery. The history buffs search through libraries and state records and come up with a prime suspect: Elmer McCurdy, alias Elmer McCuardy, Elmer McAudry, Frank Curtis, and Frank Davidson. Profession? Outlaw. They find one final clue that only a mummy could solve. Elmer had a scar two inches long on the back of his right wrist.

35 Elmer's age and height match up with the mummy. And then, even though his skin is now hard and cracked, the two-inch scar can still be seen on the wrist just as described in the prison records.

Now that Elmer McCurdy is identified, the police manage to gather some details about how he died. As the story goes, he joined a gang that robbed a train in Kansas. The gang 40 hoped to get several thousand dollars being sent as a payment to Indian tribes, but they picked the wrong train. Instead they got forty-six dollars and some whiskey.

Elmer drank some of the whiskey and slept in a hayloft until the posse found him early the next morning. There was a gun battle, and three times Elmer was asked to give up. He refused every time and was eventually killed on October 7, 1911. Since no one
45 claimed the body, the coroner preserved him in arsenic and for a nickel allowed the curious to take a peek at Elmer, who became known as the "Bandit Who Wouldn't Give Up." After five years carnival owners posing as "relatives" claimed him and got him started in sideshows and circuses. Eventually he became an attraction without a name.

After he was identified in 1977, Elmer was given a eulogy on television and flown back
50 to Oklahoma on a jet never seen in his lifetime. He is buried there under two cubic yards of concrete just in case anyone might think about digging him up and looking at him one more time.

—by Brenda Z. Guiberson

20. The final resting place of Elmer McCurdy is

   A. the Hollywood Wax Museum

   B. The March of Crime

   C. Oklahoma

   D. Kansas

21. In the phrase "a prime suspect: Elmer McCurdy, alias Elmer McCuardy, Elmer McAudry," (lines 31–32) the word "alias" means

   A. incognito

   B. anonymous

   C. also known as

   D. secret identity

22. The fact the Mount Rushmore returned the mummy to the Hollywood Wax Museum because it was not "lifelike enough" is **most likely** an example of

   A. irony

   B. the ridiculous

   C. foreshadowing

   D. a rhetorical situation

23. Elmer McCurdy earned the moniker the "Bandit Who Wouldn't Give Up" because he was very

   A. carefree

   B. obstinate

   C. desperate

   D. disgruntled

24. How many years passed between McCurdy's death and his burial?

    A. 50

    B. 55

    C. 60

    D. 66

Read the following passage to answer questions 25 to 29.

LOCHINVAR

O, young Lochinvar is come out of the west,
Through all the wide Border his steed was the best,
And save his good broadsword he weapons had none;
He rode all unarmed, and he rode all alone.
5 So faithful in love, and so dauntless in war,
There never was knight like the young Lochinvar.
He stayed not for brake, and he stopped not for stone,
He swam the Eske river where ford there was none;
But, ere he alighted at Netherby gate,
10 The bride had consented, the gallant came late:
For a laggard in love, and a dastard in war,
Was to wed the fair Ellen of brave Lochinvar.
So boldly he entered the Netherby hall,
Among bridesmen and kinsmen, and brothers and all:
15 Then spoke the bride's father, his hand on his sword
(For the poor craven bridegroom said never a word),
"O come ye in peace here, or come ye in war,
Or to dance at our bridal, young Lord Lochinvar?"
"I long wooed your daughter, my suit you denied;—
20 Love swells like the Solway, but ebbs like its tide—
And now I am come, with this lost love of mine,
To lead but one measure, drink one cup of wine.
There are maidens in Scotland more lovely by far,
That would gladly be bride to the young Lochinvar."
25 The bride kissed the goblet; the knight took it up,
He quaffed off the wine, and he threw down the cup,
She looked down to blush, and she looked up to sigh,
With a smile on her lips and a tear in her eye.
He took her soft hand, ere her mother could bar,—
30 "Now tread we a measure!" said young Lochinvar.
So stately his form, and so lovely her face,
That never a hall such a galliard did grace;
While her mother did fret, and her father did fume,
And the bridegroom stood dangling his bonnet and plume;
35 And the bridemaidens whispered, "'Twere better by far
To have matched our fair cousin with young Lochinvar."
One touch to her hand, and one word in her ear,
When they reached the hall-door, and the charger stood near:
So light to the croupe the fair lady he swung,
40 So light to the saddle before her he sprung!

> "She is won! we are gone, over bank, bush, and scaur;
> They'll have fleet steeds that follow," quoth young Lochinvar.
> There was mounting 'mong Graemes of the Netherby clan;
> Forsters, Fenwicks, and Musgraves, they rode and they ran;
> 45 There was racing, and chasing, on Cannobie Lee,
> But the lost bride of Netherby ne'er did they see.
> So daring in love, and so dauntless in war,
> Have ye e'er heard of gallant like young Lochinvar?
>
> —*by* Sir Walter Scott

25. The adjectives that best describe Lochinvar are

A. lonely but dependable

B. adventurous and wild

C. confident and valiant

D. cocky but likeable

26. As it is used in the quotation "For the poor craven bridegroom," the word "craven" means

A. extroverted

B. cowardly

C. assertive

D. brave

27. This selection is best referred to as

A. a lyric

B. an epic

C. a ballad

D. a narrative

28. The theme **most prevalent** throughout the selection is one of

A. war

B. love

C. hatred

D. tragedy

29. The main conflict that Lochinvar encounters is man versus

A. man

B. himself

C. environment

D. the unknown

ANSWERS AND SOLUTIONS—UNIT TEST

1. A	7. B	13. A	19. C	25. C
2. D	8. A	14. A	20. C	26. B
3. A	9. D	15. B	21. C	27. D
4. A	10. C	16. B	22. A	28. B
5. D	11. A	17. B	23. B	29. A
6. B	12. A	18. C	24. D	

1. A

Oliver was accused of theft. He had supposedly been caught stealing a handkerchief from an old man (lines 11–12).

2. D

When the police officer says, "Must go before the magistrate now, sir … Now, young gallows!" it was not really an invitation; it was a command.

3. A

The fact that nothing was found on Oliver when he was searched, combined with the fact that the old gentleman was unsure of Oliver's guilt and did not want to press charges, means it is likely that Oliver was innocent.

4. A

In this passage, the plot is primarily developed through the dialogue between the old gentleman and the jailer, as well as the old gentleman's internal dialogue.

5. D

In the phrase "a vast amphitheatre of faces over which a dusky curtain had hung for many years," the "vast amphitheatre of faces" symbolically refers to all of the people the old gentleman has known, and the "dusky curtain" that "had hung for many years" refers to the fact that the people are from long ago in the past, and he has not thought of them in years.

6. B

The old gentleman is kind (he does not believe that Oliver is guilty and would prefer not to press charges) and sympathetic (he was able to put himself in Oliver's shoes, and he felt sad for the boy when he was led into the cell).

7. B

At the very beginning of the passage the reader is told that hunger was the ruling instinct of the Labrador. The dog ate two frogs but he was not satisfied until he had eaten the rabbit. Since the Labrador was a young dog, he was probably bored, restless, and playful, but none of these was the motivating reason for him to leave his companions.

8. A

The actions and motivations of the key characters result from the conflict with nature. The animals in the story have to overcome many difficulties in order to be reunited with their family but, in this excerpt, all the opposition is found in nature. The animals have no contact with humans, nor do they brush with society. No animal has internal conflict.

9. D

The writer compares the grebe that pops out of the water near the moose with a jack-in-the-box. It would be the sudden movement and the quickness by which it comes out of the water that surprises all. The other three responses are not similes as nothing is being compared in them.

10. C

This excerpt is an example of the adventures that the three animals experienced as they travelled through northern Canada in search of their family. The fact that this is a true account does not make it historical and it is not a fable or a legend.

11. A

The reason for the italics as a structural feature is to show that Sheila Burnford, who wrote the story, did not write this introduction. The introduction written by the editors to give the reader some insight into what the passage was about.

12. A

This question addresses mood and tone, and how they are achieved. Throughout the excerpt, the reader feels optimistic for the animals: they survive an attack, they find some food to eat, they rest and rebuild their strength, and they recognize humans and the possibility of being fed. At no time do the animals show any signs of despair, and they have not yet failed in their quest to find their owners.

13. A

Tenacious means persistent in maintaining or adhering to something valued as habitual. The writer is stating that all living things are persistent in keeping their life which they highly value. It is rare for a living thing to give up and die without doing whatever is possible in order to survive. In order to maintain life, living things do need to be able to adapt, be strong and determined to live and know how to survive, but it is their tenacity (or will to live) that enables them to stay alive.

14. A

In spite of all the marvelous things that were discovered about Mars, the scientists were surprised that there appeared to be no signs of life—even water and they were disappointed to discover that Mars was a dead planet! Scientists had expected Mars to be similar to Earth, but it was the total lack of any life forms that most disappointed the scientists.

15. B

Ultraviolet light produces radiation which kills germs and other unwanted organisms. It is used to sterilize surgical tools and, in radiation form, to kill diseased cells in the body. Since the ultraviolet light would kill living organisms, it would destroy anything that attempted to live on Mars and so would be dangerous to all living things. It is used for sterilizing on Earth.

16. B

It is so cold on Mars that "at the polar caps, Mars' atmosphere had begun to freeze into dry ice." When the atmosphere begins to freeze there is no liquid water anywhere to be found; any that might have been present would also freeze. Mars is dead because there is no water on it and all living things need water; the greenhouse effect warmed up Mars in its younger days and the rivers dried up when Mars began to get colder and the water disappeared.

17. B

The title suggests that, at this time, it is not known if there has ever been life on Mars. Scientists do want to find out more about Mars whether the information confirms or refutes the fact that at one time there had been some form of life present on the planet. The question mark in the title suggests the unknown factor about whether life exists on Mars or not.

18. C

The study of the planets is one of many science disciplines. Therefore it is most likely that this article would have been written for a scientific magazine. There is a possibility that an article such as this could be found in a science textbook and be of interest to future astronauts, but most likely the article would have been found in a science magazine. This is not fiction.

19. C

The main idea of the passage is to suggest that there is the possibility that there may have been water life on Mars in the past. This further suggests there is the possibility of finding evidence of other life forms.

20. C

At the end of its travels, the body was returned to Tulsa, Oklahoma, where it was buried under two cubic yards of concrete.

21. C

As noted in the passage, Elmer McCurdy used various other names. The term "alias" is another way of saying "also known as." Elmer McCurdy was known by many names.

22. A

It is ironic that the mummy was returned to the Wax Museum for not being lifelike enough since it was perfectly lifelike, being the dead body of a real person.

23. B

McCurdy was very stubborn when cornered by authorities. By refusing to give up, he proved to be obstinate in the face of the law.

24. D

According to the passage, McCurdy died in 1911 and was finally buried in 1977. This represents a total of 66 years between his death and his burial.

25. C

Lochinvar rides alone unarmed and is viewed to be faithful in love and fearless in war; he is confident in who and what he is, along with being a valiant/brave knight (lines 3–6).

26. B

To be craven is to be cowardly or timorous.

27. D

A narrative poem tells a story, usually about people of high position.

28. B

The love Lochinvar and fair Ellen share surfaces despite the fact Ellen's father has chosen a husband for her and their wedding is being celebrated. Lochinvar's determination to rescue Ellen and take her away with him, despite the fact he could meet with opposition, also reinforces the theme of love.

29. A

Lochinvar confronts Ellen's parents and many family guests who support the marriage Ellen's father has arranged. Despite this physical threat, Lochinvar proceeds to secure his love, Ellen, as his own.

Manage Ideas and Information

MANAGE IDEAS AND INFORMATION

PLAN AND FOCUS

3.1.1.1 synthesize ideas and information from a variety of sources to develop own opinions, points of view, and general impressions

SYNTHESIZING

Synthesizing is the process of sorting through information in a text so that it makes sense. Synthesizing involves putting elements together to form a whole. To help you synthesize the information in any text, try asking yourself any of the following questions:

• What was the author's purpose in writing the text?
• What was the main idea of the text?
• What clues in the text helped me to determine the main idea?
• How do different parts of the text connect with one another?
• Has my thinking changed after reading the text?
• Can I think of a new title for the text?
• Are there any discrepancies in the text?
• From what perspective has the author written this text?

As you synthesize, be watchful for biased writing. Any of the texts you choose for research may have a bias or contain more opinion than fact. All authors can be prejudiced or partial to certain opinions. Authors sometimes try to influence their audience or persuade them to share their opinions.

When synthesizing research material, it is important to:

• Examine many different sources of information on a topic
• Consider different points of view
• Describe your general impression
• Draw conclusions and develop your own opinions

The following passage relates to working conditions in 19th century England and the issues that led to change. The passage describes the life of Charles Dickens. Dickens suffered directly from the poor working conditions in England at the time, and he wrote about them to try and provoke change in his novels.

CHARLES DICKENS—CHRONICLER OF HIS TIMES

Charles Dickens, one of the great English novelists of the nineteenth century, was a keen observer of life in his times. Dickens often drew on his own experiences to write his books about life in England during the Industrial Revolution. Born of a poor father who spent time in prison for debt, Dickens himself knew what poverty was like. He worked at age 12 in a London factory, pasting labels on shoe polish bottles. Later, he worked as a newspaper reporter, and he gained fame as a novelist. Dickens had great energy. He wrote, went to the theatre, toured as a dramatic reader, and busied himself with many charities. He would often walk for hours to wear off his nervous energy. This is perhaps how he came to know the streets and alleys of London better than most people of his time.

Many of Charles Dickens' books describe life in British industrial cities. In his book Hard Times, he describes life in Coketown:

It was a town of red brick ... inhabited by people equally like one another, who all went in and out at the same hours, with the same sound upon the same pavements, to do the same work, and to whom every day was the same as yesterday and tomorrow, and every year the counterpart of the last and the next.

You can synthesize general ideas about the 19th century from this document, such as the fact that

- workers were harshly treated
- workers were usually restricted to a life of labour. People of remarkable talent and ambition, such as Dickens, could move beyond working class labour, but most people born into working class conditions in England would remain in the working class for their entire lives.

The more information you read about a single topic, the better understanding you will have of that topic. To demonstrate comprehension of the issues of the working conditions that led to change, you could further examine the two articles and read one of Dickens' novels. In any project you are assigned at school, synthesis of information is necessary. The following example contains information about a student project that required the synthesis of information.

SYNTHESIS EXAMPLE ONE

Two students are given a news article to use for a two-week project for Current Events. They are asked to identify an issue raised in the news article, track the issue for two weeks, consider perspectives and possible outcomes, and engage their classmates in the issue at the end of the two weeks.

The article the students are given is about an airport safety issue arising from a recent crash landing at Pearson International Airport (Toronto) that could have resulted in a tragic loss of lives. According to the article, an Air France jet carrying 309 passengers and crew had landed halfway down the runway during a summer rainstorm. Overshooting the 90 metre buffer zone at the end of the runway, the plane careened over a bank and finally came to a full stop. Fortunately, before the damaged aircraft burst into flames, everyone on board was safely evacuated and removed from danger. The accident was caused by human error, but the issue arising from this incident involves passenger safety and accident prevention: should the runway buffer zone be extended to 300 metres, the required length at most major European airports?

The students decide to provide a tracking log to record what they did to clarify or extend their understanding of this story and the issue it raised over the two-week period.

Example

---

1. We collected stories on the topic for about two weeks, from newspapers, television, and Internet. In the end, we had 21 news items.

2. We recorded repeated facts or messages common to all the stories:

   - The Pearson runway has a 90 metre buffer zone
   - The weather conditions were severe
   - The pilot landed halfway down the runway
   - Incidents such as this happen more frequently than is commonly believed

3. We looked for public reactions at the news comment page and on the editorial page, and we recorded repeated responses:

   - Safety is of major concern
   - The expense of extending the runway is worthwhile
   - Why should Toronto not maintain an international standard?

4. We watched for different perspectives on the issue and found opinion articles from:

   - The pilots' association (safety standards)
   - City and provincial governments (funding issues)

---

5. Based on all that we found, we tried to predict an outcome:

   • A runway extension will be built over the next two years, funded by the province

6. While the issue was not resolved in two weeks, it was under review by a transportation committee.

7. We summarized our findings and prepared our class presentation. After our presentation, we will lead a brief discussion on the issue. We will then ask Miss Fergusen to review business letter format and take us to the computer lab to write letters to the Transportation Safety Board of Canada, to be forwarded to the Honourable Lawrence Cannon, Minister of Transport, Ottawa. The purpose of the letters will be to request mandatory lengthened buffer zones for major Canadian Airport runways.

Concluding Comments

Through reading, research, and discussion, we clarified and extended our understanding of an important and newsworthy safety issue. We came to have a strong personal interest in the outcome of this issue because, like most Canadians, we will use air travel throughout our lives. If a short-sighted decision is made, we ourselves could someday be victims.

The students who analyzed the article synthesized a lot of information. They took information from various sources—not just the article they were asked to read—and drew conclusions. They also recorded their process, which is another helpful method. Recording your synthesis process for research material keeps you organized. Organizing your conclusions and information as you research ensures that you do not forget anything. The more information you can use to synthesize and process a topic or issue, the better your conclusions will be.

3.1.1.2 assess adequacy, accuracy, detail, and appropriateness of oral, print, and other media texts to support or further develop arguments, opinions, or points of view

ADEQUACY AND ACCURACY

How do you know if an author is expressing fact or opinion? Opinion and fact can be confused, especially if an author is trying to persuade you to believe his or her opinion. The statement "paper is made from trees" is a fact. The statement "oak trees produce the most beautiful wood" is an opinion. Since the word "beautiful" is subjective, it is not a word that can be easily used to express fact.

In election campaigns, many voters are influenced by how well the speaker appeals to their emotions. Voters can be fooled because candidates say what the voters want to hear rather than expressing facts. In newspapers, news items report facts, and some editorial items express opinions. Sometimes news stories are coloured by the reporter's opinion. This is not good journalism because readers might have difficulty deciding what is fact and what is opinion. Some newspapers contain more opinionated or biased journalism than others.

If you are writing a letter or an essay to express your opinion about something, you should always state the facts first and then present your opinions based on facts.

When you are reading, make sure to look for any inconsistent facts presented by the author. Statements that sound wrong should alert you that the information you are reading could be inaccurate.

Factual statements are clear, accurate, and verifiable (can be proven). Much of what is read has not been tested, but is accepted because it appears to be true or a trustworthy source maintains that it is true.

Magazines, books, newspapers, websites, bulletin boards, and blogs should not be trusted until the author's knowledge and experience on the subject has been verified. Faulty conclusions are often made because texts may be based either on incorrect observations or observations that are prejudiced, wishful, or imaginative.

Look at the following chart about fictional pop star named Tiffany Jones, who, for the purpose of this exercise, is known to everyone through magazines, interviews, etc. Some aspects of her public persona are fact, while other aspects are the opinions of her fans, agent, parents, magazine writers, interviewers, and others.

Tiffany Jones	
Fact	**Opinion**
She is 19-years-old and was born in High Level, Alberta.	She is the richest 19-year-old in Alberta.
She was overweight as a young child.	She probably suffers from anorexia.
She chews gum.	She is a chronic gum chewer.
She grants interviews only when she is launching a tour or new CD.	She is reclusive and hates giving interviews to the media.
She has blond hair	She probably dyes her hair.
Her parents are divorced.	She is angry because of her parents' divorce.
She has sold thousands of CDs.	She is jealous of Jennifer Bright, another pop star, who has sold more CDs.
She opened an orphanage in Rwanda.	She opened the orphanage to make Jennifer Bright look bad.

In order to decide what is fact and what is opinion about Tiffany Jones, you must verify every one of the statements. For example, it could be a fact that Tiffany chews gum, but whether her gum chewing is chronic is one person's opinion. To some, her gum chewing might be considered excessive; to others, however, it might be considered moderate.

Opinions often contain words such as best, better, interesting should, important, beautiful, worst, and nicest. Try to distinguish factual statements and opinion statements when you are reading.

DETERMINING CREDIBILITY

In order to determine the credibility of what you are reading, examine it using the following aspects of text as a guide.

Author's viewpoint: Who is the author? What does he or she stand to gain or lose? A reference, for example, to Tiffany's anorexia written by her mother would be more credible than the same information posted by a fan on a blog.

Text structure: Is the information well presented? Are the arguments easy to understand, logical, and supported by reasonable evidence?

Author's word choice: Do the author's words seem chosen to best express ideas and convey facts, or are they meant to inflame readers' emotions? Does the tone of the writer seem balanced or angry?

USEFUL REFERENCE MATERIAL

The following list contains reference material that is ideal for research work. Printed reference material is usually very reliable.

- Almanacs: give brief information about the years
- Encyclopedias: give information on many subjects
- Dictionaries: list words and their meanings alphabetically
- Atlases: contain maps of the world

Opinions are found everywhere—advertisements, editorials, conversations, letters, and even textbooks. If you think that what you are reading is an opinion, ask yourself the following questions:

- Can this statement be proven?
- Is this statement supported by examples?
- Do I disagree?
- Might someone disagree?
- Do I need more information?
- Is the author of the opinion an expert on the subject?

Primary and secondary sources sometimes determine the degree of accuracy and reliability.

Example

Primary Source	Secondary Source
Autobiography	Biography
Interview with a *Titanic* survivor	News story written after the *Titanic* sank
Original manuscript of a book	Translated or revised edition of a book, like a child's version of *Treasure Island*

Interviews can be either primary or secondary sources of information.

FINAL TIPS ON RELIABILITY AND ACCURACY

- Compare facts in various resources and watch for differences or contradictions
- Consider the publishing date, if applicable
- Consider expertise, reputation, or source of author. If there is no author listed, for example, on a website, check the style of writing. Does it sound professional?
- Watch for biases. Is the information objective or does it favour/criticize a particular group?
- Double-check Internet sources. Is there proof of the author's expertise? Is the host organization reliable? How recent is the information on the website? Is the website educational (e.g., a university website) or commercial in nature?

Accurate information provides the support for plausible opinions. Learn to discard unreliable or questionable sources of information. The more you research a topic, the more viewpoints and facts you will be able to use to form your own opinion.

SELECT AND PROCESS

3.1.4.1 obtain information reflecting multiple perspectives from a variety of sources, such as expository essays, graphs, diagrams, online catalogues, periodical indices, film libraries, electronic databases and the Internet, when conducting research

FINDING INFORMATION

Information is all around you. Following are some examples of documents in which you can locate information.

Consumer Documents	Workplace Documents	Public Documents
Consumer reports	Safety policies	Clean Air Act
Guarantees	Dress codes	Safe Water Act
Warranties	Emergency evacuation procedures	Highways Act
Recall announcements		Littering laws
Advertisements	Internet use rules	Driver's Handbook
	E-mail policies	Library policies

Following are some examples of information books that are recognizable by their formats:

- Encyclopedias
- Atlases
- Dictionaries
- Almanacs
- Thesauruses
- Textbooks

The following table contains examples of information sources.

Goal	Possible Information Sources
To find the meaning of a word	Dictionary
To plan a trip	Internet, travel brochure, travel guide, map
To find annual weather patterns	Almanac
To find current sports information	Newspaper, Internet
To find information about replacing a broken DVD player	Warranty, guarantee
To order some camping equipment	Catalogue, Internet
To check the course options at your school	School Handbook

When you need to locate any type of information, there is usually an appropriate source close at hand. Ask yourself the following questions:

- What do I need to find out?
- Where am I most likely to find this information?
- Who could help me if I am unable to find the information?

3.2.1.2 distinguish between primary and secondary sources, and determine the usefulness of each for research purposes

RESEARCH SOURCES

When you write a research paper, you express your opinion about a subject and support your views using primary and secondary sources. Before you begin, it is a good idea to create a chart labelled "What I Know" and "What I Want to Know" about the subject. This will help you to create clear, concise, and pertinent research questions. Then, you will be ready to begin your research.

PRIMARY SOURCES

A source is considered primary if it is created by a person with direct, personal knowledge of the event. A primary source is a document such as a letter, a speech, or a photograph created by a primary participant in the event at the time it occurred.

Examples

- Interviews: you might decide to interview an astronaut from one of the Apollo Missions. How would you conduct the interview? Would you do it over the phone, via e-mail, or in person? Remember to prepare open-ended questions that are specific to the topic and your interviewee's experiences. Take notes or use a recording device as you speak to the astronaut. Finally, remember to write a thank-you letter after the interview.
- Photos: you might be able to find firsthand photographic accounts that you could use to support your research.
- Eyewitnesses: you might be able to interview someone who witnessed one of the Apollo spaceships as it took off for its mission.
- Original documents: any original, authentic documents (such as newspaper and magazine articles, pamphlets, and blueprints) that were created by a person involved in the launch of one of the Apollo spaceships.
- Autobiographies: are written by the author about the author and his or her life.

SECONDARY SOURCES

A source is considered secondary if it uses primary sources or other secondary sources to report information. A secondary source usually reports, paraphrases, or evaluates events from the past. Quotations from primary sources are often found in secondary sources.

Examples

- Libraries: catalogues in libraries have print and electronic resources listed under the headings author, title, and subject to make it easier for you to find the information you require.
- Internet sites: while the Internet has many sites from which you can gather more information about your subject, be aware that anyone can post information on a website, so even though the information may be more up-to-date than encyclopedias and textbooks, it may not always be accurate. Always check your facts using other sources.
- Books and encyclopedias: provide useful secondary source information.

A student investigates a medical career using both primary and secondary sources of information. The following chart illustrates some distinctions between the kinds of information available.

Secondary Sources (career pamphlet, career website, university handbook, career catalogue)	Primary Source (interview with family physician)
Provide generalized information: • Education requirements • Specialties • Salary range • Personal aptitudes • Range of career opportunities • Professional skills • Professional development	Provides personal, practical information: • Hardships: long hours, on-call disrupts life, tiring, demanding, limited family time, competition for hospital privileges, large patient load • Benefits: small town friendliness, valued, respected, known in community, involved in community, good salary

ORGANIZE, RECORD, AND EVALUATE

3.3.1.1 organize ideas and information by developing and selecting appropriate categories and organizational structures

ORGANIZING INFORMATION

Organizing the information you have to write about is essential to creating clear, interesting essays and stories. Try to find an organizing strategy that works for you. Some strategies that help you sort and organize information include:

• Webbing
• Outlining
• Tree diagrams
• Venn diagrams

Once you have read a variety of sources and are ready to develop your writing, you will need to organize your information into categories. When you write based on an organized plan, your writing tends to flow more logically and coherently.

Select the type of graphic organizer that best suits your purpose. The following graphic organizers are commonly used.

WEBBING

Webbing means putting information in boxes or circles. These boxes or circles are connected by arrows to show relationships between ideas, themes, etc. Following are five examples of webbing: chronological sequence, cause and effect chart, comparison/contrast chart, concept pattern, and an episode chart. Webbing organizers help you to see all the information you have collected in a more visual way.

Chronological Sequence organizes events in the order in which they occur.

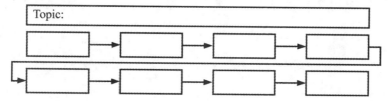

Cause and Effect Charts organize information into a series of steps that lead to a specific idea or outcome.

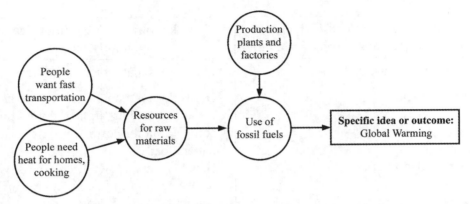

Comparison/Contrast Charts organize information according to the similarities and differences of two or more topics.

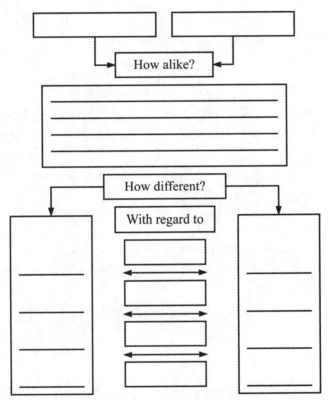

Use a **similar/different chart** to list things that are the same and things that are different.

Topic_____

Similarities	Differences

Use a KWL chart to organize your thoughts so you can stay focused and on topic.

Topic_____

What I Know	What I Want to Know	What I Learned

Tree Diagrams

A network tree uses boxes or circles to identify and link main ideas. The words that describe the relationships between the concepts are written beside the lines.

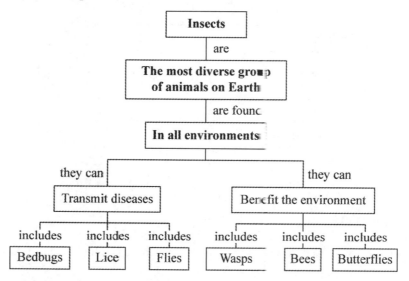

Concept Patterns are best used to organize general information about people, places, things, and events.

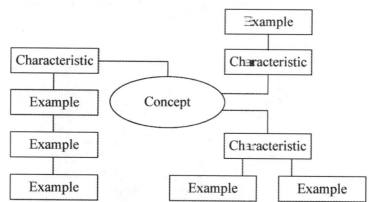

Episode Charts organize information about specific events.

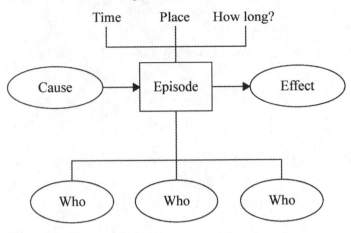

Use a **sequence chart** to show cause-and-effect relationships.

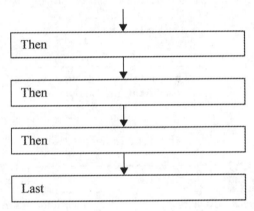

VENN DIAGRAMS

Venn diagrams are a useful way to compare and contrast two things. The overlapping part of the two circles shows the similarities.

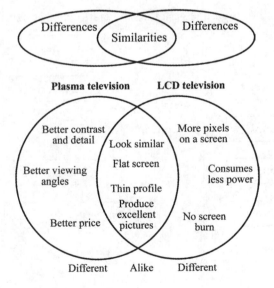

The next time you have to record information, try to organize t with one of the graphic organizers described. If you are going to present your information, be sure to organize it in an outline before writing your essay or presentation.

3.3.1.3 develop coherence by relating all key ideas to the overall purpose of the oral, print, or other media text

DEVELOPING COHERENCE

The word coherence means logically connected or consistent. Coherent writing is clear, easily followed and does not confuse the reader. To improve coherence in your writing, practise the following strategies:

- Use organizers before your writing to find the best way to organize your writing
- Use logical transition words when connecting ideas
- Revise paragraphs to make them more coherent
- Create topic sentences that connect back to the main topic

Transitions

It is important to establish and maintain coherence in your writing with transitions. Transitions are words and phrases that connect your ideas in logical ways so that they do not seem scrambled or appear as random lists. Following are effective and commonly used transitions.

Purpose	Transition Words and Phrases			
To show differences	on the other hand	in contrast	whereas	in comparison
	instead	unlike	however	
To show similarities	just as important	not unlike	also	
	in the same manner	similarly		
To indicate time	at the same time	immediately	soon	
	in subsequent months	hereafter	next	
To indicate more	in addition to	furthermore	moreover	
	another example of			

COHERENT PARAGRAPHS

In order to write a well-organized paragraph, you need a plan. Earlier in this *KEY*, an example of a method to organize your essay, the Hamburger Plan, has been described in detail as a useful tool to plan your paragraphs before you begin to write them out.

Begin with a topic sentence that introduces the main idea of the paragraph. Write several sentences that develop the idea introduced in the first sentence. These sentences contain observations, comments, or insights about the main idea. In these sentences, you might also present supporting details, list evidence or examples, present an anecdote, give an explanation, or advance an argument. Finish off a paragraph with a concluding sentence that restates the controlling idea.

PARAGRAPH REVISION

Revising, or checking your work, is very important. Reread your paragraphs carefully, and revise your writing in order to:

- Improve the organization
- Improve your use of transition words
- Make your ideas consistent
- Check your verb tenses
- Clarify your ideas
- Make your details more precise

Following is an example of a student's paragraph, followed by the student's revision of the paragraph.

Example

> Groups of large ocean waves may slam into an ocean current passing in the other direction. Several storm waves pile up to form freak waves. These waves could be more than 100 feet tall and can sink cargo ships beneath the water. The waves are most common off the coasts of Japan, Florida, and Alaska. Over the next few years, oceanographers hope to study these satellite images to help them better understand why such waves occur. Currently, a project known as WaveAtlas studies the oceans with satellites.

Following is an example of the same paragraph after the student revised it:

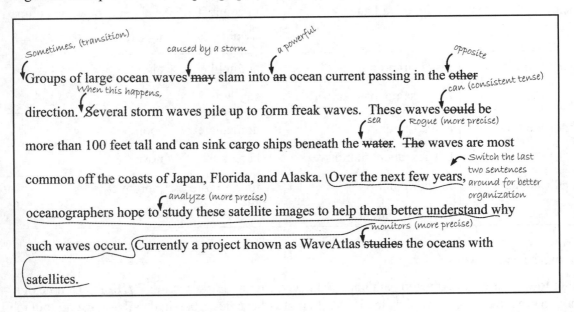

3.3.2.3 choose specific vocabulary, and use conventions accurately and effectively to enhance credibility

VOCABULARY AND CONVENTIONS

Whether you are speaking or writing, people will pay more attention if you:

- Choose appropriate, specific, and effective language
- Use language conventions correctly in your usage, including punctuation, capitalization, spelling, and sentence structure

The role of vocabulary should not be underestimated. Use vivid language and a variety of words. Try and think of the most exciting or descriptive way to describe something. Chances are if you try and make your writing exciting, you will use unique and descriptive words. Your reader will pay attention to your ideas if you present them using the most descriptive vocabulary possible.

EFFECTIVE USE OF LANGUAGE

The best writing is precise. Using a thesaurus and a dictionary, you will be able to find more specific words that will convey to your reader exactly what you mean.

Example

Simple Word	More Specific Words
Hide	disappear, conceal, discrete, confine, seclude, obscure, suppress, disguise, camouflage
Beautiful	lovely, fair, radiant, pretty, attractive, photogenic, scenic, picturesque, exquisite, ornamental

Synonyms are words that have the same or similar meanings as other words. Antonyms are words that have opposite meanings. A thesaurus lists words with their synonyms and, usually, their antonyms.

Words in a thesaurus are arranged in alphabetical order. The following example contains a dictionary entry for the word bright.

> **bright:** ADJS (adjectives/synonyms) 1. sunny, fair, mild, balmy; brilliant, vivid, resplendent
> 2. smart, brainy, brilliant, clever, gifted, talented, sharp keen
> (antonyms) 1. dull, flat, dingy, cloudy, faded, leaden, dim, pale, weak, faint 2. slow-witted, dim, slow, thick-headed, bland, desensitized

Thesauruses are useful for finding precise vocabulary. Do you need a synonym or an antonym? Do you want the literal (denotative) meaning, such as *sunny*, or a more connotative (associated) meaning, such as *brainy*? A thesaurus will help you to find a variety of words, but avoid choosing words simply because they are bigger or less well known.

How can a thesaurus help you to choose specific vocabulary? Read the following paragraph created by a student writer. Notice the underlined words:

> Jeremy <u>thought carefully about</u> his <u>great</u> idea. It could work! If he <u>planned</u> his disappearance <u>carefully</u>, the wedding would <u>continue</u> as planned, because his sister, the bride, would be too <u>busy</u> to notice his absence, and Jeremy would be well along the path to the river on his bike before anyone missed him. Of course, he needed to <u>return</u> before the reception buffet started; Mom would be <u>looking</u> for him in the food line and would be on the phone to the RCMP if she didn't <u>see</u> him heaping up his plate. A perfect July afternoon shouldn't be wasted at a garden wedding reception when the fish were biting and the river was <u>calling him!</u>

Here is the same paragraph after the student used a thesaurus to find more interesting and specific words to replace the underlined ones:

> Jeremy <u>considered</u> his <u>brilliant</u> idea. It could work! If he staged his disappearance <u>craftily</u>, the wedding would <u>proceed</u> as planned, because his sister, the bride, would be too <u>preoccupied</u> to notice his absence, and Jeremy would be well along the path to the river on his bike before anyone missed him. Of course, he needed to <u>reappear</u> before the reception buffet began; Mom would be <u>checking</u> for him in the food line and would be on the phone to the RCMP if she didn't <u>spot</u> him heaping up his plate. A perfect July afternoon shouldn't be wasted at a garden wedding reception when the fish were biting and the river was <u>beckoning</u>!

You should consider your vocabulary, or diction, when you are drafting, editing, revising your work, and even when you are in the planning stages of your writing. The role of language conventions is to make your ideas credible and understandable to a wide audience. Writing rules are followed for a reason: clarity.

PROOFREADING

When you have finished writing, revising, and rewriting, make sure to edit and proofread your final draft. When you proofread, ensure that your grammar, punctuation, capitalization, and spelling are correct. Errors will make it harder for your reader to understand your writing.

Grammar includes all aspects and rules of language:

- Verb Tense
- Subject/Verb Agreement
- Complete Sentences
- Comparative and Superlative Forms of Adjectives and Adverbs
- Subordinate Clauses and Coordinating Conjunctions
- Modifier Placement
- Correct Word Usage

VERB TENSE

The tense of a verb tells when the action happens. The most common verb tenses you will use in your writing are the past tense (before), the present tense (now), and the future tense (later).

Following is an example of the three tenses of the verb to work.

Example

Past tense	Present tense	Future tense
He worked	He works	He will work

When you plan a story, think about when it takes place: the past, the present, the future, or some combination of these timeframes. You may decide to begin your story in the present and include flashback sequences. Make sure that when you are writing in the present that your verbs reflect the present tense. When you use a flashback sequence, make sure that the verbs are written in the past tense. Whatever you decide, make sure that you are consistent with the verb tenses you use in your writing. If you jump back and forth between present tense and past tense, for example, your readers will have a difficult time understanding what is going on.

SUBJECT-VERB AGREEMENT

The following examples show the subject and the verb of a sentence agreeing:

Examples

- It *is* ready.
- They *are* ready.
- Samson and Delilah *are* no longer friends.

If the subject is singular, so is the verb. Similarly, if the subject is plural, so is the verb. Most of the difficulties in subject-verb agreement are caused by difficulties in recognizing singular and plural subjects. When subjects are joined by *or* or *nor*, the verb agrees with the nearest subject.

Examples

- Either Miller or Smith is guilty.
- Neither Miller nor Smith wants to confess.
- Neither the speaker nor the listeners are aware of the irony.

When one part of the verb is singular and the other plural, write the sentence so that the plural part is nearest the verb.

Example

- Weak: Neither band members nor the conductor is satisfied.
- Better: Neither the conductor nor the band members are satisfied.

Nothing that comes between a singular subject and its verb can make that subject plural.

Example

- Our school basketball team, the Gerbils, is victorious again.
- The prime minister, accompanied by several cabinet ministers, arrives at the airport shortly.
- Either Miller or Jones—both are suspects—is guilty.
- The contestant with the most votes is now on stage.
- One of the girls sings better.
- The ringleader who was at the head of the rebellious miners is sorry.

Indefinite pronouns such as *each, each one, either, neither, everyone, everybody, anybody, anyone, nobody, somebody, someone,* and *no one* are singular.

Example

- Each of the contestants wins a prize.
- Everybody near the river is in danger.
- No one who wants to be successful in the exams is likely to be late.

Collective nouns are singular unless there is a reason to consider them as plurals.

Example

- The group works well.
- The company is bankrupt.
- The jury is deliberating its verdict.
- The jury are arguing among themselves.

Using the correct pronoun is often a problem because the form of a pronoun varies depending on how the pronoun is used.

Use *I*, *you*, *he/she/it*, *we*, *you*, *they*, *who* as the subject of a sentence or clause and for the complement of a linking verb.

Example

- You have been chosen.
- We will be the last of the contestants.
- Who is going to be next?
- It is she who will be chosen.

Use me, you, him/her/it, us, you, them, and whom as direct or indirect objects of verbs or as the object of a preposition.

Example

- Give it to me.
- Hit the ball to them.
- Ask them the time.
- The child next to him laughed suddenly.

Use *my*, *your*, *his/her/its*, *our*, *their*, and *whose* as adjectives.

Example

- my car
- your umbrella
- its fur

Use *mine*, *yours*, *his/hers/its*, *ours*, *theirs*, and *whose* as subjects of sentences or as the complement of a linking verb.

Example

- Yours is the one on the left.
- This is mine.
- Theirs is next.

Remember that the possessive pronouns my, your, his, hers, its, our, yours, theirs, and whose never use an apostrophe to show possession.

Complete Sentences

As a general rule, all sentences should be complete sentences.

- Incorrect: He went ahead with his plan. Even though it was faulty.
- Correct: He went ahead with his plan, even though it was faulty.

Occasionally, an incomplete sentence is used deliberately for effect. Fragments that are used deliberately are sometimes called minor sentences.

- Is anyone in favor of dictatorship? No? Well, of course not.

Dialogue and reported speech are exceptions to the fragments rule.

- "Ready yet?"
- "Not yet."
- "Well then—!"

The error that is opposite of a sentence fragment is the run-on sentence. A run-on sentence results from either punctuation between sentences being omitted or a comma used to combine two sentences.

Example

- We went to Calgary we decided to visit the zoo.
  These errors can be fixed by correcting the punctuation or by rewriting.
- We went to Calgary. We decided to visit the zoo.
- We went to Calgary. Then, we decided to visit the zoo.
- We went to Calgary, and then we decided to visit the zoo.

COMPARATIVE AND SUPERLATIVE FORMS OF ADJECTIVES AND ADVERBS

Comparatives and superlatives are special forms of adjectives and adverbs. They are used to compare things. When two things are compared, use the comparative form.

- A car is much more expensive than a lollipop.
- Five plus five is greater than four plus four.

When more than two things are compared, use the superlative form.

- That was the best movie I have ever seen.
- I wanted to buy the largest dog in the window.

The following chart provides some examples that compare the base form of an adjective or adverb with the comparative and **superlatives forms of the same word.**

Base	Comparative	Superlative
Fast	Faster	Fastest
Good	Better	Best
Wide	Wider	Widest
Bad	Worse	Worst
Quickly	More quickly	Most quickly
Harmful	More harmful	Most harmful

SUBORDINATE CLAUSES AND COORDINATING CONJUNCTIONS

A clause is a group of words containing a subject and a predicate. A subordinate clause is a group of words that cannot stand alone as a sentence. Using subordinate clauses allows you to create interesting sentences by combining ideas.

Example

- My sister, *who is a doctor*, has four children.
- While I *clean my room*, I like to listen to music.

The clauses "who is a doctor" and "while I clean my room" cannot stand alone as sentences and are therefore called subordinate clauses. Subordinate clauses add information to a sentence but are not complete ideas on their own.

Coordinating conjunctions are words used to join two clauses together. Some examples of coordinating conjunctions are for, and, not, but, or, yet, and so. These simple words can be used to join ideas and create complex sentences.

Example

- Wendy loved to read books but did not enjoy magazines.
- John heard the weather report and hurried home.
- The sun was shining brightly, yet the air was still cold.

Modifier Placement

As a general rule, a modifier, which is usually an adjective or an adverb, should be placed as closely as possible to the word being modified.

Example

Vague: Entering the room, the door was shut by mother.

Clear: Entering the room, mother shut the door.

Vague: At six years of age, my parents started me in piano.

Clear: [At six years of age], I started taking piano lessons.

CORRECT WORD USAGE

Consult a dictionary if you are unsure of what a word means or how it is spelled. The following words are frequently confused:

Lie, which means "to recline"
Lay, which means "to place"
- Father would lie down for a ten-minute nap after lunch.
- We were asked to lay our uniforms neatly on the shelf.

Accept, which means "to receive"
Except, which means "with the exception of"
- Jeremy will accept the reward on behalf of his brother.
- Everyone in the family except Nolan came down with the flu.

Its, which is a possessive pronoun
It's, which is a contraction of "it is"
- The cat injured its front paw.
- It's been snowing for three days.

Can, which means "are able to"
May, which means "are allowed to"
- Most children *can* print their own name.
- You *may* watch a movie on Saturday.

Whose, which means "belonging to whom"
Who's, which is a contraction of "who is"
- I don't know *whose* wallet is missing.
- *Who's* willing to help pick up this litter?

To, too, and two
- We need *to* decide whether *two* pies will be *too* much.

Their, there, they're
- The students will take their final exam on Friday morning.
- We decided there were enough people present to take a vote.
- The Smith family lived there for eight years.
- If they're arriving Tuesday, someone should meet them at the airport.

Punctuation

In your writing, try to follow the basic rules of correct punctuation to make your ideas clear. The following section explains usage for different punctuation marks.

Brackets and Parenthesis are similar, but they have slightly different uses.

Brackets [ ] enclose words that are inserted into direct quotations but are not part of the original quotation:

- "Once I found the stolen goods, I arrested [the accused] immediately," explained the officer.

Parentheses ( ) are used to include extra information that contributes to the meaning of a sentence but does not belong in the normal structure of the sentence.

- At that moment, in walked (she said earlier that she wouldn't be caught dead at Derek's house) my sister.

Em dashes are used to show a sudden break in the sentence, to separate an interrupting word from the rest of the sentence, to clearly set off an appositive phrase:

- I want to tell you first—so shut the door quickly.
- Marley shrugged off her uniform—lab coat, goggles, and rubber gloves—before entering the lab.
- Sam Gunther—the newly elected mayor—stepped up to the podium.

Hyphens are shorter than em dashes and are used differently. Hyphens are used to join the parts of some compound words, to separate parts of a compound modifier, in compound numbers from twenty-one to ninety-nine, to divide words at margins, and after some prefixes:

- Sister-in-law
- Great-aunt
- Half-hearted attempt
- Half-sister
- Forty-three

Semicolons connect independent clauses and form one sentence. A semicolon is useful when two clauses are closely related:

Example

- (two sentences) Lightning flashed. Thunder shook the valley.
- (compound sentence) Lightning flashed and thunder shook the valley.
- (semicolon) Lightning flashed; thunder shook the valley.

Capitalization

Although there are many special rules for capitalization, the following rules are the most important to practise for now:

- Capitalize the first words of sentence, including sentences used in quotations.
- Capitalize proper nouns, including any specific person or place (Jon Doe, Calgary, December).
- Always capitalize the word "I."
- Capitalize some abbreviations. For example, R.S.V.P. (please respond), WWF (World Wildlife Federation), Ave. (Avenue), Dr. (Doctor).
- Capitalize the main words in a title, such as "The Cat in the Hat" or "My Summer in Mexico."

Spelling

The following list contains words that are commonly misspelled:

- *Neighbour*
- *Definitely*
- *Occasionally*
- *Possession*
- *Column*
- *Calendar*
- *Committed*
- *Relevant*
- *Conscience*
- *Restaurant*
- *Rhyme*
- *Discipline*
- *Rhythm*
- *Embarrass*
- *Schedule*
- *Experience*
- *Foreign*
- *Weird*
- *Friend*
- *Mischievous*
- *Professional*

While computer programs often feature a spelling and grammar check, it is best to do your final check by reading your work out loud. Computer spelling and grammar checks will usually find obvious mistakes, but they should not be used as a substitute for reviewing your work yourself.

When reviewing your work, ask the following questions:

- Does it sound right?
- Does it look right?
- Does it make good sense?
- Does it flow logically from one idea to the next?

It is a good idea to print out your final draft . Leave it for a day or two, and then go back and read it again. You may notice some things you missed. You can fix these errors, and when you are happy with it, you can print a final draft to submit to your teacher. If you don't have the time to do this, ask your parents or a classmate to go over your work. Sometimes a fresh pair of eyes can spot mistakes you may have missed.

Enhance the Clarity
of Communication

ENHANCE THE CLARITY OF COMMUNICATION

ENHANCE AND IMPROVE

4.1.4.1 distinguish between the denotative and connotative meaning of words, and discuss effectiveness for achieving purpose and affecting audience

DENOTATION AND CONNOTATION

The dictionary definition of a word is its denotation. The alternate definitions a word may have associated with it refer to that word's connotation. Connotations of words come about and change over time, and they can be negative or positive.

When you read the word "spider," do you have an emotional response like "Yuck! Get it out of here! Step on it!" Or do you see spiders as fly killers, and beneficial to people? Your emotional response to a word is its connotative meaning. Thus, you can see how words can mean different things to different people.

In the following dictionary definition for the word cool, the denotative meaning is defined in numbers 1–6, 8, 9, and 10. The connotative meaning is defined in 7a and 7b.

cool (kŏŏl), *adj.* –er, -est, n., v. *–adj.* **1.** moderately cold. **2.** permitting relief from heat; a cool dress. **3.** not excited; calm. **4.** lacking in cordiality. **5.** calmly audacious. **6.** unresponsive; indifferent. **7.** Slang. a. great; excellent. b. socially adept. –n. **8.** a cool part, place, or time: *the cool of the evening.* **9.** calmness; composure. –v.i., v.t. **10.** to become or make cool

Usually, the denotative meaning of a word is easy to understand, because you have used it yourself, heard it or read it in context, or looked it up in a dictionary to discover its meaning. Connotative meanings of a word usually take some experience hearing that word used in a new and different way in order to understand it. Sometimes connotative meanings of a word will be so obscure that they might be classified as slang. For example, the word "bread" can be used to refer to money. Someone learning English as a second language, however, would probably be very confused if you used the word "bread" to refer to money without explaining it to them first.

The negative or positive connotations of some words depend on the context in which they are written. For example, look at a dictionary definition of the word "cheap":

cheap (chēp), *adj., -*er, -est, *adv —adj.* **1.** inexpensive. **2.** shoddy or inferior. **3.** costing little labor or trouble: *Talk is cheap.* **4.** mean or contemptible. **5.** of little value: *Life was cheap.* **6.** stingy; miserly. *—adv.* **7.** at a low price. **—cheap'ly**, *adv.* **—cheap'ness**, n.

A dictionary definition will always include denotative meanings of a word. But in this example, the second and fourth entries have very definite negative connotations. You might buy a cheap (inexpensive) pair of shoes, but that does not necessarily mean that they are cheap (shoddy or inferior). Or, the carpenter who came to remodel your kitchen may have been quite cheap (charging little for his labor), but he was by no means cheap (stingy or miserly). It is important that you always consider the denotative and connotative meanings of words in both your reading and your writing.

Connotative meanings of words are often biased. The writer using the word wants you to form the same opinion that he or she has. Bias is frequently a part of advertising and propaganda (the deliberate spreading of ideas or information to promote or harm a cause).

In advertising, words and visual images are carefully chosen, in order to persuade people to want and buy products. The following chart contains examples to illustrate the denotative and connotative meaning of words.

Word(s)	Denotative meaning	Connotative meaning
Dove	1. Any of numerous pigeons, esp. small wild pigeon 2. A gentle woman or child	Symbolizes peace and harmony
Rose	1. Any of a genus of usually prickly shrubs, with pinnate leaves and showy flowers having five petals in the wild state 2. The flower of a rose	Symbolizes love, especially when it is red

If you remember that the denotative meaning is the dictionary meaning because both words begin with "d", and the connotative meaning is the symbolic or emotional meaning, you will have no trouble distinguishing between the two.

Because connotative meanings can have positive or negative effects, they are often used for propaganda and persuasive purposes. You need to read carefully to make sure you are not influenced by a connotative meaning.

Think about the words "guerilla," "mercenary," "freedom-fighter," and "soldier." They can all refer to an individual participating in a military operation, but they all have very different connotations.

The word "guerilla," for example, sounds much more evil than "soldier" or "freedom-fighter."

The following list of words also contain different connotations: suffering, anguish, agony, heartache, and melancholy. The word "agony" sounds like a much worse state to be in than the words "heartache" or "melancholy."

EVERYDAY CONNOTATIONS

In everyday life, connotations, associations, experiences, and attitudes are attached to such terms as:

- Names of seasonal holidays and special days
  - Christmas
  - Birthday
  - Vacation
- Terms reflecting school life
  - Homework
  - Interviews
  - Essays
  - Detentions
  - Early dismissal
  - Spring break

As you can see, connotations can be either positive or negative. So while you can use your thesaurus to find words that have very similar meanings, connotations between words that are similar will vary a great deal. The best way to understand connotations is to read as much as possible. You will see different words used in many different ways and will get used to using words in different situations with different connotations.

Connotations in Advertising

Because advertising deliberately sets out to influence people emotionally rather than logically, connotations play an important role in how words are used in ads and commercials.

The term "glittering generality" is an advertising term that refers to words that are "loaded with positive connotations. Words and phrases such as "sparkling freshness," "whiter than white," and "top of the line" all have very positive associations. Using glittering generalities such as the words and phrases above automatically plants a positive response in the mind of the reader.

Negative Connotation

Negative connotations play on people's fears. You will see negative connotation in:

- Insurance advertising
- Health ads
- Warning ads such as anti-smoking commercials
- Recall documents

THINKING ABOUT CONNOTATIVE MEANING

The context in which a word is used provides clues to the intended meaning, whether it be denotative or connotative. Try one of the following as a simple mental exercise in thinking about connotations:

1. Look at three different magazine ads. Pick out words and phrases that seem to have connotations that would persuade people to buy the product or service. Try to explain the intended effect of those words and phrases.

2. Think of five words, such as "silver, father, friend, money, and genuine." Brainstorm some different connotative meanings associated with those words.

4.1.4.2 explore the derivation and use of words, phrases, and jargon, including variations in language, accent and dialect in Canadian communities and regions

GREEK AND LATIN ROOTS

Often, more than one Greek or Latin root is found when words are separated into parts or syllables. Thinking about the meanings of these roots can help you to figure out the meanings of more complex words.

For example, consider the word "manufacture." Broken down into syllables, it is man/u/fac/ture. Since "man" means hand, and "fac" means make, you can recognize the combined meaning of "make by hand." By breaking the word down, you come much closer to understanding the meaning of a fairly complex four-syllable word.

If you know the meaning of Greek and Latin prefixes, suffixes, and root words, you will be able to figure out the meaning of many unfamiliar words.

Remember that prefixes (*pre* = before) are placed before the stem and suffixes (*suf* = under) are placed after the stem.

Example

- incredible = in/cred/ible = in (not), cred (believe), ible (deserving) = seems to be impossible or unbelievable

Once you become familiar with commonly used prefixes and suffixes, your vocabulary will increase as you read more complex text.

FREQUENTLY USED FOREIGN WORDS

English is a language of borrowed words. As you have already seen, the majority of English words are derived from Greek, Latin, or Old English origins. As the English language has spread throughout the world through travel, trade, and settlement, many other cultures have also contributed words to the English language. A sampling of familiar foreign words has been provided, along with their culture of origin.

Dutch		African		French	
Ahoy	Apartheid	Banana	Jazz	Abhor	Able
Cruiser	Deck	Banjo	Jive	Force	Machine
Boss	Dock	Bongo	Jukebox	Account	Police
Bow	Drive	Coffee	Tango	Adolescence	Publicity
Bundle	Etch	Chimpanzee	Trek	Role	Routine
Buoy	Easel	Gumbo	Zebra	Art	Table
Clove	Freight				
Cookie	Gas				

German		Irish		Indian (Hindi)	
Frankfurter	Sauerkraut	Bog	Crag	Bangle	Guru
Hamburger	Strudel	Bother	Dig	Bandana	Karma
Kindergarten	Wiener	Boycott	Drum	Bungalow	Loot
Pretzel	Wurst	Brogue	Galore	Caravan	Pajamas
		Clan		Chai	Path
Hawaiian				Cheetah	Punch
Hula	Luau			Cot	Shampoo
Kahuna	Aloha			Cushy	Verandah

You might be surprised at the number of familiar words derived from a wide variety of languages. "Bagel" is Yiddish. American Native groups have contributed words like "Caribou" and "toboggan." The English language is constantly adopting new words from many different sources.

FREQUENTLY USED FOREIGN PHRASES

French, Latin, and Spanish phrases have become common in the English language. You probably use some of these phrases without considering their origin.

French	Latin	Spanish
à la carte—according to the menu, ordering individual items from the menu as opposed to complete dinners *bonjour*—good day, hello *bon voyage*—have a good trip *c'est la vie*—such is life *cul de sac*—dead end *n'est ce pas*—isn't that so? *toute de suite*—immediately	*e pluribus unum*—one from many *ad nauseum*—to the point of disgust *mea culpa*—my fault *status quo*—the way things are *sub rosa*—secret or confidential	*hasta la vista*—see you later *mi casa es su casa*—my house is your house

DIALECT

Dialect refers to a variety of language within a language that has its own pronunciations and can even use different words and phrases. Many people in Quebec, for example, speak a dialect of French that is different from the French spoken in France. A dialect is usually a product of the speaker's cultural or regional background.

Cockney, for example, is a dialect used by people native to south London. The musical My Fair Lady, based on the play *Pygmalion* by George Bernard Shaw, provides a wealth of examples of Cockney dialect from its main character, Eliza Doolittle. In an opening scene of the musical, Professor Higgins, a linguistics professor, is hiding behind a nearby pillar, copying every word she says. He is intrigued by how different Eliza's dialect is from formal English. Eliza is heard to remark, "I say, capt'n' n'baw ya flahr orf a pore gel," which Higgins translates into formal English as "I say, captain, now buy yourself a flower off a poor girl."

Writers employ dialect to make their characters more believable according to the setting in which the story takes place. Sometimes writers will even spell words according to how they sound in a certain dialect.

I say, capt'n' n'baw ya flahr orf a pore gel

ATTEND TO CONVENTIONS

4.2.1.3 use a variety of strategies to make effective transitions between sentences and paragraphs in our writing

TRANSITIONAL PHRASES

A transitional phrase is a way to show your reader the relationship between your ideas. These phrases unify your paragraphs and your entire essay because they tell your reader how an idea fits with the rest of the essay. If you were contrasting the study habits of boys and girls, you could signal this contrast with "however". If you were showing the way their study habits are alike, you could signal this relation with "similarly." If you were adding one idea to another, you could signal this with "also." You may be familiar with many of the transitional phrases that are used in good essay writing.

Transitional phrases are also known as transitional devices.

Transitional devices are words and phrases like: *because, also, in addition, nevertheless,* and *as a result.* These words show the relationship between ideas in the following example:

- In addition, the witness has already admitted to lying. Therefore, you must consider whether or not any of her evidence can be believed. On the other hand, other witnesses have confirmed some of her statements.

Careful writers use transitional devices to make the relationships between sections of an essay clear. Transitional devices can be used to show a sequence or to begin a paragraph by showing how the ideas in the paragraph are related to the ideas in the preceding paragraph.

- As you consider the evidence, you will have to keep in mind the fact that the witness has admitted to lying on three occasions. First, Next, And finally,…

- On the other hand, her evidence about the escape vehicle has been confirmed by…Therefore, you will have to decide how much weight to give to her statements about…

- To conclude, it seems that we can agree…

In a play, transition is provided through scene changes. In a novel, you begin a new chapter. Sometimes the chapter begins with a transitional phrase. A short story writer may use a transitional technique like starting a new paragraph to indicate a change in the plot or setting.

4.2.2.1 demonstrate the deliberate, conscientious, and independent application of a variety of editing and proofreading strategies to confirm spelling in own writing

SPELLING

By Grade 9, you are familiar with common English spelling patterns, learned basic spelling rules, and have been taught to use spelling resources like dictionaries and the spellcheck feature on computer. Use that knowledge to spell words correctly when writing. Keep personal lists for correct spelling, such as:

- Words misspelled in writing assignments
- Terms specific to different subjects

Spell the words that you use correctly in everyday life, not just for school assignments. Correct spelling is one of the attributes of a good communicator. The following section will provide some spelling review.

Basic Spelling Rules

ei or *ie*

- If the sound is a long e, put *i* before e except after *c*.
- If the sound is a long *a* (as in weigh), reverse this order.

Example

- long *e*: niece, thief, piece, perceive, receipt, receive
- long *a*: weight, vein, sleigh, veil, neighbour
- exceptions: height, science, either, their, weird

Doubling the Consonant

If the word is one syllable with one vowel and one final consonant, double the final consonant before an ending (except when the word ends in *x*).

Example

- shop + -*ed* = shopped
- wet + -*est* = wettest
- sun + -*y* = sunny
- tar + -*ed* = tarred
- wax + -*ed* = waxed

In words of more than one syllable, follow this rule if the final syllable is stressed.

Example

- begin + -*ing* = beginning
- occur + -*ed* = occurred
- permit + -*ing* = permitting

e + Ending with a Vowel

If the base word ends in a silent e, drop the e before adding an ending that begins with a vowel.

Example

- excite + -*able* = excitable
- love + -*ing* = loving

Exceptions are words that end in *ce* or *ge*; then the *e* stays.

Example

- courage + -*ous* = courageous
- change + -*able* = changeable
- notice + -*able* = noticeable

Changing *y* to i

When the base word ends in y, change the *y* to *i* before adding endings.

Example

- baby + *es* = babies
- carry + *es* = carries
- try + *ed* = tried

Forming Noun Plurals

Generally you add *s* to a noun to make it plural. However, there are a few exceptions that you need to learn.

If the noun ends in *s*, *ss*, *ch*, *sh*, *x*, or *z*, you add *es*.

Example

- glasses
- bushes
- foxes

If the noun ends in *y* with a consonant in front, you change the *y* to *i* and add *es*.

Example

- baby to babies
- sky to skies

Some nouns ending in f are changed to v before adding *es*.

Example,

- leaf to leaves
- dwarf to dwarves

If the noun ends in *o* with a consonant in front of the *o*, you add *es* unless the noun is a musical term.

Example

- potato to potatoes
- tomato to tomatoes
- but piano to pianos

Some words need a different word in the plural. These plurals are called irregular.

- mouse = mice
- tooth = teeth

Some words stay the same.

- sheep = sheep
- deer = deer
- fish = fish

ROOTS, AFFIXES, SYLLABLES, AND SPELLING

The root of a word is its most basic part.

Example

- Root word "act" related words "reaction," "transaction"
- An affix is anything that is added to the root of a word. An affix can be a prefix or a suffix.

A prefix is added on to the beginning of a word.

Example

- <u>pro</u> active
- <u>re</u> action

A suffix is added on to the end of a word.

Example

- practi<u>cal</u>
- beaut<u>ify</u>

A syllable is a component of a word that only has a single vowel sound.

Example

- beau/ti/fy 3 syllables
- con/trast 2 syllables

The spelling of a root may change when an affix is added.

Example

- excite<u>ment</u>   no change
- exci<u>ting</u>   silent e dropped

SPELLING TIPS WITH COMMON PREFIXES

- *ad* sometimes changes to *a*: amend, arise, ascend
- *ex* sometimes changes to *e*: emission, elastic
- *in* sometimes changes to
  - *il* before root words beginning with *l*: illegal, illogical
  - *im* before root words beginning with *m* or *p*: immovable, immeasurable
  - *ir* before root words beginning with *r*: irresponsible

Spelling Rules for Adding Suffixes

a) Drop the *e*.

Examples:

- imagine = imaginable
- excite = exciting

b) Keep the *e*.

Examples

- excite = excitement
- notice = noticeable

c) Double the final consonant (usually when it is preceded by a short vowel).

Example

- admit = admitted
- sag = sagged

d) Do not double the final consonant.

Examples

- defeat = defeated
- regret = regretful
- invert = inverting

e) Change the *y* to *i*.

Example

- friendly = friendliness
- carry = carried

f) Do not change the *y* to *i*.

Examples

- enjoy = enjoying
- cry = crying

Using syllables to break a word into natural parts helps you to spell more correctly.

Example

- dis – ap – point – ment

Syllable rules for diving words into parts

- after a prefix   dis/
- between double consonants   ap / point
- before a suffix   /ment

SOUNDING THE SYLLABLES

When you sound out the natural parts, or syllables, of a word, you are more likely to spell the word correctly.

Example

- mountain = mount/ain, NOT mount/i/an

Syllables and Inflection

Pay attention to the pronunciation of the word present in the following two sentences:

- Sylvia must present her report on Tuesday.

    The correct pronunciation is prē-sent

- The teacher saw that everyone was present.

    The correct pronunciation is prĕ-sent

The word present sounds different in each sentences, but both words are spelled the same. Another word for different pronunciation is inflection. Recognizing different inflections also helps you to spell words correctly.

Unaccented Syllable Patterns

Many English words belong to families of words with similar spelling patterns. When you keep this in mind when spelling, it can be easier to remember the patterns like pictures in your head, and to spell these groups correctly. The following examples have unaccented syllables with similar spelling patterns:

Examples

- Remark<u>able</u>, cap<u>able</u>, port<u>able</u>
- Ac<u>tive</u>, reac<u>tive</u>, mo<u>tive</u>
- Joy<u>ous</u>, por<u>ous</u>, marvel<u>ous</u>
- Tri<u>ckle</u>, fi<u>ckle</u>, pi<u>ckle</u>
- Nick<u>el</u>, weas<u>el</u>, dies<u>el</u>
- Loca<u>tion</u>, vaca<u>tion</u>, reac<u>tion</u>
- Loc<u>al</u>, voc<u>al</u>, verb<u>al</u>
- Disappoint<u>ment</u>, merri<u>ment</u>, experi<u>ment</u>
- Audi<u>ence</u>, experi<u>ence</u>, magnific<u>ence</u>

4.2.3.1 use quotation marks to distinguish words being discussed in own writing

REVIEW OF QUOTATION MARKS AND DASHES

QUOTATION MARKS

Use quotation marks at the beginning and end of all words in a **direct quotation** (someone's exact words). Watch for the use of quotation marks before and after a speech tag. Also notice the use of the comma after the speech tag (Alfred said) as in the first example.

Example

- Alfred said, "We are ready."
- "I'm finished the job," said Alfred. "We can go now."
- "When we are ready," said Alfred, "we will go."

Also notice that the closing quotation mark is placed after a comma or a period.

Closing quotation marks are also used with exclamation marks and question marks. When these punctuation marks belong to the sentence, they are placed outside the closing quotation marks.

Example

- Didn't you hear him say, "I'm in trouble"?

If the question mark belongs to the quotation, it is placed inside the quotation marks.

Example

- He said sadly, "Why is it always me?"

The same rules apply to end punctuation used for other purposes. Periods and commas belong inside the quotation marks. Exclamation and quotation marks belong either outside or inside the quotation marks, depending on whether they belong to the sentence as a whole or to the words inside the quotation marks.

- You could say that her acting was "over the top."
- I can't believe that's your "best effort."

Indirect quotations, or quotations that do not repeat exact words, never require quotation marks.

- Alfred asked if we were ready.
- Alfred said that he had finished the job and that we could go.

Quotation marks are also used to set off the titles of short stories and poems.

- Marjorie Pickthall wrote "Stars."

Quotation marks indicate that a word is being used in an unusual sense.

- "Housekeeping" on the space station is challenging.

Quotation marks can also show that a word is used **ironically**. When a word is used ironically, it has a meaning opposite to its literal meaning.

- It seems that your "help" has put this project three weeks behind.

QUOTES WITHIN QUOTES

It is seldom that you will have to quote something within a quotation.

Example

- When responding to the short story, "The Gift of the Magi," a student wrote, "When Della's hair is described as 'rippling and shining like a cascade of brown water,' it makes me realize even more how hard it must have been to make the decision to cut it."

Notice that sets of single quotation marks ('') are used within material that is already being quoted.

4.2.3.2 use dashes to show sentence breaks or interrupted speech, where appropriate in own writing

DASHES

The use of dashes has been explained elsewhere in your **KEY**, under "Vocabulary and Conventions" (3.3.2.3). Some further examples to illustrate sentence breaks and interrupted speech are shown below. Remember to use dashes sparingly.

Example

- Large numbers of immigrants from Eastern Europe—Russia, Poland, and Hungary—came to Canada after 1912.

KEY Strategies for Success on Tests

KEY STRATEGIES FOR SUCCESS ON TESTS

AN OVERVIEW OF THE TEST

This section is all about the skills and strategies you need to be successful on the Alberta Provincial Achievement Test for Grade 9 English Language Arts. It is designed for you to use together with your classroom learning and assignments.

FINDING OUT ABOUT THE TEST

Here are some questions you may wish to discuss with your teacher to help you prepare for the Provincial Achievement Test for Grade 9 English Language Arts:

1.	What is the format of the test?	The examination has two parts: Part A: Written Response and Part B: Reading. Each part is worth 50% of the total test.
2.	What will I be tested on?	Part A consists of two written assignments: one narrative or essay and one functional. Part B consists of questions based on reading selections from fiction, non-fiction, drama, poetry, and visual/non-fiction media.
3.	What must I bring for the test?	For Part A you may bring a print version of commercially published dictionaries or thesauri. For Part B no resources are allowed.
4.	Will there be graphics?	Yes, diagrams, pictures, and illustrations.
5.	How many types of each question are there?	Part A will have a narrative or essay writing prompt and a functional writing prompt. Part B will have 55 multiple-choice questions.

Having a good understanding of effective test taking skills can help you do well on the test. Being familiar with the question format may help you in preparing for quizzes, unit tests, or year-end tests.

THINGS TO CONSIDER WHEN TAKING A TEST

It is normal to feel anxious before you write a test. You can manage this anxiety by using the following strategies:

- Think positive thoughts. Imagine yourself doing well on the test.

- Make a conscious effort to relax by taking several slow, deep, controlled breaths. Concentrate on the air going in and out of your body.

- Before you begin the test, ask questions if you are unsure of anything.

- Jot down key words or phrases from any instructions your teacher gives you.

- Look over the entire test to find out the number and kinds of questions on the test.

- Read each question closely, and reread if necessary.

- Pay close attention to key vocabulary words. Sometimes, these words are **bolded** or *italicized*, and they are usually important words in the question.

- If you are putting your answers on an answer sheet, mark your answers carefully. Always print clearly. If you wish to change an answer, erase the mark completely, and ensure that your final answer is darker than the one you have erased.

- Use highlighting to note directions, key words, and vocabulary that you find confusing or that are important to answering the question.

- Double-check to make sure you have answered everything before handing in your test.

- When taking tests, students often overlook the easy words. Failure to pay close attention to these words can result in an incorrect answer. One way to avoid this is to be aware of these words and to underline, circle, or highlight them while you are taking the test.

- Even though some words are easy to understand, they can change the meaning of the entire question, so it is important that you pay attention to them. Here are some examples.

all	always	most likely	probably	best	not
difference	usually	except	most	unlikely	likely

Example

1. During the race, Susan is **most likely** feeling

    A. sad

    B. weak

    C. scared

    D. determined

HELPFUL STRATEGIES FOR ANSWERING MULTIPLE-CHOICE QUESTIONS

A multiple-choice question gives you some information and then asks you to select an answer from four choices. Each question has one correct answer. The other choices are distractors, which are incorrect. The following strategies can help you when answering multiple-choice questions:

- Quickly skim through the entire test. Find out how many questions there are, and plan your time accordingly.

- Read and reread questions carefully. Underline key words, and try to think of an answer before looking at the choices.

- If there is a graphic, look at the graphic, read the question, and go back to the graphic. Then, you may want to underline the important information from the question.

- Carefully read the choices. Read the question first and then each choice that goes with it.

- When choosing an answer, try to eliminate those choices that are clearly wrong or do not make sense.

- Some questions may ask you to select the best answer. These questions will always include words like *best*, *most appropriate*, or *most likely*. All of the choices will be correct to some degree, but one of the choices will be better than the others in some way. Carefully read all four choices before choosing the answer you think is the best.

- If you do not know the answer, or if the question does not make sense to you, it is better to guess than to leave it blank.

- Do not spend too much time on any one question. Make a mark (*) beside a difficult question, and come back to it later. If you are leaving a question to come back to later, make sure you also leave the space on the answer sheet, if you are using one.

- Remember to go back to the difficult questions at the end of the test; sometimes, clues are given throughout the test that will provide you with answers.

- Note any negative words like *no* or *not*, and be sure your answer fits the question.

- Before changing an answer, be sure you have a very good reason to do so.

- Do not look for patterns on your answer sheet, if you are using one.

HELPFUL STRATEGIES FOR ANSWERING WRITTEN-RESPONSE QUESTIONS

A written response requires you to respond to a question or directive indicated by words such as *explain*, *predict*, *list*, *describe*, *show your work*, *solve*, or *calculate*. The following strategies can help you when answering written-response questions:

- Read and reread the question carefully.

- Recognize and pay close attention to directing words such as *explain*, *show your work*, and *describe*.

- Underline key words and phrases that indicate what is required in your answer, such as *explain*, *estimate*, *answer*, *calculate*, or *show your work*.

- Write down rough, point-form notes regarding the information you want to include in your answer.

- Think about what you want to say, and organize information and ideas in a coherent and concise manner within the time limit you have for the question.

- Be sure to answer every part of the question that is asked.

- Include as much information as you can when you are asked to explain your thinking.

- Include a picture or diagram if it will help to explain your thinking.

- Try to put your final answer to a problem in a complete sentence to be sure it is reasonable.

- Reread your response to ensure you have answered the question.

- Ask yourself if your answer makes sense.

- Ask yourself if your answer sounds right.

- Use appropriate subject vocabulary and terms in your response

TEST PREPARATION COUNTDOWN

If you develop a plan for studying and test preparation, you will perform well on tests.

Here is a general plan to follow seven days before you write a test.

COUNTDOWN: 7 DAYS BEFORE THE TEST

1. Use "Finding Out about the Test" to help you make your own personal test preparation plan.

2. Review the following information:

    – Areas to be included on the test

    – Types of test items

    – General and specific test tips

3. Start preparing for the test at least seven days before the test. Develop your test preparation plan, and set time aside to prepare and study.

COUNTDOWN: 6, 5, 4, 3, 2 DAYS BEFORE THE TEST

1. Review old homework assignments, quizzes, and tests.

2. Rework problems on quizzes and tests to make sure you still know how to solve them.

3. Correct any errors made on quizzes and tests.

4. Review key concepts, processes, formulas, and vocabulary.

5. Create practice test questions for yourself, and answer them. Work out many sample problems.

COUNTDOWN: THE NIGHT BEFORE THE TEST

1. Use the night before the test for final preparation, which includes reviewing and gathering materials needed for the test before going to bed.

2. Most importantly, get a good night's rest, and know you have done everything possible to do well on the test.

TEST DAY

1. Eat a healthy and nutritious breakfast.

2. Ensure you have all the necessary materials.

3. Think positive thoughts, such as "I can do this," "I am ready," and "I know I can do well."

4. Arrive at your school early, so you are not rushing, which can cause you anxiety and stress.

SUMMARY OF HOW TO BE SUCCESSFUL DURING A TEST

You may find some of the following strategies useful for writing a test:

- Take two or three deep breaths to help you relax.

- Read the directions carefully, and underline, circle, or highlight any important words.

- Look over the entire test to understand what you will need to do.

- Budget your time.

- Begin with an easy question or a question you know you can answer correctly rather than follow the numerical question order of the test.

- If you cannot remember how to answer a question, try repeating the deep breathing and physical relaxation activities. Then, move on to visualization and positive self-talk to get yourself going.

- When answering questions with graphics (pictures, diagrams, tables, or graphs), look at the question carefully, and use the following steps:

  1. Read the title of the graphic and any key words.

  2. Read the test question carefully to figure out what information you need to find in the graphic.

  3. Go back to the graphic to find the information you need.

- Write down anything you remember about the subject on the reverse side of your test paper. This activity sometimes helps to remind you that you do know something and are capable of writing the test.

- Look over your test when you have finished, and double-check your answers to be sure you did not forget anything.

NOTES

Writing the Provincial Achievement Test—Part A

WRITING THE PROVINCIAL ACHIEVEMENT TEST—PART A

WRITING TASKS

Your Grade 9 Provincial Writing Achievement Test (Part A) consists of two writing assignments:

1. Narrative/Essay Assignment

2. Functional Writing Assignment

NARRATIVE/ESSAY ASSIGNMENT

After reading a writing prompt, you will be asked to write either a narrative (story) or an essay that is related to the prompt.

Tip: Be sure your writing is related to the prompt. If you are off topic, your story or essay will be penalized with a lower mark in the content category.

The marking categories for this assignment include five separate categories:
- Content
- Organization
- Sentence structure
- Vocabulary
- Conventions

Content and organization are weighted to be worth twice as much as the the other scoring categories.

FUNCTIONAL WRITING ASSIGNMENT

This piece of writing will measure your skill in practical, "real-life" writing. You will be asked to write a business letter on an assigned topic, and to address a blank envelope correctly.

Tip: Use correct business letter format, and be sure your letter follows the topic.

If your letter is off topic, it will receive a mark of **insufficient**, which translates as zero. Small mistakes in formatting can result in a lower grade. Double-check your formatting for this section to ensure that everything has been done correctly.

There are only two marking categories for the letter:
- Content
- Content management

IMPROVING YOUR WRITING

In this section of your *KEY*, you will find the following learning tools:
- Writing rubrics to show you how the two writing assignments are marked.
- "Exemplars" or writing samples of narratives, essays, and business letters, on several different topics and at three levels of writing.

Level 3: Acceptable standard

Level 4: Approaching Standard of Excellence

Level 5: Meeting or Exceeding Standard of Excellence
- Marking rationales for all the writing samples, explaining how each mark was achieved.

Think about what is common among all of the high-scoring examples. Descriptive, precise writing and attention to details like spelling and punctuation will be rewarded with a higher score. If you have time during the test, read your writing over in your head. You will often catch mistakes like missing words or incomplete sentences using this technique.

Using the writing examples as a guide, try to recognize what you can do to improve the level of your own writing. You can achieve a higher level of performance whether or not you find writing difficult. Practise the type of writing you see in the level 4 and 5 assignments. Markers are specifically looking for the skills suggested in the marking rubrics.

TIPS FOR TAKING PROVINCIAL TESTS

Keep in mind that these tips will work for many other tests as well.

1. General Tips
   - Overview
   - Make sure you know the time limits.
   - Check that you have all the materials you will need, such as pencil, eraser, calculator, thesaurus, etc.
   - Skim over test booklet to see sections, headings, types of questions, etc.

2. Read instructions thoroughly, paying attention to key words and phrases.

3. Ask questions if you cannot understand the instructions or working of a question, etc.

4. Answer easier questions first. Sometimes they will help you understand the harder ones, or at least you can give them more time and attention.

5. After finishing, skim back over the test to make sure you have not missed anything.

TIPS FOR MULTIPLE-CHOICE TESTS

1. Skim first. Once you see the total number of questions, you can budget your time.

2. If a question is slowing you down, circle the number of the question for later. Be sure you have entered an answer, even if it is a guess, before handing your answer key in.

3. As you read the question, underline key words, and cover the choices. Try to think of the answer before you look at the alternatives.

4. Look at the choices. Which one seems closest to the one you came up with yourself?

5. If more than one answer looks right, cross out any you know to be incorrect. This narrows down your choices to make the final choice easier.

6. Be sure to check back for any missed questions. If you have time, check your answer key against the questions before handing it in to the supervisor.

FUNCTIONAL WRITING TIPS

HOW TO FORMAT A LETTER

There are three standard formats used when writing a letter. In the test, you may select any one of these three, but be careful to use the chosen format consistently throughout the letter. The consistent application of one format makes the letter appear attractive and professional to the reader.

Block Format

Notice that every letter part lines up along the left margin. Paragraphs in the body are not indented. Divisions (between parts, paragraphs) are indicated with double spaces.

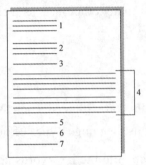

Semi-block Format

The only difference in this format is that the paragraphs in the body are indented.

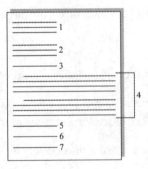

Modified Block Format

The entire letter remains in block format. The heading, closing, and signature are "modified" by being moved to run along the right margin.

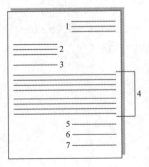

Parts of the Business Letter

The numbers in the headings correspond to the diagrams on the preceding page.

Note: Students should double-space word-processed work in order to make revisions more easily. This should be applied only to the body of the letter and not to the other parts.

1. Heading

The heading consists of your address and the date.

PO Box 4216 Toronto ON L4P 1S2 May 19, 2011	212-13936 16 St Toronto ON L4P 1S2 May 19, 2011

2. Inside Address

The inside address consists of the name and address of the person to whom you are writing. It usually appears four lines below the heading if a word processor is used or one line below if it is handwritten.

> Olivia Millar, President
> The Reading Room
> 14216 57 Ave
> Toronto ON L2T 6H4

3. Salutation

The most traditional salutation or greeting for a business letter is Dear followed by Mr., Ms., Mrs., or Miss, and the person's last name, followed by a colon.

Dear Mr. Smith:	Dear Mrs. Brown:
Dear F. Black:	Dear Miss Green:

4. Body

The body is the main part of the letter in which you write what you have to say to the addressee. Skip one line after the salutation.

- Be concise. Ensure that sufficient information is given so that your purpose is clearly understood and your request is well received.
- Business letters are usually formal, so the language that you use should also be formal.

5. Closing

The closing is the ending to your letter. It appears at the bottom of the letter, directly under the body. Only the first word in the closing should be capitalized. It is always followed by a comma.

Yours truly,	Sincerely,

6. Signature

The signature is your full name signed. Your signature should appear directly below the closing. It should always be written in ink.

7. Your Name Printed

Addressing an Envelope

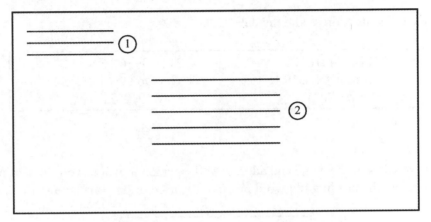

1. Return Address

The return address is the name and address of the person sending the letter. The return address appears in the top left corner of the envelope and consists of your name, post office box number (if applicable), apartment or unit number followed by a hyphen (if applicable), street address (if applicable), city or town, province, and postal code.

SAM RYAN PO BOX 4216 TORONTO ON L4P 1S2 MAY 19, 2011	SAM RYAN 212-13936 16 ST TORONTO ON L4P 1S2 MAY 19, 2011

2. Mailing Address

The mailing address is the name and address to which the letter is being sent. It always appears in the centre of the envelope. In a business letter, the address on the envelope is the same as the inside address of the letter. There may be separate lines for the title of the addressee (Editor, Director, President), the division or department in which the person works, and the name of his or her company, business, or organization.

OLIVIA MILLAR, PRESIDENT
THE READING ROOM
14216 57 AVE
TORONTO ON L2T 6H4

Envelope Format

- Addresses should be typed or written in upper-case or block letters.
- All lines of the addresses must be formatted with a uniform left margin.
- Punctuation marks (such as commas and periods) should not be used unless they are part of a place name (e.g., ST. JOHN'S).
- The postal code should always appear on the same line as the municipality and province or territory name, and should be separated from the province by two spaces.
- The two-letter abbreviation for the province name should be used wherever possible; abbreviations for street (ST), avenue (AVE), and boulevard (BLVD) should also be used.
- The return address should be formatted in the same way as the mailing address.

For more information, refer to the "Addressing Guidelines" in the Canada Postal Guide on the Canada Post website at www.canadapost.ca.

The following list contains the correct Canada Post abbreviations for Canadian provinces and territories:

Example

Province	Abbreviation
Alberta	AB
British Columbia	BC
Manitoba	MB
New Brunswick	NB
Newfoundland and Labrador	NL
Northwest Territories	NT
Nova Scotia	NS
Nunavut	NU
Ontario	ON
Prince Edward Island	PE
Quebec	QC or PQ
Saskatchewan	SK
Yukon	YT

REVIEWING AND REVISING YOUR WORK

It is important to review and revise all of your written work. There are many methods that can be helpful. You may wish to use a memory device or mnemonic device to help revise your work. The example given below is referred to as the RADS device. It is one method of reviewing your work. Use RADS device to analyze your written piece as a whole (for an essay, narrative, or business letter) and to analyze each individual paragraph.

R—Rearrange

- Are my ideas in the best possible order?
- Is there a better order (such as time or importance) that I should use?
- Does one idea flow logically to another?
- Are any ideas out of place?

A—Add

- Do I need to add ideas to make my position more convincing?
- Do I need to add detail?
- Do I need to add examples?
- Do I need to add description by including adjectives, adverbs and interesting verbs?
- Do I need to create a stronger effect by adding imagery, similes, or metaphors?
- Do I need to add some transition words or phrases to help link ideas?

D—Delete

- Do I need to delete any ideas that do not support my main idea in each paragraph?
- Do I need to delete any ideas that do not contribute to the point I am trying to make?
- Do I need to delete any words that are not appropriate for the tone I want to set in my writing?
- Do I need to delete any repetitive words or ideas?

S—Substitute

- Can I substitute any ideas I have recently thought of that are better than the ones I have written down?
- Can I substitute a stronger idea for a weak idea?
- Can I substitute better words for ordinary or unsuitable words by using a thesaurus to help me?
- Can I substitute better linking words or phrases with those that are not as effective?

NARRATIVE/ESSAY SCORING RUBRIC

Your writing will be marked using the following scoring rubric:

Content

> #### *Focus*
>
> When marking **Content** appropriate for the Grade 9 Narrative/Essay Writing Assignment, the marker should consider how effectively the student
> - explores the topic
> - establishes a purpose
> - presents ideas
> - supports the response
> - considers the reader

Excellent **E**	• The student's exploration of the topic is insightful and/or imaginative. • The student's purpose, whether stated or implied, is deliberate. • The ideas presented by the student are perceptive and/or carefully chosen. • Supporting details are precise and/or original. • The writing is confident and/or creative and holds the reader's interest.
Proficient **Pf**	• The student's exploration of the topic is adept and/or plausible. • The student's purpose, whether stated or implied, is intentional. • The ideas presented by the student are thoughtful and/or sound. • Supporting details are specific and/or apt. • The writing is considered and/or elaborated and draws the reader's interest.
Satisfactory **S**	• The student's exploration of the topic is clear and/or logical. • The student's purpose, whether stated or implied, is evident. • The ideas presented by the student are appropriate and/or predictable. • Supporting details are relevant and/or generic. • The writing is straightforward and/or generalized and occasionally appeals to the reader's interest.
Limited **L**	• The student's exploration of the topic is tenuous and/or simplistic. • The student's purpose, whether stated or implied, is vague. • The ideas presented by the student are superficial and/or ambiguous. • Supporting details are imprecise and/or abbreviated. • The writing is uncertain and/or incomplete and does not appeal to the reader's interest.

Poor **P**	• The student's exploration of the topic is minimal and/or tangential. • The student's purpose, whether stated or implied, is insubstantial. • The ideas presented by the student are overgeneralized and/or underdeveloped. • Supporting details are irrelevant and/or scant. • The writing is confusing and/or lacks validity and does not interest the reader.
Insufficient **INS**	• The marker can discern no evidence of an attempt to address the task presented in the assignment, or the student has written so little that it is not possible to assess **Content**.

Note: Content and Organization are weighted to be worth twice as much as the other scoring categories.

Student work must address the task presented in the assignment. Responses that are completely unrelated to the topic and/or prompts will be awarded a score of Insufficient.

Organization

> ### *Focus*
>
> When marking **Organization** appropriate for the Grade 9 Narrative/Essay Writing Assignment, the marker should consider how effectively the writing demonstrates
> • focus
> • coherent order
> • connections between events and/or details
> • closure

Excellent **E**	• The introduction is engaging and skillfully establishes a focus that is consistently sustained. • Events and/or details are developed in a judicious order, and coherence is maintained. • Transitions, either explicit or implicit, fluently connect events and/or details within sentences and/or between paragraphs. • Closure is effective and related to the focus.
Proficient **Pf**	• The introduction is purposeful and clearly establishes a focus that is capably sustained. • Events and/or details are developed in a sensible order, and coherence is generally maintained. • Transitions, either explicit or implicit, clearly connect events and/or details within sentences and/or between paragraphs. • Closure is appropriate and related to the focus.

Satisfactory **S**	• The introduction is functional and establishes a focus that is generally sustained. • Events and/or details are developed in a discernible order, although coherence may falter occasionally. • Transitions, either explicit or implicit, tend to be mechanical and are generally • used to connect events and/or details within sentences and/or between paragraphs. • Closure is related to the focus and is mechanical and/or artificial.
Limited **L**	• The introduction lacks purpose and/or is not functional; any focus established provides little direction and/or is not sustained. • The development of events and/or details is not clearly discernible, and coherence falters frequently. • Transitions, either explicit or implicit, are lacking and/or indiscriminately used to connect events and/or details within sentences and/or between paragraphs. • Closure is abrupt, contrived, and/or unrelated to the focus.
Poor **P**	• The introduction, if present, is obscure and/or ineffective; any focus established provides no direction and/or is undeveloped. • The development of events and/or details is haphazard and/or incoherent. • Transitions, either explicit or implicit, are absent and/or inappropriately used to connect events and/or details within sentences and/or between paragraphs. • Closure is ineffectual or missing.
Insufficient **INS**	• The response has been awarded an **INS** for **Content**

Note: Content and Organization are weighted to be worth twice as much as the other scoring categories.

Sentence Structure

> ## *Focus*
>
> When marking **Sentence Structure** appropriate for the Grade 9 Narrative/Essay Writing Assignment, the marker should consider the extent to which
> - sentence structure is controlled
> - sentence type and sentence length are effective and varied
> - sentence beginnings are varied
>
> **Proportion of error to length and complexity of response must be considered.**

Excellent **E**	• Sentence structure is effectively and consistently controlled. • Sentence type and sentence length are consistently effective and varied. • Sentence beginnings are consistently varied.
Proficient **Pf**	• Sentence structure is consistently controlled. • Sentence type and sentence length are usually effective and varied. • Sentence beginnings are often varied.
Satisfactory **S**	• Sentence structure is generally controlled, but lapses may occasionally impede meaning. • Sentence type and sentence length are sometimes effective and/or varied. • Some variety of sentence beginnings is evident.
Limited **L**	• Sentence structure often lacks control, and this may impede meaning. • Sentence type and sentence length are seldom effective and/or varied; syntactic structures are frequently awkward. • There is little variety of sentence beginnings.
Poor **P**	• Sentence structure generally lacks control, and this often impedes meaning. • There is essentially no variation in sentence type or sentence length; syntactic structures are unintelligible. • There is essentially no variety of sentence beginnings.
Insufficient **INS**	• The response has been awarded an **INS** for **Content**.

Vocabulary

> ### *Focus*
>
> When marking **Vocabulary** appropriate for the Grade 9 Narrative/Essay Writing Assignment, the marker should consider the
> - accuracy of the words and expressions
> - effectiveness of the words and expressions
> - appropriateness and effectiveness of the voice/tone created by the student
>
> **Proportion of error to length and complexity of response must be considered.**

Excellent **E**	• Words and expressions are used accurately and deliberately. • Precise words and expressions are used to create vivid images and/or to enrich details. • The voice/tone created by the student is convincing.
Proficient **Pf**	• Words and expressions are often used accurately. • Specific words and expressions show some evidence of careful selection and/or some awareness of connotative effect. • The voice/tone created by the student is distinct.
Satisfactory **S**	• Words and expressions are generally used appropriately. • General words and expressions are used adequately to clarify meaning. • The voice/tone created by the student is discernible but may be inconsistent or uneven.
Limited **L**	• Words and expressions are often used inexactly. • Imprecise words and expressions predominate; specific words, if present, may be improperly used. • The voice/tone created by the student is not clearly established or is indistinct.
Poor **P**	• Words and expressions are generally used inaccurately. • Ineffective words and expressions predominate; specific words, if present, are frequently misused. • The voice/tone created by the student is not evident or is indiscreet.
Insufficient **INS**	• The response has been awarded an **INS** for **Content**.

Conventions

> ### *Focus*
>
> When marking **Conventions** appropriate for the Grade 9 Narrative/Essay Writing Assignment, the marker should consider the extent to which the student has control of
> - mechanics (spelling, punctuation, capitalization, indentation for new speakers, etc.) and usage (subject-verb agreement, pronoun-antecedent agreement, etc.)
> - clarity and flow of the response
>
> **Proportion of error to length and complexity of response must be considered.**

Excellent **E**	• The quality of the writing is enhanced because it is essentially error-free. • Any errors that are present do not reduce clarity and/or do not interrupt the flow of the response.
Proficient **Pf**	• The quality of the writing is sustained because it contains only minor convention errors. • Any errors that are present rarely reduce clarity and/or seldom interrupt the flow of the response.
Satisfactory **S**	• The quality of the writing is sustained through generally correct use of conventions. • Errors occasionally reduce clarity and/or sometimes interrupt the flow of the response.
Limited **L**	• The quality of the writing is weakened by the frequently incorrect use of conventions. • Errors blur clarity and/or interrupt the flow of the response.
Poor **P**	• The quality of the writing is impaired by the consistently incorrect use of conventions. • Errors severely reduce clarity and/or impede the flow of the response.
Insufficient **INS**	• The response has been awarded an **INS** for **Content**.

FUNCTIONAL WRITING SCORING RUBRIC

Your writing will be marked using the following scoring rubric:

Content

> #### *Focus*
>
> When marking Content appropriate for the Grade 9 Functional Writing Assignment, the marker should consider the extent to which ideas and development of the topic are effective
> - the purpose of the assignment is fulfilled with complete and relevant information
> - the tone is appropriate for a business letter, and awareness of audience is evident

Excellent **E**	• The ideas are perceptive, and development of the topic is clear and effective. • Pertinent information is presented, and this information is enhanced by precise details that effectively fulfill the purpose of the assignment. • A tone appropriate for the addressee is skillfully maintained.
Proficient **Pf**	• The ideas are thoughtful, and development of the topic is generally effective. • Significant information is presented, and this information is substantiated by specific details that fulfill the purpose of the assignment. • A tone appropriate for the addressee is clearly maintained.
Satisfactory **S**	• The ideas are appropriate, and development of the topic is adequate. • Relevant information is presented, and this information is supported by enough detail to fulfill the purpose of the assignment • A tone appropriate for the addressee is generally maintained.
Limited **L**	• The ideas are superficial and/or flawed, and development of the topic is inadequate. • Information presented is imprecise and/or undiscerning. Supporting details are insignificant and/or lacking. The purpose of the assignment is only partially fulfilled. • A tone appropriate for the addressee is evident but not maintained.
Poor **P**	• The ideas are overgeneralized and/or misconstrued, and development of the topic is ineffective. • Information is irrelevant and/or missing. Supporting details are obscure and/or absent. The purpose of the assignment is not fulfilled. • Little awareness of a tone appropriate for the addressee is evident.
Insufficient **INS**	• The marker can discern no evidence of an attempt to address the task presented in the assignment, or the student has written so little that it is not possible to assess **Content**.

Note: Content and Content Management are equally weighted.

> Student work must address the task presented in the assignment. Letters that are completely unrelated to the context established in the assignment will be awarded a score of **Insufficient**.

Content Management

	Focus
	When marking Content Management appropriate for the Grade 9 Functional Writing Assignment, the marker should consider the extent to which • words and expressions are used accurately and effectively • sentence structure, usage, and mechanics (spelling, punctuation, etc.) are controlled • the formats of an envelope and a business letter are consistently applied **Proportion of error to length and complexity of response must be considered.**

Excellent **E**	• Words and expressions used are consistently accurate and effective. • The writing demonstrates confident and consistent control of correct sentence structure, usage, and mechanics. Errors that may be present do not impede meaning. • The envelope and letter are essentially free from format errors and/or omissions.
Proficient **Pf**	• Words and expressions used are usually accurate and effective. • The writing demonstrates competent and generally consistent control of correct sentence structure, usage, and mechanics. Errors that are present rarely impede meaning. • The envelope and letter contain few format errors and/or omissions.
Satisfactory **S**	• Words and expressions used are generally accurate and occasionally effective. • The writing demonstrates basic control of correct sentence structure, usage, and mechanics. Errors may occasionally impede meaning. • The envelope and letter contain occasional format errors and/or omissions.
Limited **L**	• Words and expressions used are frequently vague and/or inexact. • The writing demonstrates faltering control of correct sentence structure, usage, and mechanics. Errors frequently impede meaning. • The envelope and letter contain frequent format errors and/or omissions.
Poor **P**	• Words and expressions used are inaccurate and/or misused. • The writing demonstrates a lack of control of correct sentence structure, usage, and mechanics. Errors severely impede meaning. • The envelope and letter contain numerous and glaring format errors and/or omissions.
Insufficient **INS**	• The response has been awarded an **INS** for **Content**.

Note: Content and Content Management are equally weighted.

NARRATIVE WRITING PROMPT ONE

Assignment

Write a narrative or essay to show how a negative situation can be turned into something positive. You may write about yourself or other people, real or fictional. You may set your writing in the past, present, or future.

Ideas

The following material may give you ideas for your writing. **You do not have to use any of it.** Consider your own ideas gained through reading, listening, viewing, discussing, thinking, or imagining.

- You break a leg and end up in hospital—this experience so moves you that you decide to become a doctor.

- You are fired from you job—you find a much better one two days later that has more opportunity for you to learn and grow.

- You fail the end-of-year exams and your parents make you go to summer school—you meet new and great friends who are a positive influence on you.

- Your parents ground you for the weekend—home alone, you catch a robber entering your house and you are hailed a hero by the neighbourhood.

- Your team loses a very important sports game—your team is picked for the tournament's "Best Sportsmanship" trophy and you go to the next tournament anyway.

- You are out hiking with some friends and you take a wrong turn in the forest—you find two orphaned bear cubs that would surely have died if you had not been there to rescue them.

- Your parents move to another town/city/country and, against your wishes, you are made to go with them—at your new home you discover there are opportunities for you to do things/play sports/join clubs that were never present in your previous town/city/country.

- While driving the family car, you are in a minor car accident that damages the car—your parents insist that you help pay for the repairs so you get a job at a garage where you learn all about car maintenance, as well as being paid.

- The option course that you want to take is full so you have to take another course instead—by moving out of your comfort zone, you discover that you have hidden talents of which you were unaware.

- You are in an accident that leaves you in a wheelchair—you join a sports league for paraplegics and make the Canadian Olympic team for one of the sports. Not only do you get to go to the Olympic games but you also do a lot of traveling with your sport.

- You have to forfeit a winning prize for four to Los Angeles (all expenses paid) because your parents can't get time off work—when the promoters hear the reason, they give you a seven-day Caribbean cruise at a time when your parents will be able to accompany you.

When writing, be sure to:
- Consider your **audience**
- Focus on your purpose and **point of view**
- **Organize** your thoughts appropriately in sentences and paragraphs
- Use **vocabulary** that is interesting and effective
- **Edit** your work directly on your writing
- **Budget** your time

STUDENT EXEMPLARS AND RATIONALES NARRATIVE WRITING PROMPT ONE

EXEMPLAR SCORE SATISFACTORY—NARRATIVE

TURNABOUT

Usually Sarah Gustafson paid close attention in Miss Monahan's English class. This time, Sarah had no idea what the question was that Miss Monahan had just asked her. Sarah was thinking about the message she had read on her phone when she left to use the washroom.

Most of the students used washroom breaks to quickly check their text messages. Most were from friends—but today was different. On Sarah's phone was a mean text message about her being overweight.

Who could have sent the text? Sarah looked around the room. Everyone seemed busy over their work, but her eyes rested on Marnie Solomon. Marnie did come across as kind of snobby, but…

At noon, Sarah shared her concerns with her best friends, Larry and Karen. "And besides, this isn't the first time. When I was in our chat room on the weekend, someone had typed: 'Who looks like this?' followed by a piggy flying. They then typed: S.G. —my initials—with two smiles. Sure, I'm a bit overweight, but Mom told me not to worry because it runs in her family. She says I'll be thinner by the end of my teens, like she was." Larry suggested bringing the message up at the rap session that Miss Monahan allowed during Homeroom Period every Friday. She allowed pretty much any topic of discussion. The student who raised the issue would host the discussion, and everyone could participate.

"Good idea, Larry," agreed Karen. They headed off to ask Miss Monahan if they could lead the topic together.

Finally, it was Friday afternoon, last period. Everyone stared as Karen, Larry, and Sarah headed to the front of the class. Why were three people leading today, and what was the topic? Sarah noticed that Marnie was looking down at her hands.

"This is kind of unusual…." Larry spoke first… "Karen and I are here to support our friend Sarah. I'm going to let Sarah tell you herself what happened last weekend."

Sarah was a bit nervous to begin with, because the topic was so personal. However, she ended up leading an interesting discussion of how a message can hurt someone. When the bell rang, no one was anxious to leave.

On the way home, Marnie ran till she was out of breath to catch up with Sarah. "How did you know it was me?"

"I didn't." Sarah kept looking down.

"But how…. I was just sure you knew!"

"Not really…. I did think a few things about you, but then I told myself that I was being silly."

"You weren't being silly. "I was actually getting quite jealous of you and Larry and Karen. You seemed to be having fun and I wasn't. When my best friend Rosemary moved to Calgary there was no one special at school for me. I guess I was feeling sorry for myself…"

Sarah raised her head to stop Marnie. "I'm no better. I was calling you a snob to myself. I'm sorry about Rosemary. How about joining our research team… Karen and Larry and I need another person."

"Really?" Giggling and talking like old friends, the two girls moved off down the street together. Everything was going to be just fine from now on.

RATIONALE FOR STUDENT EXEMPLAR SATISFACTORY NARRATIVE

Title: Turnabout

Score	Reporting Category
S	**Content** • **The student's exploration of the topic is clear and logical.** A student deals positively with a negative situation caused by a rude text message. • **The student's purpose** (to show how a teenager deals with the hurt and anger she feels as a 'victim') is **implied** but **evident**. • **The ideas presented by the student** (a girl receives a demeaning text message, gains the support of her two best friends and a sympathetic teacher, and conducts a class discussion dealing with issues of respect for peers) are **appropriate** and **predictable**. • **Supporting details**, such as "mean text message" and "Sure, I'm a bit overweight" are **relevant** but **generic**. • **The writing is straightforward** and **generalized** as in "Larry suggested bringing the message up at the rap session that Miss Monahan allowed…" and **occasionally appeals to the reader's interest** through a detail such as "Everyone stared as Karen, Larry, and Sarah headed to the front of the class."
S	**Organization** • **The introduction is functional and establishes a focus** by establishing the reason for Sarah's lack of attention upon returning from the washroom, and the focus on Sarah's plight is **generally sustained.** • **Events are developed in a discernible order** through Sarah's being thrown off by the message, asking friends for advice at noon, and proceeding with a plan to request the class rap session for discussing peer relationships with classmates. **Coherence may falter occasionally** due to the cursory progression of the plot and absence of details. • **Transitions** such as "At noon," and "Finally it was Friday afternoon" are **generally used to connect details within sentences and between paragraphs,** but tend to be **mechanical.** • **Closure is related to the focus** but sounds **artificial and mechanical**— "Giggling and talking like old friends, the two girls moved off down the street together. Everything was going to be just fine from now on."
S	**Sentence Structure** • **Sentence structure is generally controlled.** • **Sentence type and length are sometimes effective** ("Sarah was thinking about…" **and/or varied** ("Who could have sent the text?"). • **Some variety of sentence beginnings is evident** as in "When I was in…" and "I'm going to let Sarah…" **Proportion of error to length and complexity of response has been considered.**

S	**Vocabulary** • **Words and expressions** are **generally used appropriately** throughout the story. • **General words and expressions are used adequately to clarify meaning** ("paid close attention," "everyone could participate," "kind of unusual"). • **The voice/tone created by the student is discernible** ("Most of the students used washroom breaks to quickly check their text messages," and "Sure, I'm a bit overweight"). It may be slightly **inconsistent or uneven**, when the peer voice extends to the narration ("mean text message"). **Proportion of error to length and complexity of response has been considered.**
S	**Conventions** • **The quality of the writing is sustained through generally correct use of conventions** • **Errors occasionally reduce clarity** (such as the comma omission after "Calgary") and awkward wording may sometimes **interrupt the flow of the response** ("However, she ended up leading an interesting discussion of how a message can hurt someone"). **Proportion of error to length and complexity of response has been considered.**

EXEMPLAR SCORE SATISFACTORY—ESSAY

LIFE IS A BOX OF CHOCOLATES

Life is like a box of chocolates you can eat the nice ones and when you come to one you don't like you can put it back and eat another one instead. This is the same for negative things that happen to you you can put them to one side and then work at achieving your goals. Lot's of bad things can happen to you in your life, like you can break up with your girl friend and you can fail a math test in school and you can break your leg and not make the basketball team. Your job is to take responsibility for how you face these situations.

When you and your girlfriend break up you have to believe in yourself and not get depressed. It happens to everyone and there are other thing you can do to make yourself happy like skateboarding or going to movies or just hanging out with your friends. Choose another chocolate from the box and give up on your girlfriend. You might find that it is easy to go on with life and you wonder why you couldn't do it before and it is because you didn't give it a try.

Because you did not study for the math test you will fail and then everyone like your parents and your teachers are mad at you but this mistake can be good because you can learn from it and make better choices in the future to study for your test and get better marks on your test, you can also decide to go to the teacher for extra help after school and then your marks will get better and you will pass your test.

When you break a leg and can't play on the schools basketball team you will be sad and depressed. Look at the box of chocolates, you have to take responsibility for your choice and then you can choose another thing to do instead like play in the school band or help the team by being the manager. You have to do what you can to make your life positive and not negitive.

Those are some of the bad things that can happen to you. You have to take responsibility for thing that happen to you and you can choose another chocolate from the box and make things better.

RATIONALE FOR STUDENT EXEMPLAR SATISFACTORY ESSAY

Title: Life is a Box of Chocolates

Score	Reporting Category
S	**Content** • **The student's exploration of the topic** in the discussion of how "Life is like a box of chocolates" where one can "take responsibility for how you face" negative situations and turn them into positive is **clear** and **logical**. • **The student's purpose** to examine how negative situations can be turned into positive one **is evident.** • **The ideas presented by the student** such as "Lot's of bad things can happen to you in your life," and "you have to take responsibility for your choice" are appropriate and predictable. • **Supporting details** such as "skateboarding or going to movies," "go to the teacher for extra help after school," and "another thing to do instead like play in the school band" are **relevant but generic.** • **The writing is straightforward** as in "this mistake can be good because you can learn from it" and **generalized** as in "Those are some of the bad things that can happen to you." and **occasionally appeals to the reader's interest** through the comparison of negative and positive situations to the chocolates in a box of chocolates.
S	**Organization** • **The introduction** "Lot's of bad things can happen to you in your life, like you can break up with your girl friend and you can fail a math test in school and you can break your leg and not make the basketball team. Your job is to take responsibility for how you face these situations" **is functional and establishes a focus** on how negative situations can have positive outcomes that is **generally sustained.** • **Details are developed in a discernible order** that lists the three examples of negative situations **although coherence** as in "you wonder why you couldn't do it before and it is because you didn't give it a try." **may falter occasionally.** • **Transitions** such as "When you and your girlfriend " "and you wonder why," and "Because you did not study" **tend to be mechanical and are generally used to connect details within sentences and between paragraphs.** • **Closure** "You have to take responsibility for thing that happen to you and you can choose another chocolate from the box and make things better" **is related to the focus and is mechanical.**
S	**Sentence Structure** • **Sentence structure is generally controlled but lapses** such as "study for your test and get better marks on your test, you can also decide to go to the teacher for extra help after school and then your marks will get better and you will pass your test" **may occasionally impede meaning.** • **Sentence type and sentence length** such as "Look at the box of chocolates, you have to take responsibility for your choice and then you can choose another thing to do instead like play in the school band or help the team by being the manager" and "Those are some of the bad things that can happen to you" **are sometimes effective and varied.** • **Some variety of sentence beginnings** as in "This is the same," "Your job is to," and "You have to take" **is evident.** **Proportion of error to length and complexity of response has been considered.**

S	**Vocabulary** • **Words and expressions** such as "just hanging out with your friends." and "you can choose another chocolate from the box" **are generally used appropriately.** • **General words and expressions** such as "this mistake can be good because you can learn from it and make better choices in the future," and "you will be sad and depressed" **are used adequately to clarify meaning.** • **The tone created by the student is discernible** as in "Choose another chocolate from the box and give up on your girlfriend" **but may be uneven.** **Proportion of error to length and complexity of response has been considered.**
S	**Conventions** • **The quality of the writing is sustained through generally correct use of conventions** as demonstrated in "Life is like a box of chocolates you can eat the nice ones and when you come to one you don't like you can put it back and eat another one instead." • **Errors** such as "negative," "Lot's of," and "the schools basketball team" **occasionally reduce clarity and sometimes interrupt the flow of the response** . **Proportion of error to length and complexity of response has been considered.**

EXEMPLAR SCORE PROFICIENT—NARRATIVE

TURNABOUT

Sarah Gustafson looked up guiltily as she heard Miss Monahan call on her by name. Usually Sarah paid close attention in Miss Monahan's English class. Miss Monahan's philosophy of life was that if you didn't like something, you tried to change it for the better. She would use examples like Joan of Arc or Charles Dickens. Miss Monahan had just asked Sarah about Charles Dickens, but Sarah had no idea what the question was. Sarah was thinking about her recent trip to the washroom, and the message she had read there.

Like most of the students in her school, Sarah used her washroom breaks to quickly check her text messages. Most were from her friends—but today was different. On her phone was a brief but nasty text message: **UR A FT PIG**

Who could have sent the text? Sarah looked around the room. Everyone was hunched over their work, but her eyes lingered on Marnie Solomon. Marnie did come across as a bit of a snob, but…for the rest of the period, Sarah tried to concentrate on the literature questions in front of her.

At noon, Sarah shared her concerns with her best friends, Larry and Karen. "I don't believe it." That was Larry speaking.

Karen was a little more helpful. "Yeah, Larry, but something happens to some kids when they hit Grade 9. I dunno…they watch too much TV, and start imitating stuff they've seen. Sometimes, there's no better reason for stupidity like this."

"This isn't the first time. When I was in our chat room on the weekend, someone had typed: 'Who looks like this?' followed by a piggy flying. They then typed: S.G.—my initials—with two smiles. I remember thinking 'How rude—but then I sort of forgot about it till today. Sure, I'm a bit overweight, but Mom told me not to worry. It evidently runs in her family to be a slightly chubby teenager."

Larry suggested bringing it up at the rap session that Miss Monahan hosted during Homeroom Period every Friday. She allowed pretty much any topic of discussion, part of her philosophy of changing the world, one small step at a time. Miss Monahan would have the student who raised the issue host the discussion. Most of the students looked forward to the Friday sessions.

"Good idea, Lar," agreed Karen. "Maybe we should tell Miss Monahan what has happened, and see if she'll let the three of us stand up there together."

Finally, it was Friday afternoon, last period. Everyone stared as Karen, Larry, and Sarah headed to the front of the class. Why were three people leading today, and what was the topic? Sarah noticed that Marnie was suddenly very interested in her fingernails.

"Uh, this is kind of unusual. …" Larry spoke first … "Karen and I are here to support our friend Sarah, because something weird happened to her this week. I think we all respect each other in this class, so that's why Sarah was extremely surprised by what happened. I'm going to let Sarah tell you herself. …"

Sarah stammered a little to begin with, because the topic was so personal. However, she ended up leading an interesting discussion of how a message can hurt someone, even if it is only sent originally as a joke. When the bell rang, no one was anxious to leave. Several of the girls hugged Sarah as they left class, and thanked her for bringing up a topic which had touched some of them, too.

On the way home, Marnie was running to catch up with Sarah. "Sarah… ..Sa-a-rah! Wait up!" "How did you know it was me?"

"I didn't." Sarah kept looking down.

"But how…. I was just sure you knew!"

"Not really…. I did think a few things about you, but then I told myself that I was being silly."

"You weren't being silly." Marnie was breathing quickly and nervously. "I was actually getting quite jealous of you and Larry and Karen. You seemed to be having fun at school. Remember when Rosemary moved to Calgary at the end of September? Well, she had been my best friend since Grade 2, and suddenly there was no one special at school for me. I guess I was feeling sorry for myself…"

Sarah raised her hand to stop Marnie. "I'm no better. I was calling you a snob to myself, not realizing you were missing Rosemary. Hey, how about joining our research team… Karen and Larry and I need a fourth person."

"Really?" Marnie was trying to sound casual. "What's the topic?" Chattering like longtime friends, the two girls moved off down the street together.

RATIONALE FOR STUDENT EXEMPLAR PROFICIENT NARRATIVE

Title: Turnabout

Score	Reporting Category
Pf	**Content** • **The student's exploration of the topic** (turning a negative situation into something positive) is both **adept** and **plausible**. A teenage girl is encouraged by her friends to address her classroom peers on a sensitive issue—a negative text message. • **The student's purpose** (to demonstrate how a teenager can turn a negative situation in their favor and help others to learn from it) is **intentional** as **implied by** the story. • **The ideas presented by the student** (trying to concentrate in school when emotions are in turmoil, using peer and adult support in times of distress, sharing personal feelings and values with peers) are **thoughtful and sound.** • **Supporting details**, such as "Joan of Arc or Charles Dickens," and "It evidently runs in her family to be a slightly chubby teenager" are **apt** and **specific**. • The content is **elaborated** upon through the use of sufficient details about Sarah's situation and the specifically-expressed reactions of her friends to **draw the reader's interest** from the beginning to the end of the story.
Pf	**Organization** • **The introduction**, using the incident of inattention in English class is **purposeful and clearly establishes a focus** by describing the negative situation causing Sarah the inner turmoil and self-doubt that affects her normally positive outlook on life. This focus is **capably sustained** through a progression of events that do not deviate from the focus established in the introduction. • **Details** about the way Sarah handles the negative situation are **developed in a sensible order** through an initial response of shock and disbelief, a time of confiding in good friends, and Sarah's subsequent decision to create a positive outcome in the form of a discussion with her classmates. **Coherence is generally maintained throughout the story.** The chronological sequence of events is clear. • **Transitions**, both **explicit** ("At noon,") and **implicit** ("Sarah noticed that Marnie was suddenly very interested in her fingernails.") **clearly connect events and details within sentences and between paragraphs.** • **Closure is appropriate and related to the focus** ("Chattering like longtime friends, the two girls moved off down the street together.").
Pf	**Sentence Structure** • **Sentence structure is consistently controlled** throughout the story. • **Sentence type and length are usually effective and varied:** ("Sarah looked up guiltily as she heard Miss Monahan call on her by name."; "Who could have seen the text?"; "When I was in our chat room on the weekend…" • **Sentence beginnings are often varied** ("Like most of the students", "Sure, I'm…," "Sarah stammered a little…"). **Proportion of error to length and complexity of response has been considered.**

	Vocabulary
Pf	• **Words and expressions are often used accurately** throughout the story ("looked up guiltily," "hunched over their work"). • **Specific and expressions show some evidence of careful selection** ("philosophy of life," "brief but nasty") and **some awareness of connotative effect** ("eyes lingered on Marnie Solomon"). • **The voice/tone created by the student is distinct** ("bit of a snob," "stupidity like this," "I remember thinking 'How rude'"). **Proportion of error to length and complexity of response has been considered.**
Pf	**Conventions** • **The quality of the writing is sustained because it contains only minor convention errors**. • **Any errors that are present** (such as the absence of a question mark after "Hey, how about joining our research team") **rarely reduce clarity and seldom interrupt the flow of the response.** **Proportion of error to length and complexity of response has been considered**.

EXEMPLAR SCORE PROFICIENT ESSAY

TWO NEGATIVES MAKE A POSITIVE

In math we are taught that two negatives make a positive. If we want the same can be said about our lives. We all make mistakes but by making good choices we can change these mistakes into positive experiences. The way we face difficulties in life shape us to be who we are. You and your girl friend can break up or you can fail a test at school or you can break a leg just before important sports tryouts. Whatever happens good might come out of these bad experiences.

Imagine that you and your girl friend who you have been dating since Grade 8 breaks up. You could be really sad and mope around the house and not do your home work and be pretty miserable to everyone you know or you can take control of your life and move on. Just because you have broken up it is not the end of the world and you can do things with other friends or with your family. You can still go to movies or use facebook to spend time with other people. You can get your brother to spend time with you even if it only skateboarding or skiing. Without a girl friend you will soon enough discover that you are free to do whatever you want whenever you want to.

Some school tests are really important and if you fail one of these then you could be in deep trouble. Your parents will be really mad at you and you might end up being grounded or denied priveges like your computer or movies. How can you make this terrible situation into something positive? Well you might learn the value of education, or you might discover a good book to read because you aren't allowed to watch TV, or you might even realize that spending time with your family instead of online can be sort of fun. Whatever happens you can turn this negative into a positive if you want to.

Let's say that your passion is basket ball and you're pretty good at it and you wanted to make the senior team in Grade 9. One of the worst things that could happen to you is for you to break your leg just two weeks before the tryouts. You would not have a chance now of making the team and you would have to spend the rest of the year watching your friends play while you sit on the side lines half-heartedly cheering them on. How can this negative situation be turned into a positive? Well, you will have time on your hands because you can't be on your legs so you might discover other interests like joining the school band or the drama club or the woodwork club. There are lots of things other than sports for people to do and all you would have to do is to find out what other talents you have besides basketball.

With so many negative things that can happen to you or your family or friends it might be hard to discover how to turn these negatives into positive situations. In the end, we have to remember that we are the final decision makers and we can make anything come out of any situation. Look on the bright side, things could always be worse and it is our job to make sure that we remember that two negatives make a positive, and we have control over how negative experiences affect us.

RATIONALE FOR STUDENT EXEMPLAR PROFICIENT ESSAY

Title: Two Negatives make a Positive

Score	Reporting Category
Pf	**Content** • **The student's exploration of the topic is adept** as demonstrated in "We all make mistakes but by making good choices we can change these mistakes into positive experiences." and **plausible**. • **The student's purpose** to recognize how some negative situations can become positive outcomes in life **is intentional**. • **The ideas presented by the student are thoughtful** as in "you might discover a good book to read because you aren't allowed to watch TV or you might even realize that spending time with your family instead of online can be sort of fun." • **Supporting details** such as "use facebook to spend time with other people," "you might end up being grounded" and "sit on the side lines" **are apt and specific.** • **The writing is considered and elaborated** as demonstrated in "there are lots of things other than sports for people to do and all you would have to do is to find out what other talents you have besides basketball." and **draws the reader's interest** as shown in "The way we face difficulties in life shape us to be who we are."

Pf	**Organization** • **The introduction** "In math we are taught that two negatives make a positive. If we want the same can be said about our lives. We all make mistakes but by making good choices we can change these mistakes into positive experiences" **is purposeful and clearly establishes a focus that is capably sustained** through the discussion on how negative situations can be turned into positive results. • **Details** such as "Just because you have broken up it is not the end of the world and you can do things with other friends or with your family," "Some school tests are really important and if you fail one of these then you can be in deep trouble," and "One of the worst things that could happen to you is for you to break your leg just two weeks before the tryouts" **are developed in a sensible order, and coherence is generally maintained.** • **Transitions** such as "Well you might learn," "With so many negative things," and "In the end," **clearly connect details within sentences and between paragraphs.** • **Closure** "In the end, we have to remember that we are the final decision makers and we can make anything come out of any situation. Look on the bright side, things could always be worse and it is our job to make sure that we remember that two negatives make a positive, and we have control over how negative experiences affect us" **is appropriate and related to the focus.**
Pf	**Sentence Structure** • **Sentence structure is consistently controlled** as in "Well you might learn the value of education, or you might discover a good book to read because you aren't allowed to watch TV, or you might even realize that spending time with your family instead of online can be sort of fun." • **Sentence type**, as in "How can you make this terrible situation into something positive?" and **sentence length** as in "Whatever happens good might come out of these bad experiences," and "There are lots of things other than sports for people to do and all you would have to do is to find out what other talents you have besides basketball." **are usually effective and varied.** • **Sentence beginnings** such as "The way we face," "Just because you have," "One of the worst things," and "Look on the bright side," **are often varied.**
Pf	**Vocabulary** • **Words and expressions**, such as "be really sad and mope around the house" and "sit on the side lines half-heartedly cheering them on" **are often used accurately.** • **Specific words and expressions** such as "it is not the end of the world," "you will have time on your hands because you can't be on your legs," and "Look on the bright side, things could always be worse" show **some evidence of careful selection** and **some awareness of connotative effect.** • **The tone created by the student** as in "you might even realize that spending time with your family instead of on line can be sort of fun" **is distinct.** **Proportion of error to length and complexity of response has been considered**

Pf	**Conventions** • **The quality of the writing is sustained because it contains only minor convention errors** such as "The way we face difficulties in life shape us to be who we are," and "you and your girlfriend who you have been dating since Grade 8 breaks up." • **Any errors that are present** such as "priveges" and "If we want the same can be said about our lives." and "spend time with you even if it only skateboarding" **rarely reduce clarity and seldom interrupt the flow of the response.** **Proportion of error to length and complexity of response has been considered.**

EXEMPLAR SCORE EXCELLENT NARRATIVE

Turnabout

"Sarah…"

"Miss Monahan?" Sarah Gustafson looked up guiltily at the sound of her name.

"I was just asking if you thought Charles Dickens made an important impact on British society when he wrote <u>Oliver Twist?</u>"

"Oh ye…I. .uh…Would you mind repeating the question?"

Usually Sarah didn't mind English, at least not the way Miss Monahan taught it. Miss Monahan's basic philosophy of life was that if you didn't like something, you thought of ways to change what you didn't like. She was always referring to people from history like Joan of Arc, or Charles Dickens, or that Iraqi-Canadian journalist who was murdered in Iraq for trying to send home photos of human rights violations. But today was different. Sarah was thinking about her recent trip to the washroom. Or, more accurately, what she had seen there.

Like most of the students at Colson, Sarah used her washroom breaks to quickly check her text messages. Most were from her friends—just the normal stuff kids text back and forth to get through the long day at school. Twenty minutes earlier, she had opened up her phone, turned it on and been met with a not-so-subtle message: **UR A FT PIG**

Sarah was still in shock. Who could it be? She looked around the room. By now, everyone was bent over the journal writing Miss Monahan had just assigned about child labor in Britain and how Charles Dickens wrote fiction to get the right people fired up over the terrible conditions, dangers, and rampant poverty that stalked the streets of London. Marnie? She's a bit of a jealous snob? No, I don't think she's that mean…I'll ask Karen and Larry at lunch.

"I don't believe it." That was Larry speaking, hunched over his coke and fries in the cafeteria. "Like, we don't have any mean dudes in Grade 9. Most of us have been together since Grade 1, for Pete's sake."

Karen, her best friend, was a little more skeptical, as usual. "Yeah, Larry, but something happens to some kids when they hit Grade 9. I dunno…they watch too much 'Degrassi' or something. They start imitating incidents they see on TV, whether there's any reason for it or not."

"Wait, you guys…this isn't the first time." Sarah had been morosely brooding over her peanut butter and honey sandwich, but now she looked directly at her two concerned friends. "When I was in our regular chat room on the weekend, someone had typed: 'Who looks like this?' followed by an animated piggy flying. They then typed: **S.G.**—my initials—with two smiles. I remember thinking 'How rude—must be one of the guys trying to impress his buddies with his twisted sense of humor', but then I forgot about it till today. I know I'm a bit overweight, but Mom told me not to worry, that she was just like me in her teens before she slimmed down at 20. It runs in the family."

"Let's bring it up at 'Cheap Shots' on Friday afternoon." Larry was referring to the rap session that Miss Monahan hosted during Homeroom Period every Friday. She allowed pretty much any topic of discussion, as long as it was legitimate. If no one could think of anything, she was pretty good at initiating a topic herself—something from the local news that week, or an issue of importance to teens. Sarah was secretly convinced Miss Monahan came prepared. It was part of her philosophy of changing the world, one small step at a time. Miss Monahan usually had the student who raised the issue host the discussion. Most of the students had become quite comfortable speaking their thoughts on different topics, and looked forward to the Friday sessions.

"Good idea, Lar," chimed in Karen. "Just to be on the safe side, why don't we fill Miss Monahan in before Friday on what has happened, and see if the three of us can host the topic together?"

An awkward silence rippled through the room as Karen, Larry, and Sarah headed to the front of the class on Friday at 2:45 pm. Everyone stared. Miss Monahan usually had people raise their hands to suggest a topic, then advance to the front to lead the discussion if she picked them. What was going on? Sarah noted that Marnie had suddenly become fascinated by her fingernails.

"Uh, this is kind of unusual…." Larry, bless his heart, had agreed to speak first… "Karen and I are here to support our friend Sarah, because something weird happened to her this week. Like me and Karen, Sarah looks on all of you as her friends. I think we have become especially closer this last year in junior high, and it's mostly because of these Friday afternoon sessions Miss Monahan started. That's why Sarah was so surprised by what happened. I'm going to let Sarah tell you herself…."

And that's how it all came out. Sarah, at first stammering a little, for she was usually quite self confident and mature in front of people, found herself sharing personal details in front of her classmates, her friends, her supporters. That led to a very interesting discussion of how a message, maybe intended lightly or as a joke, can be received quite differently. When Sarah got to the part about the family traits and what her mother had told her, she saw three of her classmates nodding their heads vigorously in agreement. For once, the closing bell, when it jangled insistently, was an annoying intruder instead of a welcome arrival. Miss Monahan didn't even have time to bring the discussion to a proper conclusion. Several of the girls gave Sarah a quick hug on the way to the lockers.

"Sarah…. Sa-a-rah! Wait up!"

Sarah turned slowly from halfway down the first block home. She knew that voice. Marnie was huffing and gasping as she struggled to catch up without losing her heavy backpack.

"How did you know it was me?"

"I didn't." Sarah was looking down, kicking absently at a loose twig on the sidewalk.

"But how…. I was just sure you knew!"

"Not really…. I admit I did think a few things about you, but then I told myself that I was being silly. You've been just like everyone else in class."

"Not quite like everyone else ..." Marnie was breathing quickly now, and not from the running. "I was actually getting quite jealous of you and Larry and Karen. You were always chuckling in the cafeteria over lunch, and seemed to be having fun at school. Remember when Rosemary moved to Calgary at the end of September? Well, she had been my best friend since Grade 2, and suddenly there was no one special at school for me. Everyone else seemed to be having a good time. I guess I was feeling sorry for myself ..."

Sarah raised her hand to stop Marnie. "Hey, I'm no better. I was calling you a snob to myself, not realizing you were missing Rosemary. To change the subject, why don't you join our research team ... it's just me and Karen and Larry right now, but we need a fourth person. I won't say anything about what you told me today. Anyhow, the topic we are thinking of doing is 'Cyber-bullying'...."

RATIONALE FOR STUDENT EXEMPLAR EXCELLENT NARRATIVE

Title: Turnabout

Score	Reporting Category
E	**Content** • **The student's exploration of the topic** is **insightful** (following a teenage girl's negative experience with a form of cyber-bullying from initial awareness to being proactive) and **imaginative** (beginning the story with a familiar scenario that would capture the imagination of most young readers). • **The student's purpose** (to illustrate how a young person can reverse a negative situation and develop problem-solving skills) is **deliberate**. The story is intended to inspire young people to be proactive rather than reactive, and to learn coping skills during difficult situations. • **The ideas presented by the student** (the discovery of the nasty text message, the response, the confiding in friends, and the choice of a proactive solution to the situation) are **carefully chosen and perceptive.** • **Supporting details**, such as "Iraqi-Canadian journalist," "recent trip to the washroom," and "had suddenly become fascinated by her fingernails" are **precise and original.** • **The writing is confident, creative, and holds the reader's interest** with personalized details and a plausible plot that addresses the topic through the eyes of an "average teenager."
E	**Organization** • **The introduction**, using a dramatized reproduction of dialogue between a teacher and an inattentive student, **is engaging and skillfully establishes a focus** on the topic that is **consistently sustained** through the progression of events that culminate in a class discussion on a sensitive topic. • **Events and details are developed in a judicious order** (The student writer creates a catchy initial incident, exposes a conflict or problem, and leads the main character through a series of events to a plausible outcome and resolution of the conflict). **Coherence is maintained** through a clearly evident chronological sequence of events. • **Transitions, both explicit** ("Twenty minutes earlier") and **implicit** ("Sarah was still in shock") **fluently connect events and details** within sentences and between paragraphs. • **Closure is effective and related to the focus** ("Anyhow, the topic we are thinking of doing is 'Cyber-bullying'...").

E	**Sentence Structure** • **Sentence structure is effectively and consistently controlled** throughout the story. • **Sentence type and length are consistently effective and varied** ("Sarah looked up guiltily…," "Like most of the students…," "I don't believe it." • **Sentence beginnings are consistently varied** ("That was Larry speaking…," "When I was in…," "If no one could think of anything,"). **Proportion of error to length and complexity of response has been considered.**
E	**Vocabulary** • **Words and expressions are used accurately and deliberately** throughout the story ("looked up guiltily," "a cryptic message," "skeptical"). • **Precise words and expressions are used to create vivid images and to enrich details** ("rampant poverty that stalked the streets of London," "they watch too much 'Degrassi,'" "An awkward silence rippled through the room"). • **The voice/tone created by the student is convincing** ("Oh yes … I … uh," "just the normal stuff kids text," "Like, we don't have any mean dudes in Grade 9"). **Proportion of error to length and complexity of response has been considered.**
E	**Conventions** • **The quality of the writing is enhanced because it is essentially error-free.** • **Any errors that are present** (such as the missing question mark after "To change the subject, why don't you join our research team") **do not reduce clarity and do not interrupt the flow of the response.** **Proportion of error to length and complexity of response has been considered.**

EXEMPLAR SCORE EXCELLENT—ESSAY

THE CHOICE IS ALL YOURS

Robert Frost wrote something like, "Two roads diverged in a wood, and I—I took the one less travelled by and that has made all the difference." Robert Frost did not say whether one road would be difficult and have many problems along the way and the other road would be easier to travel, but that could be the case. For every choice there is an outcome and the outcome can be negative or positive. It is how we look at the negative situations in our lives and how we can do something to turn them into positive results that help us to grow and mature. Some negative things that can occur in your life such as your girl friend breaking up with you, you failing a really important test, you breaking your leg skateboarding just before football try-outs, or you missing the bus and having to walk five kilometers to school in a snow storm would be pretty bad, but they might have positive outcomes if you open your mind to all possibilities. You do not know what good may happen to you as a result of these negative situations that you found yourself in. Good can come out of bad as you will see in this essay.

Suppose you had been dating this girl since Grade 8 and she breaks up with you just before the Easter break. You would be really disappointed because you had been planning on going snowboarding with her and you had hoped she would invite you to her family's cabin by the lake where you could have gone ski-doing and cross-country skiing and snow shoeing. You have a choice. You can mope around your house all of the break and make life miserable for yourself and the rest of your family or you can shut the door on that chapter of your life (my mother's wise saying) and get out and do some fun activities with other friends. You can still snow-board, cross country ski, snow-shoe. You just can't ski-do because you don't know anyone else who has one. But so what? It isn't the end of the world. You might even meet new and exciting friends. You might find that life is freer if you don't have a girl friend. Now you can do what you want, when you want, and with who you want.

Failing important tests in school can be serious and is definitely a wake-up call. Why did you fail? Perhaps it means you are not studying hard enough. Maybe you were spending too much time with the girlfriend (who just broke up with you) so it is a good thing that you two are not going out any more. Your parents and teachers will be disappointed because they expect better from you; so not only are you surprised but so are your parents and teachers. It doesn't matter if you fail one test in Junior High as long as you learn from it and realize that some tests (like your Grade 12 diplomas to get into University) are extremely important. The positive that came out of you failing a test is that you will learn how important it is to study for all tests.

You always wanted to make the high school junior football team. The senior team nearly always wins the city championships and you know that if you make the junior team you are pretty sure of a place on the senior team in Grade 11 or 12. How do you feel if the week before try-outs, you go flying down a flight of stairs while skateboarding (with a new friend that you met since you are no longer dating the girlfriend) and you end up in hospital with a badly broken leg? Imagine your frustration and anger.

Now that you will have no chance to make the junior team, it is unlikely that you will make the senior team in a year's time. What good can come out of this? you wonder. Well, your new friend suggests that, since you can't do anything too active for the next two months, the two of you get together with some others and form a rock band. You like this idea as you already know how to play the guitar and can now put it to some use. Five of you (a drummer, two regular guitarists, a bass guitarist, and a saxophone player) form a band called The Frivolous Five. You have so much fun that you are almost glad you broke your leg. In Grade 12 you will be able to play in gigs around the city.

It is not likely that you will ever have to walk five kilometers to school in a snow storm. I know our parents tell us they had to (and back home, and up-hill both ways) but they exaggerate to try and make us think that our life is too easy. I think I would freeze my toes.

This essay has tried to show how positive things can result from negative situations. Maybe we learn from our mistakes (which is a positive result), or maybe new and unexpected things come our way because of the negative situation. We never know what lies ahead so when times are bad, we must never give up because as one door closes, another always opens (another of my mother's wise sayings), and new and exciting and positive life experiences could be just around the corner.

RATIONALE FOR STUDENT EXEMPLAR EXCELLENT ESSAY

Title: The Choice is All Yours

Reporting Category
Content • **The student's exploration of the topic** ("As we walk along the road of life, we do not know where each path will lead us. Good can come out of bad as you will see in this essay," and "The positive that came out of you failing a test is that you will learn how important it is to study for all tests," and "Maybe we learn from our mistakes (which is a positive result), or maybe new and unexpected things come our way because of the negative situation" **is insightful.** • **The student's purpose**—to recognize how the results of unfortunate and negative situations may lead to unexpected but positive results—**is deliberate.** • **The ideas presented by the student are perceptive** (as in, "You can mope around your house all of the break and make life miserable for yourself and the rest of your family or you can shut the door on that chapter of your life (my mother's wise saying) and get out and do some fun activities with other friends.") and **carefully chosen** (as in, "How do you feel if the week before try-outs, you go flying down a flight of stairs while skateboarding"). • **Supporting details** such as, "your new friend suggests that, since you can't do anything too active for the next two months, the two of you get together with some others and form a rock band. You like this idea as you already know how to play the guitar and can now put it to some use" are **precise and original**—in so much as the student acknowledges some of the outcomes that might create a positive experience from a negative situation. • **The writing is confident and holds the reader's interest** (as in, "It is not likely that you will ever have to walk five kilometers to school in a snow storm. I know our parents tell us they had to (and back home, and up-hill both ways) but they exaggerate to try and make us think that our life is too easy. I think I would freeze my toes").
Organization • **The introduction is engaging and skillfully establishes a focus**—"It is how we look at the negative situations in our lives and how we can do something to turn them into positive results that help us to grow and mature. Some negative things that can occur in your life such as your girl friend breaking up with you, you failing a really important test, you breaking your leg skateboarding just before football try-outs, or you missing the bus and having to walk five kilometers to school in a snow storm would be pretty bad, but they might have positive outcomes if you open your mind to all possibilities."—**that is consistently sustained** (by the elaboration of the examples given in the introduction. • **Details are developed in a judicious order**, evident in each paragraph's detail and examples (such as "You can still snow-board, cross country ski, snow-shoe. You just can't ski-do" and "the two of you get together with some others and form a rock band.") of how positive results have come out of negative situations. **Coherence is maintained** by the presentation of three different situations. • **Transitions fluently connect details within sentences** ("Now you can do what you want, when you want, and with who you want.") **and between paragraphs**—as in, "Suppose you had been dating this girl since Grade 8 and she breaks up with you just before the Easter break" and "You always wanted to make the high school junior football team." • **Closure is effective and related to the focus**—"We never know what lies ahead so when times are bad, we must never give up because as one door closes, another always opens (another of my mother's wise sayings), and new and exciting and positive life experiences could be just around the corner."

E	**Sentence Structure** • **Sentence Structure is effective and consistently controlled**—as in, "Some negative things that can occur in your life such as your girl friend braking up with you, you failing a really important test, you breaking your leg skateboarding just before football try-outs, or you missing the bus and having to walk five kilometers to school in a snow storm would be pretty bad, but they might have positive outcomes if you open your mind to all possibilities." • **Sentence type** ("But so what? It isn't the end of the world.") and **sentence length** ("It doesn't matter if you fail one test in Junior High as long as you learn form it and realize that some tests (like your Grade 12 diplomas to get into University) are extremely important.") **are consistently effective and varied.** • **Sentence beginnings** such as "For every choice there is an outcome…" and "Why did you fail?" and "Well, your new friend suggests that…" **are consistently varied.** **Proportion of error to length and complexity of response has been considered.**
E	**Vocabulary** • **Words and expressions** ("You can mope around your house all of the break and make life miserable for yourself and the rest of your family") **are accurately and deliberately** ("Maybe you were spending too much time with the girlfriend (who just broke up with you…") **used.** • **Precise words and expressions** ("you can shut the door on that chapter of your life (my mother's wise saying…") **are used to create vivid images** ("a drummer, two regular guitarists, a bass guitarist, and a saxophone player form a band called The Frivolous Five.") **and enrich details.** • **The tone created by the student is convincing**, as in "Now you can do what you want, when you want, and with who you want" and "I know our parents tell us they had to (and back home, and up-hill both ways) but they exaggerate to try and make us think that our life is too easy. I think I would freeze my toes." **Proportion of error to length and complexity of response has been considered.**
E	**Conventions** • **The quality of the writing is enhanced because it is essentially error free** as demonstrated in "Robert Frost wrote something like, 'Two roads diverged in a wood, and I—I took the one less travelled by and that has made all the difference'", and "How do you feel if the week before tryouts, you go flying down a flight of stairs while skateboarding (with a new friend that you met since you are no longer dating the girlfriend) and you end up in the hospital with a badly broken leg?" • **Any errors that are present** (in usage, such as, "you can do what you want, when you want, and with who you want" and, "Maybe we learn from our mistakes (which is a positive result)…" **do not reduce clarity and do not interrupt the flow of the response.** **Proportion of error to length and complexity of response has been considered.**

NARRATIVE WRITING PROMPT TWO

ASSIGNMENT

Write a narrative or essay that conveys what you think are some of the main issues teenagers face in today's society. You may write about yourself, or other people, real or fictional. You may set your writing in the past, present, or future.

Ideas

The following material may give you ideas for your writing. **You do not have to use any of it.** Consider your own ideas gained through reading, listening, viewing, discussing, thinking, or imagining.

- Friends and friendships

- Cliques

- Dating

- Having fun

- Parental expectations

- Smoking

- Sports

- Music

When writing, **be sure to:**
- Consider your **audience**
- Focus on your purpose and **point of view**
- **Organize** your thoughts appropriately in sentences and paragraphs
- Use **vocabulary** that is interesting and effective
- **Edit** your work directly on your writing
- **Budget** your time

EXEMPLAR SCORE SATISFACTORY NARRATIVE

THE BOX

When Ian saw a large box on the sidewalk move in New York, he realized there was a homeless person inside. Although, he did not actually see the person under the box. Mom explained, back at the hotel, that some people live outside because they are homeless. It might not be their fault. Ian thought for a long time about what his mother had said.

After they arrived home from their vacation, Mom decided to bring the family downtown for the Inner City Thanksgiving March. The walk was supposed to show the richer people poverty and homelessness in the city. Ian was curious ever since New York, so he didn't mind, even though it happened on his favorite day to relax, Saturday.

The marchers were quiet as the march went through the downtown neighborhood. They saw places where homeless people could get warm clothes, hot coffee, or a place to sleep. They saw several homeless people standing on the sidewalk. It was interesting to Ian, but sad at the same time.

Ian kept quiet on the way home. When they arrived home he asked his mom where the camping stuff was stored. She told him he would find most of it in the basement storage area. Ian went downstairs to see if he could find something to donate.

Later, Ian looked over the stuff piled on his bed: sleeping bags, some toques, a few gloves, and several blankets. He asked his Mom if it was ok to take them to school to start up his donation idea, she said, "fine".

Once Ian took his idea to school, things happened pretty fast. Before he knew it, his picture was in the paper beside all the clothes and blankets they had collected. The article with the picture explained how the students, and especially one student, decided to donate winter clothing to the homeless.

Ian is just a normal guy. But, he did something about poverty. Ian thought homelessness was an important issue faced by teenagers in today's society. He tried to make a difference.

RATIONALE FOR STUDENT EXEMPLAR SATISFACTORY NARRATIVE

Title: The Box

Score	Reporting Category
S	**Content** • **The student's exploration of the topic** of an issue that faces teenagers in today's society (issues and problems connected to homelessness) is **clear** and **logical**. • **The student's purpose** (to present homeless issues within the context of a story) **is evident**. • **The ideas presented by the student** (homeless people lack the essentials of food and shelter, and often depend on charity) are **appropriate and predictable.** • **Supporting details**, such as "marchers were quiet" and "homeless people could get warm clothes, hot coffee, or a place to sleep" are **relevant** but **generic**. • The writing is **straightforward** as in "Mom decided to bring the family downtown for the Inner City Thanksgiving March" and **generalized** as in "Ian looked over the stuff piled on his bed" and **occasionally appeals to the reader's interest through a details** such as "Ian saw a large box on the sidewalk move in New York".

S	**Organization** • **The introduction is functional** and **establishes a focus** by briefly relating the main character's first exposure to a homeless person, and this focus is **generally sustained**. • **Details** about the character's exposure to homelessness in his own city are **developed in a discernible order** through a march, collection of items, and donation initiative at school. **Coherence may falter occasionally** due to the cursory progression of the plot and absence of details. • **Transitions** such as "After they arrived home", "When they arrived home" and "Later" which are **generally used to connect details within sentences and between paragraphs** tend to be **mechanical**. • **Closure is related to the focus** but **mechanical** in that it sounds **artificial**—"Ian thought homelessness was an important issue" and "He tried to make a difference."
S	**Sentence Structure** • **Sentence structure** is **generally controlled but lapses** (such as "Although, he did not actually see the person under the box.") **may occasionally impede meaning.** • **Sentence type and length** are **sometimes effective** ("Mom explained, back at the hotel, that some people live outside because they are homeless.") **and/or varied** ("It might not be their fault"). • **Some variety of sentence beginnings is evident** as in "After they arrived home," and "Ian is just." **Proportion of error to length and complexity of response has been considered.**
S	**Vocabulary** • **Words and expressions** are **generally used appropriately** throughout the story. • **General words and expressions are used adequately to clarify meaning** ("homeless person," "interesting …but sad", "his donation idea"). • **The voice/tone created by the student is discernible** ("his favorite day to relax," "He asked his Mom if it was ok"). **Proportion of error to length and complexity of response has been considered.**
S	**Conventions** • The **quality** of the writing is **sustained** through **generally correct use of conventions**. • **Errors occasionally reduce clarity** (such as incorrectly capitalizing "Mom" and failing to capitalize "fine" when used as the mother's quoted response). Errors **sometimes interrupt the flow of the response** (such as "But, he did something about poverty"). **Proportion of error to length and complexity of response has been considered.**

EXEMPLAR SCORE SATISFACTORY ESSAY

Teenagers face many different issues in today's society. Some of those issues are whether to smoke or not, some are whether to go to parties where there might be drinking and smoking, and some issues are parents.

Smoking is bad for you but many teenagers do it because they see big kids and rock stars and atheletes doing it. In school teenagers are given programs to help them not to smoke but when you're friends are smoking then it is difficult to say no. Who remembers a silly health class lesson when you are with you're friends? Anyway lots of our parants smoke too and that makes it difficult for teenagers not to smoke. That is one issue teenagers face in today's society.

When you're friends are having a party and you get to go along with them it is an issue because there might be drinking and smoking at the party. Also at parties sometimes the adults are not there and then trouble can begin. Older teenagers can gatecrash and fighting might start. People get hurt and even stabbed at some parties. I know a boy who was only 14 and he got stabbed at a party and he nearly died and his parents told him not to go to the party. Parties is a issue that teenagers face in today's society.

Parents are a BIG issue for teenagers. They tell you to go to bed when you don't want to. They tell you to do your homework and you want to watch tv or listen to you're music. They tell you when to come home and you want to be out with you're friends. They make you tidy you're room when you like it the way it is. They make you eat you're dinner when chips and pop and pizza and hamburgers are nicer for teenagers. As you can see parents are a big issue for teenagers in today's society.

There are so many issues that teenagers have to face in today's society and I have told you about three, smoking, parties and parents. We are lucky if we don't have too many issues to face because they surley do make life difficult for teenagers.

RATIONALE FOR STUDENT EXEMPLAR LEVEL SATISFACTORY ESSAY

Title:

Score	Reporting Category
S	**Content** • **The student's exploration of the topic** in the discussion of issues that face teenagers in today's society (whether to smoke or not, whether to go to parties, and parents) is **clear** and **logical**. • **The student's purpose** (to look at these issues) is **evident**. • **The ideas presented by the student**, as in that teenagers smoke because they see "big kids, and rock stars and atheletes" as well as parents smoking; teenagers go to parties to be with their friends; and parents are forever telling teenagers what to do, are **appropriate** and **predictable**. • **Supporting details**, such as "Also at parties sometimes the adults are not there and then trouble can begin" and the list of things parents expect of their teenagers, are **relevant** but **generic**. • The writing is **straightforward** as in, ("There are so many issues that teenagers have to face in today's society and I have told you about three,") and **generalized** as in, ("Smoking is bad for you" and "there might be drinking and smoking at the party") and **occasionally appeals to the reader's interest** through a couple of personal details ("I know a boy who was only 14 and he got stabbed at a party and nearly died").

S	**Organization** • **The introduction** is **functional and establishes a focus** by listing the three issues teenagers have to face in today's society that the student elaborates on and this **focus** is **generally sustained.** • **Details** about the issues that teenagers have to face are **developed in a discernible order** though **coherence may falter occasionally** as in "Parents are a BIG issue for teenagers." • **Transitions** such as "Anyway lots of…," "When your friends…" and "As you can see…" which are **generally used to connect details within sentences and between paragraphs** tend to be **mechanical.** • **Closure** is **related to the focus,** "We are lucky if we don't have too many issues to face because the surley do make life difficult for teenagers" and **mechanical.**
S	**Sentence Structure** • **Sentence structure** is **generally controlled** as in "Anyway lots of our parants smoke too and that makes it difficult for teenagers not to smoke" and "Older teenagers can gatecrash and fighting might start" but **lapses** (such as "I know a boy who was only 14 and he got stabbed at a party and he nearly died and his parents told him not to go to the party") **may occasionally impede meaning.** • **Sentence type and length are sometimes effective** ("They tell you to go to bed when you don't want to. They tell you to do your homework and you want to watch tv or listen to you're music.") **and/or varied** ("Who remembers a silly class health lesson when you are with you're friends?"). • **Some variety of sentence beginnings is evident** as in "Who remembers…," "Also at parties…," and "As you can see…" **Proportion of error to length and complexity of response has been considered.**
S	**Vocabulary** • **Words**—such as "gatecrash", "chips and pop and pizza and hamburgers"—expressions—such as "but when you're friends are smoking then it is difficult to say no." and "People get hurt and even stabbed at some parties." —are **generally used appropriately.** • **General words and expressions are used adequately to clarify meaning**—such as "Teenagers face many different issues in today's society." and "you want to be out with you're friends". • **The voice/tone created by the student is discernible** (as in, "Smoking is bad for you but many teenagers do it because they see big kids and rock stars and atheletes doing it." and "We are lucky if we don't have too many issues to face because they surley do make life difficult for teenagers." but **uneven.** **Proportion of error to length and complexity of response has been considered.**

	Conventions
S	• **The quality of the writing is sustained through generally correct use of conventions,** as in "Teenagers face many different issues in today's society. Some of those issues are whether to smoke or not, some are whether to go to parties where there might be drinking and smoking, and some issues are parents." • **Errors occasionally reduce clarity** (such as the consistent misspelling of "you're" and in verb subject agreement as in, "Parties is a issue") **and sometimes interrupt the flow of the response** (such as "parents are a big issue for teenagers in today's society." —parents themselves are not the issue,; it is their demands they make on their teenagers that are the issue. **Proportion of error to length and complexity of response has been considered.**

EXEMPLAR SCORE PROFICIENT NARRATIVE

THE BOX

Ian's first experience with a homeless person happened in New York, when he saw a large box on the sidewalk move. Although he did not see the person under the box, he could not forget how startled he was. Mom had explained, back at the hotel, that some people, not just in New York, but in most large cities, sometimes lived outside because they were homeless. The homelessness was not always their fault. She said that there were many causes, and that it was wrong to judge people for their poverty.

Just before Thanksgiving, Mom decided to bring the family downtown for the Inner City Thanksgiving March. The walk would take the marchers through the blocks most familiar to homeless citizens. For some reason, Ian didn't mind the change to his normal Saturday routine. He had been curious ever since the experience in New York.

The procession of volunteers was rather quiet for such a large group. Each group of five or six had a "guide", who provided a commentary as the march wound through the downtown neighborhood: "That building is the Co-op, where people can pick up warmer clothes as the weather gets colder.... . An important item for all of these centers is donated coffee. On the coldest nights, we try to provide enough sleeping bags for everyone to sleep in public areas like underground walkways by the subway stations. We don't want anyone to freeze. We do our best to help the homeless survive, without taking away hope and human dignity."

Ian was uncharacteristically quiet on the way home. They were barely in the door when he asked, "Mom, where do we keep the camping stuff?"

"Uh...it's down in the storage area beside the family room, hon." She didn't even ask Ian why he wanted to know.

Some time later, Ian leaned against the doorway of his room, counting the stuff piled on his bed: two sleeping bags, three toques, five pairs of gloves, and three blankets. He called out, "Hey, Ma...could you come here for a minute?"

Once Ian took his idea to school, things happened faster than he could have ever imagined. Last week, Ian's junior high school was shown on the City Page of the local newspaper. The picture showed Ian and about 25 other students posing beside a huge pile of donated winter wear. The article under the picture explained how the students, and especially one student, decided to put his thoughts into actions.

To Ian's family, classmates, and teachers, Ian is just a normal guy. He gets decent grades, minds his own business, and occasionally argues with his parents, just like most teenagers. Ian is only in Grade 9, and doesn't yet have clear future plans. However, because of that box, Ian will probably stay tuned in all his life to issues in society that come to his attention.

RATIONALE FOR STUDENT EXEMPLAR PROFICIENT NARRATIVE

Score	Reporting Category
Pf	**Content** • **The student's exploration of** the **topic** of an issue that faces teenagers in today's society (issues and problems connected to homelessness) is both **adept** and **plausible**. A teenage boy is motivated to help the homeless after his mother has the family participate in a walk through the inner city with a guide. • **The student's purpose** (to clarify homeless issues within the context of a story) is **intentional** as implied by the story. • **The ideas presented by the student** (the quietness of the volunteers, the uncharacteristic quiet of the boy on the way home) are **thoughtful and sound.** • **Supporting details**, such as "That building is the Co-op" and "two sleeping bags, three toques, five pairs of gloves, and three blankets" are **apt** and **specific**. • The writing is **elaborated** with sufficient details about Ian's first experience in New York and his decision to act following the Thanksgiving March to continue to **draw the reader's interest** from the beginning to the end of the story.
Pf	**Organization** • **The introduction**, using the anecdote from New York, is **purposeful and clearly establishes a focus** by describing the main character's first exposure to a homeless person. **This focus** is **capably sustained** through a progression of events that do not deviate from the focus. • **Details** about the character's exposure to homelessness in his own city are **developed in a sensible order** through a march at Thanksgiving time, description of the character's emotional response to what he sees, and his subsequent decision to act on what he has seen. **Coherence is generally maintained** throughout the story. The chronological sequence of events is clear. • **Transitions**, both **explicit** ("Just before Thanksgiving") and **implicit** ("Ian was uncharacteristically quiet on the way home") **clearly connect events and details** within sentences and between paragraphs. • **Closure is appropriate and related to the focus** ("However, because of that box, Ian will probably stay tuned in all his life to issues in society that come to his attention").

Pf	**Sentence Structure** • **Sentence structure** is **consistently controlled** throughout the story. • **Sentence type and length are usually effective and varied** ("The walk would take the marchers through the blocks most familiar to homeless citizens. For some reason, Ian didn't mind the change to his normal Saturday routine" "Mom, where do we keep the camping stuff?"). • **Sentence beginnings are often varied** ("Although he did not see," "He had been curious," "On the coldest nights"). **Proportion of error to length and complexity of response has been considered.**
Pf	**Vocabulary** • **Words and expressions** are **often used accurately** throughout the story ("most familiar to," "human dignity"). • **Specific and expressions show some evidence of careful selection** ("procession of volunteers," "normal Saturday routine") and **some awareness of connotative effect** ("march wound through," "uncharacteristically quiet"). • **The voice/tone created by the student is distinct** ("Mom had explained," "Mom, where do we keep the camping stuff?" "Ian is just a normal guy"). **Proportion of error to length and complexity of response has been considered.**
E	**Conventions** • **The quality of the writing is enhanced because it is essentially error-free.** **Proportion of error to length and complexity of response has been considered.**

EXEMPLAR PROFICIENT ESSAY

The difficulties of being a teenager

Teenagers have to face issues every day of their lives which makes life a lot more difficult than adults think. Often these issues come from our parents and families, teachers, friends, and peer pressure. Most teens are very insecure about themselves and this makes it difficult for them to deal with the many issues in front of them.

The issue of parents and teachers is that they do not always say what they mean and they send teens mixed messages. How do you think it would feel to be told your not old enough to do something and then be expected to babysit your younger siblings because your parents want to go out? This sort of thing happens to teens every day. As we get older we want to have responsibility and start making our own decisions but we are only allowed to do it when it suits our parents. We all know how to be responsible and make good decisions and we have arguments with our parents because they want to control us. This is another issue teens have to face in their lives.

You would not expect friends to be an issue because they are meant to be there for you, but they are. Often your friends will turn their back on you because you said something or did something that they don't like. Sometimes you do not even know what the problem is but you have to try and work it out which is impossible because your friends aren't talking to you. You might find out through school gossip, or someone might email you and tell you but it goes to show that friends can be an issue in the life of a teenager and when your friends turn against you it is really the worst feeling.

One of the worst issues that teenagers have to face is peer pressure. In our world there are so many things that are bad for us and there are so many people telling us that it is cool to smoke or try grass. When teens have a party often there is alcohol which an older brother or friend has got, and there is always someone ready to give you a drink. Imagine how hard it is to stick to coke or pepsi when all the others are trying alcohol. Peer pressure isn't just about smoking and drinking it is also about getting in to cars with a person who doesn't have his licence, and pretending to your parents you are going to a friend's house when you are really going somewhere else and not going home straight after school. There are too many peer pressures in today's society and they are everywhere for teens to face.

Just like peer pressure, parents and friends cause enormous issues for teens to deal with in their lives in today's society. It is difficult to be a teenager when there are all these issues to be faced but teens can overcome these problems and make decisions that are best for themselves no matter what the pressures they have to face.

RATIONALE FOR STUDENT EXEMPLAR PROFICIENT

Title: The difficulties of being a teenager

Score	Reporting Category
Pf	**Content** • **The student's exploration of the topic** regarding the many issues that teenagers have to face in today's society (but especially those issues relating to parents, friends and peer pressure) **is adept and plausible.** • **The student's purpose** to examine the issues teens have to face when conflict arises between parents, friends and peers "which makes life a lot more difficult than adults think" **is intentional.** • **Ideas presented by the student are thoughtful,** as in "your friends will turn their back on you because you said something or did something that they don't like" and "coke or pepsi" **and sound** as in "As we get older we want to have responsibility and start making our own decisions but we are only allowed to do it when it suits our parents" and "we have arguements with our parents because they want to control us." • **Supporting details,** such as "Peer pressure isn't just about smoking and drinking it is also about getting in to cars with a person who doesn't have his licence," and "pretending to your parents you are going to a friend's house when you are really going somewhere else" **are apt and specific.** • **The writing is considered,** as shown in "Most teens are very insecure about themselves and this makes it difficult for them to deal with the many issues in front of them" **and elaborated,** as demonstrated in "You might find out through school gossip, or someone might email you and tell you but it goes to show that friends can be an issue in the life of a teenager and when your friends turn against you it is really the worst feeling" **and draws the reader's interest** by detailing the many issues that teens have to face in today's society.

Pf	**Organization** • **The introduction** as demonstrated in "Teenagers have to face issues every day of their lives which makes life a lot more difficult than adults think" **is purposeful and clearly establishes a focus** that "these issues come from our parents and families, teachers, friends, and peer pressure" that is capably sustained. • **Details are developed in paragraphs in a sensible order** (evident in the manner in which the student discusses the issues of "parents and families, teachers, friends, and peer pressure.") **and coherence is generally maintained.** • **Transitions** in statements such as "Often these issues come from", "We all know how to be responsible", and "but it goes to show that" **clearly connect details** within sentences and between paragraphs. • **Closure is appropriate,** as demonstrated in "Just like peer pressure, parents and friends cause enormous issues for teens to deal with in their lives in today's society" **and related to the focus** by acknowledging that "It is difficult to be a teenager when there are all these issues to be faced."
Pf	**Sentence Structure** • **Sentence structure**, as demonstrated in "Most teens are very insecure about themselves and this makes it difficult for them to deal with the many issues in front of them" and "There are too many peer pressures in today's society and they are everywhere for teens to face" is **consistently controlled.** • **Sentence type,** as in "How do you think it would feel to be told your not old enough to do something and then be expected to babysit your younger sibling because your parents want to go out?" and **sentence length,** as in "This sort of thing happens to teens every day," "You might find out through school gossip, or someone might email you and tell you but it goes to show that friends can be an issue in the life of a teenager and when your friends turn against you it is really the worst feeling" are **usually effective and varied.** • **Sentence beginnings,** such as "We all know how to be," "Often your friends will turn their back" and "Imagine how hard it is" **are often varied.** **Proportion of error to length and complexity of response has been considered.**
Pf	**Vocabulary** • **Words and expressions,** such as "younger siblings", "responsible and make good decisions", and "school gossip" **are often used accurately.** • **Specific words and expressions,** such as "send teens mixed messages" and "they want to control us." **show some evidence of careful selection and connotative effect,** as in "that it is cool to smoke or try grass." • **The voice created by the student,** as demonstrated in "when your friends turn against you it is really the worst feeling" and "Imagine how hard it is to stick to coke or pepsi" **is distinct.** **Proportion of error to length and complexity of response has been considered.**

	Conventions
Pf	• **The quality of the writing is sustained because it contains only minor convention errors,** as illustrated in "face issues every day of their lives which makes" and "we want to have responsibility and start making our own decisions but we are only allowed to do it when it suits our parents." • **Any errors that are present** "licence," "told your not old" and "You would not expect friends to be an issue because they are meant to be there for you, but they are" **rarely reduce clarity and seldom interrupt the flow of the response.** • **Proportion of error to length and complexity of response has been considered.**

Exemplar Score Excellent Narrative

THE BOX

Ian stamps his feet impatiently against the pavement to stir his tingling toes. Although the sun is shining from a brilliant blue sky, it is unseasonably cold for October. Ian's mind is not on the cold. He is thinking about the box.

"What's that big box doing there in the middle of a busy street? Hey...it's moving! What the...?"
Ian was standing with his mom just outside the Manhattan Macy's department store in New York City, waiting to cross a busy street. As they waited for the light to change, Ian had noticed the box. There it was, just ahead of him on the concrete island which divided the wide thoroughfare. The box was turned upside down, as though someone had carelessly unpacked a washer or dryer and just left the box by the road. Had it really moved, or was Ian imagining things?

That had been Ian's first experience with a homeless person. He had not really seen an actual person. The image of that moving box, however, had etched a sharp and disturbing impression on his 14 year old mind. Mom had explained, back at the hotel, that some people, not just in New York, but in most large cities, even in Canada, had only a box to call "home".

Today is the Saturday before Thanksgiving. It is Mom's idea to bring the family downtown for the Edmonton Inner City Thanksgiving March. The one kilometer walk will take the marchers through the blocks most familiar to Edmonton's homeless citizens, past the Hope Mission, and ending back at the Mustard Seed Church for coffee and donuts. For some reason, Ian doesn't mind the change to his normal Saturday routine of sleeping in and playing with his Wii games. He has been curious ever since the incident in New York last summer. He looks over at his mother, father, and younger sister. Like him, they are warmly bundled, blank, waiting.

The procession of two hundred or so volunteers, once it finally begins, is strangely silent. The sociable chatter among these amiable, middle class marchers vaporizes like early morning smoke in the crisp fall air. Each group of five or six has a "guide", who quietly provides a conversational commentary as the march winds through the downtown neighborhood: "That building houses the Boyle Street Co-op, where people can pick up warmer clothes as the weather gets colder... . A big ticket item for all of these centers is donated coffee. We go through lots, especially on the coldest days. People use their cups as temporary hand-warmers. ... Down below this street is the City Center LRT Station. The city cordons off overflow sleeping space on the floor down in the tunnel to the Winspear for people who need it on the coldest nights. We try to provide enough sleeping bags for everyone. We don't want anyone to freeze.

Beyond the Hope Mission, you can see the empty lot where we allowed homeless people to set up a tent city for a few months last summer. … The two men standing over by the A and P store are Mike and Reg. I don't know their last names, but they come regularly to the Mustard Seed Food Bank. Reg told me the worst thing about being homeless is that people on the street avoid making eye contact with them, afraid they will be asked for money or something. I tell Reg that I was homeless two years ago, and that he can make it too. You can't give up on hope."

Ian appreciates the coffee and donuts that mark the end of the tour, but he can't wait to get home. He is thinking about that box again, but he is thinking about something else too. The trip home to Mill Woods is pretty quiet. Everyone is lost in their own thoughts. It has been overwhelming.

"Mom, where do we keep the camping stuff?" Ian is shrugging out of his ski jacket in the front hallway.

"Uh…it's down in the storage area beside the family room, hon." She doesn't even ask Ian why he wants to know.

An hour later, Ian is leaning against the doorjamb of his room, surveying the heap on his bed. Two down-filled sleeping bags. Three ski toques. Five pairs of various gloves and mittens. Three plaid woolen blankets from the cottage. Two scarves. Ian thrusts his head around the doorjamb and cups his hand to the side of his mouth. "Hey, Ma…could you come here for a minute?"

That is essentially how it started. Last week, Ian's junior high school was featured on the City Page of the Edmonton Journal. The picture accompanying the article shows Ian and about 25 other students posing beside a huge pile of donated winter wear, blankets, and sleeping bags, just before it is to be picked up by the Hope Mission truck. The principal looks fondly and proudly on…but the article is not about the principal or the teachers. It is about the students, and especially about one student who decided to put his thoughts into actions.

How would Ian's family, classmates, and teachers describe him? Just as a normal guy, who gets decent (not exceptional) grades, generally minds his own business, causes his parents a bit of grief once in awhile by arguing about chores or homework. Enjoys his Wii. A loyal Oilers fan. What will he become? Who knows? Ian is only in Grade 9. One thing is sure, though. Ian will be an observer, but he will also be a participant. There will always be a moving box to keep him on his toes.

RATIONALE FOR STUDENT EXEMPLAR EXCELLENT NARRATIVE

TITLE: The Box

Score	Reporting Category
E	**Content** • **The student's exploration of the topic is insightful** (tracking a boy's experience with an issue from initial awareness to action) and **imaginative** (using an italicized anecdote from another time frame as the motivating incident in the plot of the story). • **The student's purpose** (to address the importance of awareness and involvement in issues such as homelessness) is **deliberate**. The story is orchestrated to inspire young people to be active participants in positive actions. • **The ideas presented by the student** (the startling impression in New York, the boy's emotional response to the experiences and sights during the march, and his practical response to the needs he saw) **are carefully chosen and perceptive.** • **Supporting details**, such as "Manhattan Macy's," "Hope Mission," and "Wii games" are **precise and original.** • The writing is **confident, creative**, and **holds the reader's interest** with personalized details and a plausible plot that addresses the topic through the eyes of an "average teenager."
E	**Organization** • **The introduction**, using the 'present to past' time switch with the italicized anecdote from New York, is **engaging and skillfully establishes a focus** on the issue of homelessness **that is consistently sustained** through the progression of events that culminate in a donation project at the main character's school. • **Events and details** are **developed in a judicious order** (The main character experiences a flashback which makes his current situation much more meaningful to him, he responds emotionally to the evidences of poverty and homelessness in his city, and finally decides to act on what he has heard and seen.) **Coherence is maintained** throughout the story, through a clearly evident chronological sequence of events. • **Transitions, both explicit** ("Today is the Saturday before Thanksgiving") and **implicit** ("he can't wait to get home") **fluently connect events and details within sentences and between paragraphs.** • **Closure is effective and related to the focus** ("Ian will be an observer, but he will also be a participant. There will always be a moving box to keep him on his toes").
E	**Sentence Structure** • **Sentence structure** is **effectively and consistently controlled** throughout the story. Occasional sentences that are technical 'fragments' ("Just as a normal guy…") seem to have been deliberately crafted for effect. • **Sentence type and length are consistently effective and varied** ("Ian stamps his feet impatiently…", "Although the sun is shining…", "He is thinking about the box.", "Mom, where do we keep the camping stuff?") • **Sentence beginnings are consistently varied** ("The image of that moving box", "For some reason", "How would Ian's family"). **Proportion of error to length and complexity of response has been considered.**

E	**Vocabulary** • **Words and expressions are used accurately and deliberately** throughout the story ("brilliant blue sky," "unseasonably cold", "wide thoroughfare"). • **Precise words and expressions are used to create vivid images and to enrich details** ("as though someone had carelessly unpacked a washer or dryer and just left the box," "one kilometer walk," "warmly bundled, blank, waiting"). • **The voice/tone created by the student is convincing** ("It is Mom's idea to bring the family downtown…," "The procession…once it finally begins, is strangely silent," "A big ticket item for all of these centers is…"). The student uses present tense and different 'voices' (such as the guide commentary on the march) effectively in crafting voice and tone. **Proportion of error to length and complexity of response has been considered.**
E	**Conventions** • **The quality of the writing is enhanced because it is essentially error-free.** • **Any errors that are present** (such as the absence of capitals on "department store") **do not reduce clarity and do not interrupt the flow of the response.** **Proportion of error to length and complexity of response has been considered.**

EXEMPLAR SCORE EXCELLENT ESSAY

Too many to handle

Living as a teenager in today's society is one of the most difficult things anyone has to do. Yet, those of us who are teenagers have to face problems and difficulties that our parents and grandparents only dreamed about. Just think for a moment about some of the everyday issues we have to deal with. One minute our parents are telling us to "grow up" and the next minute they are telling us "to act our age" (which is 14). Then at school we have to face kids who were our friends last week, but have turned against us for reasons we don't even know. Shall I spend all my money on clothes? Or shall I go to this or that party? Or shall I go to the mall, or drive in a car with an unqualified driver, or do poorly in school, or smoke, or drink, or do drugs, or date just to be popular? These are the sorts of questions all teenagers face every day of their lives.

Facing the many problems that confront teenagers in today's society is a difficult task. Parents and teachers do not mean to make life more difficult for teenagers but sometimes they do. How often has your mother or father told you to grow up, only to tell you a little while later that you can't do something because you are "not old enough"? I ask you, what are teenagers to think? How old do we have to be before our parents consider us "old enough"? Teachers, too, expect you to act in a mature manner and keep doing your work quietly when they leave the room or speak to another teacher and to take responsibility for your work and your actions, yet they do not think you are mature enough to be left alone in a classroom before or after school because they say they do not know what you will be up to or to go off campus at lunch break. Do they think that half an hour is enough time to rob a bank? No wonder the life of a teenager is hard. We do not know who we are or whether we are old enough.

As if parents and teacher are not trouble enough, friends make life difficult as well. Imagine how difficult it is to go to school every day and see the same group of so called friends ignore you and you don't know the reason why. You wonder about everything it might be. Is it because you chose to go camping with your family and missed a sleep over? Is it because you had to babysit your little sister so you couldn't go to the mall with them? Or is it because you got an A on your science report and they didn't. You are faced with two major issues: one, your friends are not talking to you, and two, you do not know why. Adults never have to face issues like this and they seem to have forgotten what it was like when they were teenagers and had the same problems because when you try and talk to them about it they say, "You must have other friends." or, "They will soon get sick of their behaviour." or, "Ignore them,." Life is sometimes full of issues for teenagers to deal with but issues relating to friends are the most important because with friends life is so much easier and more fun, and without friends life is really, really hard.

Questions about how to live, where to go, and what to do, can cause major issues that teenagers must deal with in today's society. We are always wondering whether we should do something or go somewhere with our friends. Teens need the strength to resist when peer pressure is used to make them think about underage drinking, drugs, substance abuse, and smoking. The idea that everyone is doing it makes teens feel that the only way to fit in is to do the same. The greatest issue here for teens is that they are worried that they will not be accepted or have friends if they do not give in to peer pressure. Can you imagine how hard to is to resist temptation when you are afraid of being called names like, chicken or wimp, or cry-baby? As you can see these are serious issues for teenagers to have to face. However with the help of counselors, teachers, parents, and good friends, teenagers do not need to deal with these issues alone; this takes the weight of the problem away from the teens themselves.

It is easy to see that teenagers face many different and difficult issues in their daily lives. Life is not easy for teenagers and I think everyone would agree that teens face more issues in today's society than our parents and grandparents did in their day. Life for teenagers would be easier if they accepted responsibility for their actions, respected the adults in their lives as people who have had more experiences than they have had, and learned that with parents, teachers and friends life can be fun and these problems and issues can be faced and dealt with without too much hassle.

RATIONALE FOR STUDENT EXEMPLAR EXCELLENT ESSAY

Title: Too many to handle

Score	Reporting Category
E	**Content** • **The student's exploration of the topic** ("Parents and teachers do not mean to make life more difficult for teenagers but sometimes they do." and, "Imagine how difficult it is to go to school every day and see the same group of so called friends ignore you and you don't know the reason why." and, "Teens need the strength to resist when peer pressure is used to make them think about underage drinking, drugs, substance abuse, and smoking." **is insightful.** • **The student's purpose**—to recognize how difficult it is for teenagers to live in today's society because of the issues they have to face—**is deliberate.** • **The ideas presented by the student are perceptive** (as in, "How often has your mother or father told you to grow up, only to tell you a little while later that you can't do something because you are "not old enough?" I ask you, what are teenagers to think?") and **carefully chosen** (as in, "Imagine how difficult it is to go to school every day and see the same group of so called friends ignore you and you don't know the reason why."). • **Supporting details** such as, "Shall I spend all my money on clothes? Or shall I go to this or that party? Or shall I go to the mall, or drive in a car with an unqualified driver, or do poorly in school, or smoke, or drink, or do drugs, or date just to be popular?" **are precise** —in so much as the student acknowledges the pertinent issues that teenagers have to face. • **The writing is confident** (as in, "Yet, those of us who are teenagers have to face problems and difficulties that our parents and grandparents only dreamed about." and, "I ask you, what are teenagers to think?") **and holds the reader's interest** (as in, "How often has your mother or father told you to grow up, only to tell you a little while later that you can't do something because you are "not old enough"?")
E	**Organization** • **The introduction is engaging and skillfully establishes a focus** "Living as a teenager in today's society is one of the most difficult things anyone has to do. Yet, those of us who are teenagers have to face problems and difficulties that our parents and grandparents only dreamed about" **that is consistently sustained** (by discussing the many issues teenagers have to face in today's society). • **Details are developed in a judicious order** (by discussing some of the common everyday issues that teenagers have to face—the behavior of "Parents and teachers," "friends (who) make life difficult," and "peer pressure" **and coherence is maintained** by the presentation of issues teen have to face. • **Transitions fluently connect details within sentences** ("yet they do not think you are mature enough" and "As you can see these are serious issues") **and between paragraphs** as in," Facing the many problems that confront teenagers in today's society is a difficult task." and, "As if parents and teacher are not trouble enough, friends make life difficult as well." • **Closure is effective and related to the focus** "Life is not easy for teenagers and I think everyone would agree that teens face more issues in today's society than our parents and grandparents did in their day" and by mentioning that teenagers would find life easier if they were responsible and recognized that adults were available to help.

E	**Sentence Structure** • **Sentence structure is effectively and consistently controlled** as in "Then at school we have to face kids who were our friends last week, but have turned against us for reasons we don't even know" and "However with parents, teachers and friends life can be fun and we can face these problems and issues without too much hassle." • **Sentence type** ("Shall I spend all my money on clothes? Or shall I go to this or that party?") and **sentence length** ("You wonder about everything it might be" and "Adults never have to face issues like this and they seem to have forgotten what it was like when they were teenagers and had the same problems because when you try and talk to them about it they say…" and "You must have other friends." or, "They will soon get sick of their behaviour" or "Ignore them,.") **are consistently effective and varied.** • **Sentence beginnings** such as "Imagine how difficult…" "The greatest issue here…" and "As you can see…" **are consistently varied.** **Proportion of error to length and complexity of response has been considered.**
E	**Vocabulary** • **Words and expressions** ("Just think for a moment about some of the everyday issues" and "Teens need the strength to resist when peer pressure is used") are accurately and **deliberately** ("problems that confront teenagers," and "to take responsibility for your work and your actions") **and accurately used**. • **Precise words and expressions** ("to act our age" and "you got an A on your science report") **are used to create vivid images** ("Do they think that half an hour is enough time to rob a bank?") **and enrich details** ("chicken, or wimp, or cry-baby?") • **The tone created by the student is convincing** (as in "One minute our parents are telling us to "grow up" and the next minute they are telling us "to act our age" (which is 14)" and "The greatest issue here for teens is that they are worried that they will not be accepted or have friends if they do not give in to peer pressure"). **Proportion of error to length and complexity of response has been considered.**
E	**Conventions** • **The quality of the writing is enhanced because it is essentially error free** as demonstrated in "One minute our parents are telling us to "grow up" and the next minute they are telling us "to act our age" (which is 14)." and "You are faced with two major issues: one, your friends are not talking to you, and two, you do not know why." • **Any errors that are present** (the lack of capitals in the title, "Too many to handle") **do not reduce clarity** and **do not interrupt the flow of the response**. **Proportion of error to length and complexity of response has been considered.**

NARRATIVE WRITING PROMPT THREE

Assignment

Write a narrative or essay to show how a book you have read, a movie you have seen, or music you have listened to has changed your perspective on life. You may write about yourself, or other people, real or fictional. You may set your writing in the past, present, or future.

Ideas

The following material may give you ideas for your writing. **You do not have to use any of it**. Consider your own ideas gained through reading, listening, viewing, discussing, thinking, or imagining. You can also reference ideas from books, movies, music, or any other media.

Books

- Racism
- War
- Solitude
- Secrecy
- Tolerance
- Friendship
- Power
- Cooperation
- Helping others

Movies

- Survival
- Independence
- Integrity
- Environmental issues

Music

- Love
- Faithfulness
- Hope
- Belief
- Acceptance
- Moving on
- Following Dreams

When writing, **be sure to:**
- Consider your **audience**
- Focus on your **purpose** and **point of view**
- **Organize** your thoughts appropriately in sentences and paragraphs
- Use **vocabulary** that is interesting and effective
- **Edit** your work directly on your writing
- **Budget** your time

STUDENT EXEMPLARS AND RATIONALES NARRATIVE WRITING PROMPT THREE

EXEMPLAR SCORE SATISFACTORY NARRATIVE

DIARY OF A READING NERD

Sometimes my best friend Suri calls me a nerd just to tease me. But, anyone else should be careful cause my big brother, Aaron would go after them. He's in Grade 9, captain of the boys' basketball team, and probably the most popular guy in the school.

My mom would say that I'm another story. I am short, not tall like Aaron," have this best friend who happens to be a girl, hate basketball, and love reading. That's right—give me a good story and a few hours of free time, and you won't hear "boo" from me till you force me to eat dinner or start my chores. I guess that makes me a reading nerd

I hadn't told Aaron yet about "Macho Jack", the bully from our home room. Jack moved to our school in January. He is pretty big for his age, and already has his own little gang of "tough guys". They all hate school, and most of all, anything to do with reading. They love to mock people who like reading class: "Woo-woo…we get to read another chapter in Touching Spirit Bear! Bet Suri and her super-nerd boyfriend can hardly wait!"

Jack and his gang started to hang out in the lunch room near where we were reading ahead in our novel. We were getting to the part where Cole has to be on the island with the boy he has beaten up. Jack would take a seat on the next table with his so-called friends and say stuff like, "Well, if it isn't the grannies' noon hour book club!" Then he would wave his arms and roll his eyes sarcastically.

Both times, Suri and I pretended to read until they finally got bored with annoying us. That night I told Aaron. He listened, then told me not to worry. He said that I should just meet Suri for lunch the next day as usual. I didn't know what he was planning, but I heard him talking on his cell for quite a long time.

The next day, same thing, when all of the sudden, Aaron and five of his buddies came into the lunchroom and sat at the next table. Jack's back was to the door, so he didn't see them, until it was too late. They slid into the benches on both sides of the table he was sitting on, without saying a word. Next, they opened six copies of The Lord of the Rings. Jack was completely surrounded, so he didn't dare move. They just sat there and read, for about three minutes. Finally, Aaron looked up.

"How ya doin' there, little brother? Whatcha readin'? I remember when we did that novel in Grade 7. Best novel we ever had to read, right, guys?" He looked at his five friends and they nodded in agreement. Jack didn't dare move a muscle. After about five more minutes, the grade 9's closed their novels and left the lunchroom. Jack followed them without a word.

After that day, Jack started to change. He really wasn't so tough. When Mrs. Carlson put him in my oral reading group with two other boys the next week, he got all embarrassed, because he couldn't read very well. I told Jack we would help him with words he didn't know. Jack got more comfortable. When he stumbled over a hard word, we helped him.

I decided to get to know Jack better. We were both from single parent homes, so I told Aaron that I thought Jack respected me now. It wasn't just because my brother was the most popular guy in the school. I think Jack realized that even reading nerds are worth listening to sometimes.

The End

RATIONALE FOR STUDENT EXEMPLAR SATISFACTORY NARRATIVE

Title: Diary of a Reading Nerd

Score	Reporting Category
S	**Content** • **The student's exploration of the topic** is **clear** and **logical**. A student has been influenced by books by the time he reaches Grade 7, and is able to impact a bully's negative attitude toward reading. • **The student's purpose** (to show how attitudes toward books can change) is **implied** but **evident**. • **The ideas presented by the student** (a boy and his female friend endure teasing at school related to their love of reading books) are **appropriate** and **predictable**. • **Supporting details**, such as "Aaron would go after them" and "Jack and his gang started to hang out in the lunch room near where we were reading" are **relevant** but **generic**. • The writing is **straightforward and generalized** as in "I guess that makes me a reading nerd" and occasionally **appeals to the reader's interest** through a detail such as "Jack didn't dare move a muscle."
S	**Organization** • **The introduction** is **functional and establishes a focus** by creating the contrast between the main character and his more athletic older brother, and **the focus** on books and their role in the Grade 7 boy's life is **generally sustained.** • **Events** are **developed in a discernible order** with the boy being verbally bullied for reading his novel at noon, telling his older brother, and the lunchroom lesson for the bully. **Coherence may falter occasionally** due to the cursory progression of the plot and absence of details, but in the end, the "reading nerd" is able to help Jack change his perspective on reading and bullying. • **Transitions** such as "Both times," and "The next day," and "Next," are **generally used to connect details within sentences and between paragraphs**, but tend to be **mechanical**. • **Closure is related to the focus** ("I think Jack realized that even reading nerds are worth listening to sometimes") but somewhat **mechanical**.
S	**Sentence Structure** • Sentence structure is **generally controlled.** • Sentence **type and length are sometimes effective** ("Sometimes my best friend Suri calls me a nerd just to tease me") **and/or varied** ("That's right—give me a good story and a few hours of free time…"). • **Some variety of sentence beginnings is evident** as in "Both times," and "How ya doin' there…?" **Proportion of error to length and complexity of response has been considered.**

S	**Vocabulary** • **Words and expressions are generally used appropriately** throughout the story. • **General words and expressions are used adequately to clarify meaning** ("probably the most popular guy in the school," "love to mock people who like reading class"). • **The voice/tone created by the student is discernible** ("I…have this best friend who happens to be a girl"). **Proportion of error to length and complexity of response has been considered.**
S	**Conventions** • **The quality of the writing is sustained through generally correct use of conventions.** • **Errors occasionally reduce clarity and sometimes interrupt the flow of the response** ("The next day, the same thing, when all of the sudden, Aaron and five of his buddies came into the lunchroom and sat at the next table…"). **Proportion of error to length and complexity of response has been considered.**

EXEMPLAR SATISFACTORY ESSAY

The Diary of Anne Frank

I have just finished reading Anne Frank: *The Diary of a Young Girl* and I think it was one of the best books I have ever read. Anne died in a concentration camp for jews during the war and she never gave up hope of being saved and believing that people are really born good and she kept on writing in her diary even though she was really sick and she was dying. Anne has made me realize that it is important to be positive in life and not to be miserable even when things are not going your way.

I have never met any jews but if Anne is an example of what a jew is like then she seems like any one else. This probably means that muslims and Indians, and all kids from sudan are just like regular kids too. I always thought they were a bit different because sometimes they wear different cloths and they talk a different language but Anne did not speak English. She wrote her book in Dutch but it was translated in English so that we could read it and learn from Anne how to be tolerent and how to like people who were mean to you.

Can you imagine being shut up in an attic for more than two years and not being allowed out and having to live with your parents and these other people who you do not like very much and every one knowing all your busness. Day after day was the same. Nothing ever changed. Anne must have missed her school friends and spending time with them. But that was what it was like for Anne when they were hiding from Germans in the war. It was a good thing that Peter was in the attic and Anne and Peter could have some good talks together. Anne did complain a bit though but not all the time.

I think Anne was an amazing girl to put up with so much and even dying and still be positive about all the bad things she experienced. I am glad her father published her book so that we could all read it and learn how to be tolerent like Anne and not complain too much when life is hard. I will try to be a better person like Anne now that I have read her diary.

RATIONALE FOR STUDENT EXEMPLAR SATISFACTORY ESSAY

Title: The Diary of Anne Frank

Score	Reporting Category
S	**Content** • **The student's exploration of the topic** in how nonfiction work *Anne Frank: The Diary of a Young Girl*, has made the writer think about people from different backgrounds and in different situations is clear and logical. • **The student's purpose** (to examine how Anne suffered but remained positive throughout her life) **is evident.** • **The ideas presented by the student,** as in "This probably means that muslims and Indians, and all kids from sudan are just like regular kids too" and "Can you imagine being shut up in an attic for more than two years and not being allowed out…" **are appropriate and predictable.** • **Supporting details,** such as "they wear different clothes and they talk a different language" and "Anne must have missed her school friends and spending time with them" **are relevant but generic.** • **The writing is straightforward** as in, ("I have just finished reading Anne Frank: the Diary of a Young Girl and I think it was one of the best books I have ever read") **and generalized** as in, ("I think Anne was a amazing girl to put up with so much") **and occasionally appeals to the reader's interest** as in "Anne died in a concentration camp for jews during the war and she never gave up hope of being saved and believing that people are really born good."
S	**Organization** • **The introduction is functional and establishes a focus** "Anne has made me realize that it is important to be positive in life and not to be miserable even when things are not going your way." **that is generally sustained.** • **Details** such as, "if Anne is an example of what a jew is like then she seems like any one else" and "that was what it was like for Anne when they were hiding from the Germans in the war" **are developed in a discernible order though coherence may falter occasionally** as in "It was a good thing that Peter was in the attic." • **Transitions** such as "This probably means…," "But that was what it was like…" **which are generally used to connect details within sentences and between paragraphs tend to be mechanical.** • **Closure is related to the focus,** "I am glad her father published her book so that we could all read it and learn how to be tolerant like Anne and not complain too much when life is hard. I will try to be a better person like Anne now that I have read her diary" **and mechanical.**

S	**Sentence Structure** • **Sentence structure is generally controlled** as in "She wrote her book in Dutch but it was translated into English so that we could read it and learn from Anne how to be tolerant and how to like people who were mean to you" but **lapses** (such as the run on sentence—"Anne died in a concentration camp for jews during the war and she never gave up hope of being saved and believing that people are really born good and she kept on writing in her diary even though she was really sick and was dying..") **may occasionally impede meaning.** • **Sentence type and length are sometimes effective** ("Nothing ever changed." and "But that was what it was like for Anne when they were hiding from the Germans in the war.") and/or varied ("Can you imagine being shut up in an attic for more than two years…"). • **Some variety of sentence beginnings is evident** as in "This probably means…," and "Day after day…," and "I think Anne was…" **Proportion of error to length and complexity of response has been considered.**
S	**Vocabulary** • **Words** such as "tolerent", "amazing girl" and expressions such as "important to be positive in life," and "Anne did complain a bit" **are generally used appropriately.** • **General words and expressions are used adequately to clarify meaning**—such as "they wear different clothes and they talk a different language," and "Anne and Peter could have some good talks together." • **The voice/tone created by the student is discernible** (as in, "I think Anne was a amazing girl to put up with so much and still be positive about all the bad things she experienced") but **uneven.** **Proportion of error to length and complexity of response has been considered.**
S	**Conventions** • **The quality of the writing is sustained through generally correct use of conventions,** as in "But that was what it was like for Anne when they were hiding from the Germans in the war." • **Errors occasionally reduce clarity** (such as the lack of capitals for proper nouns and the incorrect spelling of "tolerent" and "busness") and sometimes **interrupt the flow of the response** as in the concluding paragraph where the student writes about Anne "dying and still be positive about all the bad things she experienced." **Proportion of error to length and complexity of response has been considered.**

DIARY OF A READING NERD

Some people would call me a nerd. Sometimes my best friend Suri does, just to tease me. But, you'd better not use that word around my big brother, Aaron. He's in Grade 9, 5'10", captain of the senior boys' basketball team, a straight A student, and probably the most popular guy in the school.

Now, me, I'm another story, as our mom would tell you. Besides the fact that I am still 5'2" half way through Grade 7, have this best friend who happens to be a girl, and don't enjoy any sports except the virtual kind, I love reading. That's right: give me a good story and a few hours of free time, and you won't hear "boo" from me till you force me to eat dinner or start my chores. I guess that makes me a reading nerd. Aaron sometimes looks into the family room and mutters "Weird!" as he heads out the door on a sunny day, but he doesn't really mind. I know he would challenge anyone who would give me a rough time for being who I am. He has always been there to protect his kid brother, especially since Dad died, when I was four.

Well, on with my story…

The truth is, I hadn't told Aaron yet about "Macho Jack", my own personal bully from our home room. Suri and me couldn't figure him out. Jack moved to our school in January. He is pretty big for his age, kind of nasty, and already has his own little gang of "tough guys". They all hate school, and most of all, anything to do with reading. That includes mocking people who like reading class: "Here come the Class 7A super-nerd couple. … all excited because we are coming in to LA class again. Woo-woo…we get to read another chapter in <u>Touching Spirit Bear!</u>"

By Tuesday this week, I was fed up. Jack and his gang were starting to hang out in the lunch room corner where we were reading ahead in our novel, because we were getting to the part where Cole has to be on the island with the boy he had beaten up. This main character, Cole, is starting to change, so Suri and I were talking about the things in his life that had made him so mean, like his abusive father. We didn't see Jack take a seat on the next table with his so-called friends. Jack started saying stuff like, "Well, well, if it isn't the grannies' noon hour book club!" Jack perched his chin on his fist and rolled his eyes at the ceiling, for the full effect. Tuesday was basically a replay of Monday.

Both times, Suri and I pretended to read until they finally got bored with annoying us and moved off. That night I told Aaron. He listened, then he told me not to worry—just to meet Suri for lunch the next day as usual. "I'll be by." I didn't know what he had planned, but I heard him talking on his cell in the next room.

The next day, same thing, when all of a sudden, one of Jack's buddies whispered "Uh-oh," and slid off the bench to leave. Jack's back was to the door, so he didn't see Aaron and five of Aaron's friends from the basketball team, until it was too late. They slid into the benches on both sides of the table he was sitting on, and without saying a word, and opened six copies of The Lord of the Rings by J.R.R. Tolkien. Jack was completely surrounded. They just sat there and read, for about three long minutes, while Jack watched wordlessly. Finally, Aaron glanced up.

"How ya doin' there, little brother? Whatcha readin'? I remember when we did that novel in Grade 7. Best novel we ever read in school up to that point, right, guys?" He looked at his five friends, who nodded enthusiastically. "After we read that book, most of us guys realized that there were actually some good books written for boys!"

Jack just sat like a statue. He didn't dare move a muscle. After about five more minutes, the grade 9's closed their novels, slipped back off the benches, and strolled out of the lunchroom. Jack followed them without a word.

That day marked a turning point for Jack. Turns out the new, "tough" kid wasn't so tough after all. Mrs. Carlson assigned him to my oral reading group with two other boys that Friday. When it was Jack's turn to read, he got all embarrassed, because he couldn't read very well. "Don't worry about it," I said. "We can help you with words you don't know. Mrs. C. lets us read in these small groups so we feel more relaxed about reading out loud." You could see Jack get more comfortable. When he stumbled, we helped him with the pronunciation.

I decided to get to know Jack better. We were both from single parent homes, even though his was from divorce, not a parent dying, like mine. I told my brother that Jack was a lot like Cole. We could never be best friends, like me and Suri, but I told Aaron that I thought Jack respected me now, and not just because my brother was top dude in the school. I think Jack recognized that even reading nerds have something worthwhile to say.

RATIONALE FOR STUDENT EXEMPLAR PROFICIENT NARRATIVE

Title: Diary of a Reading Nerd

Score	Reporting Category
Pf	**Content** • **The student's exploration of the topic** (how books change someone's perspective on life) is both **adept** and **plausible**. • **The student's purpose** (to demonstrate how teenagers like the main character and his brother can influence others to be less negative toward people who like to read) is **intentional** as implied by the story. • **The ideas presented by the student** (trying to be yourself even if others don't agree that reading books is a valid or worthwhile activity) are **thoughtful and sound.** • **Supporting details**, such as "don't enjoy any sports except the virtual kind" and "mocking people who like reading class" are **apt** and **specific.** • The writing is **elaborated** with sufficient details about the mental bullying situation and the older brother's intervention to **draw the reader's interest** from the beginning to the end of the story.
Pf	**Organization** • **The introduction** is **purposeful and clearly establishes a focus** by providing background for the protagonist's experience later in the story. This **focus is capably sustained** through a progression of events that do not deviate from the focus established in the introduction. • **Details are developed in a sensible order** through background information about the reading nerd, introduction of the bully, older brother's intervention, and turning point in the bully's attitude. **Coherence is generally maintained** because the chronological sequence of events is clear. • **Transitions, both explicit** ("By Tuesday this week") and **implicit** ("We didn't see Jack take a seat...") **clearly connect events and details within sentences and between paragraphs.** • **Closure is appropriate and related to the focus** ("I think Jack recognized that even reading nerds have something worthwhile to say").

Pf	**Sentence Structure** • **Sentence structure is consistently controlled** throughout the story. • **Sentence type and length are usually effective and varied** ("Some people would call me a nerd," "Besides the fact that…"). • **Sentence beginnings are often varied** ("The truth is," "How ya doin' there"). **Proportion of error to length and complexity of response has been considered.**
Pf	**Vocabulary** • **Words and expressions** are often **used accurately** throughout the story ("would challenge anyone," "his abusive father"). • **Specific and expressions show some evidence of careful selection** ("my own personal bully," "perched his chin on his fist") and **some awareness of connotative effect** ("mutters 'Weird!'"). • **The voice/tone created by the student is distinct** ("I was fed up," "starting to hang out," "saying stuff like"). **Proportion of error to length and complexity of response has been considered.**
Pf	**Conventions** • **The quality of the writing is sustained because it contains only minor convention errors.** • **Any errors that are present** (such as "Suri and me couldn't figure him out.") **rarely reduce clarity and seldom interrupt the flow of the response.** **Proportion of error to length and complexity of response has been considered.**

EXEMPLAR SCORE PROFICIENT ESSAY

THE DIARY OF ANNE FRANK

The Diary of Anne Frank is one book that has had an overwhelming effect on me. I have both read the book and seen the movie and they both influenced me greatly. The fact that the book is true and that Anne had to overcome so many difficulties makes me realize how important it is to be grateful for what we have but also to look at the positive things in our lives.

Anne Frank was a Jew who was born in Germany. When Hitler and the Nazis came to power the Frank family escaped to Holland. In Holland she went to school like all of us, had friends, and spent time going to movies or talking with her friends. However when the Nazis came to Holland Jewish children were not allowed to go to school and after a while they were not allowed to do many things like go out at night, eat in restaurants, or have a business. When Anne was thirteen, she and her family had to go into hiding to escape from the Nazis. They with another family and a friend hid in the attic of Mr. Frank's office. They stayed hidden in these little rooms for more than two years. What is truly amazing is that during this time Anne did not give up hope that one day she would be rescued and she wrote in her diary that she did not believe that the whole world was bad and that there was good in the world.

Anne wrote her diary during her time in the attic. She wrote about everything she felt, like how she got fed up with the other people in the attic and she didn't like her mother, and how she loved her father best. She also wrote about how she fell in love with Peter and when they first kissed. I don't think Anne meant to have her diary read by so many people because she wrote some really personal things, but since she died her father decided to publish the diary. I think her father had the diary published so that people can read about how difficult life was for Anne and the family but how Anne kept being positive and would not let life get her down.

Another way the book has affected me is that it has made me realize that racism is wrong. Anne was a Jew but she was just the same as all other girls her age. She liked the same things as other girls, she collected pictures of movie stars, and she liked to read and write. Jew is a religion and it is just what church they go to which is the synagog. So really when the Jews were persecuted by Hitler it wasn't really racism it was religionism. I don't think it matters what church you go to or how you pray, what matters is if you are a kind, thoughtful, and positive person like Anne. I will always remember the book The Diary of Anne Frank and it will effect me in how I make decisions and how I behave towards other people. We need to be positive like Anne and treat people as we would like to be treated because it doesn't matter what you believe or what race you are. All teenagers are alike in many ways. Anne has shown me this even though I never met her and I will remember to do what I think is right for myself and those who are near to me.

RATIONALE FOR STUDENT EXEMPLAR PROFICIENT ESSAY

Title: The Diary of Anne Frank

Score	Reporting Category
Pf	**Content** • **The student's exploration of the topic** in the examination of how the nonfiction work *Anne Frank: the Diary of a Young Girl* "has had an overwhelming effect on me" is **adept** and **plausible**. • **The student's purpose** to explain the need for racial harmony and how in spite of difficulties Anne remained a positive person is **intentional**. • **The ideas presented by the student** such as "during this time Anne did not give up hope that one day she would be rescued" and "people can read about how difficult life was for Anne" **are thoughtful and sound.** • **Supporting details** such as "They were not allowed to do many things like go out at night, eat in restaurants, or have a business," "how she got fed up with the other people in the attic" and "she collected pictures of movie stars, and she liked to read and write" are **apt and specific.** • **The writing is considered** as demonstrated in "Anne Frank was a Jew who was born in Germany. When Hitler and the Nazis came to power the Frank family escaped to Holland" and **elaborated and draws the reader's interest** by recognizing that Anne Frank did overcome many difficulties in her life.

Pf	**Organization** • **The introduction** "The fact that the book is true and that Anne had to overcome so many difficulties makes me realize how important it is to be grateful for what we have but also to look at the positive things in our lives" is purposeful and clearly establishes a focus relating to how *The Diary of Anne Frank* has influenced the student that **is capably sustained.** • **Details are developed in a sensible order** as is evident in how the student gives a brief preview of the book before discussing the areas of the novel that had the greatest impact and **coherence is generally maintained.** • **Transitions** such as "However when the Nazis came to Holland," "She also wrote about," and "Another way the book" **clearly connect details within sentences and between paragraphs.** • **Closure is appropriate** as in "We need to be positive like Anne and treat people as we would like to be treated because it doesn't matter what you believe or what rave you are. All teenagers are alike in many ways. Anne has shown me this even though I never met her and I will remember to do what I think is right for myself and those who are near to me" **and related to the focus.**
Pf	**Sentence Structure** • **Sentence structure** as in "She wrote about everything she felt, like how she got fed up with.other people in the attic and she didn't like her mother, and how she loved her father best" is **consistently controlled.** • **Sentence type** as in "What is truly amazing is that during this time Anne did not give up hope that one day she would be rescued and she wrote in her diary that she did not believe that the whole world was bad and that there was good in the world" and **sentence length** as in "Anne wrote her diary during her time in the attic" and "I think her father had the diary published so that people can read about how difficult life was for Anne and the family but how Anne kept being positive and would not let life get her down" **are usually effective and varied.** • **Sentence beginnings** such as "Anne Frank was a Jew," "When Anne was thirteen," "I think her father" and "Another way the book" are **often varied.** **Proportion of error to length and complexity of response has been considered**
Pf	**Vocabulary** • **Words and expressions** such as "Anne had to overcome so many difficulties" and "They stayed hidden in these little rooms for more than two years" **are often used accurately.** • **Specific words and expressions** such as "What is truly amazing is that during this time Anne did not give up hope," "she wrote some really personal things," and "when the Jews were persecuted by Hitler it wasn't really racism it was religionism" **show some evidence of careful selection and some awareness of connotative effec**t as in "I don't think it matters what church you go to or how you pray." • **The tone created by the student** as demonstrated in "I don't think it matters what church you go to or how you pray, what matters is if you are a kind, thoughtful, and positive person like Anne" **is distinct.** **Proportion of error to length and complexity of response has been considered.**

Pf	**Conventions** • **The quality of the writing is sustained because it contains only minor convention errors** such as "I don't think it matters what church you go to or how you pray, what matters is…" • Any errors that are present in mechanics "synagog" and "religionism" and the usage "it will effect me" and "do what I think is right for myself" rarely reduce clarity and seldom interrupt the flow of the response. **Proportion of error to length and complexity of response has been considered.**

EXEMPLAR EXCELLENT NARRATIVE

DIARY OF A READING NERD

It's ok if I call myself, Angus J. Bradley, a nerd. I don't mind if my best friend Suri does, either. Sometimes she does, just to tease me or get me going. We play these little "insult games" with each other. Mostly, other people don't know who or what we are talking about, which is ok with me, most of the time. But you'd better watch your mouth around my big brother, Aaron. He's in Grade 9, 5'10", captain of the senior boys' basketball team, a straight A student, and probably the most popular guy in the school. The girls practically drool when he walks by with his buddies and even glances their way, more so if he just smiles their way

Now, me, I'm another story, as our mom would tell you. She's been a single parent ever since my dad died of cancer two years ago, and her favorite expression seems to be, "I declare, Angus, I think you broke the mold! I sure can't figure you out! I thought I knew what to expect from boys by the time Aaron was two years old….then you came along!"

Anyhow, that's a bit off topic. You see, besides the fact that I am still 5'2" half way through Grade 7, have this best friend who happens to be a girl, and don't enjoy any sports unless they involve a hand-held controller or a computer mouse, I am a big fan of reading. That's right, folks! Take it or leave it—give me a good story or a new author, my comfy chair in the family room, and a few hours of free time, and you won't hear "boo" from me till you force me to eat dinner or start my chores. I guess that makes me a reading nerd. Aaron sometimes looks into the family room and mutters "Weird!" as he heads out the door on a sunny day to play football with his friends, but other than that he pretty much leaves me be. I know he would be happy to take on anyone who would dare to give me a rough time for being who I am. Mom says he was her right hand man when I was little, taking me for rides in the stroller or playing with me outside to give her a bit of free time. I can't remember that far back.

Well, on with my story. I seem to get sidetracked. Before I tell you what happened this week, I have to tell you about a story we read in class back in November. It was called something like "First Fall of Snow", and it was in our Grade 7 reader. In the story, some grade 7 boys are being bullied and harassed by some Grade 9 boys. The main boy in the story deserts his friend when they are being bullied, then really feels bad about it. In the end, he watches some shadows moving on the fresh snow in the park, and imagines getting major revenge on the "bully boys".

When we read the story, I thought to myself, "My brother Aaron would never let something like that happen to me. Aaron and his friends would see to it that no one could bully us grade 7 kids like that."

The truth is, I hadn't told Aaron yet about "Macho Jack", my own personal bully from our home room. Suri and me couldn't figure him out. Jack moved to our school in January after his parents split up. He is pretty big for his age; in fact, Suri said she heard him tell someone he got held back a grade. He's kind of nasty and mean, and already has himself this little posse of would-be tough guys. The thing they all seem to have in common is that they all hate school, and most of all, anything to do with reading. That includes mocking people who like reading class: "Here come the Class 7A super-nerd couple….all excited because we are coming in to LA class again. Woo-woo…we get to read another chapter in <u>Touching Spirit Bear!</u> Let's hope tough guy Cole finally gets chomped by a bear so we can bury him and the stupid book too!"

By Tuesday this week, I told Suri that I was telling Aaron. Enough is enough. Since Monday, Jack and his posse of three were starting to hang out in the lunch room corner where we were reading ahead in our novel, because we were getting to the part where Cole has to be on the island with the boy he had beaten up and injured so badly that he had to be hospitalized. This main character, Cole, is starting to change at this point, so Suri and I were talking about the things in his life that had made him so mean, like his abusive father, his alcoholic mother, and the way his parents threw money at him instead of love and real parenting. We didn't see Jack until he perched on the next table. With his so-called friends chortling in fake admiration, Jack started saying stuff like, "Well, well, if it isn't the grannies' noon hour book club! My, my…isn't that Cole just the most fascinating character! I could just talk about him for hou..urs!!" As he droned out the words, Jack perched his chin on his fist and rolled his eyes at the ceiling, for the full dramatic effect. Tuesday was basically a replay of Monday.

Both times, Suri and I quit talking and pretended to read until they finally got bored with annoying us and moved off. That night I finally told Aaron. He just listened, without saying anything. Then he told me not to worry—just to meet Suri for lunch the next day as though nothing had happened. "Do what you normally do; I'll be by." I didn't know what he had planned, but I heard him talking on his cell in the next room. The day had been quite exhausting. I think I fell asleep when Aaron was still talking on the phone.

The next day, same thing. It was beginning to sound like a duplicate of Tuesday, when all of a sudden, one of Jack's buddies whispered "Uh-oh," and slid off the bench to make a casual exit. Jack's back was to the door, so he didn't see Aaron and five of Aaron's friends from the basketball team, until it was too late. They slid into the benches on both sides of the table he was sitting on, and without saying a word, opened six copies of The Lord of the Rings by J.R.R. Tolkien. "Macho boy" couldn't do a thing. He was completely surrounded. They just sat there and read, for about three long minutes, while Jack's eyes about popped out of his head. After what seemed an eternity, Aaron glanced up as if he was seeing me and Suri for the first time.

"Hey, how ya doin' there, little brother? Whatcha readin'? I remember when we did that novel in Grade 7. Best novel we ever read in school up to that point, right, guys?" He looked at his five friends, who nodded with exaggerated enthusiasm. "After we read that book, most of us guys realized that there were actually some good books written for boys, and Mrs. Carlson gave us that book list."

Jack just sat there and gawked. He didn't dare move a muscle. After about five more minutes, the grade 9's closed their novels, slipped back off the benches, and sauntered gracefully out of the lunchroom. Jack followed them without a word.

That day marked a kind of turning point for Jack. Turns out the new, "tough" kid wasn't so tough after all. Mrs. Carlson assigned him to my oral reading group with two other boys that Friday. When it was Jack's turn to read, he got all flustered and embarrassed, and admitted that he couldn't read very well. "Don't worry about it," I said. "We can help you with words you don't know. Mrs. C. lets us read in these small groups so we feel more relaxed about reading out loud." You could see Jack get more comfortable, and he didn't stumble all that much. When he did, we helped him with the pronunciation.

I decided to make an effort to get to know Jack better. We were both from single parent homes, even though his was from divorce, not a parent dying, like mine. I told my brother that Jack was a lot like Cole. We could never be best friends, like me and Suri. We just didn't have enough in common. I also told Aaron that I thought Jack respected me now, and not just because my brother was top dude in the school. I think Jack recognized that reading nerds have something worthwhile to say. Everybody matters, even the nerds and the Coles of this world.

RATIONALE FOR STUDENT EXEMPLAR EXCELLENT NARRATIVE

Title: Diary of a Reading Nerd

Score	Reporting Category
E	**Content** • **The student's exploration of the topic is insightful** (taking a behind-the-scenes look at an avid reader) and **imaginative** (addressing the woes of "reading nerds," who are sometimes mocked by peers, in a humorous way). • **The student's purpose** (to illustrate how attitudes toward reading can change) is **deliberate.** The story is intended to show how a reader can positively influence a reluctant reader's perspective on life. • **The ideas presented by the student** (a way of dealing with bullying that is harmless and not vengeful) are **carefully chosen and perceptive.** • **Supporting details**, such as "girls practically drool," "looks into the family room," and "First Fall of Snow" are **precise and original.** • The writing is **confident, creative, and holds the reader's interest** with personalized details and a plausible but light-hearted plot.
E	**Organization** • **The introduction**, which introduces the main character and his loyal brother in a chatty, informal way, is **engaging and skillfully establishes a focus** on the topic that is **consistently sustained** through the progression of events which culminate in a positive outcome for the all, including the reading bully. • **Events and details** are **developed in a judicious order** (The student writer creates a catchy initial incident, exposes a conflict or problem, and leads the main character through a series of events to a plausible outcome and resolution of the conflict). **Coherence is maintained** through a clearly evident chronological sequence of events. • **Transitions, both explicit** ("Well, on with my story") **and implicit** ("Before I tell you what happened this week") **fluently connect events and details within sentences and between paragraphs.** • **Closure is effective and related to the focus** ("I think Jack recognized that reading nerds have something to say. Everybody matters, even the nerds and the Coles of this world").

E	**Sentence Structure** • **Sentence structure** is **effectively and consistently controlled** throughout the story. • **Sentence type and length are consistently effective and varied** ("We play these little "insult" games with each other." "That's right, folks!" "After what seemed an eternity…"). • **Sentence beginnings are consistently varied** ("As he droned out the words…," "Tuesday was…," "When it was Jack's turn to read…"). **Proportion of error to length and complexity of response has been considered.**
E	**Vocabulary** • **Words and expressions are used accurately and deliberately** throughout the story ("favorite expression," "hand-held controller," "bullied and harassed"). • **Precise words and expressions are used to create vivid images and to enrich details** ("my comfy chair in the family room," "little posse of would-be tough guys,", "chortling in fake admiration"). • **The voice/tone created by the student is convincing** ("which is ok with me, most of the time," "have this best friend who happens to be a girl," "I seem to get sidetracked"). **Proportion of error to length and complexity of response has been considered.**
E	**Conventions** • **The quality of the writing is enhanced because it is essentially error-free.** • **Any errors that are present do not reduce clarity and do not interrupt the flow of the response.** Occasional sentence fragments such as "The next day, same thing" seem to be deliberate because of the overall quality of the writing. **Proportion of error to length and complexity of response has been considered.**

EXEMPLAR EXCELLENT ESSAY

WHAT I HAVE LEARNED FROM ANNE FRANK: THE DIARY OF A YOUNG GIRL

Anne Frank: The Diary of a Young Girl is the true story of a Jewish girl who spent most of the teenage years in hiding from the Nazis and in concentration camps. The book and the movie had an overwhelming effect on me because they made me realize how important it is to be positive in life and how we need to be tolerant of others and grateful for all the good things in our lives. Anne shows us how not to give up and how to appreciate the many small and apparently unimportant events in our lives.

Anne Frank was born in Germany just before Hitler came to power to an ordinary Jewish family. When Hitler and the Nazis came to power the Frank family had to escape to Holland because Mr. Frank realize that things were going to become very difficult for Jews living in Germany. Once in Holland Anne and her sister went to school like everyone else, they had friends and spent time going to movies or visiting friends after school. However when the Nazis came to Holland many restrictions were placed on the Jews such as: Jewish children were not allowed to go to school, Jews were not allowed to own a business, or a car, or a telephone, or eat in restaurants and Jews were not allowed out at night. As things got more and more difficult Mr. Frank decided to take his family and another family and a friend into hiding in an attic at the back of his shop. At that time Anne was only thirteen and her sister was fifteen. They stayed hidden in these small rooms not making a sound during the day for more than two years. It is hard to imagine what that would be like, but in spite of these difficulties, Anne never gave up hope that one day she would be rescued and she continued to believe that the world was really a good place.

While Anne lived and ate and slept in this overcrowded attic she wrote her diary. She wrote about how she felt about her life and what was going on in the world. She wrote about the kind people who visited them and bought them food and news, she wrote about how she was frustrated with her mother and preferred her father, she wrote about how some of the other people in the attic annoyed her and made her angry because of their greed and selfishness, and she wrote about her growing love for Peter and their first kiss. Anne wrote about everything and she did not think anything was too insignificant not to be mentioned. I don't think she meant to have her whole diary read by so many people because she wrote some very personal things, but her father decided to publish the diary so that people could read about how difficult life was for Anne and the family, and how Anne continued to be positive and would not let the difficulties in her life get her down.

This book also makes the reader think about racism and what it means. Hitler persecuted the Jews because he was racist, but being a Jew is being a religion like being United or Catholic or Mormon. It doesn't matter what religion you are because most of the time you are just a Canadian or a German (like Anne) or an American. By reading this book we come to realize that we all have the same interests regardless of our religion. Anne liked to collect pictures of movie stars and decorate where she slept by sticking them up on the wall above her bed. Lot's of teenagers today collect pictures of their heroes and put them up in their rooms.

Anne Frank: The Diary of a Young Girl has affected me by making me think about how I make decisions and how I behave towards other people. Anne was positive throughout her terrible teenage years and never gave up and thought life wasn't worth living. She also treated the others in the attic with respect and kindness even though they made her mad. This book has made me realize how bad things were for people during the war and that all teenagers are alike regardless of their race or religion.

RATIONALE FOR STUDENT EXEMPLAR EXCELLENT ESSAY

Title: **What I have learned from The Diary of Anne Frank**

Score	Reporting Category
E	**Content** • **The student's exploration of the topic** in the discussion of how it is important "to be positive in life and how we need to be tolerant of others and be grateful for all the good things in our lives" in relation to what has been learned from the nonfiction work *Anne Frank: The Diary of a Young Girl* is insightful. • **The student's purpose** to examine how the book *Anne Frank: The Diary of a Young Girl* changed the student's outlook on life is **deliberate**. • **The ideas presented by the student are perceptive** as in "It is hard to imagine what that would be like, but in spite of the difficulties, Anne never gave up hope," "While Anne lived and ate and slept in this overcrowded attic she wrote her diary", and "her father decided to publish the diary so that people could read about how difficult life was for Anne and the family," **and carefully chosen** as in "Anne was positive throughout her terrible teenage years." • **Supporting details** such as "Jewish children were not allowed to go to school, Jews were not allowed to own a business, or a car, or a telephone, or eat in restaurants and Jews were not allowed out at night," "she wrote about how she was frustrated with her mother and preferred her father," and "but being a Jew is being a religion like being United or Catholic or Mormon" **are precise and original.** • **The writing is confident** and **holds the reader's interest** through repetition such as "She wrote about the kind people who visited them and bought them food and news, she wrote about how she was frustrated with her mother and preferred her father, she wrote about how some of the people in the attic annoyed her and made her angry because of their greed and selfishness, and she wrote about her growing love for Peter and their first kiss."
E	**Organization** • **The introduction** "The book and the movie had an overwhelming effect on me because they made me realize how important it is to be positive in life and how we need to be tolerant of others and grateful for all the good things in our lives" **is engaging and skillfully establishes a focus that is consistently sustained.** • **Details are developed in a judicious order** as is evident in how the student gives a brief preview of the book before discussing the areas of the novel that had the greatest impact **and coherence is maintained.** • **Transitions fluently connect details within sentences** such as in "However when the Nazis came to Holland many restrictions were placed on the Jews such as:" and "This book also makes the reader think about racism" **and between paragraphs** as in "While Anne lived and ate and slept in this overcrowded attic." • **Closure** "*Anne Frank: The Diary of a Young Girl* has affected me by making me think about how I make decisions and how I behave towards other people" and "This book has made me realize how bad things were for people during the war and that all teenagers are alike regardless of their race or religion" **is effective and related to the focus.**

E	**Sentence Structure** • **Sentence structure is effectively and consistently controlled** as shown in "When Hitler and the Nazis came to power the Frank family had to escape to Holland because Mr. Frank realize that things were going to become very difficult for Jews living in Germany." • **Sentence type** such as "However when the Nazis came to Holland many restrictions were placed on the Jews such as: Jewish children were not allowed to go to school, Jews were not allowed to own a business, or a car, or a telephone, or eat in restaurants and Jews were not allowed out at night" **and sentence length** as in "It is hard to imagine what that would be like, but in spite of these difficulties, Anne never gave up hope that one day she would be rescued and she continued to believe that the world was really a good place" and "This book also makes the reader think about racism and what it means." **are consistently effective and varied.** • **Sentence beginnings** such as "Anne shows us," "As things got more and more difficult," "I don't think she meant to have" and "By reading this book" are **consistently varied**. **Proportion of error to length and complexity of response has been considered.**
E	**Vocabulary** • **Words and expressions** such as "how to appreciate the many small and apparently unimportant events in our lives" "to an ordinary Jewish family." and "They stayed hidden in these small rooms not making a sound during the day" **are used accurately and deliberately.** • **Precise words and expressions** such as "many restrictions were placed on the Jews" and "other people in the attics annoyed her and made her angry because of their greed and selfishness" and "Anne liked to collect pictures of movies stars and decorate where she slept by sticking them up on the wall above her bed." **are used to enrich details.** • **The tone created by the student** as in "*Anne Frank: The Diary of a Young Girl* has affected me by making me think about how I make decisions and how I behave towards other people" **is convincing.** **Proportion of error to length and complexity of response has been considered.**
E	**Conventions** • **The quality of the writing is enhanced because it is essentially error free** as demonstrated in "I don't think she meant to have her whole diary read by so many people because she wrote some very personal things, but her father decided to publish the diary so that people could read about how difficult life was for Anne and the family, and how Anne continued to be positive and would not let the difficulties in her life get her down." • **Any errors that are present** such as "Lot's of teenagers," "overwhelming effect on me," "Mr. Frank realize that things" and "bought them food and news," **do not reduce clarity and do not interrupt the flow of the response.** **Proportion of error to length and complexity of response has been considered.**

FUNCTIONAL WRITING PROMPT ONE

THANKING A PRESENTER FOR HIS ANTI-BULLYING PRESENTATION

Read about the situation below and complete the assignment that follows.

The Situation

Imagine you are Nicky Quinn, a grade 9 student at the fictional Lynwood Junior High School. The school has just had an Anti-bullying presentation from Jimmy Spencer who, having grown up as a bully, changed his ways and now spends his spare time talking about why people bully, how it can be stopped, and helping victims of bullying reach out to those who can help them. Your English teacher has asked you to write to Jimmy Spencer to thank him for his lively, realistic, and interesting presentation. Your letter should show how much you and the students of your school appreciated Jimmy Spencer's honesty and real-life examples and how his presentation will benefit everyone in your school.

Assignment

Write a business letter to Jimmy Spencer thanking him for his Anti-bullying Presentation.
In your letter make sure that you tell him how much his presentation was appreciated and what programs the school is planning to implement in order to make your school a bully-free school.

In your writing, be sure to:
- **Identify** the purpose of your letter
- **Explain** the details of the situation
- **Organize** your thoughts appropriately in sentences and paragraphs
- Use **vocabulary** that is appropriate and effective
- **Sign** your letter Nicky Quinn—**do not sign your own name**
- **Address** the envelope

Note: Use your imagination to make up reasonable and realistic details about Jimmy Spencer and the anti-bullying programs your school is planning to implement.

Address Information

Use the following information for your letter and to address the envelopes below:

Jimmy Spencer
Jimmy Spencer lives in rural Ontario. His address is R.R. 3, Loon Lake. His postal code is P7C 6H8.

Nicky Quinn
Nicky Quinn attends Lynwood School in Pascal, Alberta. The address is 975 Coronation Street. The postal code is T4S 7D4.

Envelope

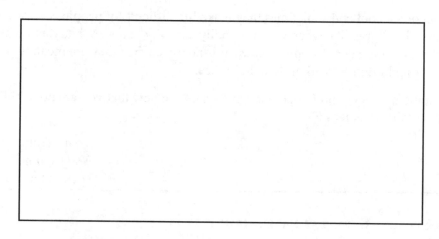

STUDENT EXEMPLARS AND RATIONALES FUNCTIONAL WRITING PROMPT ONE

STUDENT EXEMPLAR SCORE SATISFACTORY

Envelope

Nicky Quinn
Lynwood School
Pascal AB T4S 7D4

Jimmy Spencer
R.R.3 Loon Lake
Ontario P7C 6H8

Nicky Quinn
Lynwood School
Pascal AB T4S 7D4
May 5 2009

Jimmy Spencer
R.R.3 Loon Lake
Ontario P7C 6H8

Dear Jimmy Spencer,

Thank you for your intresting talk on bullying. I an Nicky Quinn a grade 9 student who listened to you giving the speech and my teacher asked me to write and than you. Your speech was very intresting.

We have bullys in our school and sometimes they make life difficult for people, so it was good that you talked to us about what it was like when you were bully and why you were bully and why you stopped. I hope that the bullys in our school stop it because it is not nice when they are mean to people. All the kids liked your talk and I think it will make a difference.

Than you for reading my letter and I hope you have a safe life now that you are not a bully. I wish you lots of luck in your talks to other kids.

Yours Truly,
Nicky Quinn
Nicky Quinn

RATIONALE FOR STUDENT EXEMPLAR SATISFACTORY

Score	Reporting Category
S	**Content** • **The ideas are appropriate** as illustrated in "Thank you for your intresting talk on bullying" and **development of the topic is adequate** as demonstrated in "I am Nicky Quinn a grade 9 student who listened to you giving the speech and my teacher asked me to write and than you. Your speech was very intresting." • **Relevant information is presented** such as "We have bullys in our school and sometimes they make life difficult for people" **and this information is supported by enough detail** as in "so it was good that you talked to us about what it was like when you were bully and why you were bully and why you stopped" and "All the kids liked your talk and I think it will make a diffrence" **to fulfill the purpose.** • **A tone appropriate for the addressee** as in "Thank you for reading my letter" **is generally maintained.**

S	**Content Management** • **Words and expressions used are generally accurate** as in "Your speech was very intresting" and "We have bullys in our school and sometimes they make life difficult for people" **and occasionally effective** as shown in "All the kids liked your talk and I think it will make a diffrence." • **The writing demonstrates basic control of correct sentence structure** as in "I am Nicky Quinn a grade 9 student who listened to you giving the speech and my teacher asked me to write and than you," **usage,** as in "student who listened to you giving the speech," and **mechanics** as in "difficult for people, so it was good." **Errors** such as "intresting," "bullys," "when you were bully and why you were bully," and "diffrence" **occasionally impede meaning.** • **Occasional format errors and omissions are contained in the envelope** such as the omission of the street in the return address and the incorrect format for the mailing address **and letter** with the same errors as the envelope as well as the omission of a space before the date, the inclusion of the Christian name in the salutation, the comma in the salutation, and the closing "Yours Truly." **Proportion of error to length and complexity of response has been considered.**

STUDENT EXEMPLAR SCORE PROFICIENT

Envelope

```
┌─────────────────────────────────────────────┐
│  Nicky Quinn                                  │
│  Lynwood School                               │
│  975 Coronation street                        │
│  Pascal AB T4S 7D4                            │
│                                               │
│                    Jimmy Spencer              │
│                    R.R.3, Loon Lake           │
│                    Ontario P7C 6H8            │
│                                               │
│                                               │
└─────────────────────────────────────────────┘
```

Nicky Quinn
Lynwood School
975 Coronation street
Pascal AB T4S 7D4

Jimmy Spencer
R.R. 3, Loon Lake
Ontario P7C 6H8

Dear Mr. Spencer:

I am Nicky Quinn and my teacher has asked me to write and thank you for the Anti-Bullying presentation that you gave to the students of Lynwood School last Tuesday. It was most interesting and we all enjoyed listening to the stories about your life and what made you change from being a bully.

Your many examples of how you bullied when you were in Junior High such as calling kids who were smaller than you wimp and baby, helped us understand that what goes around comes around.
Your parents really should have stopped your older brothers being so mean to you when you were little and then you would not have been a bully. Your story about how you changed because you found this little girl crying in the playground, made us realize that when we bully we hurt someone. This little girl made you realize how sad it is to be bullyed.

Because of your talk, the student council and the teachers at Lynwood have decided to start up a peer support group to help people who are being bullyed. The bullyed kids can go to anyone on the team and tell their story and they will remain aninomous to the bully. We hope this will help.

Thank you for coming to talk to the students at school and telling all your great stories because we learned so much from your presentation.

Yours truly,

Nicky Quinn

Nicky Quinn

RATIONALE FOR STUDENT EXEMPLAR PROFICIENT

Score	Reporting Category
Pf	**Content** • **The ideas are thoughtful** as evident in "It was most interesting and we all enjoyed listening to the stories about your life and what made you change from being a bully" and the development of the topic in statements such as "write and thank you for the Anti-Bullying presentation that you gave to the students of Lynwood School last Tuesday" is generally effective. • **Significant information** as in "many examples of how you bullied" **is presented and this information is substantiated by specific details** such as "such as calling kids who were smaller than you wimp and baby," "should have stopped your older brothers being so mean to you when you were little and then you would not have been a bully," "Your story about how you changed because you found this little girl crying in the playground," and "the student council and the teachers at Lynwood have decided to start up a peer support group to help people who are being bullied" **that fulfill the purpose of the assignment.** • A **tone** as in "we all enjoyed listening to the stories about your life" and "Thank you for coming to talk to the students at school and telling all your great stories because we learned so much from your presentation." **appropriate for the addressee is clearly maintained.**
Pf	**Content Management** • **Words and expressions used are usually accurate** as in "enjoyed listening to the stories" and "made you realize how sad it is to be bullied" **and effective** as in "calling kids who were smaller than you wimp and baby," and "what goes around comes around." • **The writing demonstrates competent and generally consistent control of correct sentence structure,** as in "Your parents really should have stopped your older brothers being so mean to you when you were little and then you would not have been a bully" **usage,** as in "Because of your talk, the student council," **and mechanics,** as in "Your story about how you changed because you found this little girl crying in the playground, made us realize" **Errors that are present** such as "bullyed" and "aninomous" **rarely impede meaning.** • **The envelope and letter contain few format errors** such as the incorrect format for the mailing address, and omissions such as the lack of a capital letter in "Coronation street," the date, and the printed name. **Proportion of error to length and complexity of response has been considered.**

STUDENT EXEMPLAR SCORE EXCELLENT

Envelope

Nicky Quinn
Lynwood School
975 Coronation Street
Pascal AB T4S 7D4

        Mr. Jimmy Spencer
        R.R.3
        Loon Lake ON P7C 6H8

Lynwood School
975 Coronation street
Pascal AB T4S 7D4

Mr. Jimmy Spencer
R.R.3
Loon Lake ON P7C 6H8

Dear Mr. Spencer:

Last Friday I, and the student body of Lynwood School, attended your wonderful Anti-bullying presentation. We are all very grateful to you for bringing such a very important issue to our attention in a most interesting way and I would like to thank you on behalf of everyone at our school for your presentation.

Your slide show of all the different types of bullying that goes on, from name calling, to ignoring someone, to giving mean looks, to taking away people's possessions, and to fighting made us all aware that bullying can be dangerous to those who bully as well as those who are bullied. Your stories from your childhood about how mean you were to others, and then the experience that made you realize that you could change, were most interesting. I had always thought that once someone was a bully they would never change.

I think you are doing a great job going around the different schools and talking about bullying. As you said, the more it is talked about and the more it is reported the sooner it will stop. At our school we do have an anti bullying program but there are still bullies around. Since your presentation, we have decided to have student buddies in the hallways to watch for things like pushing into lockers, taking things out of lockers, name calling and swearing. We hope this will help because two eyes are always better than one and those who are being bullied will feel there is someone there for them.

Thank you again for a truly great presentation on bullying. I think people like you will one day bring a stop to school bullying and life will be happier for everyone. Keep up the good work!

Yours sincerely,

Nicky Quinn

Nicky Quinn

RATIONALE FOR STUDENT EXEMPLAR EXCELLENT

Score	Reporting Category
E	**Content** • **The ideas are perceptive,** as illustrated in "We are all very grateful to you for bringing such a very important issue to our attention in a most interesting way" and "I think people like you will one day bring a stop to school bullying" **and development of the topic is clear** as evident in "thank you on behalf of everyone at our school for your presentation" and **effective**, as in "I think you are doing a great job going around the different schools and talking about bullying." • **Pertinent information** such as "your wonderful Anti-bullying presentation" **is presented and this information is enhanced by precise details** such as "from name calling, to ignoring someone, to giving mean looks, to taking away people's possessions, and to fighting made us all aware that bullying can be dangerous to those who bully as well as those who are bullied" and "we have decided to have student buddies in the hallways to watch for things like pushing into lockers, taking things out of lockers, name calling and swearing" that **effectively fulfill the purpose of the assignment.** • **A tone appropriate for the addressee** as in "Thank you again for a truly great presentation on bullying" and "Keep up the good work!" **is skilfully maintained.**
E	**Content Management** • **Words and expressions used are consistently accurate** such as "your wonderful Anti-bullying presentation" and "bullying can be dangerous to those who bully as well as those who are bullied" **and effective**, as in "two eyes are always better than one and those who are being bullied will feel there is someone there for them." • **The writing demonstrates confident and consistent control of correct sentence structure** as demonstrated in "Your stories from your childhood about how mean you were to others, and then the experience that made you realize that you could change, were most interesting, **usage**, as in "from name calling, to ignoring someone, to giving mean looks, to taking away people's possessions, and to fighting," **and mechanics** as in "Keep up the good work!" **Errors that are present** such as "Last Friday I, and the student body of Lynwood School, attended" **do not impede meaning.** • **The envelope and letter are free from format errors.** **Proportion of error to length and complexity of response has been considered.**

FUNCTIONAL WRITING PROMPT TWO

INVITING GRADE 6 STUDENTS

Read about the situation below and complete the assignment that follows.

The Situation

Imagine you are Alex Clayton, a Grade 9 student at Woodley Junior High School. Your Grade 9 class has been asked by the principal to write to the Grade 6 students at nearby elementary schools inviting them to spend a day at your school in order for them to see how junior high is different from elementary school, to become knowledgeable about some of the options your school has to offer, and to meet the teachers and the school principal. The day will start with a morning assembly and then the Grade 6 students will buddy up with a Grade 9 student and shadow them for morning classes. In the afternoon the Grade 6 students will have the opportunity to visit three option classes of their choice. Your letter should give information about your school in order to promote it to the incoming Grade 6 students. Each Grade 9 student has been given a specific Grade 6 student to invite. The Grade 6 student you have been assigned to write to is Kelly Smith.

Assignment

Write a business letter to Kelly Smith a Grade 6 student at Longridge Elementary School inviting Kelly to your Junior High school's open house. In your letter explain the purpose of the open house, and give details about how the day will be spent. Encourage Kelly to attend.

When writing, **be sure to:**

- **Identify** the purpose of your letter

- **Explain** the details of the situation

- **Organize** your thoughts appropriately in sentences and paragraphs

- Use **vocabulary** that is appropriate and effective

- Sign your letter Alex Clayton—**do not sign your own name**

- **Address** the envelope

Note: Use your imagination to make up reasonable details about how your school's open house will be conducted.

ADDRESS INFORMATION

Use the following information for your letter and to address the envelopes below:

Kelly Smith

Kelly Smith is a Grade 6 student at Longridge Elementary School in Aspen, Alberta. The postal code is T5F 6D7. The elementary school is located at 847 Birch Road.

Alex Clayton

Alex Clayton attends Woodley Junior High School in Aspen, Alberta. The school is located at 1209 Sycamore Street and the postal code is T5S 3M8.

Envelope

STUDENT EXEMPLARS AND RATIONALES FUNCTIONAL WRITING PROMPT TWO

STUDENT EXEMPLAR SCORE SATISFACTORY

Envelope

Alex Clayton
Woodley Junior High School
1209 Sycamore Street
Aspen, Alberta, T5S 3M8

Kelly Smith
Longridge Elementary School
Aspen, Alberta, T5F 6D7

Alex Clayton
Woodley Junior High School
1209 Sycamore Street
Aspen, Alberta, T5S 3M8

Kelly Smith
Longridge Elementary School
Aspen, Alberta, T5F 6D7

Dear Kelly,

Hi. I am your buddy Alex Clayton and I am inviting you to come to our school for the day to see what junior high is like when you spent a day with us. It is like an open house. You will be comming on June 13.

You will get to meet the teachers and the principle and come to my classes with me. I have math and LA when you are here. You can go to some options if you want like band and drama and sculpture. It will be a cool day and i hope u can come.

you can let me know if you comming by writting back to me at my school.

See you then.

truly yours

Alex Clayton

RATIONALE FOR STUDENT EXEMPLAR SATISFACTORY

Score	Reporting Category
S	**Content** • **The ideas are appropriate** as demonstrated in "I am inviting you to come to our school for the day to see what junior high is like" and the **development of the topic** in such statements as "It is like an open house" and "You will be comming on June 13." **is adequate.** • **Relevant information** such as "You will get to meet the teachers and the principle and come to my classes with me" **is presented, and this information is supported by enough detail** as in "I have math and LA when you are here" and "You can go to some options if you want like band and drama and sculpture" **to fulfill the purpose of the assignment**. • **A tone appropriate for the addressee** in that it is one student writing to another student "i hope u can come" **is generally maintained.**

S	**Content** • **Words and expressions used are generally accurate** as in "come to our school for the day to see what junior high is like" **and occasionally effective** as seen in "It will be a cool day." • **The writing demonstrates basic control of correct sentence structure** as in "You will get to meet the teachers and the principle and come to my classes with me," **usage** as in "Hi. I am your buddy", **and mechanics. Errors** such as "when you spent a day with us," "coming," "i hope u can come," and "you comming by writting back " **occasionally impede meaning.** • **The letter and the envelope contain occasional format errors** such as "Aspen, Alberta," "Kelly," and "truly yours" **and omissions** such as "847 Birch Road" from both the envelope and the inside address, the date, the comma after "truly yours," and the signature for Alex Clayton. **Proportion of error to length and complexity of response has been considered.**

STUDENT EXEMPLAR SCORE PROFICIENT

Envelope

```
+---------------------------------------------------------------+
|                                                               |
|   Alex Clayton                                                |
|   Woodley Junior High School                                  |
|   1209 Sycamore Street                                        |
|   Aspen, AB T5S 3M8                                           |
|                                                               |
|                     Kelly Smith                               |
|                     Longridge Elementary School              |
|                     847 Birch Road                            |
|                     Aspen, AB T5F 6D7                         |
|                                                               |
|                                                               |
+---------------------------------------------------------------+
```

Alex Clayton
Woodley Junior High School
1209 Sycamore Street
Aspen, AB T5S 3M8
May 9, 2009

Kelly Smith
Longridge Elementary School
847 Birch Road
Aspen, AB T5F 6D7

Dear Kelly Smith;

I am Alex Clayton, a grade 9 student, and I am writing to invite you to our school's open house on June 13th. Mr. Griffin, our principal, thought it would be a good idea for all grade 6 students in Aspen to come and see our school and find out a bit about it before they come here in September. I choose your name to write to you and then to be your buddy on June 13th.

The day will start at 10:00 am with an assembly in the gym where Mr. Griffin will give a talk about the school and the teachers will tell you interesting information about themselves and what they teach. After that we will go to my regular classes so you can see what they are like. You and me will have math and social. In social we are presenting our projects so it will be pretty interesting. After lunch, which you can have with your own friends, you will be able to go and visit three option classes. Options are great and you will enjoy finding out all our different options like art, drama, band, debate, and French or Spanish. Your day will end when you go back to your school at 2:00 pm.

I hope you come to our open house and I look forward to being your buddy for the day and helping you find out about Junior High school. You can email me at aclay@hotmail.com to let me know if you are coming.

See you on June 13th.

Sincerely

Alex Clayton

Alex Clayton

RATIONALE FOR STUDENT EXEMPLAR PROFICIENT

Score	Reporting Category
Pf	**Content** • **The ideas are thoughtful** as is evident in "I am writing to invite you to our school's open house on June 13th." **and the development of the topic** in statements such as "our principal, thought it would be a good idea for all grade 6 students in Aspen to come and see our school and find out a bit about it before they come here in September." **is generally effective**. • **Significant information** such as "The day will start at 10.00 am with an assembly in the gym where Mr. Griffin will give a talk about the school and the teachers will tell you interesting information about themselves and what they teach" **is presented and this information is substantiated by specific details** such as "In social we are presenting our projects so it will be pretty interesting" and "Options are great and you will enjoy finding out all our different options like art, drama, band, debate, and French or Spanish" **that fulfill the purpose of the assignment.** • **A tone appropriate for the addressee** as demonstrated in "I hope you come to our open house and I look forward to being your buddy for the day and helping you find out about Junior High school" is **clearly maintained**.

Pf	**Content Management** • **Words and expressions used are usually accurate** such as "come and see our school and find out a bit about it" and "In social we are presenting our projects so it will be pretty interesting" **and effective** such as "teachers will tell you interesting information about themselves and what they teach" and "Options are great." • The writing demonstrates **competent and generally consistent control of correct sentence structure**, such as "After lunch, which you can have with your own friends, you will be able to go and visit three option classes," **usage**, such as "like art, drama, band, debate, and French or Spanish," **and mechanics**, such as "I am Alex Clayton, a grade 9 student." **Errors that are present** such as "I choose your name to write to you" and "You and me will have math and social" **rarely impede meaning.** • **The envelope and letter contain few format errors** such as "Dear Kelly Smith;" and a comma in "Aspen, AB," and omissions such as the comma after "Sincerely." **Proportion of error to length and complexity of response has been considered.**

STUDENT EXEMPLAR SCORE EXCELLENT

Envelope

Alex Clayton
Woodley Junior High School
1209 Sycamore Street
Aspen, AB T5S 3M8

Kelly Smith
Grade 6
Longridge Elementary School
1209 Sycamore Street
Aspen, AB T5F 6D7

Woodley Junior High School

1209 Sycamore Street

Aspen, AB T5S 3M8

May 26, 2009

Kelly Smith
Grade 6
Longridge Elementary School
1209 Sycamore Street
Aspen, AB T5F 6D7

Dear Kelly:

Mr. Snowden, the principal of Woodley Junior High, has asked the Grade 9 students to write to a Grade 6 student from your school in order to invite you to a special open house that we have planned in order to introduce you to some of the differences between junior high and elementary school. I selected your name, and I am writing to invite you to come to our open house on Friday, June 13th. I will be your buddy for the day so you will feel quite at home and I am positive we will have a wonderful day.

The day will start off at about 9.30 am with an assembly where you will meet Mr. Snowden, the guidance counselor, and most of the teachers. The teachers will tell you a little bit about what they teach and what homerooms they have, and Mr. Snowden will inform you about the school itself, its discipline policy and other school activities such as school teams and clubs. You will find the first part of the morning most informative. You will also have the chance to ask questions, if you want to.

After the assembly, you and me will buddy up and spend the rest of the morning going to my regular classes. Luckily, it is a Day 5 so I have science and LA. Both these classes are cool, especially science where we are dissecting frogs. After lunch with your own friends, you will have the opportunity to go for a 20 minute visit to any three option classes. This will give you a chance to discover what options might interest you and what actually happens during these classes. Some of the options you can choose from are: home ec., computers, drama, band, art, technical studies, speech and debate, and different outdoor activities. Your day will finish at about 2.00 pm when you will return to your own school.

As you can see we have a full and exciting day planned for you and your grade 6 class. I do hope you will come as it will give you a great introduction to junior high and I will be able to answer many of your questions and assure you that junior high can be a fun place. Please let me know through your teacher or by emailing me at abclayton

I look forward to meeting you.

Yours truly,
Alex Clayton

Alex Clayton

RATIONALE FOR STUDENT EXEMPLAR EXCELLENT

Score	Reporting Category
E	**Content** • **The ideas are perceptive** as in "Mr. Snowden, the principal of Woodley Junior High, has asked the Grade 9 students to write to a Grade 6 student from your school in order to invite you to a special open house" **and the development of the topic is clear** as demonstrated in "I am writing to invite you to come to our open house on Friday, June 13th. I will be your buddy for the day so you will feel quite at home and I am positive we will have a wonderful day" **and effective** as in "in order to introduce you to some of the differences between Junior High and elementary school. I selected your name." • **Pertinent information** such as "The day will start off at about 9.30 am with an assembly where you will meet Mr. Snowden, the guidance counselor, and most of the teachers. The teachers will tell you a little bit about what they teach and what home rooms they have, and Mr. Snowden will inform you about the school itself, its discipline policy and other school activities such as school teams and clubs" **is presented, and this information is enhanced by precise details** such as "After the assembly, you and me will buddy up and spend the rest of the morning going to my regular classes...science and LA. Both these classes are cool, especially science where we are dissecting frogs" and "you will have the opportunity to go for a 20 minute visit each to any three option classes…home ec., computers, drama, band, art, technical studies, speech and debate, and different outdoor activities" **that effectively fulfill the purpose of the assignment.** • **A tone appropriate for the addressee** as illustrated in "I do hope you will come as it will give you a great introduction to Junior High and I will be able to answer many of your questions" and "I look forward to meeting you" **is skilfully maintained.**
E	**Content Management** • **Words and expressions used are consistently accurate** as illustrated in "introduce you to some of the differences between Junior High and elementary school" and "Both these classes are cool, especially science" **and effective** as illustrated in "you will feel quite at home and I am positive we will have a wonderful day," "I will be able to answer many of your questions and assure you that Junior High can be a fun place." and "As you can see we have a full and exciting day planned for you." • **The writing demonstrates confident and consistent control of correct sentence structure,** as in "The teachers will tell you a little bit about what they teach and what home rooms they have, and Mr. Snowden will inform you about the school itself, its discipline policy and other school activities such as school teams and clubs," **usage,** as in "choose from are: home ec., computers, drama, band, art, technical studies, speech and debate, and different outdoor activities," and **mechanics,** as in "Mr. Snowden, the principal of Woodley Junior High, has." **Errors that are present** such as "you and me will buddy up" **do not impede meaning.** • **The envelope and letter are essentially free from format errors** other than the inclusion of a comma in "Aspen, AB." **Proportion of error to length and complexity of response has been considered.**

FUNCTIONAL WRITING PROMPT THREE

REQUESTING SCHOOL CLUBS

Read about the situation below and complete the assignment that follows.

The Situation

Your name is Tory Knowles and you are a member of your school's Student Council. The students in your school have approached the student council asking that they formally ask the school's administration if there can be extra-curricular clubs in the school other than sports teams. There are many students in the school who do not play on sports teams but would like to experience the competitive spirit and the comradeship that members of sports teams often experience. Some of the clubs could be competitive with matches against other schools or they could be solely within the school with competitions taking place internally. Since sports teams often play and practice after school, you feel it would not be unreasonable to have these other clubs held after school.

You understand that there can never be enough clubs to satisfy everyone's interests, but "Club Day" could encompass more than one activity, according to the interest and commitment of the students who participate.

Ideas for Clubs			
Chess	Arts and crafts	Book club	Movie club
Debate and speech	Board games such as Monopoly, Settlers, Risk, Scrabble		

Assignment

Write a business letter to Mrs. Phillips, the principal of your school, requesting that extra-curricular clubs be started in your school for those students who do not wish to, or do not get selected to participate in school sports teams. In your letter, recognize that it may be difficult to find staff to facilitate the clubs and provide information that will help to promote your point of view regarding this issue.

When writing, **be sure to:**

• **Identify** the purpose of your letter

• **Explain** the details of the situation

• **Organize** your thoughts appropriately in sentences and paragraphs

• Use **vocabulary** that is appropriate and effective

• **Sign** your letter Tory Knowles—**do not sign your own name**

• **Address** the envelope

Note: Use your imagination to make up reasonable details about the types of clubs students might like to have and activities that may take place.

Address Information

Use the following information for your letter and to address the envelopes below.

| **Joan Phillips** |
| Joan Phillips is the principal of your school, Crofton Downs Junior High. The school is located on Springtime Avenue. R.R. 6. Alberta. The postal code is T9X 0L7. |
| **Tory Knowles** |
| Tory Knowles attends the school where Mrs. Phillips is principal. The address would be the same since the letter is being written regarding school activities. |

Envelope

STUDENT EXEMPLARS AND RATIONALES FUNCTIONAL WRITING PROMPT THREE

STUDENT EXEMPLAR SCORE SATISFACTORY

Envelope

Crofton Downs Junior High School
Springtime Avenue, R.R.6
Alberta, T9X 0L7

       Joan Phillips
       Crofton Downs Junior High School
       Springtime Avenue, R.R 6
       Alberta, T9X 0L7

Crofton Downs Junior High School
Springtime Avenue, R.R.6
Alberta, T9X 0L7

Joan Phillips
The Principal
Crofton Downs Junior High School
Springtime Avenue, R.R.6
Alberta, T9X 0L7

Dear Miss Phillips:

as a student in your school who is on student counsel, we want to ask you to let us have more Clubs in the school. We all ready have lots of sports teams and that is too much but we want other Clubs to make it more fun for the kids who do not make the sports teams.

We would like it if we can have chess and arts and crafts and book club and movie club and debate and board games. It would be lots of fun to have these Clubs and many students would like it if they don't make the team. Some of the Clubs like chess could have teams to play against other schools. Debate could do the same. Some teachers could be happy to help us have Clubs and that is good for the students and the school.

You can find me in room 9G so please get back to me and student counsel about your answer.

I thank you for taking the time to read this letter.

Your Student,

Tory Knowles

Tory Knowles

RATIONALE FOR STUDENT EXEMPLAR SATISFACTORY

Score	Reporting Category
S	**Content** • **The ideas are appropriate** as demonstrated in "we want to ask you to let us have more Clubs in the school" and **the development of the topic** in statements such as "we want other Clubs to make it more fun for the kids who do not make the sports teams." **is adequate.** • **Relevant information** such as "We would like it if we can have chess and arts and crafts and book club and movie club and debate and board games" **is presented, and this information is supported by enough detail** such as "many students would like it," "Some of the Clubs like chess could have teams to play against other schools," and "Some teachers could be happy to help us have Clubs" to **fulfill the purpose of the assignment.** • **A tone appropriate for the addressee** as in "we want to ask you to let us have" and "I thank you for taking the time to read this letter" is **generally maintained**.

S	**Content Management** • **Words and expressions used are generally accurate** as seen in "we want to ask you to let us have more Clubs" and "we want other Clubs to make it more fun for the kids" **and occasionally effective** as seen in "It would be lots of fun to have these Clubs" and "You can find me in room 9G so please get back to me and student counsel about your answer." • **The writing demonstrates basic control of correct sentence structure** as in "It would be lots of fun to have these Clubs and many students would like it if they don't make the team" **usage**, as in "many students would like it if they don't make the team." **Errors** such as "as a student in your school who is on student counsel,", "We all ready have," "many students would like it if they don't make the team," **occasionally impede meaning.** • **The envelope and letter contain occasional format errors** such as the placement of "R.R.6" and "Alberta, T9X 0L7," "Your Student," and the inconsistent use of block format **and omissions** such as "Tory Knowles" above the return address on the envelope and the date. **Proportion of error to length and complexity of response has been considered.**

STUDENT EXEMPLAR SCORE PROFICIENT

Envelope

Tory Knowles
Crofton Downs Junior High School
Springtime Avenue
R.R.6.
AB, T9X 0L7

>   Ms. J. Phillips
>   The Principal
>   Crofton Downs Junior High School
>   Springtime Avenue
>   R.R.6.
>   AB, T9X 0L7

Tory Knowles
Crofton Downs Junior High School
Springtime Avenue
R.R.6.
AB T9X 0L7
May 5, 2009

Mrs. J. Phillips, The Principal
Crofton Downs Junior High School
Springtime Avenue
R.R.6.
AB T9X 0L7

Dear Ms. Phillips:

I am a student in your school and I am a member of student council. I am writing to you ask if the school's students can have more clubs held after school that are not sports teams. There are many students in the school who would like to be able to do things after school in a club, but there is not the opportunity right now.

Some of the suggestions for clubs that student have made are for there to be a book club or a movie club, or an art club. Some students would even like it if we can have a debate club or a chess club where there will be the chance to have competitions with other student or other schools. We think we might even win; because Andrew and Paul are always arguing in class and Miss Jackson said they should take up debate.

The student council knows that it might be difficult to have teachers give up their time after school to run these clubs, but if we can get parents to help us then there would be less stress for the teachers. We hope you will agree to letting us have more clubs as that will make lots of students very happy.

Thank you for taking the time to read this letter. You can contact me or student council at any time but we would really appreciate it if you would let us know your response before the end of next week.

Yours truly,

Tory Knowles

Tory Knowles

RATIONALE FOR STUDENT EXEMPLAR PROFICIENT

Score	Reporting Category
Pf	**Content** • **The ideas are thoughtful** as is evident in "I am writing to you ask if the school's students can have more clubs held after school that are not sports' teams," **and the development of the topic** in statements such a "There are many students in the school who would like to be able to do things after school in a club, but there is not the opportunity right now" is **generally effective**. • **Significant information** such as "Some of the suggestions for clubs that student have made are for there to be a book club or a movie club, or an art club" **is presented, and this information is substantiated by specific details** such as "Some students would even like it if we can have a debate club or a chess club where there will be the chance to have competitions with other student or other schools," and "Andrew and Paul are always arguing in class and Miss Jackson said they should take up debate" **that fulfill the purpose of the assignment.** • A **tone appropriate for the addressee** as demonstrated in "Thank you for taking the time to read this letter. You can contact me or student council at any time" is **clearly maintained**.
Pf	**Content Management** • **Words and expressions used are usually accurate** as in "Some of the suggestions for clubs that student have made are" and "as that will make lots of students very happy" and **effective** as in "there is not the opportunity right now," "there would be less stress for the teachers" and "we would really appreciate it." • **The writing demonstrates competent and generally consistent control of correct sentence structure** as in "Some students would even like it if we can have a debate club or a chess club where there will be the chance to have competitions with other student or other schools," **usage** as in "We think we might even win; because Andrew and Paul," **and mechanics** as in "the school's students can have more clubs held after school that are not sports teams.". **Errors that are present** such as "I am writing to you ask" and "to have competitions with other student" **rarely impede meaning.** • The envelope and letter contain few format errors such as the consistently incorrect placement of "AB T9X 0L7" and the placement of the inside address along the right margin rather than the left margin. **Proportion of error to length and complexity of response has been considered.**

STUDENT EXEMPLAR SCORE EXCELLENT

Envelope

Tory Knowles
Crofton Downs Junior High School
Springtime Avenue
R.R.6. AB T9X 0L7

> Mrs. J. Phillips, The Principal
> Crofton Downs Junior High School
> Springtime Avenue
> R.R.6. AB, T9X 0L7

Crofton Downs Junior High School
Springtime Avenue
R.R.6. AB T9X 0L7
May 5, 2009

Mrs. J. Phillips, The Principal
Crofton Downs Junior High School
Springtime Avenue
R.R.6. AB T9X 0L7

Dear Mrs. Phillips:

On behalf of the school's student council, I am writing to request that you consider the idea of promoting non-sport school clubs in the school. The idea behind this is that only a small percentage of the students actually play on a sports team and there are many students who would like to be involved in other school activities.

The student council feels that two hours one afternoon a week after school, could be put aside for Clubs. This could be on the same day as sports practices or on another day. The clubs would have to depend on student interest and on teacher experience but some ideas for clubs that has been brought forward by the students are: a book club, a club for playing board games such as monopoly or settlers, a movie club or an art club. Some of the more competitive students would like the opportunity to have a chess club or a debate club where they could compete against other schools. This would give the school the opportunity to show its academic ability as well as its athletic talent. We already have three students who play chess competitively outside of school and have won a few matches.

The student council realizes that the teachers already work very hard, so we thought we could advertise for parent volunteers to help run these clubs so that all the extra work does not have to be done by teachers. Hopefully this would help make your response favourable to us, as there is a great interest in these clubs.

I would appreciate it if you could get back to student council and let us know your decision before our next meeting on May 20th. If you wish to discuss these clubs with us, please contact me or any member of student council.

Thank you for taking the time to read this letter.

Your student,

Tory Knowles

Tory Knowles

RATIONALE FOR STUDENT EXEMPLAR EXCELLENT

Score	Reporting Category
E	**Content** • **The ideas are perceptive** as is evident in "I am writing to request that you consider the idea of promoting non-sport school clubs in the school" **and the development of the topic is clear** as demonstrated in "a small percentage of the students actually play on a sports' team and there are many students who would like to be involved in other school activities" and **effective** as in "The student council feels that two hours one afternoon a week after school, could be put aside for Clubs." • **Pertinent information** such as "The clubs would have to depend on student interest and on teacher experience but some ideas for clubs that has been brought forward by the students are: a book club, a club for playing board games such as monopoly or settlers, a movie club or an art club**." is presented, and this information is enhanced by precise details**, such as "Some of the more competitive students would like the opportunity to have a chess club or a debate club where they could compete against other schools" and "we thought we could advertise for parent volunteers to help run these clubs" that **effectively fulfill the purpose of the assignment.** • **A tone appropriate for the addressee** as illustrated in "I would appreciate it if you could get back to student council and let us know your decision" and "Thank you for taking the time to read this letter" is **skilfully maintained**.
E	**Content Management** • **Words and expressions used are consistently accurate** as illustrated in "would have to depend on student interest and on teacher experience" and "The student council realizes that the teachers already work very hard, so we thought we could advertise for parent volunteers" and **effective** as illustrated in "give the school the opportunity to show its academic ability as well as its athletic talent" and "help make your response favourable to us." • **The writing demonstrates confident and consistent control of correct sentence structure,** as in "On behalf of the school's student council, I am writing to request that you consider the idea of promoting non-sport school clubs in the school.", **usage** as in "been brought forward by the students are: a book club, a club for playing board games such as monopoly or settlers, a movie club or an art club," **and mechanics**, as in "play on a sports' team." **Errors that are present** such as "but some ideas for clubs that has been brought forward by the students are" **do not impede meaning.** • **The envelope and letter are free from format errors.** **Proportion of error to length and complexity of response has been considered.**

NOTES

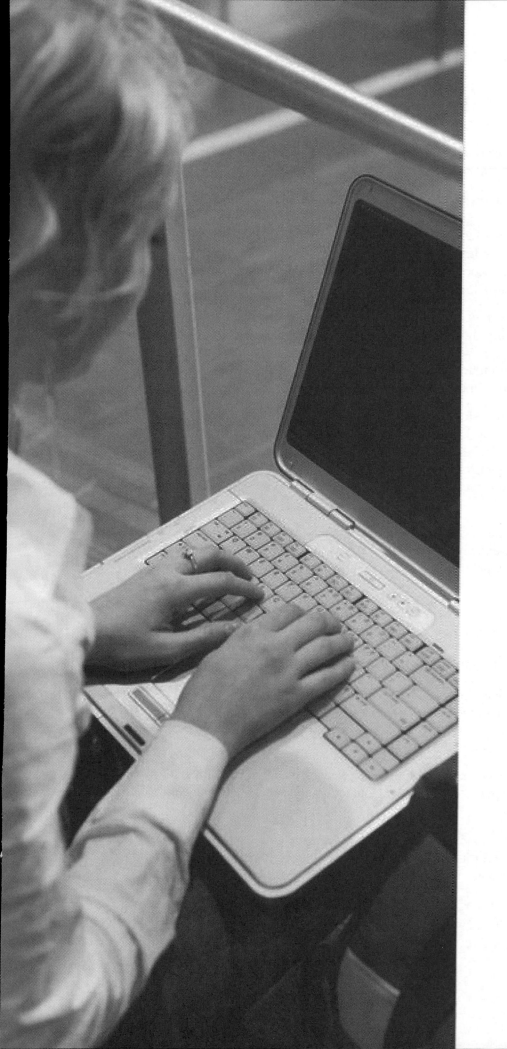

Provincial Achievement Tests—Part B

2000 PROVINCIAL ACHIEVEMENT TEST—PART B

Read the short story excerpt below and answer questions 1 to 8.

THE VISITOR

The mayor called a town meeting to discuss Spruce. Once people found out that the mayor was thinking about getting rid of the moose they began to take sides. It was all they could talk about for a week. Petitions were sent around and signs were posted in front yards and along fences, some saying Let Him Be and others saying He's Got To
5 Go. I'd never seen people get so worked up over something. No one protested this much when the mines closed.

The council meeting was moved from the municipal office, a small room in the basement of the library, to the union hall so everyone could attend. There was a reporter from the St. John's newspaper, which never before bothered with small town council meetings.
10 The reporter wasn't much older than me. He didn't even try to hide his boredom, just yawned and doodled in his steno book.

The moose issue was shuffled to the bottom of the evening's agenda. I think the mayor hoped people would get bored and leave the meeting before it ended. His nerves were frazzled, speaking in front of so many people, and he kept shuffling the papers in front of
15 him. He'd never seen so many bodies at a council meeting. The only people who usually attended the meetings were a couple of old-timers with nothing better to do and the editor of the town paper.

My father asked me to go to the meeting with him. He said it was an important issue for the town, and it went beyond a simple decision to let Spruce stay or to force him out. I
20 agreed to go partly because I was feeling guilty for the way I had been treating him the past few weeks.

After passing motions to recruit another volunteer firefighter, start collecting a dog tax, and approve a letter requesting the donation of library books, they finally reached the end of the agenda. A group of men, followed by a haze of their own cigarette smoke, stepped
25 into the stifling hall, and everyone else stopped shuffling and whispering.

The discussion about Spruce started off respectfully enough. Representatives from both sides of the issue carefully stated their case as we sat in silence. My father looked over at me once, and started to smile but changed his mind and looked down at a piece of folded up paper he was holding.

30 The mayor, in an attempt at a compromise, asked the audience, "Why don't we get one of them tranquilizer guns, knock him out and let him go somewhere one hundred kilometres from here?"

A man in the back stood up. I'd seen him before, standing outside the Legion every afternoon, waiting for it to open. "We're some stunned to be sitting here arguing about
35 this moose. Why don't we just kill it and get a nice bunch of steaks out of him."

"Yes, bye, we do that and we'll have them peace freaks and animals rights activists accusing us of cruelty to animals," said a woman from the middle of the crowd.

"What harm is he doing to ye. I say we just let him do his thing and leave him alone. It's the proper thing," said Mrs. Tilley. Her husband sat beside her shaking his head.

40 Then one of the old-timers jumped up and yelled, "Kill him before he tramples some poor child." Someone else in the back yelled, "Let the poor thing alone." The St. John's reporter jerked his head up and began writing madly. Then everyone got into it. People were yelling back and forth at each other. The mayor kept banging his gavel on the table, but everyone ignored him. The reporter stopped his frantic writing for an instant to take a
45 picture of the mayor yelling at everyone to shut up.

In the middle of the yelling and screaming my father stood up slowly. He never said a word in any sort of public meeting. I wanted to slip into the cracks of the floor and disappear. He unfolded his piece of paper and looked at it quickly. Then he folded it back up and held it tightly in his hand. The people around us stopped talking and looked
50 at my father. Like a wave, silence gradually fell over the rest of the hall. He just stood there, waiting, gripping on to that piece of paper as if it gave him the strength to stand.

He quietly cleared his throat. His first words didn't quite make it out. Someone yelled, "Speak up, we can't hear you." He stopped. I thought he'd pack it in right there. But he didn't. He looked over at me. I couldn't help it, but I turned my eyes away and stared at
55 my shoes.

He began again, a little louder this time, "Spruce has done something for this town that no one has seen for years."

"Yeah, he's picked up the garbage regularly," some wisecracker yelled out. "Uh, that's not my point," said Dad quietly. He started to unfold his paper and look at his notes. He
60 was totally thrown off.

"Tell them about the treats," I whispered. "Tell them about all the times you and other people set out treats for Spruce, like it was Christmas or something." Dad looked down at me, nodded his head slightly and smiled. Then he released his grip on the paper and let it fall to the floor. I thought he had dropped it and when I bent down to pick it up he
65 whispered, "Leave it there."

He began again. This time his voice was loud enough the first time. "How many of us have run into our kitchens to find special treats for Spruce every time he was spotted in town? When is the last time you felt that same excitement about something?"

I look up at him, hoping he would see that I was listening to every word. "Spruce has
70 given us all a little hope, something almost magical, during a time when we don't have much of anything that's good." A few people in front of us were nodding in agreement. "I think it would be a foolish idea to get rid of him. I think we should just let him be." Dad didn't waste any time sitting down. People were still looking at him but he didn't acknowledge their stares.

75 I could tell people were stunned. No one said a word for a few seconds. The mayor screwed up his face as if he had a bad taste in his mouth. The reverend shrugged his shoulders and sighed. Once people digested everything an excited buzz spread throughout the union hall. I caught bits and pieces of the conversations around us.

"Maybe he's got a point."

80 "I can't believe Graham Percy stood up and …"

"But what if Spruce …"

"I've never heard him say that much at one time."

People were talking as much about my dad as they were about Spruce, but I didn't care. I reached down and picked up the crumpled paper my Dad had dropped and put it in
85 my pocket.

"Thanks for your help, Willy," he said.

"You would have done fine without me. People really listened to what you had to say." I looked straight at him. For the first time I noticed the flecks of gold in his deep brown eyes. I had those same flecks.

90 "You think so?" He really didn't know. It was like he was a kid looking for someone to say he did the right thing.

"I know so," I said.

—*by* Christine Pinsent-Johnson

1. The meeting described in this excerpt was bigger than most town meetings because
   A. the mayor was anxious to have as many people attend as possible
   B. a reporter from the St. John's newspaper was attending
   C. all the townspeople were upset with the mayor
   D. many people had an interest in the issue

2. During the meeting, the newspaper reporter's attitude changed from being
   A. disinterested to motivated
   B. frustrated to involved
   C. tired to opinionated
   D. annoyed to amused

3. Graham Percy's act of dropping the paper is symbolic of his
   A. losing his temper
   B. speaking from the heart
   C. becoming nervous and forgetful
   D. giving up trying to convince people

4. The narrator's father was "totally thrown off" (line 60) because he had
   A. changed his mind about what to say
   B. been unable to get out his first words
   C. distracted himself by looking at his son
   D. been interrupted by a comment from the crowd

5. The flecks in the father's and son's eyes are mentioned in order to symbolize
   A. similarities in character between the father and his son
   B. physical similarities between the father and his son
   C. the growing closeness the son feels for his father
   D. the careful attention the son pays to every detail of his father

6. A line that shows an example of a local dialect is
   A. "'Why don't we just kill it and get a nice bunch of steaks out of him'" (lines 35)
   B. "'Yes, bye, we do that and we'll have them peace freaks…'" (line 36)
   C. "'Yeah, he's picked up the garbage regularly'" (line 58)
   D. "'I think we should just let him be'" (line 72)

7. The point of view from which this excerpt is written is
   A. first person
   B. second person
   C. third person
   D. fourth person

8. The father's character is **best** described as
   A. excited but nervous
   B. assertive but forgetful
   C. reserved and thoughtful
   D. composed and confident

Read the article excerpt below and answer questions 9 to 15.

THE WORLD'S BIGGEST PEBBLE

Rising starkly from the savage red flatlands at the dead centre of the Australian Outback is one of the most spectacular natural wonders of the world. Ayers Rock is the world's largest single stone. From the air, it
resembles an enormous kite; from the
5 ground, it is just plain overwhelming!
Rising vertically to a height of 348 metres, it
is 1.6 km wide, 2.4 km long, and measures
9 km around its base!

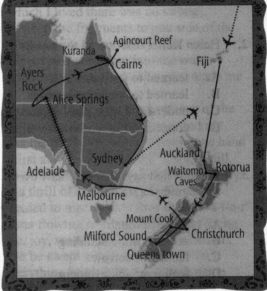

Despite its extreme remoteness, Ayers Rock
10 rivals the famous Great Barrier Reef in its
power to attract visitors—nearly 90,000
a year! The jumping-off place is Alice
Springs, familiar to readers of Nevil Shute's
novel *A Town Called Alice*.

15 Alice Springs is a tourist haven itself;
visitors can enjoy Noel Fullerton's Emily
Gap Camel Ranch, experience a corroboree
(a celebration of singing and dancing staged
by the Aborigines), or watch the "Henley-
20 on-Todd Regatta", a yacht race held each August on a dry riverbed; the participants stand in fully-rigged boats, the bottoms of which have been removed, hoist the boats to their waists and stagger off towards the finish line!

Visitors travel the 470 km from Alice Springs to Ayers Rock either by plane or road; those going the land route may spot such local wildlife as kangaroos, wild horses, camels
25 and buffalo. Upon arrival at the rock, many pilgrims stop at "Sunset Strip", an area of raised desert two km from the rock, an ideal spot from which to view it. Ayers Rock bears careful watching, as in addition to its size, it has another remarkable feature—it appears to change colour as the day wears on. Although its true hue is the harsh red of its limestone, this varies from moment to moment; at sunset it goes from a burnt red to
30 brilliant orange to crimson, and then wanders through delicate shades of purple and blue.

To the local Pitjantjatjara tribe of Aborigines, Ayers Rock is sacred, having the significance of an ancient temple.

Many of its caves are the sites of religious ceremonies, including those marking the rites of passage of children into adulthood. The Aborigines decorated many of the caves
35 with mysterious paintings depicting plant and animal life, humans, and various abstract symbols.

The Aborigines believe that Ayers Rock was produced during the Dreamtime, before men walked the earth; giants, who had slept through the time before time began, awoke and broke through the earth's crust. They set about the creation of the world; it took ten of
40 them to produce Ayers Rock, which to the Aborigines is known as "Uluru", the Place of Shade. Details were added later; Uluru Water, a deep water-hole on top, was formed from the blood of a man who died in battle, while a slab of black rock is the body of another who was burned to death as punishment for not sharing his emu meat with the tribe.

The first white man to see Ayers Rock was Ernest Giles; he spotted it from Lake
45 Amadeus, thirty km north. The year was 1872, and by the time he got back for a visit a
year later, William Gosse, a government surveyor, had led his Western Exploring
Expedition to the base of the rock. Gosse was mightily impressed, and wrote, "When I
was only two miles, distant and the hill, for the first time coming fairly into view, what
was my astonishment to find it an immense pebble, rising abruptly from the plain. This
50 rock is certainly the most wonderful natural feature I have ever seen; it appears more
wonderful every time I look at it, and I may say it is a sight worth riding over 85 miles of
spinifex sandhills to see." Gosse named
the rock after Sir Henry Ayers, premier of
South Australia, and then he climbed to
55 the top. This has become a tradition
followed by most tourists, although
many go in groups under a tour guide.
The Bush Tucker Tour is popular;
conducted by Aborigines, it includes a
60 delicious meal of witchety grubs and billy
tea with mint-flavoured gum leaves.

Although Ayers Rock has been sacred to
the Pitjantjatjara for 15,000 years, this represents but a wink of an eye in its geological
life span. Ayers Rock is between five and six million years old, and was once buried
65 beneath an inland sea. When the water receded, the rock remained, an enormous
protuberance above a surrounding moonscape. … The rock is scarred with weather-
induced gullies and lightning-scarred ridges. The overflow from infrequent rains ruins
the usual silence of the desert with the sound of cataracts three hundred metres high.

Ayers Rock is part of Uluru National Park, which also contains an impressive collection
70 of mountains located thirty kilometres due west. Collectively dubbed "The Olgas", the
most impressive of these dome-shaped formations is Mount Olga itself, its red tower
stretching to a height of 550 metres…

The next time you happen to be visiting the Red Centre of the continent of Australia, stop
by Ayers Rock and Mount Olga for a quick look. You won't regret it!

—*by* Robert Nielsen

9. Alice Springs is a "jumping-off place" (line 12) for Ayers Rock because it is

A. located just west of Ayers Rock

B. located on the top of Ayers Rock

C. the closest town to Ayers Rock

D. the best place from which to view Ayers Rock

10. In addition to its immense size, Ayers Rock is world famous for its

A. ancient ceremonial sites

B. distinctive kite shape

C. changing appearance

D. incredible age

11. Ayers Rock is sacred to the Aborigines **mainly** because it

   A. provides the only shade in the whole area

   B. contains many caves with mysterious paintings

   C. is the place of battles where many men died

   D. is related to beliefs about how the world began

12. The environment of the area close to Ayers Rock is such that

   A. rainfall is rare

   B. wild game is plentiful

   C. the weather is mild

   D. the vegetation is abundant

13. Ayers Rock was named after

   A. an Australian politician

   B. an aboriginal tradition

   C. the person who discovered it

   D. the area in which it is located

14. The word "protuberance" (line 66) means

   A. depression

   B. shadow

   C. bulge

   D. rock

15. It can be inferred from this passage that the Pitjantjatjara tribe's explanation for the formation of Ayers Rock differs from that of

   A. surveyors

   B. geologists

   C. Ernest Giles

   D. Sir Henry Ayers

Read the short story excerpt below and answer questions 16 to 22.

HISTORY LESSON

No one could remember when the tribe had begun its long journey. The land of great rolling plains that had been its first home was now no more than a half-forgotten dream.

For many years Shann and his people had been fleeing through a country of low hills and sparkling lakes, and now the mountains lay ahead. This summer they must cross them to
5 the southern lands. There was little time to lose. The white terror that had come down from the Poles, grinding continents to dust and freezing the very air before it, was less than a day's march behind.

Shann wondered if the glaciers could climb the mountains ahead, and within his heart he dared to kindle a little flame of hope. This might prove a barrier against which even the
10 remorseless ice would batter in vain. In the southern lands of which the legends spoke, his people might find refuge at last.

It took two weeks to discover a pass through which the tribe and the animals could travel. When midsummer came, they had camped in a lonely valley where the air was thin and the stars shone with a brilliance no one had ever seen before.

15 The summer was waning when Shann took his two sons and went ahead to explore the way. For three days they climbed, and for three nights slept as best they could on the freezing rocks, and on the fourth morning there was nothing ahead but a gentle rise to a cairn of gray stones built by other travelers, centuries ago.

Shann felt himself trembling, and not with cold, as they walked toward the little pyramid
20 of stones. His sons had fallen behind. No one spoke, for too much was at stake. In a little while they would know if all their hopes had been betrayed.

To the east and west, the wall of mountains curved away as if embracing the land beneath. Below lay endless miles of undulating plain, with a great river swinging across it in tremendous loops. It was a fertile land; one in which the tribe could raise crops knowing
25 that there would be no need to flee before the harvest came.

Then Shann lifted his eyes to the south, and saw the doom of all his hopes. For there at the edge of the world glimmered that deadly light he had seen so often to the north—the glint of ice below the horizon.

There was no way forward. Through all the years of flight, the glaciers from the south
30 had been advancing to meet them. Soon they would be crushed beneath the moving walls of ice…

Southern glaciers did not reach the mountains until a generation later. In that last summer the sons of Shann carried the sacred treasures of the tribe to the lonely cairn overlooking the plain. The ice that had once gleamed below the horizon was now almost at their feet.
35 By spring it would be splintering against the mountain walls.

No one understood the treasures now. They were from a past too distant for the understanding of any man alive. Their origins were lost in the mists that surrounded the Golden Age, and how they had come at last into the possession of this wandering tribe was a story that now would never be told. For it was the story of a civilization that had
40 passed beyond recall.

Once, all these pitiful relics had been treasured for some good reason, and now they had become sacred though their meaning had long been lost. The print in the old books had faded centuries ago though much of the lettering was still visible—if there had been any to read it. But many generations had passed since anyone had had a use for a
45 set of seven-figure logarithms, an atlas of the world, and the score of Sibelius' Seventh Symphony printed, according to the flyleaf, by H. K. Chu and Sons, at the City of Pekin in the year 2371 A.D.

The old books were placed reverently in the little crypt that had been made to receive them. There followed a motley collection of fragments—gold and platinum coins, a
50 broken telephoto lens, a watch, a cold-light lamp, a microphone, the cutter from an electric razor, some midget radio tubes, the flotsam that had been left behind when the great tide of civilization had ebbed forever.

—by Arthur C. Clarke

16. "Shann felt himself trembling" (line 19) because he was
    A. fearful for his sons' safety
    B. nervous about what he might see
    C. exhausted from climbing for many days
    D. overwhelmed by the sacred place

17. The phrase "doom of all his hopes" (line 26) indicates that the
    A. way north was not open
    B. crops would soon be ruined
    C. ice was advancing from the south
    D. journey could not continue immediately

18. The tribe was not aware of the relics' original purpose because the
    A. relics were only broken pieces
    B. relics had become sacred treasures
    C. people lived so far from civilization
    D. knowledge of the past was mostly lost

19. *Question Deleted*

20. The word "flotsam," as used in line 51, means
    A. gifts
    B. remains
    C. souvenirs
    D. merchandise

21. In this excerpt, the goal of the people was to
    A. continue their life of travelling in safety
    B. find a way to live comfortably beside the glaciers
    C. find a place to settle permanently and establish farms
    D. seek out all the glaciers and determine how far they had spread

22. The conflict in this passage is one of
    A. good versus evil
    B. people versus nature
    C. people versus people
    D. nature versus the supernatural

Read the poem below and answer questions 23 to 26.

THUMBPRINT

In the heel of my thumb
are whorls, whirls, wheels
in a unique design:
mine alone.
5 What a treasure to own!
My own flesh, my own feelings.
No other, however grand or base,
can ever continue the same.
My signature,
10 thumbing the pages of my time
My universe key,
my singularity.
Impress, implant,
I am myself,
15 of all my atom parts I am the sum.
And out of my blood and my brain
I make my own interior weather,
my own sun and rain.
Imprint my mark upon the world,
20 whatever I shall become.

—*by* Eve Merriam

---

23. The expression "thumbing the pages of my time" (line 10) is an example of a play on words because

   A. lines 9 and 10 are related to the title

   B. lines 9 and 10 suggest someone having fun

   C. the word "thumb" also appears in the first line

   D. the word "thumbing" has more than one meaning

24. The "sun and rain" (line 18) are symbolic of the narrator's

   A. passing time

   B. varying emotions

   C. natural environment

   D. temperature changes

25. A description of a thumbprint is contained in the words

   A. "whorls, whirls, wheels" (line 2)

   B. "What a treasure to own!" (line 5)

   C. "thumbing the pages of my time" (line 10)

   D. "Imprint my mark upon the world" (line 19)

26. The theme of this poem is one of

A. individuality

B. superiority

C. gratitude

D. solitude

Read the excerpt below and answer questions 27 to 32.

THE MISSION

I know that we reaped the benefit of those hard-earned lessons on the first attempt, and took them and used them to our advantage on this one. I think the core of people that came from the 1982 Canadian Mount Everest Expedition had a mission. We all had a mission, but they had a real mission.

—Sharon Wood

5   Suddenly, Barry let out a muffled cry from under his oxygen mask. He pointed up. Crashing down towards them like so many bowling balls were rocks the size of breadboxes. There was no time to think—only to react.

Trapped in her hypoxia-induced inertia[1], Sharon Wood dropped to the ice-anchor at her feet. She had an immediate flashback to the year before when she had been ripped off

10   her feet on the highest mountain in Peru. There, a small rock had shattered her shoulder blade in a second. She knew how much damage even the smallest rock could do, but here at 26,500 feet on the north face of the world's tallest mountain, she was powerless to do anything but pray.

Miraculously, the rocks went plummeting past.

15   Snapped from her sluggishness by a sudden surge of adrenaline[2], she became acutely lucid. Glancing around, things looked terrible. This May 19, 1986, the north face of Mount Everest was vicious. She, Barry Blanchard, Kevin Doyle and Dwayne Congdon struggled against the weight of 30-kg packs. As the wind tore at them, they staggered with every step in the rarefied air. Like some mountain-made snow gun, the gale blasted

20   snow crystals right through their zippers, driving cold to their cores. At times, Sharon would look up to see everyone face-down in the snow, cowering against the relentless force of the wind. It threatened to propel them into airborne oblivion.

"If this had been any other mountain, I would probably have turned back right there," Sharon recalls.

25   "It was like a statement from Everest: 'Commit or go home, but don't hesitate.'"

She did hesitate—they all did, if only for a moment. It seemed the whole day had been an exercise in extended agony. It had started at 9:00 A.M. in a ferocious gale and deteriorated as the day went on. Just minutes before, at 5:00 P.M., they had left the security of the three-mile-long fixed ropes. Now they were proceeding into the infamous

30   Hornbein Couloir, a massive rock gash that slashes down the north face of Everest.

---

[1] hypoxia-induced inertia—resistance to movement caused by a lack of oxygen

[2] adrenaline—a hormone secreted in response to physical or emotional stress

Varying from one to nine metres in width, it was an eerie passage. The scattered remains of old tents and shredded scraps of rope from previous expeditions hung like crystallized cobwebs from the walls. Combined with these ominous spectres of broken dreams, the couloir could have been the highest junk yard on earth.

35 The temperature was minus 35°C. With near-hurricane-force winds deep-sixing the wind chill to minus 40° and 50°C, the atmosphere of the place grew even more treacherous and sinister.

The Hornbein serves as a huge funnel for snow and debris tumbling off the top of the mountain. Perched at a 45-degree angle, it is like a gauntlet thrown at the foot of
40 climbers. It is also the gateway to the summit of "Chomolungma"—the Tibetan name for Everest, meaning "Mother Goddess of the World."

The goddess was more demonic than benevolent that day. And while the oceanic view may have been spectacular from where they were, not one of the frozen four paid any attention to it. They were too preoccupied with hanging on.

45 Time was running out. The 13-member expedition had been battling the mountain for two months and was more than a week behind schedule. Within days, the summer monsoon would be upon them, if it wasn't already. At lower elevations, the monsoon would bring torrential rains. But at this altitude, that rain would turn to horrific snowfalls that would make safe climbing impossible. Add to that the fact that the climbing permit
50 the Chinese government had granted the team would expire in about a week and things did indeed look bleak. If the climbers were to mount a summit bid, it was now or never. They literally and figuratively had their backs against the wall.

There was even more to it than time. An American team further out on the face had reached the same elevation as they had and was on a more direct line to the summit.
55 They, too, had a female member on their team—Annie Whitehouse, from Albuquerque, New Mexico. She, along with her colleagues, was also hoping to make a summit bid. If she succeeded before Sharon, she would become the first North American woman to climb Everest.

—*by* Alan Hobson

27. The word "lucid" (line 16) means that Sharon was
   A. drowsy
   B. aware
   C. confused
   D. injured

28. Sharon found climbing particularly hard on this day because
   A. the wind was so strong
   B. her shoulder hurt so much
   C. the monsoon was coming
   D. she was concerned about avalanches

29. The phrase "ominous spectres of broken dreams" (line 33) reminds the reader of the

    A. consequences of hesitating

    B. earlier attempts on Everest

    C. worn out, damaged equipment

    D. long, scary nights in the Hornbein

30. Time was running out for the climbers in the sense that the

    A. Chinese government did not want the climbers to continue

    B. other climbers had already reached the summit

    C. weather was steadily becoming worse

    D. team was almost too tired to continue

31. The word "mission" is used in this passage to imply a sense of

    A. hope

    B. interest

    C. responsibility

    D. determination

32. This passage **mostly** conveys a sense of

    A. despair

    B. hesitation

    C. panic

    D. urgency

Read the article below and answer questions 33 to 39.

ABACUS

Ever seen an abacus? You know, those centipede like things with wooden beads in rows. They're sold mostly in knickknack import shops, for wall decoration. But, in fact, an abacus is an adding machine, calculator, and computer. On second thought, that's not quite true. The abacus is just a visual record of the computations going on in the mind of
5 the person using it.

Millions of people in Asia still use the abacus daily. And it has been in use there for a couple of thousand years or more. Not only is it an effective practical tool, but it is nice to look at. Nice to hold and touch. Wood and brass and ivory. And the older they get and the longer they are handled by a human being, the lovelier they get—smooth and dark
10 and polished. They will last for a lifetime; they will never need updating; all the software needed to drive them is between your ears; and if they break they can be fixed by an eight-year-old with household tools.

The presence of the abacus puts some kinds of progress in perspective. I remember a time when a Japanese-American computer conglomerate moved into the Chinese market
15 in a big way. In order to demonstrate the value of its small pocket calculators, it arranged a contest. The great abacus–PC shoot-out. The guy who won—the guy with the abacus,

of course—was named Chan Kai Kit. Hong Kong Chinese—a senior clerk for a shipping company. It is true that the operator of the little computer did handle the pile of invoices forty-four seconds faster than Chan Kai Kit and his abacus. But the computer got the
20 wrong answer. Seems the machine operator was in too big a hurry to prove how smart his machine was and fed it fuzzy facts. Much face was lost.

Now don't get me wrong. Pocket calculators are here to stay, and they have their place. A Luddite I am not—machines are not evil in themselves. And a careful, thoughtful man like Chan Kai Kit might do even better with his own pocket calculator instead of his
25 abacus—who knows? It's just that I'm a sentimentalist about the wonders of the human hand and mind. And when I find evidence that it can still hold its own in the face of the wizardry of the electronic circuitry of little chips, I am pleased. It is comforting to know that some very old and very simple ways of getting from one place to another still work.

And I ponder the fact that an ancient and worn abacus will find its way to the walls of the
30 twentieth century as a thing of art and wonder, made lovely by its usefulness and made useful by its beauty. I have an old wooden bowl and an elderly chopping knife I would stack up against a food processor any day. It's the same story.

—by Robert Fulghum

33. The phrase "the guy with the abacus, of course" (line 16–17) is used to convey

   A. irony

   B. closure

   C. mystery

   D. foreshadowing

34. The outcome of the contest was **mostly** a result of the

   A. invoices not being printed quickly

   B. abacus operator completing the work first

   C. spectators distracting the calculator operator

   D. calculator operator entering inaccurate information

35. The sentence "Much face was lost" (line 21) means that the

   A. value of the calculator decreased

   B. calculator manufacturers were embarrassed

   C. calculator operator mysteriously disappeared

   D. information about the demonstration was destroyed

36. A "Luddite" (line 23) is a person who

   A. opposes advances in technology

   B. appreciates the dangers of technology

   C. wants humans to work with technology

   D. understands the usefulness of technology

37. The purpose of mentioning the bowl and knife (lines 31) is to

    A. generalize the discussion of the abacus to other areas

    B. suggest that technology sometimes brings improvements

    C. consider the other side of the argument about technology

    D. confirm that some possessions are more beautiful than useful

38. The author organizes his ideas **mainly** by

    A. giving reasons

    B. providing details

    C. showing cause and effect

    D. making comparisons and contrasts

39. The author's main message is that

    A. the abacus is becoming obsolete

    B. old technologies can remain useful

    C. old methods of calculation are the best

    D. the abacus is more decorative than functional

Read the poem below and answer questions 40 to 43.

SPORT

A fisherman steps
to the banks of a river
a comfortable rainbow
lies still in the water
5 and slides to the surface
to dine on the hatches
the quick eye that follows
makes perfect the target
while seeking—mouth open
10 finds steel for its dinner
the stillness is broken
by ripples exploding
implacable bamboo
arcs out to the victim
15 but short is the battle
for scales are uneven
and mesh that is anxious
awaits gleaming silver
soon two pounds of muscle
20 lies dead in a basket
and fishermen heart-beats
are proud and disdainful
the womb of the mother
is spilled by the angler
25 and ten thousand children
lie dead in the sand.

—*by* Kirk Wirsig

40. "A comfortable rainbow" (line 3) refers to

   A. a type of fish in its natural surroundings

   B. the shape of water ripples in the river

   C. the reflection of light from the sky

   D. a dying fish on the river bottom

41. The phrase "scales are uneven" (line 16) suggests that the

   A. fisherman is being unfair

   B. fish is too heavy to escape

   C. fisherman is more powerful than the fish

   D. fish's rough skin gets caught in the net

42. The last four lines of the poem present the conclusion that

   A. fishing is a battle

   B. fishing is a carefree sport

   C. killing fish is like killing children

   D. killing one fish may kill many fish

43. The **main** purpose of the poem is to

   A. describe the physical features of a fish

   B. persuade the reader to take up fishing

   C. excite the reader with battle images

   D. present a vivid picture of fishing

Read the short story excerpt below and answer questions 44 to 52.

MY NAME IS ANGIE

Angie struggled at school and suffered a lot when teachers asked questions she couldn't answer. By Grade 9, Angie had learned to stay quiet, cover up what she didn't know, and never catch the teacher's eye. Whenever she got really scared, she would quietly recite the multiplication tables she had worked so hard to learn in Grade 4. Angie rode the school
5 *bus everyday.*

Alex sat beside her—beautiful, clever, popular Alex. Alex was vice-president of the Student Council this year. Angie shifted a shy sideways glance to see whether a smile would be returned. It wouldn't; Alex was already busy, her head bent into her French text. Angie looked back out the window to the reflection of Alex coasting along in the air a few
10 feet away.

"She's so pretty and so smart … love the dangling pompom on her toque … love how it dances when we hit a bump … heard her tell her friends her grandma knit it for her. She's got so many friends, girls and boys, too … bet she even goes out with boys. She seems so brave around them, always laughing and having fun. Maybe if Mom knit me a toque with
15 a dangling pompom …" Angie drifted off into her thoughts, still looking out her window, sometimes at Alex's composed studious reflection, sometimes out past that to the fence posts, pastureland and trees sliding by …

Now they were at the top of the last big hill before the road swooped down and over the bridge on the final lap before reaching the school. All the pickups had been made. No
20 more stops now till they were there.

Angie felt the bus gathering speed as it rumbled down the hill toward the bridge. Anyone would think they'd have made the bridge a little sturdier over such an angry and hostile-looking stretch of water. It was always frothing and foaming, leaping up around the scarred banks as if intent on escaping. Even now, in the dead of winter, the stretch upriver
25 from the bridge remained open, lashing and tugging at the great, frozen chunks it had earlier thrown up in disgust on the banks. Further down, below the bridge, the surface had reluctantly frozen, but the heart of the angry blackness was alive, just inches below, ready to snatch away anything or anyone foolish enough to come close.

Any second now and they'd be on the bridge. Angie always hated the hollow rumble they
30 made as they crossed. It made the bridge seem even less substantial somehow.

If it hadn't been for the driver's quick reflexes when they hit the patch of ice on the bridge, the bus would have been right over the side. But, he did all the right things. He steered into the skid, then corrected; steered into the skid the other direction and corrected again, but it wasn't quite enough. There was a horrible, jarring crash; metal being crushed;
35 glass shattering. Finally, they slid to a quivering stop, only the back wheels left on the bridge. The front third of the bus was hanging at an angle, out over the wild water below. A sudden gust of wind moaned through the smashed guardrails and set the bus rocking, like a teeter-totter, softly rocking in a terrifying caricature of all the lovely, gentle things usually associated with being rocked.

40 Not a sound. Complete, frozen silence.

"Don't anybody move! Just sit real still, everybody. We're okay as long as we just hold tight." It was the driver's voice, a hoarse, trembling voice trying not to tremble. Angie recognized the sound of fear. She had heard it enough in her own voice many times.

"Just sit still, kids, we'll be okay. Just don't panic. A transport truck has seen us; he's
45 stopped; he'll radio for help. Just hang on kids …"

Angie was pushed forward and sideways by the angle of the bus. She could clearly see the river rushing by below, deep and dark and waiting …

"I'll just sit very, very still and be very quiet …" This terrified animal posture was nothing new to Angie; she did it every day in every class.

50 Awful, little, strangled, throaty noises from somewhere nearby… "I can't! I can't! … let me out … I want to go, I want to get out!" The voice rose almost to a scream. It was Alex. She started to get up; a shudder from the sudden movement ran the whole length of the bus. Her books slithered from her lap, hit the floor and slid several seat lengths forward, down toward the gently dipping and swaying nose of the bus. Finally, catching
55 on something, they stopped.

Alex stopped too, halfway standing, frozen. Alex on the edge of panic. Others were, too, Angie could feel it. Panic threatening—crackling through the bus, alive and awesome. They weren't listening to the driver. They were too afraid. But Angie knew how to handle fear, even this kind of fear.

60 She reached out and took Alex's hand, gently pulling her back down into the seat.

Still holding her hand, in a small but distinct voice, Angie spoke out.

"One times one is one; one times two is two; one times three is three; one times four is four…" She spoke with the same steady rhythm she had used to ease her own panic so many times before. Were they listening?

65 "… One times eleven is eleven; one times twelve is twelve; two times one is two; two times two is four; two times three is six …" on and on, her voice steady and strong. They listened; it was hypnotic. "… Six times six is thirty-six; six times seven is forty-two …" Silence except for Angie's voice. "… Eight times eight is sixty-four; eight times nine is seventy-two…"

70 Everyone listened, following the rhythmic cadences of her voice, their minds locked into the pattern of numbers, their minds turned away from fear. Some silently moved their lips in time with Angie. "… Twelve times seven is eighty-four; twelve times eight is ninety-six …" On she went, never faltering; steady, perfect rhythm, perfect calm …" twelve times ten is 120; twelve times eleven is 132; twelve times twelve is 144 …" then over 75 again, "…one times one is one; one times two is two …"

The river rushed and raged below, the bus teetered in its delicate balance, but Angie kept on, repeating over and over again the times tables—nothing else mattered, just the numbers … just the numbers …

With a violent lurch, the huge transport tow truck pulled the bus back onto the bridge. The 80 high school principal had rushed to the scene. He had watched, helpless, as his students hung on the edge of death. He was there to wait in anguish for the arrival of the tow truck. When, after an eternity, it did arrive, he had watched the cables being attached, oh so carefully, oh so gently. He had seen the police cars turning back traffic at each end of the bridge; had seen the arrival of the emergency rescue team and ambulances. Scuba divers 85 had been sent to the river's edge, waiting, ages ago. He had stared at the gently swaying bus with its load of silent, motionless young people; he had stared and wondered at their unbelievable calm.

The jolt of the two front wheels hitting solid ground broke the spell. A wild, chaotic cheer went up both from inside and outside the bus. The principal was the first to board, forcing 90 open the twisted doors and crunching up the glass-covered steps two at a time.

"Well," he said to the driver, clasping him round the shoulders in a giant bear hug, "Congratulations to you, sir!" His voice choked in relief. "You have done a wonderful thing here. But, how did you keep it so calm? How did you do it?"

"Oh, it wasn't me," said the driver with a pale smile, point back down the aisle with a 95 still-shaking hand, "It wasn't me. It was that blonde girl there, the one with the blue jacket on."

The principal turned and looked her way. "And what's your name, young lady? It seems we all owe an awful lot to you."

When the cheering and whistling and clapping had died down, she looked him straight in 100 the eye; somehow she knew that things were going to be different.

"Angie, sir," she said. "My name is Angie."

—*by* Beverly Terrell-Deutsch

44. In lines 22 to 28, the characteristic of the river that is focused on is its

    A. depth

    B. volume

    C. coldness

    D. turbulence

45. Over the years, much of Angie's fear had been connected to the

    A. pressure of peers

    B. nature of the river

    C. questions of teachers

    D. instability of the bridge

46. An example of a simile is found in the words

    A. "but the heart of the angry blackness was alive" (lines 27)

    B. "the bus rocking, like a teeter-totter, softly rocking" (lines 37–38)

    C. "as his students hung on the edge of death" (line 80–81)

    D. "His voice choked in relief" (line 92)

47. The word "caricature," as used in line 38, means

    A. bizarre imitation

    B. accurate reflection

    C. precise duplication

    D. comic exaggeration

48. The effect of Angie's recitation was to

    A. create a sense of hope

    B. pass the time more quickly

    C. develop a feeling of teamwork

    D. provide something on which to focus

49. The ellipses (…) used in lines 65 to 78 help to show

    A. the passing of time

    B. the building of tension

    C. pauses in Angie's recitation

    D. interruptions to Angie's recitation

50. The mood of this excerpt changes from danger to relief with the words

    A. "he had watched the cables being attached, oh so carefully" (lines 82–83)

    B. "he had stared and wondered at their unbelievable calm" (lines 86–87)

    C. "The jolt of the two front wheels hitting solid ground broke the spell" (line 88)

    D. "'Congratulations to you, sir!'" (line 92)

51. In this passage, it is ironic that Angie

    A. took charge of the situation

    B. rode the school bus everyday

    C. felt the panic of the other students

    D. hated the hollow rumble on the bridge

52. Angie "knew that things were going to be different" (line 100) **most likely** because she would

    A. now have the respect of other people

    B. now be able to make friends with Alex

    C. no longer be a stranger to the principal

    D. no longer have problems with her school work

Examine the cartoon below and answer questions 53 to 55.

FOR BETTER OR FOR WORSE © (1998) Lynn Johnston Productions. Dist. By Universal Press Syndicate.
Reprinted with permission. All rights reserved.

53. In frame 5, Mrs P.'s facial expression is one of

A. regret

B. concern

C. amusement

D. hopefulness

54. The driver says "that'd be great, Mrs. P.!" (frame 6) because he wants to be

A. polite

B. cynical

C. sarcastic

D. encouraging

55. By the end of this cartoon, Mrs. P. is feeling

A. resentful

B. generous

C. self-satisfied

D. misunderstood

ANSWERS AND SOLUTIONS—2000 PROVINCIAL ACHIEVEMENT TEST—PART B

1. D	12. A	23. D	34. D	45. C
2. A	13. A	24. B	35. B	46. B
3. B	14. C	25. A	36. A	47. A
4. D	15. B	26. A	37. A	48. D
5. C	16. B	27. B	38. D	49. A
6. B	17. C	28. A	39. B	50. C
7. A	18. D	29. B	40. A	51. A
8. C	19. Deleted	30. C	41. C	52. A
9. C	20. B	31. D	42. D	53. D
10. C	21. C	32. D	43. D	54. A
11. D	22. B	33. A	44. D	55. C

1. D

Many people had an interest in this issue: "I'd never seen people get so worked up over something" (line 5) and "No one protested this much when the mines closed"(line 5–6). The mayor was not anxious to have as many people attend as possible, as seen in lines 12–13 "… the mayor hoped people would get bored and leave the meeting before it ended." There is no evidence that the people went to the meeting to see the reporter, or that the townspeople were upset with the mayor. The evidence indicates that the issue is the interest of the people as "… they began to take sides. It was all they could talk about for a week" (lines 2–3). They were attending the meeting because they were interested in what could happen to Spruce.

2. A

Lines 10–11 reveal that "He didn't even try to hide his boredom, [he] just yawned and doodled in his steno book," which is evidence that the reporter was initially disinterested. Lines 41–42 state that "The St. John's reporter jerked his head up and began writing madly," which indicates that his lack of interest changed, and he became motivated.

3. B

The key word in this question is "symbolic." Lines 63–64 state, "Then he released his grip on the paper and let it fall to the floor," which implies intent. The writer has carefully selected the words "released" and "let it fall" to convey that it was intentional. In lines 50–51 we read that the father "just stood there, waiting, gripping on to that piece of paper as if it gave him the strength to stand."

By lines 63–64, the father appears to no longer need to cling to his paper for strength. Releasing the paper symbolizes the father finding his own inner strength, and speaking from the heart.

There is no evidence to suggest the father loses his temper. The father is nervous: "His nerves were frazzled, speaking in front of so many people, and he kept shuffling the papers in front of him" (lines 13–15). This may have caused him to accidentally drop the papers, but this idea is discounted in line 65 when he tells his son to leave the paper on the floor.

4. D

Line 58 confirms that the father, Graham Percy, had been interrupted by a comment from the crowd. "'Yeah, he's picked up the garbage regularly' some wisecracker yelled out." This serves as proof that he was interrupted.

5. C

The key word in this question is "symbolize." Symbolism is representation. What do the flecks in the son's and father's eyes represent within the context of this excerpt? According to line 88, "For the first time I noticed the flecks of gold in his deep brown eyes." He has known his father all his life, but this is the first time he notices those "flecks of gold." They represent the son seeing his father differently. The statement "It was like he was a kid looking for someone to say he did the right thing" indicates that the son is able to recognize a quality, or need, within his father. When the son reflects that "I had those same flecks" (line 89), there is a growing closeness that the son feels for his father.

6. B

The use of the word "bye" is an example of local dialect. The word "them" is used incorrectly but would not alone be evidence of local dialect. However, coupled with the word "bye," we can recognize this quotation it as a dialect from a specific location. The word "yeah," is a slang term that is used almost universally, so it is not an example of local dialect.

7. A

The excerpt is written from the first person point of view. Note that the narrator uses the word "I" frequently and participates in the action of the story.

8. C

There is strong support for the idea that the father is reserved. In line 46 to 47, we learn that "He never said a word in any sort of public meeting" which indicates a quiet nature. Lines 49–50 point out that "The people around us stopped talking and looked at my father." This suggests that the people were surprised to hear from him, again inferring a reserved nature. Lines 75 and 80 also support this: "I could tell people were stunned," and "'I can't believe Graham Percy stood up.'" But is he thoughtful? Although he only says a few words, you can tell they are very different from the other views shared at the meeting: "Spruce has given us all a little hope, something almost magical, during a time when we don't have much of anything that's good" (lines 69–71). This short speech by the father is heartfelt.

9. C

A "jumping-off place" is an expression used to describe a place from which to start. The fact that Ayers Rock attracts "nearly 90,000 visitors a year" is mentioned just prior to Alice Springs being referenced as the place to start, so Alice Springs is the closest town. As well, the fact that tourists travel "from Alice Spring to Ayers Rock" (line 23) also indicates this. Finally, according to the map, Alice Springs is the closest town to Ayers Rock.

According to the map, Alice Springs is east of Ayers Rock, not west, as Alternative **A** suggests. Line 41 states that there is "…Uluru Water, a deep water-hole on top," of the rock, not Alice Springs.

10. C

Lines 27–29 tell us that the rock has "another remarkable feature"—its changing appearance. This is the other feature that people from around the world come to Ayers Rock to see.

11. D

The words "mainly" and "sacred" are key to this question. Lines 37–39 state that "The Aborigines believe that Ayers Rock was produced during the Dreamtime, before men walked the earth; giants… set about the creation of the world," which is directly related to their beliefs about how the world began according to line 31–32. "Ayers Rock is sacred, having the significance of an ancient temple," which links the sacredness of the rock to the spirituality and beliefs of the people.

In lines 41–42, Ayers Rock is known as " 'Uluru,' the Place of Shade." However, that is not mainly why it is sacred. That is only a part of the story. The facts that "Many of its caves are the sites of religious ceremonies" and that the "Aborigines decorated many of the caves with mysterious paintings" (lines 34–35) are not the primary reason this rock is considered sacred.

12. A

Lines 68 and 69 offer direct proof that rainfall is rare, as "The overflow from infrequent rains ruins the usual silence of the desert."

Although we are told that visitors may "spot such local wildlife as kangaroos, wild horses, camels and buffalo," there is nothing to indicate that those animals are plentiful. The weather cannot be mild given that "The rock is scarred with weather-induced gullies and lightning-scarred ridges" (lines 67 and 68).

13. A

Lines 52–55 directly state that the rock was named after an Australian politician: "Gosse named the rock after Sir Henry Ayers, premier of South Australia, and then he climbed to the top."

14. C

Lines 65–66 state that "When the water receded, the rock remained, an enormous protuberance above a surrounding moonscape…" This tells that the water moved away from the rock and that the rock is above the surrounding moonscape. These references indicate that the bulge is the accurate answer.

15. B

Scientists who study rocks and geological formations are called geologists. Lines 62–64 are laden with facts that indicate geologists is the correct answer. "Although Ayers Rock has been sacred to the Pitjantjatjara for 15,000 years, this represents but a wink of an eye in its geological lifespan." The remainder of the paragraph details the geological reference, which differs dramatically from that of the aboriginal people, detailed in lines 37–43.

16. B

Lines 20–21, "No one spoke, for too much was at stake. In a little while they would know if all their hopes had been betrayed," reveal that Shann was nervous about what he might see.

17. C

The "doom of all his hopes" was seen as "Shann lifted his eyes to the south" (line 26), and it was evident that the ice was advancing from the south: "the glint of ice below the horizon." Lines 29–30 affirm that "the glaciers from the south had been advancing to meet them."

18. D

Lines 41–42 clarify that the knowledge of the past was mostly lost. "Once, all these pitiful relics had been treasured for some good reason, and now they had become sacred though their meaning had long been lost."

19. QUESTION DELETED

20. B

The reference to "flotsam" in lines 51–52, "the flotsam that had been left behind when the great tide of civilization had ebbed forever," informs as that it was something that was left behind. As well, the word "flotsam" is used to summarize everything left behind, so to select the best synonym for that word you must examine what was left behind. Are these items left behind gifts, remains, souvenirs, or merchandise? The items include "old books … a motley collection of fragments … broken telephoto lens … the cutter from an electric razor, some midget radio tubes." They are all remains.

A gift is something intended for a specific person, and these items were "left behind" with no person intended. Souvenirs remind us of our past, but we do not leave them behind. Merchandise has monetary value, and although some of the items ("gold and platinum coins … a watch, a cold-light lamp, [and] a microphone") may be of value, others are not ("a broken telephoto lens … the cutter from an electric razor"). Also, the fact that they are leaving them behind indicates the items have no current value.

21. C

Lines 24 to 25 state: "It was a fertile land; one in which the tribe could raise crops knowing that there would be no need to flee before the harvest came." This tells us that they are seeking a place to settle permanently and to establish farms.

From line 11, "his people might find refuge at last," it can be understood that they are seeking safety but not desiring a lifestyle of safe travel. When they determined how far the glaciers had spread, Shann "saw the doom of all his hopes," which indicates he is not happy about this discovery.

22. B

People versus nature has to be the correct answer because the glaciers that have changed the lifestyle of these people and have displaced them for years.

Glaciers are created through natural circumstances, not by the powers of the supernatural, nor through evil. There is no reference to either of those forces in this writing.

23. D

The expression a play on words refers to a word or phrase that has more than one meaning.

24. B

You must determine a "symbolic" meaning. Lines 16–18 tell you that the narrator "makes my own interior weather, / my own sun and rain." Since sun and rain are universal symbols of happiness and sadness, this question means that the narrator makes his or her own happiness or sadness.

The phrase "interior weather" refers to these emotions. Hence, the reference to varying emotions is the only possible alternative. The other three alternatives all refer to external elements.

25. A

The beginning of the poem starts with a graphic description of the thumb. "In the heel of my thumb / are whorls, whirls, wheels / in a unique design: / mine alone." The remaining alternatives do not provide descriptions.

26. A

You know that fingerprints are unique individual characteristics. The writer chose to use her thumbprint as a metaphor for her character and her individuality in this poem. She does display gratitude in her writing ("What a treasure to own!"), but it is focused on her individuality, as evidenced through her many personal references (I, me, mine alone, my signature, my singularity). There is no support for superiority as an answer because she writes, "No other, however grand or base, / can ever contain the same" which refers to those greater and lesser than she, but does not employ comparison. Finally, there are no references in the poem to suggest that the theme is solitude.

27. B

To determine the best meaning for the word "lucid," examine line 15: "Snapped from her sluggishness by a sudden surge of adrenaline, she became acutely lucid." Refer to the footnote indicated beside the word adrenaline, which reads "a hormone secreted in response to physical or emotional stress." This indicates that the adrenaline changed her state from "sluggish" to "lucid." The statement "Glancing around, things looked terrible" shows that she is aware.

28. A

Lines 18–22 introduce the wind "As the wind tore at them, they staggered with every step in the rarefied air ... the gale blasted snow crystals right through their zippers, driving cold to their cores... [they were] cowering against the relentless force." It becomes clear that the climb was particularly hard because the wind was so strong when "It threatened to propel them into airborne oblivion" and "With near-hurricane-force winds deep-sixing the wind chill to minus 40° and 50°C…"

29. B

"Spectres" can be defined as ghosts or spirits. You must read a few lines prior to the one referred to in the question to be sure of the answer. "The scattered remains of old tents and shredded scraps of rope" are from previous expeditions are the ghosts that remind her of earlier attempts on Everest. The idea of "broken dreams" is also related to failed attempts on Everest.

You know that there is worn-out damaged equipment, but the narrator combines the phrase "the highest junk yard on earth" with "these ominous spectres of broken dreams."

30. C

Time was running out because the weather was steadily becoming worse. According to lines 46–49, "Within days, the summer monsoon would be upon them, if it wasn't already. At lower elevations, the monsoon would bring torrential rains. But at this altitude, that rain would turn to horrific snowfalls that would make safe climbing impossible."

31. D

"The Mission" is the title of this piece, and is referenced in the quotation at the beginning of the passage where its purpose and meaning are clarified. We learn that some climbers have tried this mountain before, learned some "hard" lessons, and used them to do better with this second attempt. This implies a goal, and a goal is understood to be the focus of determination. Some of the climbers on this attempt (1986, as noted in line 17) were returning climbers who had failed on their 1982 attempt. They did not want to fail again. Determination grows from desire, and nothing fosters desire more than failure.

32. D

A sense of urgency is conveyed throughout the passage from the first avalanche, through finding the remains left behind by failed teams in Hornbein Couloir, to the current weather and the oncoming monsoon season, and finally, to the other team with a female member being in a better location. The last bit of information intensifies the sense of urgency developed throughout the passage.

Hesitation is mentioned only briefly from lines 25–27, so it would not be the prominent message. Panic was also experienced by the team as noted through the "sudden surge of adrenaline" in line 15, but it was not long lasting.

33. A

Irony is used to show incongruity between what is expected and what actually occurs. In this case, the contest was arranged "to demonstrate the value of its small pocket calculators" (line 15). When "The guy who won" was not the guy with the pocket calculator, but instead "the guy with the abacus, of course," the opposite of what was expected is what actually happened.

34. D

The surprising outcome occurred because the calculator operator entered wrong information This is clearly stated in lines 20 to 21. The abacus operator completed his work last, not first ("the operator of the little computer did handle the pile of invoices forty-four seconds faster than Chan Kai Kit").

35. B

To understand the meaning of the term "much face was lost," you need to understand its context in the article. The statement "the machine operator was in too big a hurry to prove how smart his machine was and fed it fuzzy facts" precedes it, so it was written in reference to the failure of the calculator as a result of human error. This would be embarrassing; thus, the calculator manufacturers were embarrassed is the answer.

36. A

"A Luddite I am not—machines are not evil in themselves." The author indicates he is not a Luddite, and then provides the definition of one in the remainder of his statement. A Luddite is one who sees machines as evil. Therefore, a Luddite opposes advancements in technology.

37. A

To establish the purpose of mentioning the bowl and knife, refer to the context from which they are extracted (line 31).

The writer is in awe of the "ancient and worn" abacus lasting this long. It has become "a thing of art and wonder, made lovely by its usefulness and made useful by its beauty." Then, the writer refers to the "old wooden bowl and an elderly chopping knife" that he owns, and says it "would stack up against a food processor any day." When he finally says "It's the same story," he is showing that the simple bowl and knife are similar to the simple but beautiful abacus. This comparison infers other simple instruments elicit the same kind of awe as the abacus. He has generalized his discussion of the abacus to other areas.

38. D

The author makes comparisons and contrasts throughout the article; for example, the abacus and the calculator, old technology and new technology, electronic "wizardry" and "simple ways," and the wooden bowl and knife and the abacus.

39. B

Old technologies can remain useful is the main message, as introduced at the beginning: "They will last for a lifetime; they will never need updating; all the software needed to drive them is between your ears; and if they break they can be fixed by an eight-year-old with household tools" (line 10–12). This idea is also reinforced when the author comments: "It's just that I'm a sentimentalist about the wonders of the human hand and mind. And when I find evidence that it can still hold its own in the face of the wizardry of the electronic circuitry of little chips, I am pleased. It is comforting to know that some very old and very simple ways of getting from one place to another still work" (lines 25–28). Finally, by relating the abacus to his bowl and knife, he reinforces the idea that old technologies can remain useful.

There is evidence that the abacus is not becoming obsolete in the article, as "Millions of people in Asia still use the abacus" (line 6). The abacus is not more decorative than functional as shown in lines 7 to 8: "Not only is it an effective practical tool, but it is nice to look at." Although the writer notes that "The presence of the abacus puts some kinds of progress in perspective" (line 13), he does not claim the old methods of calculation are best.

40. A

The phrase a "comfortable rainbow" refers to a type of fish in its natural surroundings as it "lies still in the water and slides to the surface to dine on the hatches" (lines 4–6). This expression cannot refer to the shape of the water ripples, as water ripples cannot "dine on the hatches." A reflection of light from the sky and a dying fish on the river bottom are not options for the same reason.

41. C

The "scales are uneven" is a play on words as fish have scales and scales are also used to measure weight. This suggests that the fisherman is more powerful than the fish. The fish has its "mouth open [for its dinner, and] / finds steel for its dinner" (lines 9–10). The steel is the fishing hook. At this point, the battle between the fish and the fisherman is on, but "short is the battle" (lines 15–16) because the "scales are uneven." That is, the scales give the advantage to the man over the fish.

42. D

The last four lines of the poem must be carefully examined to answer this question, as you are asked specifically what conclusion these lines present. The last four lines are "the womb of the mother / is spilled by the angler/and ten thousand children / lie dead in the sand." This imagery describes the angler, or fisherman, gutting the fish, which happens to be a female with thousands of eggs in her belly, and as he does, these eggs spill onto the sand. The use of the word "womb" refers to a human mother, as fish do not have wombs. They lay eggs. Therefore, the author is using a metaphor to compare a female fish to a human mother. This is a powerful metaphor, as it enables you to relate to the image on a very personal level, intensifying the image, of "ten thousand children dead in the sand." By catching and killing this fish, he has killed many. Killing one fish may kill many fish is the only conclusion that makes sense given the image of "ten thousand [fish lying] / dead in the sand."

43. D

The main purpose of this poem is to present a vivid picture of fishing, which the writer does through his compelling imagery. The poem does not describe the physical features of a fish. It is not a persuasive poem, and the image at the end is certainly not one that would persuade anyone to take up fishing: "ten thousand children / lie dead in the sand."

The battle imagery is written with passion, not humour: "the stillness is broken / by ripples exploding / implacable bamboo arcs out to the victim" (lines 11 to 14).

44. D

Read lines 22 to 28 carefully to establish the characteristic of the river. Is the depth, volume, coldness, or turbulence being described? "It was always frothing and foaming, leaping up around the scarred banks as if intent on escaping." This personifies the river, and addresses its turbulence through activity.

45. C

According to the preamble, Angie's fear had been connected to the questions of teachers: "Angie struggled at school and suffered a lot when teachers asked questions she couldn't answer."

46. B

A simile is a literary device that is a comparison of two unlike things using the words "like" or "as." It compares the rocking bus with a teeter-totter using the word "like."

47. A

A caricature is a cartoon-like representation in which something is exaggerated. In this reference, the bus, which is on the brink of disaster, is described as "softly rocking," but we know that this rocking is not at all like usual associations of rocking. The bus is just imitating gentle rocking, and given impending disaster, the imitation is bizarre.

48. D

Angie had used her recitation in the past to allay her fears: "Whenever she got really scared, she would quietly recite the multiplication tables" (preface). It provided her with another focus. In this incident, "Everyone listened, following the rhythmic cadences of her voice, their minds locked into the pattern of numbers, their minds turned away from fear" (lines 70–71); that is, providing something on which they could focus.

There is no reference to a sense of hope from the inside of the bus, only through the eyes of the principal watching the rescue. There is teamwork in that the students all focus on Angie, and the time passes more quickly because they are focused on her, but it is the author's use of the literary device of repetition to develop a monotonous tone that confirms the power of the focus within the bus.

49. A

"One times one is one; one times two is two; one times three is three; one times four is four...." The first ellipses are used to show that the pattern continues. "… One times eleven is eleven; one times twelve is twelve; two times one is two; two times two is four; two times three is six.. ." The second ellipses are used for the same reason, and to develop an hypnotic tone so that you are able to participate in the power of the focused experience. "… on and on, her voice steady and strong. They listened; it was hypnotic." The ellipses reinforce the author's purpose as the passing of time.

It has now become "hypnotic." The use of auditory imagery coupled with the visual placement of the ellipses within the text relates to the passing of time.

50. C

The mood of danger instantly changes to relief when "The jolt of the two front wheels hitting the solid ground broke the spell."

51. A

Irony is an incongruity between what is expected to occur and what actually occurs. It is ironic, that Angie took charge of the situation because you would have never expected her to.

The preface tells us that "… Angie had learned to stay quiet, cover up what she didn't know, and never catch the teacher's eye," , and in lines 49–50, we find that "This terrified animal posture was nothing new to Angie; she did it every day in every class." Therefore, for Angie to take charge of any situation would not be what you would expect would happen.

52. A

Angie realizes things are going to be different "When the cheering and whistling and clapping had died down…" (line 99), so the respect of other people demonstrated by their cheers, whistles, and clapping has convinced her of this. It is true that she would not be a stranger to the principal and that she might make friends with Alex, but those are not the references the writer uses to support this new awareness within her.

It is the "cheering and whistling and clapping" that are the means for this, and these are behaviours used for showing respect.

53. D

Given the words "Can I come?" and her wide open eyes with raised brows, the correct answer is hopefulness.

54. A

The teenagers are off to the beach, and Mrs. P is the mother of one of the teenagers. You know this because one of the people in the car responds, "Yeah! We've got food an' everything, Mom." When Mrs. P. says, "Sounds like fun!" and then asks to come, the car is already packed with the teenagers and their beach necessities. You know how much fun it would be to get away to the beach for a day without your mom. When the driver answers, he is just being polite. Frame 9 confirms that he was being polite when someone says, "That was close!" Thus, he was not being encouraging. Neither teen is being cynical or sarcastic, as the tone is a happy and light one.

55. C

"Every now and then, I like to shake them up a little!" is Mrs. P's final comment. Her expression is one of self-satisfaction as you realize that she is aware she had them convinced that she wanted to join them!

2001 PROVINCIAL ACHIEVEMENT TEST—PART B

The readings and questions that are repeated from the 2000 Provincial Achievement Test are NOT included in the 2001 Provincial Achievement Test printed here.

Read the short story excerpt below and answer questions 1 to 8.

THE COMING OF MUTT

During my lifetime we had owned, or had been owned by, a steady succession of dogs. As a newborn baby I had been guarded by a Border collie named Sapper, who was one day doused with boiling water by a vicious neighbour, and who went insane as a result. But there had always been other dogs during my first eight years, until we moved to the
5 west and became, for the moment, dogless. The prairies could be only half real to a boy without a dog.

I began agitating for one almost as soon as we arrived and I found a willing ally in my father—though his motives were not mine.

For many years he had been exposed to the colourful tales of my Great-uncle Frank, who
10 homesteaded in Alberta in 1900. Frank was a hunter born, and most of his stories dealt with the superlative shooting to be had on the western plains. Before we were properly settled in Saskatoon my father determined to test those tales. He bought a fine English shotgun, a shooting coat, cases of ammunition, a copy of the Saskatchewan Game Laws, and a handbook on shotgun shooting. There remained only one indispensable item—a
15 hunting dog.

One evening he arrived home from the library with such a beast in tow behind him. Its name was Crown Prince Challenge Indefatigable. It stood about as high as the dining-room table and, as far as Mother and I could judge, consisted mainly of feet and tongue. Father was annoyed at our levity and haughtily informed us that the Crown
20 Prince was an Irish setter, kennel bred and field trained, and a dog to delight the heart of any expert. We remained <u>unimpressed</u>. Purebred he may have been, and the possessor of innumerable cups and ribbons, but to my eyes he seemed a singularly useless sort of beast with but one redeeming feature: I greatly admired the way he drooled. I have never known a dog who could drool as the Crown Prince could. He never stopped, except
25 to flop his way to the kitchen sink and tank up on water. He left a wet and sticky trail wherever he went. He had little else to recommend him, for he was moronic.

Mother might have overlooked his obvious defects, had it not been for his price. She could not overlook that, for the owner was asking two hundred dollars, and we could no more afford such a sum than we could have afforded a Cadillac. Crown Prince left the
30 next morning, but Father was not discouraged, and it was clear that he would try again.

My parents had been married long enough to achieve that delicate balance of power which enables a married couple to endure each other. They were both adept in the evasive tactics of marital politics—but Mother was a little more adept.

She realized that a dog was now inevitable, and when chance brought the duck boy—as
35 we afterwards referred to him—to our door on that dusty August day, Mother showed her mettle by snatching the initiative right out of my father's hands.

By buying the duck boy's pup, she not only placed herself in a position to forestall the purchase of an expensive dog of my father's choice, but she was also able to save six cents in cash. She was never one to despise a bargain.

40 When I came home from school the bargain was installed in a soap carton in the kitchen. He looked to be a somewhat dubious buy at any price. Small, emaciated, and caked liberally with cow manure, he peered up at me in a near-sighted sort of way. But when I knelt beside him and extended an exploratory hand he roused himself and sank his puppy teeth into my thumb with such satisfactory gusto that my doubts dissolved. I knew that
45 he and I would get along.

—*by* Farley Mowat

1. When the narrator says "The prairies could be only half real to a boy without a dog" (lines 5–6), he **probably**
   A. knows that he would enjoy the prairies more with a dog
   B. realizes that he has been without a dog for too long
   C. is inspired by the hunting stories of his Great-uncle
   D. likes the prairies a lot less than his former home

2. The phrase "a willing ally in my father—though his motives were not mine" (lines 7–8) suggests that the narrator and his father
   A. were careful to avoid talking about dogs
   B. both liked dogs but could not agree on a breed
   C. were in agreement about most things except dogs
   D. both wanted to acquire a dog but for different reasons

3. In the story, the phrase "determined to test those tales" (line 12) means that the narrator's father
   A. challenged himself to learn a new skill
   B. started to dream about hunting on the prairies
   C. set about proving that Frank was exaggerating
   D. wanted to see if the hunting was as good as Frank claimed

4. Upon seeing Crown Prince for the first time, the narrator was
   A. amused
   B. enchanted
   C. concerned
   D. intimidated

5. The family did not keep Crown Prince because he was too
   A. messy
   B. stupid
   C. clumsy
   D. expensive

6. The word "adept" (lines 32 and 33) means

   A. weak

   B. skilled

   C. impressive

   D. enthusiastic

7. The narrator portrays his father as a person who

   A. did not listen to other people

   B. always got what he wanted

   C. became impatient quickly

   D. did not give up on an idea

8. The narrator knew that he would get along with the puppy because the puppy

   A. enjoyed getting dirty

   B. responded to his greeting

   C. looked up at him so cutely

   D. showed potential as a hunter

Read the newspaper articles below and answer questions 9 to 15.

In January 1998, a huge winter storm struck central Canada. These three articles appeared together in The Edmonton Journal at that time.

ICE STORM WREAKS HAVOC

Article 1

"The cold may get old, but freezing rain is much bigger pain"

I'll take 25 below, anytime.

Even after a decade living in Ottawa, I can still feel the numbing western chill that burns
5   cheeks and blurs the vision.

But the bitter cold of discomfort that has left Albertans grumbling after a week in the deep freeze is a breeze of inconvenience compared to the ice box emergency encasing central Canada following back-to-back freezing-rain storms.

The iceman cameth. And there's more to come.

10   Try getting by in winter without power overnight. When our lights flickered and then died Wednesday night, it was a bit of an adventure initially to find the candles and flashlights. For my teenage son, it was a particularly lucky strike. First the computer died and snuffed out his assignment. Then, even better, region-wide power failures and impassable roads for school buses caused schools to close for the second day this week.

15   Unlike previous outages which rarely lasted more than an hour, this one persisted. Overnight. No coffee in the morning. The temperature of the house had dipped to 13 degrees by the time power was restored 17 hours later.

Hundreds of thousands of other families haven't been so lucky. My 87-year-old uncle,
who has lived alone for the past 20 years, found refuge in a Montreal shelter after social
workers checked in on him. He was wearing three layers of clothing, but wouldn't seek
help even after the lights had been off for two days.

My brother-in-law is trying to track down a spare portable generator to pump water to his
thirsty beef cattle. His problems are compounded by the fact his farmhouse and barn are
500 metres from the section road and the driveway and fields are iced over.

For the first time ever, a state of emergency has been declared in the Ottawa-Carleton
area. The bright lightning so many people thought they'd seen light up the night sky was
in fact exploding transformers.

Universities, most government offices and some stores and shopping malls were closed
Thursday as hydro and road crews fought losing battles to repair downed lines, fix power
stations and pour salt on the slick streets. Police want everyone to stay home today,
although by Alberta standards the zero temperatures are positively balmy.

One suburban man surveying the havoc told a radio reporter he was reminded of another
disaster he experienced. He compared it to the 1987 Edmonton tornado.

A walk through my Ottawa bedroom community makes it easy to see why. Each lawn
is stacked with the twisted debris of broken tree limbs. The heavy branches swaying
high above are now laden with ice about three cm thick. It's a wondrous, mystic vision
that turns quickly ominous when the sound of crinkling ice crystals is suddenly heard,
preceding a sharp crack as a branch tumbles with a whoosh to the ground.

Walking, or should I say shuffling, the dog, on the iced roads half a block from home
Thursday morning, I came upon a shaken driver who moments before had miraculously
escaped getting crushed by a 20-metre tree that had fallen over.

With 12 tall trees in my yard, some hanging over the house, the constant crashing has
made me a light sleeper in the past three nights. A neighbour did little to settle our nerves
when she told my wife how she had watched a thick six-metre long poplar branch whistle
past our second-storey bedroom window Thursday.

More freezing rain was forecast Thursday night. We may sleep in the basement.

—*by* Norm Ovenden

Article 2

"On Ice"

Storm: First round, Monday night, drops 20 mm of icy rain. Second round starts
Wednesday, doesn't let up. Total precipitation 45 mm as of Thursday, with another 10 to
15 cm expected by Saturday.

Worst hit communities: South shore of St. Lawrence River across from Montreal as well
as Montreal Island, Ottawa, Laurentian Mountains. Ice storm described as worst in many
decades.

Effects: An estimated three million Quebecers left without power, as well as at least
50,000 in the Ottawa area. Seven storm-related deaths to date. About 800 Quebecers in
emergency shelters, number expected to double or triple.

Repairs: 3,000 Hydro-Quebec employees working 16-hour shifts, assisted by 1,000 linemen from United States and 550 Canadian soldiers. More than 2,000 other troops help out in shelters.

15 Outlook: Icy precipitation through weekend, growing number of people to seek emergency shelter, full return of power not likely until next week.

—*by* Norm Ovenden

Article 3

"Acts of kindness light up the darkness"

Jolene Barton toughed it out at her Kirkland home without electricity for two days, but with her husband out of town she threw in the towel Wednesday, packed up her two sons
5 and headed for a downtown hotel.

That's when she met her Good Samaritan, one of hundreds around the Montreal region who have been helping friends, neighbours and mostly complete strangers through the devastation of the continuing storm.

After Barton hit a pothole and blew one of the tires on her minivan, a shiny black Porsche
10 stopped and a man "dressed to the gills" followed her to a nearby car dealership. It was closed, so he changed the tire himself.

"He was wearing a dress shirt, with the white cuffs and the gold cuff links and there he was down on his knees, changing my tire," Barton said.

"All I know is his name is Chris from Kirkland and I love him dearly. He said he did it
15 because something like this happened to his wife once and a stranger stopped and helped her and he never forgot it."

All around the city, people are recounting stories like Barton's. More than the cracked and twisted trees, the bitter cold, the darkness broken only by flickering candlelight, what many Montrealers will remember about this storm is the kindness of others.

20 At makeshift shelters around the region, hundreds of volunteers pitched in to set up beds, hand out blankets, serve coffee and sandwiches and do what they could to make people comfortable. Some have been working since Tuesday with next to no sleep.

People lucky enough to still have electricity have taken in friends and neighbours who are without. Many hotels are offering special rates.

25 In Montreal West, more than a dozen volunteers worked the phones to call 2,500 households in the area to make sure no one was freezing or going without the necessities.

Residents of various neighbourhoods are calling YMCAs to offer help. The association offered free use of showers and other facilities while staff volunteered time to play with children in the gyms.

30 But disaster doesn't always bring out the best in everybody. A local tree nursery hiked the cost of a cord of wood by $10. A gas station upped its price at the pump by three cents a litre. Thieves hit a number of abandoned homes and made off with thousands of dollars worth of goods.

—*by* Monique Beaudin and Sue Montgomery

9. In Article 1, the author's son was happy about the storm because he was
   A. unable to leave his home
   B. able to spend some time alone
   C. able to take long and beautiful walks
   D. unable to continue with his normal activities

10. An example of imagery is found in the words
    A. "ice box emergency" (Article 1, line 7)
    B. "back-to-back freezing-rain storms" (Article 1, line 8)
    C. "the lights had been off for two days" (Article 1, line 21)
    D. "a thick six-metre long poplar branch" (Article 1, line 44)

11. The **most likely** reason that people were asked to stay home (article 1, line 30) was so that
    A. they would stay warm
    B. they would avoid injury
    C. the authorities could control crime
    D. the authorities could conserve energy

12. In Article 2, sentence fragments are used in order to
    A. create vivid images
    B. focus on facts and figures
    C. produce an emotional response
    D. allow for comparisons of information

13. In Article 3, line 10, the phrase "'dressed to the gills'" means
    A. prepared for any event
    B. wearing formal clothing
    C. covered from head to toe
    D. wearing warm winter clothing

14. Which of the following expressions conveys the underlying message of Barton's story in Article 3 about "Chris from Kirkland"?
    A. Don't give up hope.
    B. You get what you pay for.
    C. Pass on an act of kindness.
    D. You can't control the elements.

15. The final paragraph of Article 3 uses the technique of
    A. rebuttal
    B. contrast
    C. repetition
    D. summarization

Read the section below and answer questions 16 to 21.

ANIMATING ANIMALS

No actor finds it easy to work with animals but today's movie magic makes it easier for actors to share the screen amicably with dinosaurs, dragons, aliens, and gorillas. This is possible because of animatronics, the process of creating electronic and mechnical creatures that respond to remote control signals. Animatronics can create the unbelievable without the need for special trainers or re-takes, and the creatures can take the shape of ordinary animals, such as the gorilla in the movie Buddy (1997), or fantastic aliens and monsters from outer space. Bringing animal robots to life, however, takes months of preparation by skilled craftspeople and puppeteers. On the set, the models and costumes are strapped and harnessed with wires, rods, metal frames, and electronic sensors that together create the illusion of a living, breathing animal, with realistic skin, hair, teeth, and claws.

Dressing the part

Imitating a living animal can often lead to monkey business! For the film *Buddy*, four different model gorillas were built to show the hero of the movie as a baby, a toddler, a juvenile, and an adult ape. For the adult version an actor wears a padded muscle suit covered by an authentic "hair" suit.

The muscle suit is custom-built to fit the actor

It took one person six weeks to punch in all the hairs on Buddy's back

The flexible rubber hands fit like gloves

The "hair" suit is put on over the muscle suit—the heat inside is intense!

Velcro straps attach the ape feet to the body of the suit

The adult head is fully animatronic and worn like a crash helmet

Animating an Animatronic Ape Head

All animals convey emotion with their faces. For Buddy, the animatronic head was made to convey an array of emotions with its eyes, nose, mouth, and facial muscles. Model-makers at Jim Henson's Creature Shop developed an intricate head from observation of live gorillas. The animatornic head was worn by an actor for close-ups in the movie, and every twitch of its features was executed by remote control.

Face is sculpted from accurate reference

Each hair is individually *punched in* by hand

Eyebrow mechanism—the slightest twitch can convey profound emotions

Realistic bulge in the cornea adds to Buddy's soulfulness

A soft and fleshy silicone skin gives added realism to Buddy's facial expression

Buddy's nose can be wrinkled at anything with this sliding device

Lightweight polycarbonate shell maintains the shape of Buddy's skull under the skin

Left hand controls facial expressions

Rubber plates attach the silicone skin to the mechanisms

A complex scissor mechanism allows the corners of Buddy's mouth to simulate eating, growling, and smiling movements

Powerful jaw motors can bite hard—actors beware!

Acrylic teeth are indistinguishable from the real thing

Lower-lip mechanism

Muscle and hair suit combined with the animatronic head

The Story of Buddy

Buddy tells the true story of a baby gorilla raised by a rich American socialite. Although often dressed as a human being in the movie, Buddy's movements and actions still had to be recognizably those of an ape, so animal experts were always on hand during filming in Los Angeles to give advice.

Molding the model

Sculpting and molding are important aspects of animatronics. A model is sculpted in nondrying clay which can be worked on and blended easily without cracking. When the sculpture is complete, a mold of it is made in fibreglass. The mold is then cast in silicone or foam latex.

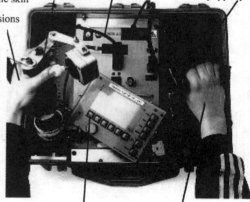

Universal joy stick controls eye movements

Cable connects puppet to control rig

Mitten control is adapted from traditional puppetry

Commands can be programmed in on site

Right hand controls mouth movements

Keeping Control

Animatronic creations are made to work by an operator who uses a remote control machine behind the camera. Sensors attached to the eyes, nose, arms, and other parts of the mechanical creature respond to electronic signals from the control panel. The animatronic creature responds to the messages sent in "real time"—in other words, the animatronic ape reacts to the signal the minute it is transmitted.

From Special Effects in Film and Television

16. According to this selection, animatronics is **most useful** when moviemakers want to

   A. avoid training animals

   B. spare animals from harm

   C. make animals seem more human

   D. protect actors from dangerous animals

17. Animatronic movements are effected by

   A. model makers

   B. animal experts

   C. fully disguised actors

   D. remote control operators

18. The heading "Animating An Animatronic Ape Head" contains an example of

   A. hyperbole

   B. alliteration

   C. onomatopoeia

   D. personification

19. In the sentence, "Each hair is individually *punched* in by hand", the phrase "punched in" means

   A. formed

   B. pierced

   C. collected

   D. embedded

20. According to the selection, Buddy's animatronic face is made of

   A. rubber

   B. silicone

   C. fibreglass

   D. polycarbonate

21. The skills of an animatronic operator are **most** like those of

   A. an actor

   B. a director

   C. a puppeteer

   D. a model maker

Read the poem below and answer questions 22 to 25.

BILLY PARIS

This term I don't have a lunch period,
Too many subjects to make up.
So while I learn new nouns in Mr. Brewer's Spanish class,
I munch on some potato chips.
5 Two days ago he laid down the law:
"No snacking while speaking Spanish."
Yesterday I got even.
I pulled out from my bag
A checkered tablecloth,
10 Two candlesticks,
One bowl,
One spoon,
And a thermos full of soup.
I slowly set the table,
15 Said a blessing (in Spanish) over the food,
And named every object with perfect accent.
Mr. Brewer stood there, dumbstruck.
Then he began to laugh.
The class joined in.
20 You know, school doesn't have to be so grim.

—*by* Mel Glenn

---

22. The **main** purpose of Billy's performance in class was to

  A. protest Mr. Brewer's rules

  B. eat a good lunch in comfort

  C. show off his perfect Spanish accent

  D. turn the students against Mr. Brewer

23. In lines 9–14, the poet's purpose is to show that Billy was

  A. feeling defiant and hostile

  B. being arrogant and conceited

  C. feeling confused and agitated

  D. being deliberate and methodical

24. Mr. Brewer's reaction to Billy's performance changed from

  A. concern to relief

  B. denial to acceptance

  C. annoyance to mockery

  D. surprise to amusement

25. The tone of this poem is

A. sarcastic

B. optimistic

C. full of regret

D. matter-of-fact

Read the poem below and answer questions 26 to 29.

BRENDA STEWART

Jill is so straight, I can't stand it.
But I need a friend who helps me touch the ground
While I chase the wind.
If I am a high-flying kite,
5   Jill is my string.
If I want to buy something outrageous,
She reminds me that it's not machine washable.
If I act like a complete idiot,
She tells me there is still hope.
10 If I have a fight with my parents,
She reminds me that it will soon blow over.
Last Saturday I wanted to go shopping with her,
But she had a game to cheer.
I went to the mall myself and
15 Walked through the aisles admiring everything.
Without thinking, I pulled a top off one of the shelves
And stuffed it into my bag.
A hand grabbed my arm.
A face asked me questions.
20 A finger dialed a phone.
I felt so embarrassed.
I kept thinking I wouldn't be in this mess
If Jill had come shopping with me.

—*by* Mel Glenn

---

26. The word "straight" (line 1) means

    A. patient

    B. helpful

    C. sensible

    D. supportive

27. The phrase "Jill is my string" (line 5) means that Jill

    A. frustrates Brenda's plans

    B. controls Brenda's thoughts

    C. moderates Brenda's actions

    D. influences Brenda's feelings

28. This poem relates how, when she went to the mall, Brenda

    A. got into trouble

    B. tried to contact Jill

    C. forgot what she was doing

    D. made the wrong purchase

29. In Brenda's life, Jill **mainly** acts as a

    A. guide

    B. leader

    C. critic

    D. rival

ANSWERS AND SOLUTIONS—2001 PROVINCIAL ACHIEVEMENT TEST

1. A	7. D	13. B	19. D	25. D
2. D	8. B	14. C	20. B	26. C
3. D	9. D	15. B	21. C	27. C
4. A	10. A	16. A	22. A	28. A
5. D	11. B	17. D	23. D	29. A
6. B	12. B	18. B	24. D	

1   A

The narrator declares "The prairies could be only half real to a boy without a dog" because he knows that he would enjoy the prairies more with a dog.

He has not been without a dog for too long: we learn in line 5 that the family was only dogless "for the moment." This indicates that for a brief period of time, he did not have a dog. In lines 9 to 10, the narrator explains that it was his father, not he himself, who was inspired by the hunting stories of his great uncle. There is no comparison offered between his new home and his old home.

2.   D

The narrator and his father both wanted to acquire a dog, but for different reasons. The statement "I found a willing ally in my father—though his motives were not mine" indicates that the father and the son both want a dog. An ally is a partner, a supporter, or a collaborator. The father and son are "allies," so they both support the idea of getting a dog. The father wants a dog to go hunting with: "There remained only one indispensable item—a hunting dog" (lines 14–15) and the son wants a dog to play with.

3.   D

The narrator's father is "determined to test those tales"; that is to see if the hunting was as good as Frank claimed. "For many years he had been exposed to the colourful tales of my Great-uncle Frank, ... and most of his stories dealt with the superlative shooting to be had ... my father determined to test those tales" (lines 9–12).

4.   A

You are asked to establish whether the narrator was amused, enchanted, concerned, or intimidated the first time he met Crown Prince. There is overwhelming evidence that the narrator was amused. In lines 16–26, the writer employs diction effectively to develop a humorous tone. For example, the father arrived with the "beast in tow," which creates a humorous image. The dog's name "Crown Prince Challenge Indefatigable" is comical as is the description of the dog consisting "mainly of feet and tongue." The most powerful humour developed when the author attempts an obvious contrast by stating that the dog does have "one redeeming feature." Rather than that feature being something admirable, it is the "way he drooled."

He may have been enchanted and concerned. He was not intimidated.

5.   D

As we learn in lines 27–29, the family did not keep the dog because he was too expensive: "Mother might have overlooked his obvious defects, had it not been for his price." Further evidence is given: "we could no more afford such a sum than we could have afforded a Cadillac."

6. B

Study the passage to determine the use of the word "adept" within the context of the writing. "My parents had been married long enough to achieve that delicate balance of power which enables a married couple to endure each other" (lines 31–32). This sentence precedes the line using the word "adept" and explains that the narrator's parents have managed to reach a "balance of power," although it is "delicate." The sentence "They were both adept in the evasive tactics of marital politics …" suggests that it is adeptness that enables them to maintain the delicate balance of power. Therefore, in this context, "adept" must mean skilled: their skill in marital politics let them maintain the balance of power.

7. D

The father is portrayed as a person who was "determined to test those tales" (line 12) before the family was properly settled, so he was eager. Lines 13–14 indicate he was well organized and thorough. In lines 29–30, we learn that even though the mother made him return Crown Prince, it was "clear that he would try again," so he was not the type to give up on an idea.

8. B

You are asked to determine why or how the narrator knew that he would get along with the puppy. The only interaction between the narrator and the puppy is at the very end of the story when the narrator got home from school: the puppy peered up at him in "a near-sighted sort of way." As the narrator held out his hand out to the puppy, the puppy awoke and "sank his puppy teeth into [the narrator's] thumb with such satisfactory gusto that [the narrator's] doubts dissolved." The puppy had responded to the narrator's greeting, and through this, the narrator knew that "he and I would get along."

There is nothing to substantiate any of the other answers.

9. D

The author's son was happy about the storm because "the computer died and snuffed out his assignment," power failures and bad roads caused "schools to close for the second day this week" (lines 12–14).

The author's son was unable to continue with his normal activities.

10. A

Imagery is a literary device that appeals to the senses. The term "ice box emergency" (Article 1, line 7) most aptly appeals to one's visual and feeling senses. This image also employs a metaphor. You visually see the image of an icebox through the use of the metaphor that compares an icebox with the weather, and you imagine a frosty sensation at the same time.

The phrase "back-to-back freezing-rain storms" (Article 1, line 6) contains well known idiom (common expression) "back to back," but does not employ imagery.

11. B

Preceding the sentence in which people were asked to stay home, we learn that "Universities, most government offices and some stores and shopping malls were closed Thursday as hydro and road crews fought losing battles to repair downed lines, fix power stations and pour salt on the slick streets" (lines 28–30). You can surmise from this information that the most likely reason that people were asked to stay home was so that they would avoid injury.

12. B

In Article 2, sentence fragments are used in order to focus on facts and figures. Fragments have been used in order to eliminate any unnecessary information. The purpose of this article is to impart information quickly and clearly. For example, lines 3–5 communicate straightforward facts and figures.

13. B

This phrase is introduced in the sentence "a shiny black Porsche stopped and a man 'dressed to the gills' followed her to a nearby car dealership" (lines 9 and 10). At this point, you cannot be sure of what "dressed to the gills" means, although his "shiny black Porsche" is a clue. You know that a Porsche is a luxury sports car, and this one is "shiny black," so you could suppose the driver to be wealthy and well-dressed. In lines 12–13, we learn that "He was wearing a dress shirt, with the white cuffs and the gold cuff links and there he was down on his knees, changing my tire."

14. C

This article is about a woman who encountered a "Good Samaritan" in the middle of a snowstorm when she had a flat tire; That is, someone who helped her out by performing an act of kindness. Lines 6 to 8 state that "… hundreds around the Montreal region … have been helping friends, neighbours and mostly complete strangers through the devastation of the continuing storm," confirming that passing on an act of kindness is the underlying message of this article.

There is nothing in this article about Barton giving up hope or not.

15. B

In the final paragraph of Article 3, the authors suggest that "disaster doesn't always bring out the best in everybody." They go on to report specific incidents in which people took advantage of the disaster: "A local tree nursery hiked the cost of a cord of wood by $10. A gas station upped its price at the pump by three cents a litre. Thieves hit a number of abandoned homes and made off with thousands of dollars worth of goods." As the main message of this article is to pass on an act of kindness, the technique used in the final paragraph is contrast. A rebuttal is an argument against something, but the last paragraph does not present an argument against statements made earlier in the text.

16. A

According to the first paragraph, animatronics is most useful when moviemakers want to avoid training animals: "Animatronics can create the unbelievable without the need for special trainers."

17. D

According to the section entitled "Keeping Control," it is the remote control operators that control the movements.

18. B

The heading "Animating An Animatronic Ape Head" contains an example of alliteration. Alliteration is a literary device that uses repetition of the beginning sounds of words. The title has each of the first four words starting with the short "a" sound.

19. D

An arrow points from the sentence "Each hair is individually punched in by hand" to the hair on the picture of the gorilla's head. Embedded is what "punched in" means here, as the hairs are pushed, or embedded, into the head.

20. B

According to the section "Molding the Model," first a model is made in clay then a fibreglass mold is made, and finally the mold is "cast in silicone or foam latex."

21. C

According to the section entitled "Keeping Control," "Animatronic creations are made to work by an operator who uses a remote control machine behind the camera." The use of a remote control to manipulate the robot most closely resembles that of a puppeteer using strings to animate his puppet. "Sensors attached to the eyes, nose, arms, and other parts of the mechanical creature respond to electronic signals from the control panel." These sensors are similar to the strings tied to a puppet, and manipulated by the puppeteer. Finally, "The animatronic creature responds to the messages sent in 'real time'—in other words, the animatronic ape reacts to the signal the minute it is transmitted." This is similar to the way a puppet responds to a puppeteer.

22. A

You are asked to determine the main purpose of Billy's performance. "No snacking while speaking Spanish" is the "law" Mr. Brewer had laid down. This term in school, Billy didn't "have a lunch period," because he had "too many subjects to make up." (lines 1–2), so he ate in Mr. Brewer's Spanish class." According to line 7, he wanted to "get even" to protest Mr. Brewer's rules: "Yesterday I got even."

His purpose was not to eat a good lunch in comfort, as he had been satisfied with munching chips until Mr. Brewster proclaimed that snacking was no longer allowed. Although he did say "a blessing (in Spanish) over the food, / And named every object with perfect accent" (lines 15–16), showing off his perfect Spanish accent was not the main purpose for his performance. Turning the students against Mr. Brewster was not a motivating factor.

23. D

The words "A checkered tablecloth, / Two candlesticks, / One bowl, / One spoon, / And a thermos full of soup" are used to show Billy being deliberate and methodical. The arrangement of these words and the images they produce demonstrate methodical and deliberate behaviour. There is nothing defiant or hostile in these words. There is no arrogance, conceit, confusion, or agitation in these words.

24. D

The reason that "Mr. Brewer stood there, dumbstruck" (line 17) was that he was shocked by Billy's unexpected behaviour. "Then he began to laugh" (line 18), so his reaction changed from surprise to amusement.

25. D

The poem simply relates an incident that occurred at school and then ends, "You know, school doesn't have to be so grim" in a matter-of-fact tone.

26. C

What does "straight" mean in this context? Lines 6 to 7 read: "If I want to buy something outrageous, / She reminds me that it's not machine washable," so Jill is sensible. "But I need a friend who helps me touch the ground /While I chase the wind" (lines 2 and 3) confirms Jill's sensibility. Brenda acknowledges that quality by narrating that Jill "helps [her] touch the ground".

As seen in line 7, Jill does not support Brenda's desire to be outrageous. We also learn that when Brenda acts "like a complete idiot," Jill does not support this behaviour, but instead offers common sense: "there is still hope," so supportive is wrong.

You could think that Jill is helpful as you read, "If I am a high-flying kite, / Jill is my string" (lines 4–5). However, this comparison of Jill to the string of a kite indicates that Jill is Brenda's foundation, thus Jill's helpfulness is diminished and her sensibility becomes the focus. It is evident through all of these examples that Jill is patient, but it is not a possible meaning for the word "straight" as used in this poem.

27. C

"Jill is my string" (line 5) means that Jill moderates Brenda's actions. This metaphor compares Jill to a string. Brenda is the kite. Keeping the metaphor in mind enables you to answer this question with greater precision.

28. A

Brenda got into trouble when she went to the mall. She "… pulled a top off one of the shelves / And stuffed it into [her] bag" (lines 16–17). In lines 18–21, we learn that she was caught shoplifting.

29. A

The last lines of the poem show that Jill acts as a guide in Brenda's life. Brenda acknowledges that if Jill had been shopping with her, Brenda probably would not have gotten in "this mess." Brenda would not have shoplifted if Jill was there, and if Brenda had considered shoplifting with Jill, Jill would have advised—or guided—her not to.

It appears that neither girl is the leader, as a leader implies a follower. Jill does not follow Brenda's actions, and Brenda does not follow Jill. Jill is not a critic. There is nothing in the poem to support this idea. Jill is not Brenda's rival. There is no competition detailed in this relationship.

0211.00
0212.00
0213.00
0214.00
0215.00
0216.00
0217.00
0218.00
0219:00
0220.00
0221.00
0222:00
0223.00
0224:00

GLOSSARY OF RELEVANT TERMS

Abstract	Abstract terms and concepts name things that are not knowable through the senses; examples are love, justice, guilt, and honour.
Alliteration	Repetition of initial consonant sounds.
Allusion	Indirect or passing reference to some person, place, or event; or to a piece of literature or art. The nature of the reference is not explained because the writer relies on the reader's familiarity with it.
Analogy	A comparison that is made to explain something that is unfamiliar by presenting an example that is similar or parallel to it in some significant way.
Anecdote	A brief story of an interesting incident.
Antecedent action	Action that takes place before the story opens.
Assonance	Repetition of similar or identical vowel sounds.
Ballad	A narrative poem that tells a story, often in a straightforward and dramatic manner, and often about such universals as love, honour, and courage. Ballads were once songs. Literary ballads often have the strong rhythm and the plain rhyme schemes of songs. Songs are still written in ballad form, some old ballads are still sung, and some literary ballads have been set to music. Samuel Taylor Coleridge's "The Rime of the Ancient Mariner" is an example of a literary ballad.
Blank verse	Poetry written in unrhymed iambic pentameters.
Chronological	In order of time.
Cliché	An overused expression; one that has become stale through overuse.
Colloquial	Informal, suitable for everyday speech but not for formal writing.
Concrete	A concrete thing exists in a solid, physical way; it is knowable through the senses; trees, copper, and kangaroos are all examples of concrete things.
Connotation	Implied or additional meaning that a word or phrase imparts. Such meaning is often subjective.
Denotation	The explicit or direct meaning of a word or expression, aside from the impressions it creates. These are the meanings listed in dictionaries.
Discrepancy	Distinct difference between two things that should not be different or that should correspond.
Fantasy	A literary genre; generally contains events, characters, or settings that would not be possible in real life.
Foreshadowing	A storytelling technique; something early in the story hints at later events.

Free verse	Is usually written in variable rhythmic cadences; it may be rhymed or unrhymed, but the rhymes are likely to be irregular and may not occur at the end of lines.
Hyperbole	A figure of speech that uses exaggeration for effect.
Imagery	Language that evokes sensory impressions.
Imitative harmony	Words that seem to imitate the sounds to which they refer; buzz and whisper are examples of imitative harmony; also called ONOMATOPOEIA.
Interior monologue	Conversation-like thoughts of a character.
Irony	The difference—in actions or words—between reality and appearance. Authors use irony for both serious and humorous effects. Irony can also be a technique for indicating, through character or plot development, the writer's own attitude toward some element of the story.
Jargon	Special vocabulary of a particular group or activity; sometimes used to refer to confusing or unintelligible language.
Justification	The giving of reasons or support; for example, giving an argument or reason that shows that an action or belief is reasonable or true.
Juxtaposition (or contrast)	The deliberate contrast of characters, settings, or situations for effect; the effect may be a demonstration of character or heightening of mood.
Lyric	A poem that expresses the private emotions or thoughts of the writer; sonnets, odes, and elegies are examples of lyric poetry.
Metaphor	Comparison without using the words *like* or *as*.
Monologue	A literary form; an oral or written composition in which only one person speaks.
Mood	In a story, the atmosphere; when a writer orders the setting, action, and characters of a story so as to suggest a dominant emotion or patterns of emotions, this emotional pattern is the mood of the story. Also a person's state of mind or complex of emotions at any given time.
Ode	A poem expressing lofty emotion; odes often celebrate an event or are addressed to nature or to some admired person, place, or thing; an example is "Ode on a Grecian Urn" by John Keats.
Onomatopoeia	Words that seem to imitate the sounds to which they refer.
Oxymoron	A combination of two usually contradictory terms in a compressed paradox; for example, "the living dead." An oxymoron is like a metaphor in that it expresses in words some truth that cannot be understood literally; truthful lies is an oxymoron that describes metaphors.
Parable	A short, often simple story that teaches or explains a lesson: often a moral or religious lesson.

Paradox	An apparently self-contradictory statement that is, in fact, true.
Parallelism	The arrangement of similarly constructed clauses, verses, or sentences.
Personification	The extension of human attributes to objects or to abstract ideas.
Point of view: first person	The story is told by one of the characters in the story ("I"). The narrator is in the story. First-person narrators only know what they think, feel, do, see, and hear.
Point of view: objective	The story is told without telling any characters' thoughts and feelings. Only the characters' actions and words are told. This point of view is a lot like the camera's point of view in a movie. Objective narrators only know what a camera can record. This story-telling form suffers from the limitations of film but at the same time can produce a film-like effect.
Point of view: third person	The story is told through the eyes of one or more characters ("he, she, and they"). The narrator is outside the story, and tells what the characters think, feel, and do. Omniscient narrators know about everything that happens and what any character thinks and feels. Limited omniscient narrators only know about one character and the things that one character knows, thinks, feels, and does.
Prologue	An introduction to a play, often delivered by the chorus (in ancient Greece, a group, but in modern plays, one actor) who plays no part in the following action.
Pun	A humorous expression that depends on a double meaning, either between different senses of the same word or between two similar sounding words.
Ridicule	Contemptuous mocking or derision (contempt and mockery); ridicule may be an element of satire.
Satire	A form of writing that exposes the failings of individuals, institutions, or societies; to ridicule or scorn in order to correct or expose some evil or wrongdoing.
Simile	Comparison using the words *like* or *as*.
Sonnet	A lyric poem 14 lines long and usually written in iambic pentameter. The Shakespearean sonnet consists of three quatrains (four-line stanzas) and a couplet (two lines), all written to a strict end-rhyme scheme (abab cdcd efef gg). The development of the poet's thoughts is also structured. There are several methods: one method is to use each quatrain for different points in an argument and the couplet for the resolution of the argument. Because of the complexity of the sonnet, poets sometimes find it a suitable form for expressing the complexity of thought and emotion.

Symbol	Anything that stands for or represents something other than itself. In literature, a symbol is a word or phrase referring to an object, scene, or action that also has some further significance associated with it. For example, a rose is a common symbol of love. Many symbols, such as flags, are universally recognized. Other symbols are not so universally defined. They do not acquire a meaning until they are defined by how they are used in a story. They may even suggest more than one meaning. For example, snow might be used to symbolize goodness because of its cleanness, or cruelty because of its coldness. Symbols are often contained in story titles; in character and place names; in classical, literary, and historical allusions and references; in images or figures that appear at important points in a story; and in images that either receive special emphasis or are repeated.
Thesis	A statement that is made as the first step in an argument or a demonstration.
Tone	A particular way of speaking or writing. Tone may also describe the general feeling of a piece of work. It can demonstrate the writer's attitude toward characters, settings, conflicts, and so forth. Different tones can cause readers to experience such varying emotions as pity, fear, horror, or humour.

DIRECTING WORDS

The following list of directing words and definitions can help you plan your writing. For example, a particular discussion might include assessment, description, illustrations, or an outline of how an extended argument could be developed.

Directing Word	Definition
Agree Or Disagree	Support or contradict a statement; give the positive or negative features; express an informed opinion one way or the other; list the advantages for or against.
Assess	Estimate the value of something based on some criteria; present an informed judgement. The word "assess" strongly suggests that two schools of thought exist about a given subject. Assessing usually involves weighing the relative merit of conflicting points of view; e.g., negative versus positive, strong versus weak components, long-range versus short-term.
Compare	Point out similarities or differences; describe the relationship between two things; often used in conjunction with CONTRAST.
Contrast	Show or emphasize differences when compared.
Describe	Give a detailed or graphic account of an object, event, or sequence of events.
Discuss	Present the various points of view in a debate or argument; write at length about a given subject; engage in written discourse on a particular topic.
Explain	Give an account of what the essence of something is, how something works, or why something is the way it is; may be accomplished by paraphrasing, providing reasons or examples, or by giving a step-by-step account.
Identify	Establish the identity of something; establish the unique qualities of something; provide the name of something.
Illustrate	Give concrete examples to clarify; provide explanatory or decorative features.
List	Itemize names, ideas, or things that belong to a particular class or group.
Outline	Give a written description of only the main features; summarize the principal parts of a thing, an idea, or an event.
Show (that)	Give facts, reasons, illustrations or examples to support an idea or proposition.
State	Give the key points; declare.
Suggest	Propose alternatives, options, or solutions.
Support	Defend or agree with a particular point of view; give evidence, reasons, or examples.
Trace	Outline the development of something; describe a specified sequence.

CREDITS

Every effort has been made to provide proper acknowledgment of the original source and to comply with copyright law. However, some attempts to establish original copyright ownership may have been unsuccessful. If copyright ownership can be identified, please notify Castle Rock Research Corp so that appropriate corrective action can be taken.

Use Strategies and Cues – Respond to Texts

Canadian Press, "Father Calls Hockey Game of Butchery," reprinted by permission.

Excerpt from "The Tell-Tale-Heart", by Edgar Allan Poe.

"The Blind Men and the Elephant", by John Godfrey Saxe.

Excerpt from "The Most Dangerous Game" by Richard Connell, first published in *Colliers*, January 19, 1924

Excerpts from "The Diamond Necklace" by Guy de Maupassant

"Nancy" by Ernie Bushmiller: © United Feature Syndicate, Inc.

Use Strategies and Cues – Practice Questions

"A Winter's Walk" excerpted from *Anne of Green Gables* by L.M. Montgomery.

"Letter" by Judith Mackenzie. From *The Fourth Morningside Papers* by Peter Gzowski. (McClelland & Stewart, Toronto; 1991.)

From THE BONE DETECTIVES by Donna Jackson, with photographs by Charlie Fellenbaum. Text copyright © 1996 by Donna M. Jackson. By permission of LITTLE, BROWN AND COMPANY.

"Cook's Brook" from *An Island in the Sky: Selected Poetry of Al Pittman*, edited by Martin Ware and Stephanie McKenzie. © 2003. Published by Breakwater Books Ltd.

"The Bronte Sisters" From *In Context 8, Student Anthology* by GRAVES, CLAYTON. 1990. Reprinted with permission of Nelson, a division of Thomson Learning: www.thomsonrights.com. Fax 800-730-2215.

"Just for Today" by Mollie Moir from NO BODY'S PERFECT: STORIES BY TEENS ABOUT BODY IMAGE, SELF-ACCEPTANCE, AND THE SEARCH FOR IDENTITY by Kimberly Kirberger. Copyright © 2003 by Kimberly Kirberger. Reprinted by permission of Scholastic Inc.

Use Strategies and Cues – Unit Test

"At the Police Station" excerpted from "Oliver Twist" by Charles Dickens.

"The Delay" excerpt from *The Incredible Journey* by Sheila Burnford. (Bantam Doubleday Dell Books for Young Readers). Copyright © 1960, 1961 by Sheila Burnford. Copyright renewed © 1988 by Jonquil Graves, Juliet Pin, and Peronelle Robbins.

"Wanted – Mars ... Dead or Alive" by Geoffrey A. Landis, from ODYSSEY's January 2001 issue: 2001: A Space Odyssey, © 2001, Cobblestone Publishing, 30 Grove Street, Suite C, Peterborough, NH 03458. All Rights Reserved. Used by permission of Carus Publishing Company.

"The Outlaw Who Wouldn't Give Up" excerpted from *Mummy Mysteries: Tales from North America* by Brenda Z. Guiberson. Copyright © 1998 by Brenda Z. Guiberson. Reprinted by permission of Henry Holt and Company, LLC.

"Lochinvar" by Sir Walter Scott.

Manage Ideas and Information – Plan and Focus

"Charles Dickens – Chronicler of his Times". From *Made in the USA 1st edition* by MACKWOOD. 1990. Reprinted with permission of Nelson, a division of Thomson Learning: www.thomsonrights.com. Fax 800-730-2215.

2000 Provincial Achievement Test

"The Visitor" by Christine Pinsent-Johnson from *Notes Across the Aisle*. (Thistledown Press Ltd., 1995).

"The World's Biggest Pebble" from *Canadian Children's Annual* by Robert Nielsen. (Potlatch Publications Ltd., 1985).

Map from Westworld Alberta vol. 24, no.5, (Canada Wide Magazines and Communications Ltd., 1998).

"History Lesson" by Arthur C. Clarke. from *Echoes 3* (Oxford University Press, 1981).

"Thumbprint" from IT DOESN'T ALWAYS HAVE TO RHYME by Eve Merriam. Copyright © 1964. © Renewed 1992 Eve Merriam. Used by permission of Marian Reiner.

"The Mission" by Alan Hobson from *One Step Beyond* (Altitude Publishing, 1992).

"Abacus" from ALL I REALLY NEED TO KNOW I LEARNED IN KINDERGARTEN by Robert L. Fulghum, copyright © 1986, 1988 by Robert L. Fulghum. Used by permission of Villard Books, a division of Random House, Inc.

"Sport" by Kirk Wirsig, from *Who Owns the Earth?* (Alberta Heritage Learning Resources Project, 1979).

"My Name Is Angie" by Beverley Terrell-Deutsch, from *The Reader Writes the Story* (Prentice-Hall Canada Inc., 1992).

FOR BETTER OR FOR WORSE © 1998 Lynn Johnston Productions. Dist. By Universal Press Syndicate. Reprinted with permission. All rights reserved.

2001 Provincial Achievement Test

"The Coming of Mutt", excerpted from *The Dog Who Wouldn't Be* by Farley Mowat. Published by McClelland & Stewart Ltd, The Canadian Publishers. Copyright © 1957 by Farley Mowat.

"The cold may get old, but freezing rain is much bigger pain" by Norm Ovenden, from *The Edmonton Journal*, January 9, 1998.

"On Ice" by Norm Ovenden, from *The Edmonton Journal*, January 9, 1998.

"Acts of Kindness Light Up the Darkness" by Monique Beaudin and Sue Montgomery, from *The Montreal Gazette* as found in *The Edmonton Journal*, January 9, 1998. Material reprinted with the express permission of: "Montreal Gazette Group Inc.", a Canwest Partnership.

"Animating Animals" from *Special Effects in Film and Television* edited by Miranda Smith (Scholastic Canada Ltd., Copyright 1998 Dorling Kindersley Limited, London).

"Billy Paris" by Mel Glenn, from *Class Dismissed! High School Poems* (Clarion Books, 1982).

"Brenda Stewart" by Mel Glenn, from *Class Dismissed! High School Poems* (Clarion Books, 1982).

Some images in this document are from www.clipart.com, copyright © 2011 Jupiterimages Corp

NOTES

NOTES

ORDERING INFORMATION

SCHOOL ORDERS

Schools and school jurisdictions are eligible for our educational discount rate. Contact Castle Rock Research for more information.

THE KEY **Study Guides** are specifically designed to assist students in preparing for unit tests, final exams, and provincial examinations.

THE KEY **Study Guides**—$29.95 each plus G.S.T.

SENIOR HIGH		JUNIOR HIGH	ELEMENTARY
Biology 30	Biology 20	English Language Arts 9	English Language Arts 6
Chemistry 30	Chemistry 20	Mathematics 9	Mathematics 6
English 30-1	English 20-1	Science 9	Science 6
English 30-2	Mathematics 20-1	Social Studies 9	Social Studies 6
Mathematics 30-1	Physics 20	Mathematics 8	Mathematics 4
Mathematics 30-2	Social Studies 20-1	Mathematics 7	English Language Arts 3
Physics 30	English 10-1		Mathematics 3
Social Studies 30-1	Mathematics 10		
Social Studies 30-2	Combined		
	Science 10		
	Social Studies 10-1		

Student Notes and Problems (SNAP) Workbooks contain complete explanations of curriculum concepts, examples, and exercise questions.

SNAP Workbooks—$29.95 each plus G.S.T.

SENIOR HIGH		JUNIOR HIGH	ELEMENTARY
Biology 30	Biology 20	Mathematics 9	Mathematics 6
Chemistry 30	Chemistry 20	Science 9	Mathematics 5
Mathematics 30-1	Mathematics 20-1	Mathematics 8	Mathematics 4
Mathematics 30-2	Physics 20	Science 8	Mathematics 3
Mathematics 31	Mathematics 10	Mathematics 7	
Physics 30	Combined	Science 7	
	Science 10		

Class Notes and Problem Solved—$19.95 each plus G.S.T.

SENIOR HIGH		JUNIOR HIGH
Biology 30	Biology 20	Mathematics 9
Chemistry 30	Chemistry 20	Science 9
Mathematics 30-1	Mathematics 20-1	Mathematics 8
Mathematics 30-2	Physics 20	Science 8
Mathematics 31	Mathematics 10 Combined	Mathematics 7
Physics 30		Science 7

Visit our website for a tour of resource content and features or order resources online at
www.castlerockresearch.com/store/

#2410, 10180 – 101 Street NW
Edmonton, AB Canada T5J 3S4
e-mail: learn@castlerockresearch.com

Phone: 780.448.9619
Toll-free: 1.800.840.6224
Fax: 780.426.3917

CASTLE ROCK
RESEARCH CORP

ORDER FORM

THE KEY	QUANTITY	Student Notes and Problems Workbooks	QUANTITY SNAP Workbooks	Problem Solved and Class Notes	QUANTITY Class Notes	QUANTITY Problem Solved
Biology 30		Mathematics 31		Mathematics 31		
Chemistry 30		Biology 30		Biology 30		
English 30-1		Chemistry 30		Chemistry 30		
English 30-2		Mathematics 30-1		Mathematics 30-1		
Mathematics 30-1		Mathematics 30-2		Mathematics 30-2		
Mathematics 30-2		Physics 30		Physics 30		
Physics 30		Biology 20		Biology 20		
Social Studies 30-1		Chemistry 20		Chemistry 20		
Social Studies 30-2		Mathematics 20-1		Mathematics 20-1		
Biology 20		Physics 20		Physics 20		
Chemistry 20		Mathematics 10 Combined		Mathematics 10 Combined		
English 20-1		Science 10		Mathematics 9		
Mathematics 20-1		Mathematics 9		Science 9		
Physics 20		Science 9		Mathematics 8		
Social Studies 20-1		Mathematics 8		Science 8		
English 10-1		Science 8		Mathematics 7		
Math 10 Combined		Mathematics 7		Science 7		
Science 10		Science 7				
Social Studies 10-1		Mathematics 6				
Social Studies 9		Mathematics 5				
English Language Arts 9		Mathematics 4				
Mathematics 9		Mathematics 3				
Science 9						
Mathematics 8						
Mathematics 7						
English Language Arts 6						
Mathematics 6						
Science 6						
Social Studies 6						
Mathematics 4						
Mathematics 3						
English Language Arts 3						

Total Cost

Subtotal 1	
Subtotal 2	
Subtotal 3	
Cost Subtotal	
Shipping and Handling*	
G.S.T	
Order Total	

*(Please call for current rates)

PAYMENT AND SHIPPING INFORMATION

Name: _____
School _____
Telephone: _____
SHIP TO
School Code: _____
School: _____
Address: _____
City: _____ Postal Code: _____
PAYMENT
☐ By credit card   VISA/MC
Number: _____
Expiry Date: _____
Name on card: _____
☐ Enclosed cheque
☐ Invoice school   P.O. number: _____

CASTLE ROCK

#2410, 10180 – 101 Street NW, Edmonton, AB T5J 3S4   **Phone:** 780.448.9619   **Fax:** 780.426.3917
Email: learn@castlerockresearch.com   **Toll-free:** 1.800.840.6224

Alma Flor Ada • F. Isabel Campoy

FLYING DRAGON

ILLUSTRATORS

Fabricio Vanden Broeck
Julián Cícero
Dimitrios Gulbalis
Gabriel Gutiérrez
Claudia Legnazzi
Felipe Ugalde
Luis García-Fresquet
Alain Espinosa
Enrique Martínez
Felipe Dávalos
Rapi Diego

ALFAGUARA

YOUNG READERS
SANTILLANA

Originally published in Spanish as *Chuchurumbé*

Art Director: Felipe Dávalos
Design: Petra Ediciones
Editor: Norman Duarte

Cover: Fabricio Vanden Broeck

Text © 2000 Alma Flor Ada and F. Isabel Campoy
Edition ©2000 Santillana USA Publishing Company, Inc.

Santillana USA Publishing Company, Inc.
2105 NW 86th Avenue
Miami, FL 33122

Poetry D: *Flying Dragon*

ISBN: 1-58105-580-3

Printed in Colombia
Grupo OP S.A.

ILLUSTRATORS

JULIÁN CÍCERO: pp. 6-9
FELIPE DÁVALOS: pp. 38-39
RAPI DIEGO: pp. 44-48
ALAIN ESPINOSA: pp. 30-36
LUIS GARCÍA-FRESQUET: pp. 26-29
DIMITRIOS GULBALIS: pp. 10-13
GABRIEL GUTIÉRREZ: pp. 14-17
CLAUDIA LEGNAZZI: pp. 18-21
ENRIQUE MARTÍNEZ: p. 37
FELIPE UGALDE: pp. 22-25
FABRICIO VANDEN BROECK: pp. 40-43

ACKNOWLEDGEMENTS

The authors gratefully acknowledge the editorial assistance of Susan Baird Kanaan and Rosa Zubizarreta.

ROSA ZUBIZARRETA for the English translation of the following poems:
Alma Flor Ada, "For F. Isabel Campoy," p. 7; "To Marina Romero," p. 31; F. Isabel Campoy, "The Refrigerator Door," p. 8; "Nicaragua Old and New," p. 10; "To José Coronel Urtecho," p. 11; "Inland on the Island," p. 14; "To José Emilio González," p. 15; "My Friend, Argentina," p. 18; José Coronel Urtecho, "Circus," p. 12; José Emilio González, "Children's Choir," p.16; "The Girl and the Firefly," p. 16; "At the Circus," p. 17; José Martí, "The White Rose," p. 28; "The Leopard has a Fine Coat," p. 29; José Juan Tablada, "Watermelon," p. 24; "Flying Fish," p. 24; "A Sunny Day," p. 24; "The Moon," p. 25; "Alligator," p. 25; "The Bumblebee," p. 25; "Bees," p. 25; María Elena Walsh, "The Red Crane," p. 20; "In the Land of I-Don't-Remember," p. 20; "In a Tiny Matchbox," p. 21; Anonymous, "Croak, Croak," p. 39; "Short Stories," p. 42; "Telling Lies," p. 43; "Your Turn to Jump," p. 44; "My Beard Had Three Long Hairs," p. 47.

Translations and/or adaptations are based on the following works.
JOSÉ CORONEL URTECHO: "Plenilunio" and "Circo" from *Pol-La D'Ananta Katanta Paranta Dedójmia T'élson*. Copyright ©1993 Editorial Nueva Nicaragua. Permission to use these works is pending.
JOSÉ EMILIO GONZÁLEZ: "Coro de niños," "La niña y el cucubano," and "En el circo" from *La poesía y el niño*, compiled by Isabel Freire de Matos. Copyright ©1993 Instituto de Cultura Puertorriqueña. Permission to use these works is pending.
MARINA ROMERO: "Caballo" and "Canguro" from *Alegrías: Poemas para niños*. Copyright ©1972 Anaya, S. A. Permission to use these works is pending. "Si yo fuera" from *Poesía española para niños*, compiled by Ana Pelegrín. Copyright © Taurus Ediciones, S. A. Reprinted by permission of Taurus Ediciones, S. A.
JOSÉ JUAN TABLADA: "Sandía," "Las abejas," "Caimán," "El abejorro," Día de sol," and "La luna" from *La poesía y el niño*, compiled by Isabel Freire de Matos. Copyright ©1993 Instituto de Cultura Puertorriqueña. "Peces voladores" from *Niños y alas* by Ismael Rodríguez Bou. Copyright ©1958 Consejo Superior de Enseñanzas, Universidad de Puerto Rico. These works reprinted by permission of Sociedad General de Escritores de México.
MARÍA ELENA WALSH: "La garza colorada" from *Zoo Loco*. Copyright ©1996 Compañía Editora Espasa Calpe Argentina S. A. "En el país de Nomeacuerdo" and "En una cajita de fósforos" from *El Reino del Revés*. Copyright © Compañía Editora Espasa Calpe Argentina S. A. These works reprinted by permission of the author.

For Alma Lafuerte and
María Coronado,
examples of motherhood and love.

Contents

Latinos

Friends from Everywhere

F. Isabel Campoy

I saw you at school
and I liked your name:
José, Alberto, Juan, Rafael.
I saw you at recess
and I loved your laughter:
Marisa, Ana, Lupe, Raquel.
I saw you in the park
just the other day.
I saw you speaking Spanish
with your mom and dad.
I saw you and knew we were friends,
Hispanics,
bilingual,
Latinos,
with twice as much
to offer.

F. Isabel Campoy

She loves to play with words.
She takes big words
and makes them small,
and small ones, wonderful.
She writes poetry and plays,
and words for songs
because above all,
Isabel loves to sing.
Some of her books are *Dulce es la sal* (*Salt is Sweet*),
Primer acto (*First Act*), and *Gorrión, gorrión* (*Sparrow, Sparrow*).

6

For F. Isabel Campoy

Alma Flor Ada

On the wings of her poems,
the rooster on the weathervane
blows kisses to the sun.

On the wings of her poems,
the sun grows roots
that blossom into sunflowers.

On the wings of her poems,
you'll find a mother's love,
pride in our language,
the radiance of your eyes,
and before you know it,
you'll fly higher and higher
until, smiling at us from above,
you are the sun.

The Refrigerator Door

F. Isabel Campoy

A drawing of my face,
a photo of my sister,
a letter from my father,
everything held by a magnet.

A shopping list,
a cinnamon stick,
grandma's picture,
everything held by a magnet.

No one knows what color
our refrigerator door is,
as it's covered, top to bottom,
with photos, phone numbers, letters,
everything held by our love.

8

My Mirror

F. Isabel Campoy

How handsome the mirror
when I look at it!

A Story to Finish

F. Isabel Campoy

Page one: you sit in the sun.
Page two: a pirate looks at you.
Page three: his parrot flies free.
Page four: the pirate starts to snore.
Page five: the parrot steals his knife.
Page six: he's up to his old tricks.
Page seven: the pirate dreams he's in heaven.
Page eight: now he's awake.
Page nine: he makes a big find.
Page ten: the parrot's gone again.
Page eleven: if you want to know every detail
about the end of this fine tale,
grab a brush, a crayon, or a pen
and write or paint the story's end.

Nicaragua

Nicaragua, Old and New

F. Isabel Campoy

High, as high
as your mountains.
Green, as green
as your forests.
Nicaragua old and new,
I want to climb up to you
and sing a song to your people,
brave men and women, and children too
May you guard for all of us
the treasure of your history,
your peace, your smile, and your memory

José Coronel Urtecho

Urtecho often said that poetry is looking and seeing,
listening and hearing,
feeling and living.
He said that poetry is knowing how to love.
He died when he was ninety.
He left many beautiful poems, such as
Los parques (Parks), *Pequeña oda a Tío Coyote*
(Little Ode to Uncle Coyote), and
Luna de palo (Wooden Moon).

To José Coronel Urtecho

F. Isabel Campoy

Dear Coronel Urtecho,
I am here
to report to you,
on behalf of the children
of Africa, Europe, and
the Americas, sir.

We'd like you to know,
our colonel,
we're taking good care of poetry.
We continue to read yours every day,
and, as you had asked us to do,
to the word we've held fast and stayed true.

Circus

José Coronel Urtecho

: drums :
Boom, boom, boom!
Here come the animals!
Boom, boom, boom!
: drums :

E – The Dragon that Shows His Tongue
M – The Camel of the Desert
S – The Dancing Serpent
Q – The Lion, King of the Jungle

: drums :
Boom, boom, boom!
Here come the animals!
Boom, boom, boom!
: drums :

1

Full Moon

José Coronel Urtecho

In a farmer's field,
a hen laid a brown egg.
        She laid 1
        She laid 2
        She laid 3
        She laid 4
        She laid 5
        She laid 6
        She laid 7
        She laid 8
        She laid 9
        She laid 10
        She laid – plop! –
            The moon!

Puerto Rico

Inland on the Island

F. Isabel Campoy

Today, from the beach, I watched your hands,
those tall and tousled palm trees
that dance in the wind.
They sing
and speak very slowly.
They say, in Spanish of course,
that the pride of your people
is alive and well
inland on the island.

José Emilio González

This poet knows how to find a word that echoes like a river,
a bird, the sea.
He loves the music of the spoken word.
He feels very proud of his island, Puerto Rico.
He dedicated his book *La niña y el cucubano* (*The Girl and the Firefly*) to his daughter
and "to all her Puerto Rican brothers and sisters."

14

To José Emilio González

F. Isabel Campoy

How fun!
Your poems are all dressed up
and ready for a party.

You dress them in rain,
and we hear violins.
You dress them in white,
and they sing "Good night!"

I like to read you
again and again,
wishing your books
would never end.

15

Children's Choir

José Emilio González

Johnny Maloney,
    a handsome stick puppet.
Johnny Maloney,
    climbing up a tree.
Johnny Maloney,
    riding a white horse.
Johnny Maloney,
    singing to the stars.
Johnny Maloney,
    brave little soldier.
Johnny Maloney,
    with a magic sword.
Johnny Maloney,
    plays a game of marbles.
Johnny Maloney,
    teller of tall tales.
Johnny Maloney,
    a-singing and a-dancing
Johnny Maloney,
    laughs and laughs and laughs.
Johnny Maloney,
    playing in the circus.
Johnny Maloney,
    oh you silly clown!

The Girl and the Firefly

José Emilio González

When the girl goes to the farm,
the skies wear wool to snuggle warm.
When the girl goes out to town,
the skies put on a new blue gown.
When the girl goes to the river,
the skies dress up in glass and silver.
When the girl goes out to sea,
the skies catch fish for you and me.

At the Circus

José Emilio González

La-dee-da-dee-oh,
la-dee-da-dee-oh,
to the circus I go,
taking my heart along.

That big tall clown
walking towards me,
swaying back and forth,
looks like a giant tree.

La-dee-da-dee-oh,
la-dee-da-dee-oh,
to the circus I go,
taking my heart along.

Tigers and lions
and white elephants,
mischievous monkeys
and giraffes doing stunts.

La-dee-da-dee-oh,
la-dee-da-dee-oh,
to the circus I go,
taking my heart along.

See that doll there!
I want that clown,
that roly-poly striped one,
I want to take him home.

La-dee-da-dee-oh,
la-dee-da-dee-oh,
from the circus I go,
leaving my heart behind.

17

Argentina

My Friend, Argentina

F. Isabel Campoy

Argentina
long and sleek,
with a *pampa* hat
and icy feet.

Argentina, Argentina,
land of tangos
and concertinas,
rich and cultured,
my friend Argentina.

María Elena Walsh

Walsh is a poet and story-teller whose books
have been translated into many languages.
This great writer has received
many significant international awards.
But most importantly, she has brought joy
to hundreds of thousands of children.
Some of her books are
Tutú Marambá, El Reino del Revés (*The Backward Kingdom*),
and *Zoo Loco* (*Crazy Zoo*).

To María Elena Walsh

F. Isabel Campoy

Your swallows are scissors
shearing the fog from the sky,
and your mountain doves
weave their nests
from sunbeams and moonlight.
María Elena Walsh,
brilliant poet who helps us fly
from here to Mars
in the blink of an eye...
Thank you for your smile and your light,
and for taking us on board
that giant airplane
as your magical imagination
takes flight.

The Red Crane

María Elena Walsh

Do you know why the red crane stands
on only one leg (without any hands)?
Well, she prefers it. And, as she well knows,
if she raised them both up,
she would fall on her nose.

In the Land of I-Don't-Remember

María Elena Walsh

In the land of I-Don't-Remember
I take three steps, and can't go further.

One step over here…
(over where? oh dear!)
One step over there…
(oh dear! over where?)
One step to and fro,
and that's as far as I can go.
You see, I forgot already where I put
(goodness gracious!) my other foot.

20

In a Tiny Matchbox

María Elena Walsh

In a tiny matchbox
you can store many things.

A ray of sunshine, for example
(but we need to close it quickly,
or the shadows will gobble it up).
A few flakes of snow,
a moonsilver coin,
some buttons from the wind's jacket.

I will share a secret with you.
In my tiny matchbox
I store a single tear
where no one else can see.
It's clearly no longer of use to me.
It's true that it's quite worn out.

I know, I know, but what else can I do?
To throw it away is more than I can bear.

Perhaps grown-ups won't ever
understand about treasures.
"Garbage!" they'll say. "Junk!"
"I don't know why you keep all that."
It doesn't matter. You and I
will still keep saving
sticks, balls of lint, buttons,
thumbtacks, pencil stubs,
peach pits, bottle caps, paper,
string, empty spools, rags,
thread, bits of rubble, bugs.

In a tiny matchbox
you can store many things.
After all, things don't have mothers.

Mexico

Mexico Between Two Oceans

F. Isabel Campoy

Between two oceans
sails the ship of your history,
carrying a hundred
        different languages,
a hundred different cultures,
a hundred different races.
Such a wealthy inheritance!
Such handsome peoples!
Mexico is… presence.
Mexico is… present.

José Juan Tablada

Tablada was the author of words
so strong and deep
that each verse needed only a very few.
He was a professor and a diplomat.
He lived for many years in the United States.
Some of his books are: *Al sol y bajo la luna* (*In the Sun and Under the Moon*), *La feria* (*The Fair*), and *El florilegio* (*The Poetry Recital*).

To José Juan Tablada

F. Isabel Campoy

Your words are meteorites
streaking across the sky of your imagination,
causing seas to explode and offering
a glimpse of the entire universe
in a single star.

Haiku

José Juan Tablada

Watermelon

Cool red laughter,
summer's own;
a nice thick slice
of watermelon!

Flying Fish

The bold sun's gold
shatters the sea's glass
into shiny slivers.

A Sunny Day

A sunny day:
a butterfly
on each flower.

24

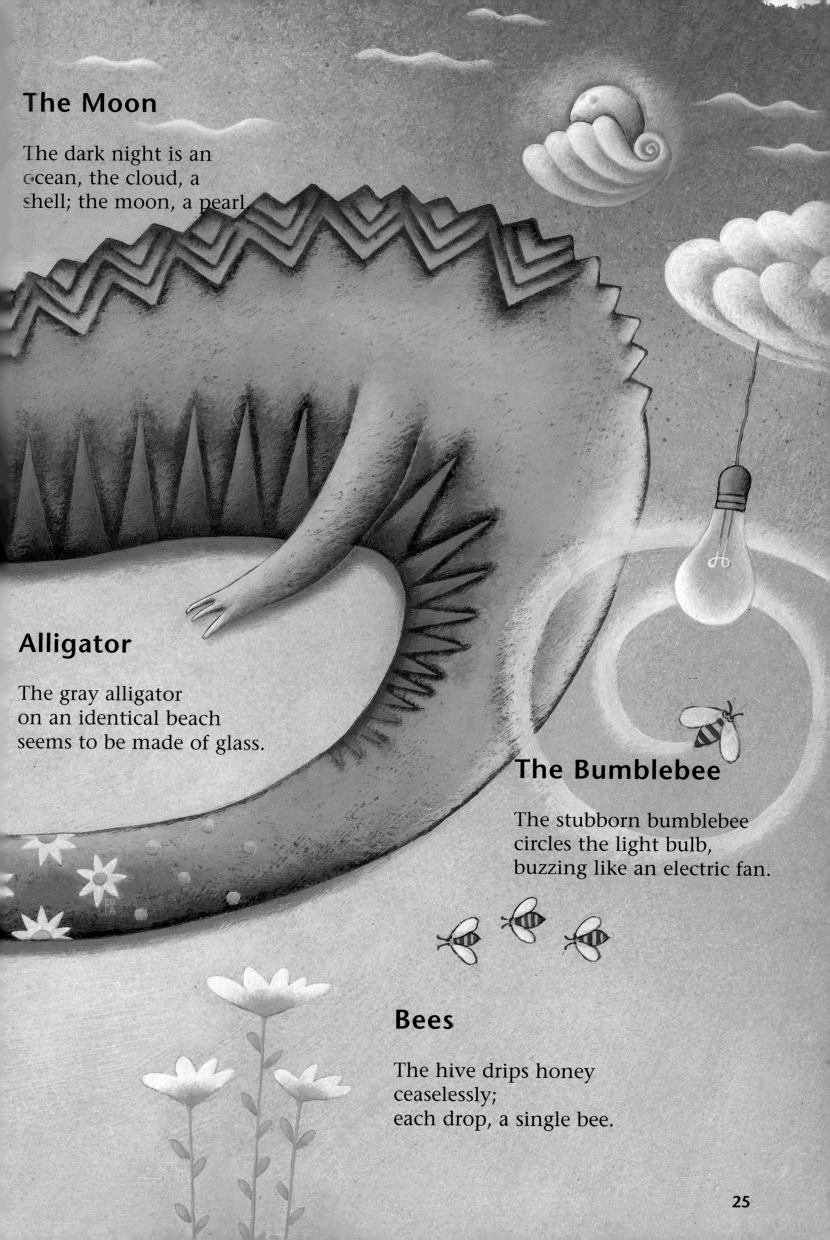

The Moon

The dark night is an
ocean, the cloud, a
shell; the moon, a pearl.

Alligator

The gray alligator
on an identical beach
seems to be made of glass.

The Bumblebee

The stubborn bumblebee
circles the light bulb,
buzzing like an electric fan.

Bees

The hive drips honey
ceaselessly;
each drop, a single bee.

25

Cuba

Green Island

Alma Flor Ada

Green island,
beautiful island,
mine,
yours,
theirs.
Cuba belongs to everyone
who loves brotherhood and sisterhood,
seeks justice for all,
and wants to learn
to sing
verses that bloom
in the shade of a bird's wing.

José Martí

Martí is the best-loved poet of Cuba,
And one of her greatest historical figures.
He loved his country, and fought for her all his life.
In New York, he created the magazine *La edad de oro*
(*The Golden Times*), for all of the girls and boys of the
Americas. You may also want to read *Versos sencillos*
(*Simple Verses*) and *Ismaelillo* (*Little Ishmael*).

To José Martí

F. Isabel Campoy

You run ahead of your horse
with two words emblazoned on your forehead:
one to use in May,
another in December.
With them, brave poet,
you walk north to south,
throughout this enormous continent.
With one hand, you offer friendship;
with the other, freedom.

The White Rose

José Martí

I carefully tend a white rose
in both January and July
for the true friend who offers
an honest and loyal hand.

And for the cruel one
who tears from me
my living and beating heart
I tend neither thistle nor thorn bush
but instead a white, white rose.

The Leopard Has a Fine Coat

José Martí

The leopard has a fine coat
in his mountains without end;
I have much more than the leopard,
for I have found a true friend.

Counts have a noble lineage,
a beggar has the bright dawn;
a bird has its wings, while I,
there in Mexico, I have a friend.

Our honorable president
has a garden with a fountain
and a treasury of gold to tend.
I have more—I have a friend!

Spain

I'll Go to Spain

F. Isabel Campoy

One day I'll go to Spain
to see if Grandpa was right.
Is it really true that people speak Spanish
in his town, too?

Marina Romero

Marina Romero likes to talk
to characters from books.
She dedicates poems to Snow White,
to the little donkey Platero, and to Peter Pan.
She also likes small flowers
and big animals. She knows how to invent imaginary worlds
that seem quite real, even if they were born in
her imagination. She has written many books,
including *Alegrías* (*Happiness*), which she dedicated
"to all children, that they may keep dreaming."

30

To Marina Romero

Alma Flor Ada

So that
children
might keep
dreaming,
you fill their days
with poetry.

Dear Marina,
so that you
might keep dreaming
too,
the children and I
send you a kiss
filled with love,
on the petals
of a rose.

31

Kangaroo

TO MARCO POLO

Marina Romero

Martinique has fish,
Iceland, Eskimos;
Florida has coconuts,
Mexico, tamales.

Australia has kangaroos,
Galicia, lots of squids;
Morroco has camels,
and India, elephants.

Colombia has emeralds,
Africa has diamonds;
Rome, the Colosseum,
and Venice, her canals.

New York City has skyscrapers,
Russia had its czars;
San Francisco has two bridges,
and Holland has tulips from here to Mars.

Paris has the Eiffel Tower,
while Seville has one built by Arabs.
Córdoba has a mosque,
and Elche has dates that grow on palms.

Valencia has paellas,
and Toledo has swords.
Havana has cigars,
while London has the Thames.

Costa Rica has macaws,
and Guatemala, quetzals;
Brazil has coffee and milk,
while Argentina has *mate*.

This story is about to end,
as I've run out of places to be.

Who can lend me a big world map
so I can fly across the sea?

33

If I Were...

Marina Romero

If I were a green cicada,
I'd play the violin
to entertain a lady.

If I were a singing cricket,
I'd play the drums.
It would be just the ticket!

If I were an agile dolphin,
I'd swim in the fish pond
and then go out golfin'.

If I were a kangaroo,
I'd hop to the city
and visit the zoo.

If I were a long centipede,
I'd put on my shoes
and run through the weeds.

If I were a bumpy camel,
I'd paint your house
with purple enamel.

If I were a porcupine…

Enough! This is the end!

35

Horse

TO CHUCHURUMBEL

Marina Romero

I do not want that
lead soldier,
nor those crystal boots,
nor that feather for my hat.

I do not want
that twelve-wheeled train,
nor a real horse,
nor those leather chaps.

I do not want
turquoise pins,
buckles on my shoes,
nor ribbons on my coat.

I do not want
colorful rainbows,
racing sailboats,
nor boxes of candy.

I do not want
a star in my wallet,
nor a shiny toy gun,
nor all the blue in the sky.

You know what I want.
I want...
I want...
I want you to give me a kiss!

Hispanic Folklore

To Play and Sing

Poems to sing
with friends or family,
at home or at school.

Songs nearly forgotten,
that we want to remember
to keep alive our memories,
our laughter, and our play.

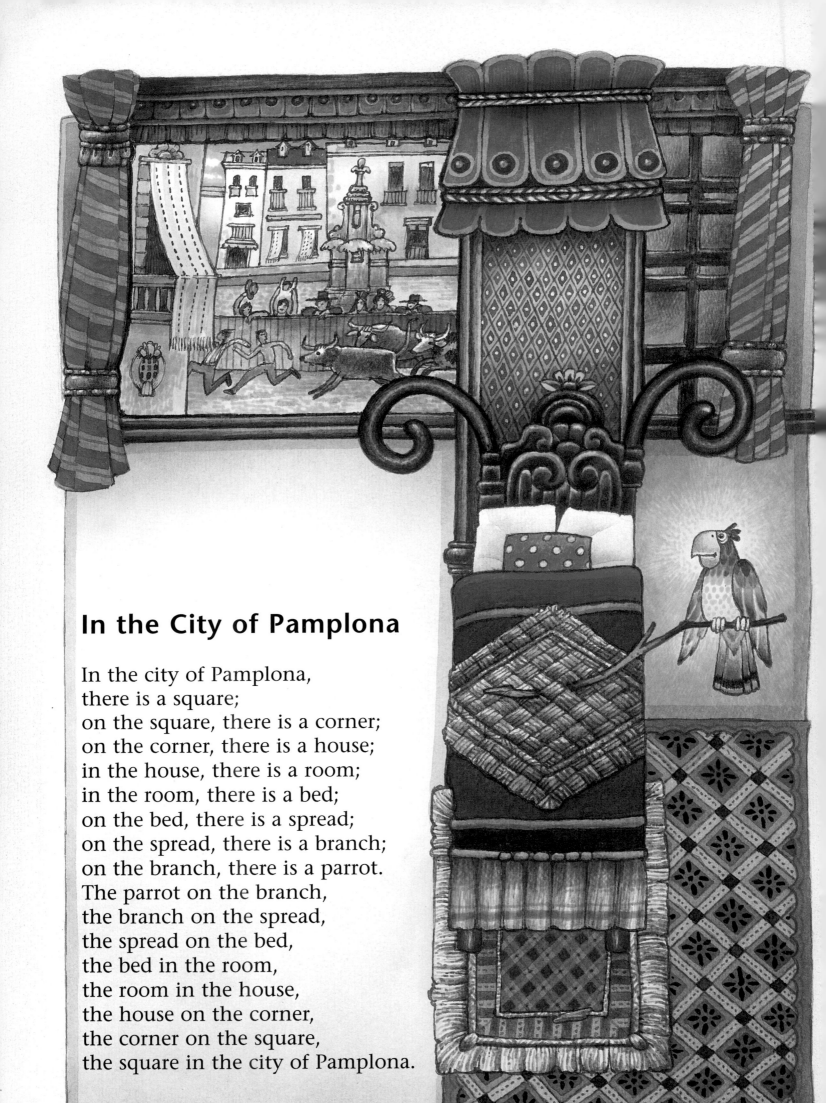

In the City of Pamplona

In the city of Pamplona,
there is a square;
on the square, there is a corner;
on the corner, there is a house;
in the house, there is a room;
in the room, there is a bed;
on the bed, there is a spread;
on the spread, there is a branch;
on the branch, there is a parrot.
The parrot on the branch,
the branch on the spread,
the spread on the bed,
the bed in the room,
the room in the house,
the house on the corner,
the corner on the square,
the square in the city of Pamplona.

Croak, Croak

Croak, croak, all day sang the frog,
croak, croak, in a watery bog.
Croak, croak, a tall man came by,
croak, croak, he had on a tie.
Croak, croak, a lady came through,
croak, croak, dressed up all in blue.

The Castle of Chuchurumbé

These are the keys
to the door
of the castle of Chuchurumbé;

this is the cord
that held the keys
to the door
of the castle of Chuchurumbé;

this is the mouse
that gnawed through the cord
that held the keys
to the door
of the castle of Chuchurumbé;

this is the cat
that chased the mouse
that gnawed through the cord
that held the keys
to the door
of the castle of Chuchurumbé;

this is the dog
that bit the cat
that chased the mouse
that gnawed through the cord
that held the keys
to the door
of the castle of Chuchurumbé;

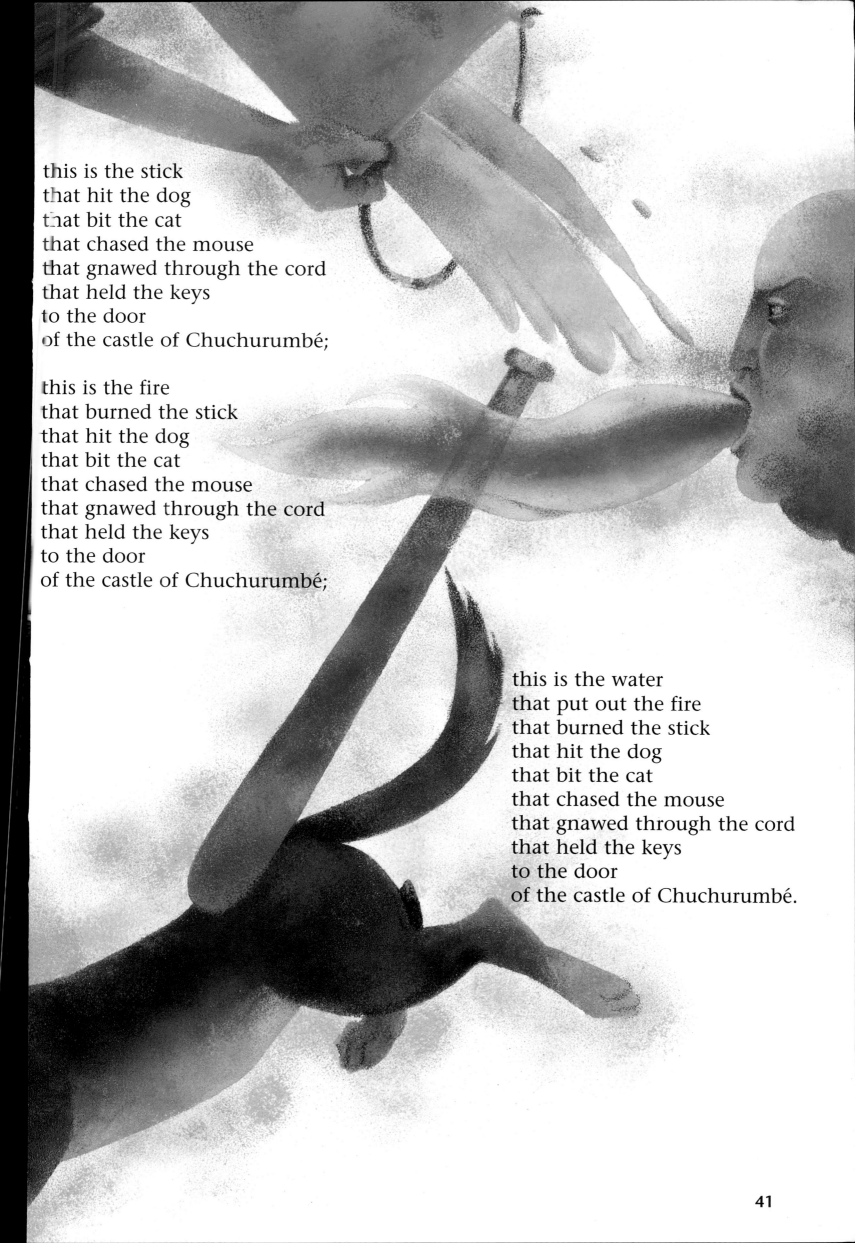

this is the stick
that hit the dog
that bit the cat
that chased the mouse
that gnawed through the cord
that held the keys
to the door
of the castle of Chuchurumbé;

this is the fire
that burned the stick
that hit the dog
that bit the cat
that chased the mouse
that gnawed through the cord
that held the keys
to the door
of the castle of Chuchurumbé;

this is the water
that put out the fire
that burned the stick
that hit the dog
that bit the cat
that chased the mouse
that gnawed through the cord
that held the keys
to the door
of the castle of Chuchurumbé.

OUI, OUI, MERCI

Short Stories

"Once upon a time, there was a dog who spoke French.
It was a most unusual thing. Would you like to hear it again?"
"Sure..."
"Well, once upon a time, there was a dog who spoke French..."

This is a story about a squirrel,
a story so little that if I start to tell it,
it will end in the middle.

This is a story about a lock with no key.
It's the shortest story ever told...
I think you will agree.

I begin to get started
I want to start right in.
I wonder if, by getting started,
I'll be able to begin.

42

Telling Lies

Now that we're walking slowly,
let's tell a lie or two:
rabbits run across the sea,
sardines like mountain views.
I left my camp six weeks ago
when I ran out of staples.
I saw a plum tree by the road,
its branches full of apples.
I started to throw rocks at it,
and almonds began to fall,

when the owner of the pear tree
came out and loudly called:
"Stop throwing rocks, child! Can't you see?
This lovely patch of melons does not
    belong to me."

43

Your Turn to Jump

It's your turn to jump now,
I've already gone.
Now it's time for you to go,
for I'm already done.

Two and two is four,
four and two is six,
six and two is eight,
and another two makes ten.

One, Two

[A BED-TIME RHYME]

One, two,
three and four,
the queen did hear
someone at the door.
Mr. Handle
blew out the candle.
"Your Royal Highness,
good night," he said.
Now count to twenty,
it's time for bed.

One, Two, Three, Polly-Pollyanna

[A GAME]

One, two, three, Polly-Pollyanna,
la bamba, la bamba, can can do.
The apple takes a walk
from the table to New York.
Don't use a knife to tickle me,
I prefer a fork.
One, two, three, four—you are out,
let's play some more.

Madam Frog

"Dear Madam Frog,"
    "Yes, my dear sir,"
"Has your husband returned from the hills?"
    "Yes, indeed, sir!"
"And what did he bring you?"
    "He brought me a shawl, sir!"
"What color shawl?"
    "Green like a lime, sir!"
"Are you coming to church?"
    "I don't have a shirt!"
"Will you come to hear the sermon?"
    "I don't have a skirt!"

The itty-bitty bottle does not have a top,
and the large old jug does not have a plug.

My Beard Had Three Long Hairs

My beard had three long hairs,
three long hairs had my beard.
Had it not had three long hairs,
it would not have been my beard.

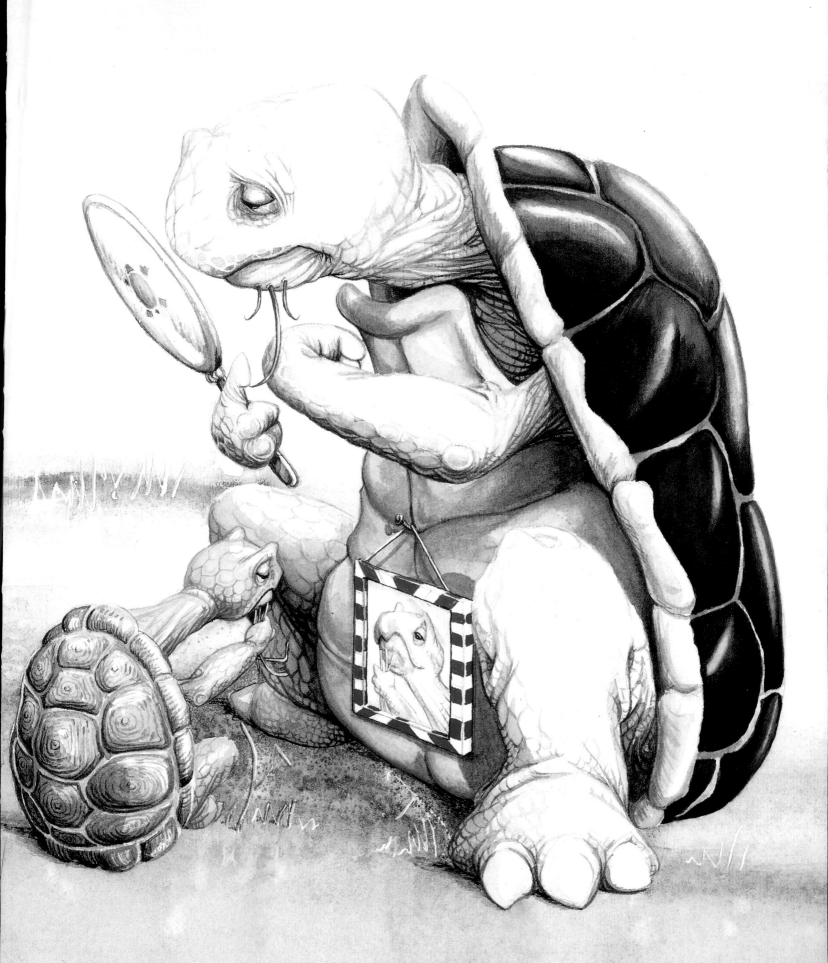

To Our Anonymous Poets

F. Isabel Campoy

Alma Flor Ada

Mothers, fathers, and grandmothers,
as they sang to us,
were our first schoolhouse.

A schoolhouse where we learned
Two and two makes four,
four and two makes six,
long cape, short pants,
and the crown of a king.

Poets without fame, teaching us
to play with rhythm and words,
that we may join in a game,
or sing while we skip rope.

Our culture lives on in those verses,
and in all who choose to remember.

SANFORD GUIDE

THE SANFORD GUIDE
To Antimicrobial Therapy
2023

53rd Edition

David N. Gilbert, M.D.
Henry F. Chambers, M.D.
Michael S. Saag, M.D.
Andrew T. Pavia, M.D.
Helen W. Boucher, M.D.

Douglas Black, Pharm.D.
David O. Freedman, M.D.
Kami Kim, M.D.
Brian S. Schwartz, M.D.